PRAISE FOR *LINUX MUSIC & SOUND*

"Finally . . . a useful book on making, processing and recording sound with Linux."

—Paul Barton-Davis, Linux audio and MIDI software developer

". . . an indispensable guide for novice and expert alike. If you are an electronic musician, this book is THE reason to install Linux on your PC!"

—Dr. Richard Boulanger, Professor of Music Synthesis
at the Berklee College of Music in Boston

". . . an invaluable guide for the Linux user interested in sound and music creation and playback but lacking the time to find and configure the numerous software packages available. . . . [the] CD-ROM in itself is worth the price of the book"

—Larry Ayers, Linux journalist and enthusiast

LINUX MUSIC & SOUND

How To Install, Configure, and Use Linux Audio Software

Dave Phillips

No Starch Press

San Francisco

Printed in the United States of America

1 2 3 4 5 6 7 8 9 10—03 02 01 00

Trademarked names are used throughout this book. Rather than use a trademark symbol with every occurrence of a trademarked name, we are using the names only in an editorial fashion and to the benefit of the trademark owner, with no intention of infringement of the trademark.

Publisher: William Pollock
Project Editor: Karol Jurado
Assistant Editor: Nick Hoff
Editorial Production Assistant: Jennifer Arter
Technical Reviewer: Nicola Bernardini
Cover and Text Design: Octapod Studios
Copyeditor: Carol Lombardi
Composition: Magnolia Studio
Proofreader: Suzanne Goraj
Indexer: Nancy Humphreys
Special thanks to Michael Gogins for permission to use his Silence composition "Tryptich" in Chapter 9.

Distributed to the book trade in the United States and Canada by Publishers Group West, 1700 Fourth St., Berkeley, CA 94710; phone: 800-788-3123; fax: 510-658-1834.

For information on translations or book distributors outside the United States, please contact No Starch Press directly:

No Starch Press
555 De Haro Street, Suite 250, San Francisco, CA 94107
phone: 415-863-9900; fax: 415-863-9950; info@nostarch.com; http://www.nostarch.com

The information in this book is distributed on an "As Is" basis, without warranty. While every precaution has been taken in the preparation of this work, neither the author nor No Starch Press shall have any liability to any person or entity with respect to any loss or damage caused or alleged to be caused directly or indirectly by the information contained in it.

Library of Congress Cataloging-in-Publication Data

Phillips, Dave, 1951–
    Linux music & sound / Dave Phillips.
        p. cm.
    Includes bibliographical references and index.
    ISBN 1-886411-34-4 (alk. paper)
    1. MIDI (Standard) 2. Linux. 3. Computer sound processing.
I. Title.
MT723.P53 2000   99-42680
784.19'0285'46--dc21

DEDICATION

To Ivy, Nick, & Renee, con amore

And to the memory of Paul A. Sanders,
1951–2000
"...in perpetuum, frater, ave atque vale"

ACKNOWLEDGMENTS

This book owes its existence to the support and encouragement of many people, some of whom may be surprised to find themselves mentioned here.

First and foremost I want to thank Donna J. Young (my mother), Robert I. Phillips (my father), and my brothers Scott, Bill, and Joe Phillips: They have willingly provided essential material and spiritual assistance whenever I needed it, which has been often enough to guarantee them all a heavenly paradise.

Enormous thanks go to the true Linux MIDI and sound wizards and gurus, including Paul Barton-Davis, Nicola Bernardini, Nick Copeland, Francois Deschelles, Fred Floberg, Guenter Geiger, Michael Gogins, Dr. Oyvind Hammer, Reine Jonsson, Richard Kent, Alexander Koenig, Matti Koskinen, Michael Krause, Jaroslav Kysela, Paul Lansky, John Lazzaro, Eric Lyon, Gabriel Maldonado, Dev Mazumdar and Hannu Savolainen, Stefan Nitschke, Jean Piche and Alexandre Burton, Maurizio Umberto Puxeddu, Juhana Sadeharju, Eric Sheirer, Bill Schottstaedt, Doug Scott, Per Sigmond and Andreas Voss, Tim Thompson, Eric Tiedemann, Dave Topper, Larry Troxler, Kai Vehmanen, Stefan Westerfeld, and Adam Williams. They have patiently endured years of my correspondence (i.e., nagging) and will probably (and unfortunately for them) endure many years more of it.

The entire cast of contributors to the Csound mail-list has been a constant inspiration, and I continue to learn from the whole crew. Special thanks go to Dr. Richard Boulanger for his tutorials, his friendship, and his decision to include my work in his own wonderful *Csound Book*. And I am deeply indebted to John ffitch, maintainer of the canonical Csound sources, who really set me off on my Csound adventure when he suggested I try compiling the sources for Linux and then let me place the results at the main Csound repository in Bath UK.

I am equally in debt to the membership of the Linux Audio Development mail-list. Special thanks must go to Erik Castro de Lopo, Richard W. E. Furse, Jorn Nettingsmeier, David Olofson, David O'Toole, Benno Sennoner, David Slomin, Erik Steffl, and (last but certainly not least) Paul Winkler.

Professor Burton Beerman kindly provided me with the opportunity to evangelize the Linux audio cause to the students in his Music Technology course at Bowling Green State University. Much gratitude to him and his students, and many thanks also to his graduate assistants Adam Zygmunt and Mark Vigoritto.

I owe special thanks to Georg Hitsch, Matt Probst, and Kenji Yasaka: They have provided mirrors for the Linux Sound & MIDI Software pages in Europe (http://www.linuxsound.at), the United States (http://sound. condorow.net), and Japan (http://www.ymo.org/linuxsound/), enabling easy access to the site at any time from anywhere in the world.

Every writer needs the occasional jump-start, and I could never have written all the words in this book without the coffee and delightful camaraderie found at Elaine Bruggeman's Main Street Deli, just downstairs from my apartment in Findlay, Ohio.

Many thanks to Deb Frye and Gearge Head, owners of the Guitar Ranch, and to my students there for putting up with suddenly cancelled lessons and my occasional complete distraction.

Thanks also to Greg Halamay and his staff at Finder's CDs and Tapes, especially Rick Clark, Stephen Conley, Kerry Dasher (now Mrs. Kerry Morris), Jan Reichenbach, and Tony Rosselet. I doubt any other employer or crew would have tolerated my wayward schedule or my general weirdness.

Great support for this project also came from Bob Baratta, Dan and Ginny Britsch, Rusty and Dina Campbell, Josh Flechtner, Fred Kwis, Kevin Lyle, Terry McClanahan, Joe Routzon, Chris Spradlin, and Phil Sugden. "From each according to his ability, to each according to his due."

This book would never have been written at all without a fateful email message from Bill Pollock, owner of No Starch Press. His encouragement and support of a totally new author has resulted in this unique book, and I hope his faith is amply rewarded. Great gratitude also to Nick Hoff, my editor, who is by now very knowledgeable about Linux MIDI and sound matters, and without whom my writing would have remained incomprehensible. Karol Jurado and Carol Lombardi guided me through the details of the finishing touches, Jennifer Arter ushered the book through its production stages, and Amanda Staab and Melissa Sherowski make sure the world learns of its existence.

As my technical editor, Nicola Bernardini did all one man could do to correct my too-frequent lapses in judgement, mistakes in expression, and errors in calculation. What faults remain in this book are certainly mine alone, and I owe Nicola great thanks for his patience and clarity. However, I owe him far greater thanks for a friendship that has inspired me with the hope that I too might someday become a truly civilized man.

Finally, deepest thanks of all to Ivy Maria: My life's light, safe haven of my soul, keeps on lifting me higher...

Dave Phillips
Findlay, OH

BRIEF CONTENTS

CONTENTS IN DETAIL

0

THE WORLD OF LINUX MUSIC & SOUND

1

BASICS OF DIGITAL AUDIO

2

SETTING UP YOUR SYSTEM

3

MIXING, PLAYING, AND RECORDING

4

SOUNDFILE EDITORS

5

MOD FILES AND LINUX

6

THE LINUX MIDI STUDIO

7

LINUX DOES MP3

8

MULTITRACK HARD-DISK RECORDING AND MIXING

9

SOFTWARE SOUND SYNTHESIS

10

REALTIME SOFTWARE SYNTHESIZERS

11

MUSIC NOTATION PROGRAMS

12

NETWORK AUDIO SOFTWARE

13

LINUX AND THE DIGITAL DJ

14

LINUX GAMES

15

OPERATING SYSTEM EMULATORS

FOREWORD

In the current situation of widely monopolized software and operating systems, whenever a new operating system emerges, the question "That's all very nice, but are there software applications written for it?" becomes the most obvious condition for acceptance on a wider basis. All the more so when we restrict the niche of applications to a smaller dedicated selection like that of sound and music packages.

However, the Linux case is somewhat different on several accounts. Linux software draws on the experience of UNIX systems (perhaps the longest-lived operating system still running successfully all over the world), it is based on a new software development model (open-source development, which is proving to have an extremely quick turnaround), and last but not least it is being developed collectively by literally several million people. *Linux Music & Sound* is an eloquent demonstration of the Linux difference: The book test drives dozens of applications in different musical fields ranging from signal processing research and contemporary music tools to virtual DJ turntables and astounding adventure games. No market considerations or business plans drive the development of these applications—just their plain sheer usefulness.

But this book was certainly not easy to write: Linux is not a closed system, and its users are always allowed to go under the hood to delve into its full depths—a liberty that gave Linux the reputation of being "user-unfriendly" (nothing farther from the truth, really). Explaining deep things in plain and concise terms requires a firm control over written language and a creative ability to devise clear explanations and solutions to difficult concepts. The reader will quickly realize that the author of this book is well endowed with the required creativity and control.

And there is more. Most of the applications described in this book can't be bought in a shop, simply because they are completely free and can be easily downloaded from the Internet—while this is a great opportunity for all users to get to try and select the applications that fit their needs best, it is a difficult endeavor to even guess which is the application that you need, let alone what its name is and where you could find it. This is where the most precious expertise of the author of this book, Dave Phillips, comes in. For several years, Dave has been managing the most widely acclaimed Web site on the planet specializing in Linux sound and MIDI (at sound.condorow.net), and his gentle and cooperative attitude has won him the friendship and esteem of all developers and specialists in the field. Many of them consider him a central figure of this social environment made of billions of ASCII characters and glyphs traversing the earth every day. Furthermore, his intense professional musicianship never allowed the technicalities of the software to obscure the ultimate musical meaning of its purpose, something which turns out to be a real bonus for those of us who set the music as the end product of our lives.

So this is what *Linux Music & Sound* turns out to be in the end: An indispensable working reference for musicians who consider computers and intelligent operating systems to be valuable musical tools. I hope you enjoy reading and using this book.

Nicola Bernardini

THE WORLD OF
LINUX MUSIC & SOUND

Do you want to record and play digital sound and music on your computer? Do you dream of distributing your music as MODs, MIDI, or MP3s? Would you like to experiment with digital signal processing software? And would you like to do all this and more with *free* applications? If so, then this book—and Linux—are for you.

This book is the first to collect and present comprehensive Linux information specifically for amateur and professional sound enthusiasts and researchers. In concise, easy-to-understand English, this book

- Clarifies the Linux audio system setup

- Describes basic and advanced use of the system

- Profiles and evaluates sound and music applications and development software

Though not written to be a textbook, this book can certainly be used as one. It is meant to inspire a hands-on attitude towards the software reviewed and encourage the reader to try and go beyond the given examples. In addition, sections on the history, current status, and possible future of the Linux audio system will help you evaluate the prospects of Linux sound and music for yourself.

The Good Stuff

At the heart of the book are evaluations of selected software packages and brief tutorials describing their installation and use. However, these examples are only a small taste of what's available: The Linux Music & Sound Applications Web page (included on this book's CD-ROM) lists hundreds of other software packages, and I sincerely hope that you will be inspired to try them out yourself.

The Absent Stuff

This book assumes that you have already set up Linux on your computer and that you have a soundcard installed in it. You should also know the difference between console and X applications, and you should understand the most basic commands in Linux. If you're already confused, fear not, since there are many excellent introductions to Linux (including *The No B.S. Guide to Red Hat Linux* published by No Starch Press).

This book is primarily a survey, and while it will certainly help you discover and explore the software profiled here, it is no substitute for reading the application documentation. Finally, although some technical information is presented, I have purposely kept the jargon to a minimum. If you're looking for exhaustive, in-depth explanations of digital audio theory or the MIDI specification, please see the bibliography for a list of relevant books and articles.

The CD-ROM

The CD-ROM contains a wealth of how-tos, FAQ sheets, programming examples, comparison charts, and other relevant documentation. It also offers most of the applications discussed in the text along with many others. (Some applications are licensed in such a way as to prohibit inclusion, Csound being the most notable omission.)

Where possible (always in the case of software protected by the GNU Public License), source code is included; packages in the popular Red Hat RPM (Red Hat Package Manager) format are provided if available; and binaries have been built for some of the packages.

A Bit of History

Linux sound support dates at least back to 1992, when Hannu Savolainen released a kernel driver for the original Sound Blaster soundcard. Regular expansions of the driver and its programming interface, provided by Hannu and other kernel hackers, were included with Linux sources throughout the kernel series 2.0.x and 2.1.x. Hannu is no longer directly involved in the development of the kernel sound driver and its API (application programming interface); kernel hacker Alan Cox now maintains that area.

Linux Arrives

In 1996, when I started maintaining a Web site that provided links to all available sound and music applications written for Linux, "all" meant about 40 links. The site now lists more than 500 Web addresses for audio and music software applications, including many for digital signal processing software, MIDI programs and tools, software synthesizers and synthesis languages, and players for virtually every popular soundfile format. Many of these powerful tools and applications can be run on both the Linux console and the X windowing system, and sound and music applications now exist for every notable window manager, GUI toolkit, and desktop environment.

Why is the world of Linux sound and music exploding with activity?

Open source code availability (letting anyone see and modify the source code behind Linux and Linux applications, which was the basis of Linux's success) has had a profound effect on the Linux audio community. Application sources coupled with straightforward sound programming interfaces provide an excellent environment for developing audio and MIDI software. As a result, Linux music and sound software has proliferated. Many projects have shown real longevity and growth, indicating a bright future for Linux as a powerful platform for audio and music application development.

. . . and Hardware Follows

Hardware vendors such as Trident, Creative Labs, and Aureal 3D have recognized the Linux phenomenon: Trident made their 4Dwave chipset specifications available for free to Linux developers, Creative Labs has developed open-source Linux drivers for their popular SBLive! soundcards, and Aureal now provides native Linux drivers for their Vortex chipsets (included on many popular soundcards, such as the Turtle Beach Montego). The ALSA open-source soundcard driver project now includes support for the RME Hammerfall digital audio board and the Mark Of The Unicorn MIDI Time Piece/AV (a complex MIDI interface/router/time-code box), while 4Front Technologies has announced forthcoming support for more professional digital audio boards for their commercially-available OSS/Linux drivers. These developments clearly indicate a continuing interest in Linux as a serious platform for audio and music software.

The Reviewer's Testing Facility

The software reviewed in this book was tested on a 486/100 PC with 16 MB (megabytes) RAM, a 486/120 PC, and a Pentium 166 (the latter two with 64 MB RAM each). Soundcards included the Media Vision Pro Audio Spectrum 16, the Creative Labs Sound Blaster 16, a generic CS4232-based card, the

Sound Blaster AWE64, the Sound Blaster PCI128, and the Music Quest MQX32M standalone MIDI interface. Other elements of the testing studio included a Casio CZ101 MIDI keyboard, two Yamaha TX802 FM synthesizers, a Yamaha DMP11 MIDI-automated mixer, and a 486/120 running MS-DOS MIDI software. A Yamaha MJC8 provided MIDI patching to connect the various pieces, and playback was through a pair of Yorkville Sound YSM-1 studio monitor speakers driven by a QSC 100-watt power amplifier.

Two Linux distributions were used: a "mongrel" libc5 system grown from a Slackware installation and hybridized through kernel 2.0.29, and a glibc (libc6) system from a more-or-less stock Red Hat 5.2 installation with Linux kernel 2.0.36. The packages profiled, though, should run under any Linux distribution. Due to slight differences in file system organization between distributions, you may find it occasionally necessary to adjust a pathname or two.

NOTE *Only Intel x86 hardware was tested. The examples throughout this book, therefore, assume a version of Linux for x86 processors.*

To those readers on a budget: Please don't consider this a shopping list. For testing purposes, we built a good, medium-powered setup. Don't be discouraged; Chapter 2 lists a "Starter Set" that will get you up and running without selling body parts.

Console or X?

This book will present software that can be used on the lowest-end Linux system (a 386SX without support for X) and on high-end systems (a multiprocessor with GUI). Where possible, I will indicate console equivalents or alternatives to selected X applications, but such alternatives may not exist for all components (soundfile editors, for example, almost always require a GUI toolkit). The X window system provides the greatest power to the serious sound hacker and presents visually appealing and useful interfaces. Applications such as Csound or RTcmix now have a variety of graphic interfaces, but they were originally designed for use at the command line (many users still prefer using the command-line versions). You can create an excellent music and sound development environment using only the Linux console, so I have intentionally profiled a number of console applications for readers who prefer working from a command line.

A Word about Versions versus the CD-ROM

Linux is a fast-moving target, with major kernel upgrades occurring frequently. New versions of applications software arrive weekly, and newer versions will not always match what is described in this book. The CD-ROM that comes with this book contains the latest versions of the software profiled in the text—but, even if this software is revised next week, compatibility issues should not be a terrible problem. You may find it necessary, though, to perform a component upgrade or two.

Graphics toolkits (such as Gtk and Qt) and desktop environments (such as GNOME and KDE) are also in continual development, and audio software authors follow those developments as well as what goes on in the newer kernels. If a new feature offers some improvement to a programmer, she will likely use it, and the resulting program may require some system upgrades. It is beyond the scope of this book to tell you how to install new libraries and other system components, but it is rarely a difficult procedure. RPMs are reliable installation utilities for updating Red Hat systems, as are DEB packages for Debian systems; other distributions offer similar means to ease the chore of updating your system.

Conventions

This section covers a few conventions used throughout this book.

Code listings are always in this font:

```
printf("This is code font\n");
```

Command sequences are represented in bold face:

tar xzvf packagename-latest.tar.gz

I use a generic manner of referencing the software packages. The form

packagename-latest.tar.gz

is a short-hand for what is usually a numbered version. Developers do not follow any strict rules in naming their packages, so the above might refer to a package actually named

packagename-091899.tgz

where the numbers indicate the release date and the .tar.gz extension has been shortened to .tgz. The numbers in

packagename-3.1.0a.tar.gz

indicate the major and minor version numbers (3.1) and the patch level (.0a).

Many ftp sites provide a link to an application's latest version in the form of *packagename-latest.tar.gz*. I have also done so for the packages on the CD-ROM bundled with this book.

Remember that case matters in Linux: Make sure program names and command-line parameters are spelled with the correct capitalization.

Where Should I Go from Here?

My advice is to simply jump in and start swimming. If you've successfully configured a Linux kernel for sound support, then you're ready to take a unique musical journey. So whether you consider yourself a newcomer or an old hand, I invite you to discover the wonder and pleasure of Linux sound and music software. Programs such as jMax, Cecilia, Quasimodo, and DAP await you, along with an incredible array of other applications and utilities. Although perhaps not the Final Frontier, Linux music and sound software is a relatively unexplored and surprisingly rich sector of the galaxy.

Welcome aboard, we leave at once. . . .

BASICS OF DIGITAL AUDIO

Essential Theory

Understanding a few key concepts will help you obtain optimum audio from your system. For more of the technical details of digital audio theory, read one of the books listed in the bibliography—I especially recommend *Computer Music: Synthesis, Composition, and Performance* by Charles Dodge and Thomas A. Jerse.[1]

Pulse-Code Modulation

PCM (pulse-code modulation), the process of converting an electrical impulse into a stream of numbers, is the cornerstone of the digital audio capabilities of your soundcard. When you record (or sample) a digital audio file using your soundcard, a microphone converts a sound pressure wave into an electrical signal and sends it to the soundcard's analog-to-digital converter (ADC),

1   Dodge, C. and Thomas A. Jerse. *Computer Music: Synthesis, Composition, and Performance.* 2ⁿᵈ ed. New York: Schirmer Books, 1997. ISBN 0-02-864682-7.

a clever device that converts the electrical (analog) current into a numerical (digital) stream. The ADC performs its magic by measuring the electrical current's voltage at regular periods of time (usually in ten-thousandths of a second); this sampling process is what signal-processing engineers call pulse-code modulation. "CD-quality" sampling, a common recording technique that uses pulse-code modulation, takes samples at a frequency of 44,100 Hz (44.1 kHz) with a resolution of 16 bits. The sampling frequency determines the upper limit of the frequencies measured (see "The Nyquist Theorem" below), and the bit resolution determines the upper limit to the dynamic range (16 bits at 6 dB per bit yields a 96 dB dynamic range).

In plain English: CD-quality recording samples an input signal for its changes 44,100 times per second and assigns each sample a 16-bit numerical value.

Not surprisingly, playing a digital audio file is simply the reverse process of recording one. A stream of numbers representing variations in an electrical impulse is sent to the soundcard's digital-to-analog converter. The DAC converts the numbers into electrical impulses that are sent to the card's speaker output jacks and on to an amplifier and speakers. The speakers are then vibrated by the electrical energy to create a sound pressure wave identical to the original recording. The sound pressure wave vibrates the membranes, hairs, and bones in your ear—and you hear the music.

Most soundcards can both record and play PCM files (the popular WAV and AIFF formats use PCM). Many cards can record with sampling rates up to 48 kHz, but playback is usually limited to 44.1 kHz. For most project recording purposes, the CD-quality sampling rate and bit-resolution will do quite well.

NOTE *Your mixer application, which adjusts the settings of your soundcard, will display faders (the sliders used to adjust settings) that control the master volume, CD player volume, PCM output strength, and (sometimes) treble and bass response—so they're all available for tweaking.*

The Nyquist Theorem

The Nyquist theorem says that for any signal's frequency range to be sampled accurately, the sampling rate must be at least twice the peak of the frequency range. Given that the normal range of our hearing is from 20 Hz to 20 kHz, a sampling frequency of 40 kHz is required to reproduce accurately the range of sound audible to the human ear. Some soundcards will record up to 48 kHz, but for most purposes, CD-spec audio (44.1 kHz) is sufficient. When a sampled frequency range extends beyond the sampling rate (recording a symphony orchestra at 11 kHz, for instance), the upper frequencies will fold back into the signal as unremovable (and probably undesirable) noise. This effect is called aliasing or foldover. Filtering cannot remove aliased sound once it is recorded, so most sampling devices place a low-pass filter before the ADC in order to eliminate such unwanted frequencies.

Dealing with Data Rates

The faster the sampling frequency and the greater the bit resolution, the higher the quality of audio sampling and reproduction. However, files recorded at higher sampling rates and bit resolution will require larger amounts of storage space (though with sharply falling prices for massive hard disks, storage is less of a problem). Nevertheless, this formula is still worth knowing: 1 minute of CD-quality stereo sound will require 10 MB of disk space. So if you want to record 12 three-minute songs, you will need almost half a GB (gigabyte) of disk space—not to mention the space needed for alternate takes, back-up versions, and permanent storage.

The management of data rates and file sizes is also critical to realtime operation (i.e., when data is streamed directly to the soundcard DAC instead of being written to disk). Only a fast CPU (a 233 MHz Pentium or faster) will maintain sufficient data-flow integrity for professional (CD-quality) audio. However, if your processor is on the slow side and if your software permits, you might be able to adjust the input/output buffer (data holders) size to better match the data output rate to your soundcard's hardware capabilities. The I/O buffers hold data until they are full, then deliver the data to the digital-to-analog converters. If a buffer setting is too large or too small, playback and recording may be choppy or even completely stalled. Depending on the application, you may be able to adjust the I/O buffer size by using a command-line option, changing a resource-file setting, or selecting an item from a menu.

Another possible solution to data-flow problems is to lower the sampling rate to reduce data log jams. Be warned, though: If your recording is rich in high frequencies, lowering the sampling rate will result in a noticeably duller sound. On the other hand, a high sampling rate is unnecessary if the audio source can be fully represented by a lowered sampling rate. A signal that contains only frequencies below 11,025 Hz, for example, can be accurately sampled at 22,050 Hz (following the Nyquist theorem of 2 X the peak frequency). However, if you plan to record audio tracks for mastering to a CD, it's better to stick with the CD standard of 44,100 Hz.

Soundcard Synthesis

Many soundcards have an on-board chip or chipset that provides a hardware synthesizer. Such cards are often complete solutions for the sound requirements of game players or the person who likes to listen to MIDI files over the Internet. On-board synthesizers are a convenient replacement for bulky external synthesizers, though their hardware is not normally up to the specs of, say, Yamaha or Roland professional studio synthesizers. Nevertheless, on-board synthesizers have become quite powerful and are capable of supplying excellent sound banks. Many soundcards also offer effects processing (such as reverberation, echo, and chorus) to enhance the on-board sounds.

FM Synthesis

The original Ad Lib and Sound Blaster soundcards (and other cards that claim Sound Blaster compatibility) have an on-board "synthesizer-on-a-chip," the Yamaha OPL3. The OPL3 performs a simple form of frequency modulation (FM) synthesis. Developed at Stanford University in 1973 by the composer John Chowning, FM synthesis controls the timbre (the tone color) of a sound by modulating the frequency of one sine wave by the frequency of another. A complete explanation of FM synthesis is beyond the scope of this book, and the interested reader should consult the Dodge & Jerse book.

Digital FM synthesis proved to be both musically expressive and computationally inexpensive (i.e., sounds could be synthesized quickly). Able to create highly evocative imitative and original sounds without the need for heavy computing resources, FM synthesis became popular with many composers working with computers. In 1975 the Yamaha Corporation licensed the technology from Stanford and ten years later the company marketed the DX7, a successful commercial digital synthesizer that created its sounds using FM synthesis.

The OPL3, however, is not a DX7 on a single chip. Designed for use on cheap, mass-produced soundcards in order to provide a common level of sounds (particularly for games), the OPL3's palette is rather limited. Consequently, it simply does not suffice for serious synthesis or MIDI file playback. In order to provide a richer palette of sounds, many cards now include a wavetable synthesizer instead of (and sometimes as well as) the OPL3.

Wavetable Synthesis

According to a strict computer-music definition, wavetable synthesis synthesizes a sound by filling a software table with a pre-calculated waveform and then reading the table through a digital oscillator. The oscillator typically adds frequency (pitch) and amplitude (volume). For example, a function table in the sound programming language Csound can store a pre-defined waveform—such as a sine wave or sawtooth wave—and make it available for processing (i.e., synthesizing) by Csound's oscillators and other tools.

To complicate matters, however, soundcard manufacturers have a different definition of wavetable synthesis; for them it is actually a type of sample playback. By this definition, playing a set of sounds pre-loaded into a soundcard's memory is wavetable synthesis. You can loop and add effects to these sounds, but do remember that the sounds used are *not* synthesized but rather are pre-recorded samples.

The Sound Blaster AWE64 is a good example of a soundcard with an on-board wavetable synthesizer, and an especially good choice for MIDI file playback. The chip that provides the synthesis engine is an EMU8000, designed by engineers from the EMU Corporation, leaders in the design of hardware samplers. It is accessible via MIDI, has expandable memory, and comes pre-loaded with a usable set of General MIDI sounds. In order to maintain compatibility with the original Sound Blaster, it also includes the ubiquitous OPL3.

Other Synthesis Methods

Many other synthesis strategies exist and can be explored using software synthesis languages such as Csound and RTcmix. These other useful methods include physical modeling, additive synthesis, subtractive synthesis, waveshaping, and analysis-based resynthesis. Each method has its strengths: Physical modeling can produce strikingly realistic instrumental timbres, subtractive synthesis recreates the sounds of vintage analog synthesizers, waveshaping is very effective for imitating brass instruments, and additive resynthesis techniques provide unique tools for warping the time and pitch of a previously recorded sound. However, most contemporary soundcards only supply hardware for the FM and wavetable methods. Although these other types of synthesis are not likely to appear soon as standard soundcard hardware, they are available now in many Linux synthesis languages (see Chapter 3).

A Few Words about MIDI

MIDI is *not* an audio format. MIDI *is* a simple switching and command protocol designed to pass on/off messages between compatible devices. It also supports the continuous data streams produced by the pitch bend wheel, mod wheel, sustain pedal, and other controllers commonly found on MIDI keyboards. MIDI simply sends and receives commands to and from devices that *do* make sounds—such as soundcards, external synthesizers, and drum machines— telling them when to play a particular sound, for how long, at what volume, and so forth. You will learn more about MIDI in Chapter 6.

2

SETTING UP YOUR SYSTEM

Before recording or playing any sounds with your computer, you must make sure that your system is prepared for audio. This chapter will help you determine what hardware and software you need to prepare your Linux sound system for digital audio as well as take you through configuring Linux for sound. After you've set up your system, the next chapter will help you install and configure some basic recording and playback software and walk you through the basic recording process.

For simple recording:

Input (microphone, CD or tape player, mixing board, MIDI synthesizer) →
Analog-to-digital converter (soundcard inputs) →
Recorder (computer writes audio data to hard-disk)

For simple playback:

Playback device (computer reads audio data from hard-disk) →
Digital-to-analog converter (soundcard outputs) →
Output (mixer to amplifier to speakers, or directly to powered speakers)

Your Budget

How much you are willing to spend on hardware will make a big difference in your system's recording and playing capabilities. You should strive to avoid compromising any aspect of your hardware. However, if your budget is tight, I recommend that you first set up a good audio playback system. A relatively slow CPU can still handle digital audio at lowered sampling rates (such as 32 kHz or lower), but your amplifier and speakers are the final link in your output chain, and they will ultimately determine how your music will sound. Buy the best soundcard you can afford and be sure to study its capabilities and how extensively it is supported by the available Linux drivers.

Hardware

Fundamental hardware considerations include your CPU type and speed, the size and speed of your hard disk, the amount of memory installed, and the components in your audio playback system. The recommendations and advice given here will prove sufficient for desktop sound and small-scale project studio purposes. If you are putting together a serious music studio, then you should consult professional audio catalogs and other reference materials.[1]

The CPU

The Linux operating system runs on CPUs ranging from the lowliest 25 MHz 386SX to the latest multi-gigahertz Athlon. Music and sound applications can make heavy demands on your CPU. If you plan on a MIDI-only system, any 386 or 486 will work, but if you want to do multitrack recording or realtime sound synthesis, you should have at least a Pentium-class CPU—the faster the better.

The two hardware listings presented here are the minimal and optimal systems for running the software profiled in this book. They are presented as guides to help match your budget to your purposes.

Minimum Requirements

To gain the most pleasure and insight from this book, you need at least the following hardware:

- A working Linux system, preferably on a Pentium 120 or better

---

1 The following books are especially recommended:
Robert E. Runstein and David Miles Huber. *Modern Recording Techniques*. 4th ed. Boston: Focal Press, 1995. ISBN: 0240803086.
Davis, Gary and Ralph Jones (contributor). *Sound Reinforcement Handbook*. 2nd ed. Milwaukee: Hal Leonard Publishing, 1990. ISBN: 0881889008.

- A working sound system (Linux-compatible soundcard with appropriate drivers, a microphone, amplifier and speakers, or powered speakers)

- A large hard disk (2 GB or better)

- At least 64 MB of RAM

- A CD-ROM drive

- A 15-inch or larger color monitor

- A MIDI interface and optional keyboard

This system will be able to run any Linux MIDI application. It will record and play popular audio formats, such as WAV and MP3 files, but its realtime synthesis capabilities (such as the realtime audio output produced by instruments created in the Csound and RTcmix environments) are minimal. Realtime synthesis software will be able to produce only a few sounds at a time and may require lower sampling rates.

Advanced System

The following list would build a system more like a digital audio workstation:

- A working Linux system on a Pentium 450 or better (preferably a dual-processor system)

- A professional multi-channel digital audio board with digital input/output

- A studio-quality playback system (mixing board, power amplifier, studio monitors, 3-way speaker system)

- A 12 GB SCSI hard disk, preferably two or more

- At least 128 MB of RAM

- A CD-ROM drive, the faster the better

- A CD recorder

- A 17-inch or larger color monitor

- A MIDI interface and keyboard

NOTE *If you want to use timing protocols such as MIDI Time Code (MTC) or SMPTE, you will need a standalone MIDI interface card, such as the Roland MPU-401 or the Music Quest MQX32M. Soundcard MIDI interfaces usually operate in what is known as UART or "dumb" mode, whereas time code requires the "intelligent" mode available only from the dedicated cards. A soundcard MIDI interface, though, should work with all the MIDI programs presented in this book.*

Serious digital audio will stress your system to its maximum potential. Heavy-duty storage, fast retrieval, large archiving space, and a very fast CPU are all required for anything approaching serious audio work.

Why So Much Disk Space?

Digital audio is a conspicuous consumer on desktop computers. In addition to the large size of audio software files, simply storing music takes up a lot of disk space. One minute of CD-quality stereo sound requires 10 MB of disk storage—which doesn't sound like much until you start calculating the real length of pieces, the need for working copies and alternate takes, and the need for permanent storage. If you have a CD burner, you can of course simply save files to a compact disc. Otherwise, you will have to consider either a larger hard disk or a removable drive.

Why So Much Memory (RAM)?

Many of the applications profiled in this book require large amounts of physical memory. Some of the soundfile editors (in Chapter 4) read from memory, limiting the file size to the amount of RAM present in your machine. For example, the Silence composition and synthesis environment (see Chapter 9) includes some very memory-intensive processes. 64 MB is workable for low-demand audio, 128 MB will satisfy most of the applications reviewed in this book, and 256 MB is best of all.

What Is a Working System?

A working Linux system here means a recent kernel with up-to-date libraries and other support software such as the components listed in the Necessary Support Software section later in this chapter. Linux audio developers may be only marginally concerned with backward compatibility, so it's best to stay current with your base system software.

NOTE *It is not the aim of this book to teach users how to install the Linux kernel. Virtually all contemporary Linux distributions include a precompiled kernel along with instructions for upgrading and installing a new one. Most users will enjoy a working system simply by carefully following the directions provided with the distribution documentation.*

System Requirements for MIDI

MIDI demands far less from a system; even a 386SX can run MIDI applications fairly well. MIDI is less demanding because it is not audio data. It is a simple messaging protocol that, in effect, sends mainly on/off switches back and forth along the MIDI cable—the actual production of the sound is carried out by the soundcard or the external synthesizer's dedicated processors.

Audio Hardware

In all audio systems, one rule holds true: The overall quality of your equipment will determine the overall quality of your results. With that rule in mind, setting up an audio system for Linux is a straightforward procedure.

Minimum Requirements

The following hardware components will give you a basic system. The first three items are required.

- Soundcard and driver
- Speakers
- Cables
- Microphone (optional)
- Amplifier (optional)
- Subwoofer (optional)

The Options

A microphone is necessary if you want to record your voice or any other external sound source. You might need an amplifier if you don't have powered speakers (speakers with built-in amplifiers) or if your soundcard does not provide a pre-amplified signal (your soundcard manual should tell you if its signal is pre-amplified or not).

Consider a subwoofer if you're using a simple multimedia audio system that was packaged with an off-the-shelf computer. These are sufficient for business and game sound, but won't provide the ideal bass response.

Digital audio is capable of producing clear signals through the entire range of human hearing—but you won't be able to hear sounds your system can't reproduce.

Medium System

My home system might give you a good overview of a medium-powered desktop audio setup:

Soundcards   For testing various pieces of audio and MIDI software, I have three soundcards in my machine: a Sound Blaster AWE64, a Music Quest MQX32M, and a Sound Blaster PCI128. The MQX is actually a standalone MIDI card and has no audio output. The other two cards are configured to produce audio output for my CD player, to provide an internal MIDI synthesizer for MIDIfile playback, and to provide full-duplex (the ability to record and play simultaneously) PCM digital audio functions.

Speakers   I use a pair of unpowered YSM-1 studio monitor speakers from Yorkville Sound.

Cables   I have shielded cable from Hosa and Rapco, with speaker cables for the monitors and regular patch cabling for all other connections except the mic (which has its own cable).

Microphone   I use a Yamaha MZ106 dynamic microphone.

Amplifier   My mixer sends its stereo output to a 100-watt power amplifier manufactured by the QSC Company.

Tape recorder   I usually record onto a 4-track analog recorder using a high tape speed and dbx noise reduction. Input to the 4-track can be routed from my MIDI synthesizers, from my computer, or from the microphone.

Mixer   Audio output from both Sound Blaster cards is fed into a Yamaha DMP11, an 8-channel digital mixer that sends the mixed signals to its stereo output jacks. (I also recommend the Mackie mixers for low to medium budgets.)

Effects processor   An inexpensive Alesis MIDIverb provides a variety of reverb, echo, and chorus effects for outboard processing (i.e., not done by the mixing board).

Advanced System

Bear in mind that more expensive gear wants more expensive accommodations, i.e., a building or room constructed specifically for the purpose of audio recording. Given the funds for such a room I would build a system like this one:

Soundcard   RME Hammerfall digital audio board with ALSA driver.

Speakers   Yamaha NSM-10 monitors, 3-way main system with speakers (I'm obviously partial to Yamaha gear, but Genelec speakers are also a preferred professional solution) dedicated to bass, midrange, and high frequencies.

Cables   Monster cables.

Microphones   An assortment of expensive dynamic and condenser mics by manufacturers such as Neumann and Groove Tube.

Amplifiers   A 3-way system requires a crossover box (splits the signal into the three frequency ranges) and amplification for each signal path. My choice would be a rack of Crown power amps.

Multitrack digital tape recorder   The Alesis ADAT is the machine of choice in many pro studios.

Mixing board   A 32-channel Neve or Yamaha board would do nicely.

Effects processor   I'd like an Eventide Ultraharmonizer, please . . .

But now to some specifics about *your* system. . . .

Soundcards

Get the best soundcard you can afford, and check to see if your choice of drivers (OSS/Free, ALSA, OSS/Linux—all discussed below) supports your card and all its features. Professional-quality cards are only beginning to get support for Linux installations, so you'll likely need to consider a consumer-grade card.

The Sound Blaster PCI128 is an excellent low-cost solution, with an external MIDI port and especially good full-duplex and CD audio. Drivers for the PCI128 are available from 4Front Technologies (OSS/Linux) and ALSA.

The Trident 4Dwave is another excellent card, with a Sony/Philips digital audio interface (S/PDIF) supported by ALSA drivers. The Trident 4Dwave is particularly recommended if you want to transfer audio from your computer to a DAT (digital audio tape) recorder or a mini-disc recorder, or if you want to record audio from a CD player with a digital output.

Physically installing your soundcard is easy, but for specific installation instructions, consult your soundcard's manual.

NOTE   *In November 1999 Creative Labs inaugurated an open-source development initiative for their popular SBLive! soundcard. This card has digital audio I/O, 4-channel sound, on-board effects processing, and an EMU101K synthesizer. Open-source drivers for this card are available from the Creative Labs Linux project Web site (http://open-source.creative.com). Both ALSA and 4Front also now provide drivers for the SBLive! card (see the soundcards directory on the CD-ROM for more information).*

More Essentials

Cables

Quality cabling is an important factor in achieving high-quality audio recordings and playback. Unfortunately, soundcards typically have small pin-jacks and consumer-grade connectors that are far from optimal. Whereas the jacks cannot be easily replaced, you can at least make sure that the connecting plugs and cables are the highest quality you can afford. Plugs should be seated firmly in the jacks: Loose or shaky connections can result in dropouts, static, and other noise conditions during recording and playback. Cables from companies such as Monster and Hosa should be good enough for home studios.

Speakers, Amplifiers, and Mixers

If you're serious about audio then it's a bit silly to compromise the audio possibilities of your dual-processor 500 MHz Linux box by connecting it to a $40 pair of powered speakers. In addition to a good set of studio-quality monitor speakers (such as those available from Yamaha and Alesis), you will also have to consider adding a power amplifier and stereo mixer if you want to enjoy high-quality sound.

For the best results I recommend a three-way system, a system that routes audio through a crossover (a device for separating the sound into two or three broad ranges) and then through a speaker system optimized for low, middle, or high frequencies. This is a rather expensive solution, requiring the crossover box, separate amplifiers for the speakers, and the speakers themselves. Typical costs can easily reach into thousands of dollars for a quality system (using Yamaha and Crown equipment, for instance).

Microphones

The cheap microphone that comes with your soundcard is usable only for low-fidelity spoken-word recording. If you're planning to record musical instruments or singers, you will need microphones optimized for the frequency and amplitude ranges of singers and instruments.

Microphones come in three types, and each type has its strengths and weaknesses.

Dynamic microphones are rugged microphones especially good at handling loud, powerful signals, but they lack a good *transient response* (the speed at which the mic responds to the changes of a sound).

Condenser and electret mics have a better sensitivity to lower-powered signals, such as acoustic guitars and light voices, but they require a separate power source and are prone to overloading.

Ribbon microphones are usually found in professional studios: They offer superior transient response, but are very fragile and expensive.

Because of the wide variance in the power and frequency ranges of even one kind of sound, it is difficult to recommend microphones. Each player plays his or her instrument in a unique fashion, so the best solution is to have at least two of the above microphone types.

Mixing Boards

Recommending hardware mixers is considerably easier than recommending mics. Mackie makes excellent low-cost mixers, and professional studio boards are available from such manufacturers as Neve, Studer, and Yamaha. Once again, your budget will determine what you get. You will have to consider how many inputs you might need for your microphones and instruments and get a board appropriate for your purposes: Mixers are available for live performances or studio recording, and each has very different specifications.

Before leaving this section I must remind the reader to set aside funds for the purchase of miscellaneous items such as mic stands, racks for rack-mountable boxes (such as synthesizer modules and effects processors), baffles for quieting a sound source, headphones, and, of course, duct tape.

Software: Soundcard Drivers

There are three main sources for Linux soundcard drivers: The OSS/Free kernel modules, the ALSA drivers, and the OSS/Linux package. Soundcards supported by these three sources are listed in the soundcards directory on the CD-ROM. For the latest installation instructions, see "Installing and Updating Drivers" below.

In this section we'll look at the pros and cons for each driver. If you already know which driver you want to use, you can skip to the "Setting Up Linux for Sound" section. If your driver is already installed, skip to the "Checking Your System for Sound Support" section. If you have no idea whether your current soundcard is supported under Linux, or if you haven't determined which card to purchase, see the soundcard support pages on the book's CD-ROM.

The OSS/Free Driver

Authors: Hannu Savolainen, Alan Cox, Thomas Sailer, et al.
Version profiled: Versions for various kernels from 1.2.13 through 2.0.36
Web site: http://www.linux.org.uk/OSS/
FTP site: n/a
Maintained: Yes
Availability: Free, included with Linux kernel
License: GPL

Modern Linux distributions usually ship with the basic kernel sound drivers (OSS/Free drivers) already compiled and ready to use as loadable modules. The Red Hat system, for example, comes with a nice configuration utility (sndconfig, shown in Figure 2-1) that provides a simple menu-driven interface for selecting and installing the driver for your card (Mandrake and SuSE offer similar sound configuration utilities). The OSS/Free modules are easy to configure, but the selection of cards they support is limited. Support for some cards' range of features may be limited as well (see the CD-ROM).

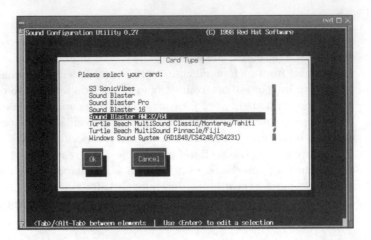

Figure 2-1: Red Hat's sndconfig utility

The ALSA Driver

Authors: Jaroslav Kysela (project leader)
Web site: http://www.alsa-project.org
FTP site: n/a
Maintained: Yes
Availability: Free, open-source
License: GPL

The ALSA (Advanced Linux Sound Architecture) project is an ambitious team effort led by developer Jaroslav Kysela. At the time of this writing, it has evolved to level $0.5.x$ and is considered by its authors to be in the alpha (first) stage of development (see the ALSA Web site for the most current status reports). Nevertheless, it is already usable and, though it lacks an amenable configuration tool, it is becoming easier to set up and install (Figure 2-2 shows ALSA's configuration utility). The ALSA drivers aim for complete implementation of their supported cards' feature sets: Full duplex is present for any card that has it, and support is available for the digital I/O of certain cards (the Hoontech 4Dwave, the RME Hammerfall, and the Creative Labs SBLive!). The ALSA drivers are free, and two very active mail lists provide excellent forums for reporting and resolving user-level and development problems.

ALSA is considered by many users to be the future of Linux kernel sound support. Its PCM audio support is already excellent, a very powerful MIDI sequencer applications programming interface (API) is nearing completion, OSS/Free emulation is almost perfect, and the number of supported chipsets is growing. Perhaps most importantly, ALSA is open-source, and many talented Linux programmers continue to lend their skills to its development. The ALSA drivers will eventually replace OSS/Free in the kernel distribution, perhaps as early as the $2.4.x$ series.

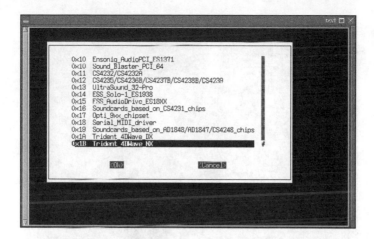

Figure 2-2: ALSA's alsaconf utility

From the 2.2.x series onward, the Linux kernel lets you configure sound system support without specifying particular driver modules. This feature makes it possible to install new drivers more easily, without having to reconfigure the entire system or rename/ remove kernel sound modules already present. This amenity is especially agreeable to the ALSA package.

The OSS/Linux Driver

Authors: Hannu Savolainen, Dev Mazumdar
Web site: http://www.4front-technologies.com
FTP site: n/a
Maintained: Yes
Availability: Commercial, binary-only
License: Copyright held by authors

The OSS/Linux driver is a commercial package available from 4Front Technologies (Figure 2-3 shows its configuration utility). It sells for a base price of $20, with extra features available at somewhat higher cost. OSS/Linux is a greatly expanded version of the original OSS/Free drivers and is thus compatible with any application written for the Linux kernel drivers. OSS/Linux supports a much greater number of cards and chipsets than OSS/Free, and its configuration utility is simple and powerful. Cards can be autodetected, manually configured, and added or removed at will (without a system reboot). The 4Front package is distributed as a binary-only package with an automated installation. Purchasing OSS/Linux entitles the user to one year of technical support and two years of free upgrades. A trial version is available from the company's Web site.

```
┌─ Select a device to be added ─────────────────────────────┐
│◀Front Tech. Virtual Mixer (includes SoftOSS)              │
│4Front Tech. Virtual Synth (SoftOSS) for 486/40           │
│4Front Tech. Virtual Synth (SoftOSS) for 486/66+          │
│4Front Tech. Virtual Synth (SoftOSS) for Alphas           │
│4Front Tech. Virtual Synth (SoftOSS) for MMX/P6/PII        │
│4Front Tech. Virtual Synth (SoftOSS) for P100+            │
│4Front Tech. Virtual Synth (SoftOSS) for PowerPCs          │
│4Front Tech. WaveLoop loopback audio device (NOT SUPPORTED ANY MORE)│
│A-Plus Sound of Music (OPL3-SA)                           │
│A-Trend Harmony 3DS724 PCI *BETA. See README.PCI-XG*      │
│A-Trend Harmony 3Ds751 (PCI)                              │
│AMD Interwave reference card                              │
│ARC Probook                                               │
│AW32 Pro (R2.2-W2)                                        │
│AW35 (CS4237)                                             │
│AW37 Pro (CS4235)                                         │
│AcerMagic S23                                             │
│Actech PCI 388-A3D *EARLY BETA. See README.Vortex*        │
│AdLib ASB 64 4D                                           │
│AdLib FM synthesizer card                                 │
│AdLib MSC 16 PnP (CS4235)                                 │
│Adaptec AME-1570 (UNSUPPORTED)                            │
│Aureal Vortex PCI *EARLY BETA. See README.Vortex*         │
│Aureal Vortex2 PCI *NOT SUPPORTED YET. See README.Vortex* │
│Avance Logic ALS300                                       │
│Aztech AZT1008 Sound Device *BETA*                        │
│Aztech AZT2320 Sound Device                               │
│Aztech AZT3000 Sound Device *NOT SUPPORTED*               │
│Aztech Sound Galaxy NX Pro                                │
│Aztech Sound Galaxy NX Pro 16                             │
│Aztech Sound Galaxy WaveRider 32+                         │
│Aztech Washington                                         │
│                                                          │
│     [ Ok ]          [ Cancel ]        [ Card Info ]       │
└──────────────────────────────────────────────────────────┘
```

Figure 2-3: 4Front's soundconf utility

Which Driver to Use?

Your soundcard may determine which package you select: If only one of the packages supports your card, your decision is made for you.

Beyond that, the answer depends on your needs and experience. The kernel modules approach (OSS/Free) has the virtue of being an "out of the box" solution, but only if you have a supported soundcard (see the CD-ROM). I recommend the OSS/Free driver if you don't want to build and install the ALSA drivers or if you don't have performance needs such as full duplex.

The ALSA drivers, like the OSS/Free, also cost nothing, but they are in heavy development and you may find them somewhat difficult to configure and install. However, I recommend the ALSA drivers if you want a cutting-edge open-source solution.

OSS/Linux supports the widest variety of cards and chips with the greatest ease, but it costs money and is not open-source. Choose OSS/Linux if you want the simplest installation and maintenance procedures, or if it's the only driver that supports your soundcard.

If you're not sure which driver package you should choose, I suggest starting with the OSS/Free kernel drivers. They are free, they are included with the kernel sources, and they are easy to configure and install.

Setting Up Linux for Sound

Now that you've chosen the driver you want to use, you're ready to configure the kernel for sound support.

It is beyond the scope of this book to go over every detail of installing the sound system software for the Linux kernel. However, some general guidance may reduce the confusion that can arise when you're setting up the software. If you've already configured your kernel properly and are sure you have the right soundcard driver, you can skip to Chapter 3.

Configuring the Linux Kernel for Audio

In this section I'll show you how to configure the kernel audio subsystem. If you already have your kernel configured (or aren't sure if it's been configured or what driver you have installed) and want to check your system to make sure everything is correct, skip to the "Checking Your System for Sound Support" section below.

Linux distributions usually include a precompiled kernel. Most distributions include a sound configuration utility that identifies, configures, and installs the appropriate modules (the OSS/Free drivers) for your audio and MIDI system. However, you may need to recompile the kernel to support new hardware, update existing drivers, or set up the system for the ALSA drivers.

Configuring and building a new kernel is not difficult, but it is beyond the scope of this book. For detailed instructions, see the Linux Kernel HOWTO at http://metalab.unc.edu/mdw/HOWTO/Kernel-HOWTO.html. When you have installed the kernel sources, read the sound system documentation in /usr/src/linux/Documentation/sound for information concerning support for your hardware.

Kernel Configuration: Tips for a Better Audio System

To make it easy to update and add drivers later, configure the kernel itself for module support.

NOTE *If you intend to use the ALSA drivers you must enable sound system support, but without selecting a soundcard.*

When configuring the kernel for sound (usually near the end of the configuration process), you will be asked to identify your soundcard and the options for its driver. Consult your card's documentation for default I/O address, IRQ (interrupt request) numbers, DMA (direct memory access) channels, and other settings. Select the appropriate options and enter the required values. You will be asked to choose whether you want the drivers to be compiled into the kernel or compiled as loadable modules. The novice may find it easiest to compile the drivers directly into the kernel, but more experienced users will want modular support. Driver modules can be removed, updated, and installed without recompiling the kernel.

You will also be asked whether you want support for /dev/dsp and /dev/audio. You do. They are the basic sound devices in Linux, and you will need them to record or play any digital audio.

Complete the configuration. Following the instructions in the kernel HOWTO, compile and install your new kernel.

After the kernel is installed, run **make modules** to create the module object files. Then run **make modules_install** to install the modules and create the necessary entries in the conf.modules file (usually found in the /etc directory).

Check for Device Files

Device files such as /dev/dsp and /dev/audio must exist for the sound devices. They are usually created during a Linux installation, and you can easily verify their existence. Enter **ls -l /dev/dsp** at the command prompt. The output should look something like this:

```
lrwxrwxrwx   1 root     root           9 Jun 13  2000 dsp -> /dev/dsp0
```

Entering **ls -l /dev/audio** should display something similar to this report:

```
lrwxrwxrwx   1 root     root          11 Jun 13  2000 audio -> /dev/audio0
```

If you didn't get the above outputs, you need to create the device files. Simply run the **/dev/MAKEDEV** script to rebuild the /dev directory contents.

Keep in mind that merely finding the device files does *not* guarantee that your sound system is operable. The correct sound driver must be loaded for the sound devices to work.

Installing and Updating Drivers

Installing and updating drivers is simple if you've enabled modular support. Follow the instructions for compiling the new driver (see the driver documentation in /usr/src/linux/documentation/drivers), then run **rmmod *old-file***. Install your new driver with **insmod *new-file***.

If you compiled your soundcard driver directly into the kernel, you have no choice but to reconfigure and recompile the kernel.

The Latest Driver Documentation

As the Linux kernel develops, procedures for configuring the sound system may change. The latest documentation for the OSS/Free kernel sound drivers can be found in /usr/src/linux/Documentation/sound, the ALSA mini-HOWTO is on-line at http://www.alsa-project.org/~valentyn/Alsa-sound-mini-HOWTO.html, and the current OSS/Linux documentation is installed in /usr/lib/oss/doc.

Configuring Plug-and-Play Soundcards

Many soundcards use the plug-and-play (PnP) protocol to configure their I/O address, IRQ, and DMA settings. Some older PnP soundcards use fixed settings or hardware jumpers: You can skip this section if you have such a card.

As of version 2.2, Linux does not have full PnP support in the kernel itself (it is expected in the 2.4 series). However, most distributions include the isapnptools utilities to provide support for PnP cards, and many distributions preconfigure those utilities.

If you want or need to do it yourself, configuring a PnP soundcard is easy. At the command prompt, enter **pnpdump > /etc/isapnp.conf**. The settings for all your PnP devices will be described in this file. You will need to uncomment the appropriate settings for your soundcard, avoiding values that conflict with other devices. Uncomment the (ACT Y) line after each device you want to activate. Finally, run the **isapnp/etc/isapnp.conf** command to let your system know about the new configuration. You will need to run **isapnp** whenever you boot your system, so you should add it to one of your startup scripts (such as .bash_profile or .bashrc in your /root or /home directory).

Configuring PCI Soundcards

PCI (personal component interface) boards are the most easily configured soundcards. You usually only need to select the driver for the card with no other special consideration, but some PCI bus conflicts have been reported. Often just moving the card to another PCI slot fixes this problem. See the Audio-Quality HOWTO For Linux in the soundcards directory of the CD-ROM of this book for more information about solving PCI card problems.

Checking Your System for Sound Support

Linux reads the contents of conf.modules when it boots and will report sound system errors, such as lost modules and incorrectly configured PnP cards. You can study the boot messages at any time by running the **dmesg** command at the prompt.

What to Look for if Your Driver Is Compiled into the Kernel

If your driver is compiled into the kernel, look for messages like these:

```
Sound initialization started
  Sound Blaster 16 (4.13) at 0x220 irq 5 dma 1,5
  Sound Blaster 16 at 0x330 irq 5 dma 0
  Yamaha OPL3 FM at 0x388
Sound initialization complete
```

If the "initialization started" and "initialization completed" lines are not displayed, the sound driver is not present in the kernel. Check that you actually installed your new kernel by entering the **uname -a** command at the prompt. If you did not update the LILO boot loader, you might still be running your previous kernel.

If nothing is printed between the initialization start and complete lines, no sound devices were found. Your card may not be supported, you may have selected and installed the wrong driver, the I/O base address may be incorrect, or you may not have configured your PnP soundcard.

Also look for any messages displayed by the sound driver during bootup that might give you a clue to potential problems.

What to Look for if You're Using Loadable Sound Driver Modules

If you are using loadable sound driver modules, look for these messages at your system startup:

```
Finding module dependencies… done
    can't locate module sound
    can't locate module midi
```

The above indicates that module dependencies were reported for sound and MIDI without error, but the actual object code modules sound.o and midi.o were not found. This error usually means that you didn't run make modules_install after compiling the kernel. On my system, the sound modules are located in /lib/modules/2.0.36/misc. If you're sure you compiled and installed the sound modules but don't know where they went, type **find * - name sound.o** (or **midi.o**) at the prompt to search your entire system for the missing modules. If found, place them in /lib/modules/(kernel-version)/misc or /lib/modules/misc.

Checking whether Audio Is Properly Configured

To check whether audio has been configured properly (or at all) for your Linux system, you can run some simple tests at the command prompt.

If you're using the OSS/Free or the OSS/Linux drivers, type **cat /dev/ sndstat** at the command prompt. On my system, this yields the following:

```
Card config:
   Ensoniq AudioPCI / Sound Blaster PCI at 0x6100 irq 11
   Roland MPU-401 at 0x330 irq 9
   Generic PnP support SoundBlaster PnP at  0x220 irq 5 drq 1,5
   Emu 8000 Synthesizer Engine at 0x620
Audio devices:
   0: Ensoniq AudioPCI (DUPLEX)
   1: Ensoniq AudioPCI  (playback only)
   2: Creative AWE64 PnP (4.16) (DUPLEX)
   3: SB secondary  device (DUPLEX)
Synth devices:
   0: AWE32-0.4.2 (RAM512k)
Midi devices:
```

```
  0: AudioPCI
  1: MPU-401 0.0  Midi interface #1
Timers:
  0: System clock
Mixers:
  0: Ensoniq AudioPCI
  1: Sound Blaster
  2: AWE32 Equalizer
```

Let's look at this report in some detail. The card configuration section tells me that I have a Sound Blaster PCI128 (also known as the Ensoniq AudioPCI), a true Roland MPU-401 MIDI interface (my MIDI Quest MQX32M standalone MIDI interface), a Sound Blaster PnP card (a Sound Blaster AWE64), and an EMU8000 (the on-board synthesizer for the AWE64). Audio I/O devices are found on the PCI128 and the AWE64, and their full-duplex status is noted. The synth device is the EMU8000 on the AWE64: It is compatible with an earlier incarnation of the card, hence the reference to the AWE32. Active MIDI ports are found on the PCI128 and the MQX32M cards. The system clock is used to coordinate audio timing signals (necessary to control the flow of audio data in and out of the audio devices). Finally, support is provided for the mixing capabilities of the PCI128, the AWE64, and a special equalizer for the AWE32 synth (the EMU8000). The default device selection is the first listed device, so firing up the aumix software mixer would report the card capabilities of the PCI128.

On a system using the ALSA drivers, type **cat /proc/asound/cards** and **cat /proc/modules** to determine what cards and services are installed. Here's the report for a system with a Sound Blaster16 installed:

```
> cat /proc/asound/cards
        0 [card1          : SB16 - Sound Blaster 16   Sound Blaster 16 at 0x220, irq 5, dma 1&5

> cat /proc/modules
    snd-pcm1-oss      4          0
    snd-sb16          1          1
    snd-sb-dsp        4    [snd-sb16]     0
    snd-pcm1          4    [snd-pcm1-oss snd-sb-dsp]      0
    snd-pcm           3    [snd-pcm1-oss snd-sb16 snd-sb-dsp snd-pcm1]      0
    snd-mixer         3    [snd-pcm1-oss snd-sb16 snd-sb-dsp]        1
    snd-mpu401-uart   1    [snd-sb16]     0
    snd-midi          4    [snd-sb16 snd-sb-dsp snd-mpu401-uart]     0
    snd-opl3          1    [snd-sb16]     0
    snd-synth         1    [snd-sb16 snd-opl3]        0
    snd-timer         1    [snd-opl3]     0
    snd               8    [snd-pcm1-oss snd-sb16 snd-sb-dsp snd-pcm1 snd-pcm snd-mixer
snd-mpu401-uart snd-midi snd-opl3 snd-synth snd-timer]      0
```

The above report tells us that a Sound Blaster16 is installed, with services including the OPL3 FM synthesizer (snd-opl3), OSS/Free emulation (snd-pcm1-oss), support for a software mixer (snd-mixer), and emulation of the MPU401 MIDI interface.

If you run these commands and receive a message that says something like "Operation not supported by device," then you do not have the audio subsystem properly installed. Try retracing the installation steps for the driver you've installed (OSS/Free, ALSA, OSS/Linux) and be sure you have followed them precisely.

Playing a Test File

You can test your audio devices at the command prompt with the UNIX cat (catenate) command. If you don't have a WAV soundfile to test, go to ftp://mustec.bgsu.edu/pub/linux and download the linus8.wav soundfile. Enter **cat linus8.wav > /dev/dsp**, and you should hear the instructive voice of Linus Torvalds, played through the default PCM audio device. If you do have a WAV file (any WAV file should work), type **cat _your_file_.wav > /dev/dsp** to hear it.

If nothing is heard, your mixer settings may be too low. Open the aumixer program by typing **aumix** (profiled in Chapter 3—most Linux distributions automatically install aumix, but if you don't have it, check your distribution documentation to see which mixer it installed). Within aumix, raise the master and PCM channel volumes and then try your WAV file again. If you still hear nothing or if the sound is distorted, then it's time to troubleshoot.

Troubleshooting

Troubleshooting my sound system has been truly humbling. From experience I have learned that the source of most problems lies with the interface between the keyboard and the chair (i.e., yours truly). Here are some of the most common problems and solutions I've encountered:

Problem 1: The command **cat /dev/sndstat** reports that everything I installed is there, but when I play a soundfile I hear nothing.

Possible solutions: Check the levels of your software mixer (described in Chapter 3). If the master volume and PCM channels are raised sufficiently (65 percent is good), then take a look at your sound system. Check to see whether all your wires and cables are connected properly. If you have powered speakers, make sure they are turned on and that their volumes are raised. All of the equipment in your audio chain (power amplifier, mixer, signal processors) must be powered on with levels up.

Problem 2: I can play CDs, but I can't play a WAV file.

Possible solutions: Run **cat /dev/sndstat** (or **cat /proc/modules** if you installed the ALSA drivers). If no audio devices are listed, then you may have failed to correctly build or install the sound support. Retrace the steps outlined above for the kernel sound configuration.

Problem 3: I can play WAVs, but I can't play CDs.

Possible solutions: Check to see if the master volume and CD channels are raised on the software mixer. You might need to open the computer to see if the CD drive is connected to the soundcard. Be sure it's connected to the appropriate socket (it should be labelled on the board or specified in your soundcard's documentation).

If the CD drive is mounted as a data drive, your CD player may not work. Unmount the CD drive by typing `umount /mnt/cdrom` (or whatever mount point you chose for the CD drive) and restart your CD player.

Problem 4: I hear sound, but it's distorted/barely audible/noisy/too thin/too booming/playing at the wrong pitch.

Possible solutions: For problems with volume, see the solutions to Problem 1.

Distortion can be caused by a variety of factors. Overdriving speakers is a common source of distortion: If the software mixer levels are already high, raising the volume of your speakers or power amplifier will overdrive and distort the sound. Conversely, if the mixer levels are too low, increasing levels on your speakers or amplifier will increase the system noise level in a sound already lacking power.

Thin or booming sound is usually due to badly set treble and bass controls. Not all soundcard mixers provide those controls, so you might need an external EQ (equalizer) to balance the high and low frequencies of your audio.

Problems with playback speed are usually the result of incorrect configuration of the player software: A soundfile recorded with a sampling rate of 44.1 kHz must be played back at the same rate to be heard at its original pitch.

Paul Winkler's HOWTO

You may also want to check out Paul Winkler's excellent HOWTO (from http://www.linuxdj.com/audio/quality), which is dedicated to improving audio quality under Linux. Following are nuggets of wisdom from his page:

Mute unused channels   Open your mixer and mute each channel to find the noisy ones. On every card I've used there's been one or more noisy channels. Turning them down to zero or muting them can dramatically decrease system noise, especially with a poorly shielded card.

Cables   Use the best cabling and connectors you can get. Better wiring usually means better insulation and conductivity. Connectors should insert solidly: Pin-jacks are notoriously unsteady, and you may have to try a few plugs to find a good fit.

Shield cards   Move or shield cards if necessary. The motherboard, the power supply, the installed cards, and all the drives are sources for noise of various sorts, including radio frequency noise. Moving the soundcard from a noise source may reduce interference. Winkler's Audio Quality HOWTO (you'll find a copy on this book's CD-ROM) describes a homebrew method of shielding that may also reduce interference, but it is a tricky and risky operation.

Post a Message to a Newsgroup

When you believe that you have exhausted your own resources, it's time to post a distress call to a relevant Usenet newsgroup. For the best response, describe your problem in detail, make clear in your message what you've done so far, list your system specifics, avoid cross-posting (sending the same message to many groups), and be polite about asking for help.

Newsgroups likely to be of assistance when you're trying to configure and install a Linux audio system include the following:

comp.os.linux.hardware

comp.os.linux.setup

comp.os.linux.misc

linux-dev.sound

If you use the ALSA drivers, you may want to subscribe to their very active users mail list. See the ALSA Web page at www.alsa-project.org for subscription details.

Necessary Support Software

The following list is not comprehensive, but it does indicate the range of support software necessary for most of the applications presented in this book:

X11	The basic libraries and headers for the X window system
SVGA library	A console graphics library needed by many games and demos
LessTif	Free replacement libraries for the often-required Motif GUI toolkit
Gtk	The GIMP ToolKit, a graphics library for GUI development
Qt	A graphics library associated with the KDE desktop GUI
KDE libraries and headers	Needed for compiling KDE-based apps
GNOME libraries and headers	Needed for compiling Gtk apps
Xforms	Another graphics toolkit
ncurses	A library for creating a text-based interface for console applications

You should try to install the most current version of a software package, but be aware that certain applications may require older or specific libraries and/or headers. Be sure to read whatever documentation comes with the package for that information.

Many of the applications profiled are packaged as source code only. In order to compile those programs, you will need the following languages and their development environments:

C/C++	Normally in the form of the GNU C compiler (GCC), needed to build the Linux kernel itself, therefore found in all Linux distributions
Java 1.2 or Java 1.1.7 with Swing extensions	Sun Microsystems' "write once, run anywhere" language, a popular cross-platform development environment (with native GUI support)
Tcl/Tk	A scripting language (Tcl, the tool command language) bound to a set of graphics widgets (Tk, the toolkit) for rapid development of a program's graphic interface
Perl	Another scripting language, widely used for processing text in Web applications
Python	Yet another scripting language gaining popularity as a general-purpose applications programming language

Fortunately, most popular distributions include the above packages (except for Java, which must be downloaded from www.javasoft.com) as a matter of choice during the installation or upgrade process. They are also all available for free over the Internet. Check your distribution for language and interface packages you may not have installed when you first installed Linux.

Internet Connection

Like Linux itself, sound and music software is a "moving target" under constant development. As toolkits improve, so do the applications built from them, thus necessitating updates and upgrades, both easily downloaded from the Net. Further, many of the applications presented in this book maintain mail lists for user feedback, and Usenet hosts a variety of newsgroups dedicated to music and sound (not necessarily Linux-specific). Consider the Internet connection a mandatory item.

3

MIXING, PLAYING, AND RECORDING

This chapter will take you through the setup of a basic playback and recording system and also step-by-step through your first Linux recording. I will profile three programs I consider to be the best of their kind: the aumix software mixer, the yarec sound recorder/player, and the SoX soundfile format converter.

The Software Mixer

An audio-device software mixer is a necessary piece of sound support software. The mixer queries your installed audio hardware for its capabilities and represents those capabilities as channels. You use faders to control the individual and combined channel levels of audio input and output.

aumix, profiled below, is a versatile mixer that is updated frequently, and I recommend it for any Linux system. I chose aumix because it requires no special graphics toolkit, and it is included with all mainstream Linux distributions. However, many software mixers are available for Linux, using virtually every popular GUI toolkit. The listing at www.metalab.unc.edu/pub/Linux/apps/sound/mixers/ is a good place to start looking for a mixer that will accommodate your favorite graphic interface. Since the list is rather long, a text file with the .lsm (Linux software map) extension is provided for each mixer listed. This file provides a brief description of the program and its requirements. Read the .lsm files—they are your friends.

aumix

Author: Various; see AUTHORS file in package
Version profiled: 1.22
Web site: http://jpj.net/~trevor/aumix.html
FTP site: n/a
Maintained: Yes
Availability: Free, open-source
License: GPL

aumix is a command-line mixer that will run either at the Linux console or in an xterm window. It automatically configures itself to the capabilities of your soundcard and is easy to build and use. Figure 3-1 shows aumix set to record from the microphone input channel of a Sound Blaster PCI128.

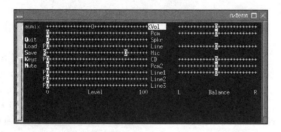

Figure 3-1: The aumix mixer

Getting It, Building It

Either retrieve the aumix-latest.tar.gz file from the FTP site listed above or from the CD-ROM that accompanies this book.

Move it to your /home or /usr/local directory and unpack it with **tar xzvf aumix-latest.tar.gz**. Move into your new aumix directory and follow the instructions there for building and installing the program. Run **./configure --help** to check the configuration options, then run **./configure**; **make**; **make install**. If all goes well, you should now have a new copy of aumix.

You will encounter the configure/make/make install *sequence of build instructions many times throughout this book. You will remain a normal user for the* configure *and* make *steps, but* make install *will require you to become the superuser by running*

su root. *You will be prompted for the root password you gave yourself when you installed Linux. If you are on a network, consult with your system administrator for access to the root account.*

./configure will inform you of any missing pieces, so once you're past that stage the make process should proceed smoothly. However, if the compiler fails, you may have a problem with outdated or conflicting versions of libraries or header files. Look closely at the output of ./configure and any error messages produced by the compiler; they can tell you exactly what's missing. Re-read the documentation included in the package, especially the INSTALL and README files, and be sure you meet the system requirements.

Use a recent stable kernel, keep your distribution up to date, and most of the time you should have no problems compiling the programs in this book.

Using aumix

aumix is very easy to use: The up and down arrow keys move the cursor to the desired channel display (mic, line, CD—all visible in Figure 3-1), the left/right arrow keys adjust the level, and the TAB key toggles between the channel levels on the left and the pan settings on the right. You can toggle the CD, microphone, and line channels between play and record states (P/R) by moving to the desired channel and pressing the space bar. If you're having trouble playing audio files, check these three mixer settings to make sure they're set properly. In Figure 3-1, all channels have been muted except for the mic input and the master volume—this setup keeps background noise to a minimum.

The Soundfile Player and Recorder

The process of recording and playing soundfiles is straightforward, so this section profiles only one: A good basic recorder and player named yarec.

yarec

Author: Ralf W. Stefan
Version profiled: 0.65
Web site: n/a
FTP site: ftp://metalab.unc.edu/pub/Linux/apps/sound/recorders/
Maintained: No
Availability: Free, open-source
License: GPL

yarec (the name stands for "Yet Another RECorder") is easy to use and works perfectly. It is a "lightweight" application, meaning that you need no special software packages in order to compile it on nearly any Linux system.

Getting It, Building It

Get the yarec-0.65.tar.gz file from the FTP site listed above. Move it to your /home or /usr/local directory. Unpack it with **tar xzvf yarec-0.65.tar.gz**, enter your newly created yarec directory, and follow the instructions there for building and installing the program. Run **./configure --help** to check the configuration options, then run **./configure**; **make**; **make install**. The program compiles quickly, and after a few minutes you will have a freshly built copy of yarec.

Launching yarec

The command

```
yarec -r 44100 -b 16 -n testrec.wav
```

launches yarec to record from the microphone (Figure 3-2). The recording will be a 16-bit file named testrec.wav, with a sampling rate of 44100 Hz.

Figure 3-2: The yarec program

Before you can record anything into yarec, you must specify the recording channel in your mixer (mic, line, or CD). The balance of this example will use the microphone input of your soundcard and aumix for setting levels.

NOTE *Setting mixer levels is very important for recording. If your input level is too low, your recording will be noisy and difficult to hear, and if it's too high the signal will distort or feedback. Make a test recording or two to find the best settings. It's also a good idea to keep your PCM audio channel set to a low value when first testing your soundcard output, bringing it up slowly to find the optimum level. If playback starts and the output setting is too high, you may damage your speakers.*

Recording with yarec

Recording with yarec is a simple six-step process:

1. At the console or xterm window prompt, open aumix, press **M** and mute all channels.

2. Move the cursor to the volume channel and use the right and left arrow keys to raise the channel level to the midpoint of the level display.

3. Move the cursor to the mic channel and toggle the P/R (play/record) mode to Record by pressing the space bar.

4. Raise the input channel level slightly higher than the midpoint.

5. Make sure the microphone is turned on and plugged into your sound-card's mic input (or a channel on your mixing board), and you should be ready to record. Quit aumix. Or, if you're working in X, you can keep aumix open and start another xterm window for yarec (see Figure 3-3). Run yarec with `yarec -r 44100 -b 16 -n testrec.wav` and press either R or ENTER on your keyboard.

6. Speak into the microphone. When you're finished, press s or the space bar to stop yarec.

You should now have a file named `testrec.wav` residing in your current directory. Press P to play it.

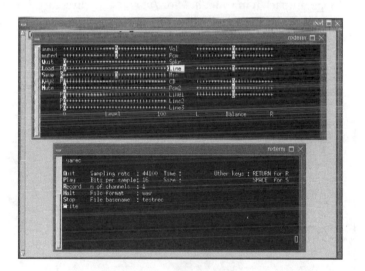

Figure 3-3: aumix and yarec set for a basic recording

General Audio Tools

The utilities presented in this section are essential tools for working with audio files. SoX, for instance, is often referred to as the "Swiss Army knife" of Linux sound tools, doing everything from recording and playback to format conversion to adding simple special effects. Other utilities are more specialized, but you will certainly want one or more of the following in your audio toolkit.

SoX

Authors: Lance Norskog, Chris Bagwell
Version profiled: 12.16
Web site: http://home.sprynet.com/~cbagwell/sox.html
FTP site: n/a
Maintained: Yes
Availability: Free, open-source
License: GPL

SoX (SOund eXchange) is a venerable Linux audio tool, especially useful for good-quality resampling (changing the soundfile sample rate), file-format conversion (such as WAV to AIFF), and handy effects processing. Converting a soundfile to another format is very easy with SoX: All you need is `sox testrec.wav testrec.aif` for a simple conversion of the file `testrec` from WAV to AIFF format.

Getting It, Building It

Download the latest package from the SoX Web site, or copy the `sox-latest.tar.gz` file from this book's CD-ROM. Once you have the SoX source code package, unpack it in your `/home` or `/usr/local/` directory. Enter the newly created SoX directory and follow the same build procedure as with aumix and yarec: `./configure`; `make`; `make install` (don't forget to `su root` for the last step!) will complete the build and installation.

Figure 3-4: The SoX manual page

Using SoX

Let's use SoX to convert the `testrec.wav` file you just recorded with yarec to an AIFF file, resample it to a lower sampling rate (22,050 Hz), and add some reverberation. Here's how it's done with SoX at the command line:

```
sox -r 44100 -t wav testrec.wav -r 22050 -t aiff testrec.aiff reverb 1 3000 500
```

The numbers after the reverb option are the values for the effect's output gain (1 is equal in intensity to the original signal with no effects added), reverb time (3000 milliseconds), and delay time (500 milliseconds). If you want to learn more about SoX, type **man sox** at the command prompt to display the SoX manual page, a portion of which is shown in Figure 3-4.

Other General Audio Tools

Basic tools   Most distributions include various basic audio tools for the console and for X. The CD-ROM bundled with this book contains as much of the profiled software as space and legality allow. To view the full range of Linux audio and MIDI tools available over the Internet, see the Linux Music & Sound Applications (http://sound.condorow.net) site. DLP's Choice (http://sound.condorow.net/dp_choice.html) is a helpful page of recommended selections from the larger listing.

Other useful tools include file compression utilities, such as Split2000 (http://heroine.linuxave.net), dedicated effects processors such as the software delay unit Tapiir (www.iua.upf.es/~mdeboer/tapiir), and dozens of audio development kits (sound.condorow.net/tools.html).

GUIs   Interfaces built with Gtk, Motif/LessTif, Qt, and other graphics toolkits give a nice appearance and ease of use in X sessions. Figure 3-5 shows a collection of audio utilities running under X.

Interface builders for the Linux console include the popular ncurses library and the SVGAlib graphics toolkit. Both are included in all mainstream Linux distributions.

Troubleshooting

If your sounds still aren't sounding, you're sure your soundcard and driver are properly installed, and Linux is properly configured on your machine (see Chapter 2), you'll need to double-check and troubleshoot everything described in the Troubleshooting section in Chapter 2. If you're having recording problems, check to make sure you've:

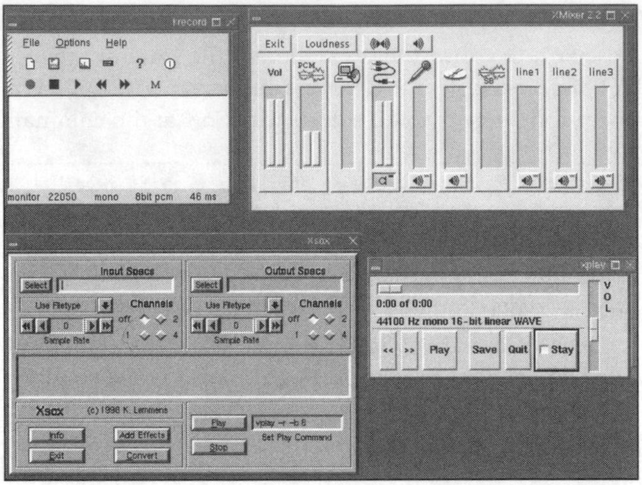

Figure 3-5: Various audio programs run in the X window environment: XForms (xsox), Qt (krecord), Xt (aifplay), and X11 (xmixer)

- Set the recording input to Record and set the recording level.

- Turned your microphone on.

- Set the playback channel level.

Managing System Load

Limit the number of open applications.

The number of programs you have running on your computer is a decisive factor in getting the most from your Linux audio system. Because Linux routinely checks various aspects of system performance, limiting unnecessary system activity can reduce the possibility of interrupted data streams. Even on a 500-MHz machine, it would probably be unwise to record four tracks of CD-quality digital audio while compiling the kernel, downloading an 80-megabyte WAV file, and watching looped MPEG animations of fractal displays. If you don't need to be online, stay off the network. On truly low-powered machines (anything less than a Pentium CPU), you may want to avoid the X window system entirely.

Going Farther

By now you should be acquainted with the basic tools of your Linux sound system, particularly SoX and your software mixer. You're ready to try out the various sound and music software packages available for Linux, and that's what the rest of this book is about. I'll be your guide on this trip, pointing out items of interest in this new world. We'll have an interesting voyage, and I hope you enjoy your journey!

4

SOUNDFILE EDITORS

A soundfile editor is required in any digital audio processing environment to perform cut/copy/paste actions, reverse files, add effects, and resample files. All of the editors presented in this chapter perform these functions and add some tricks of their own. Table 4-1 presents an overview of each editor's capabilities.

Table 4-1: Comparison of Linux Soundfile Editors

Name	File size limited by:	Recording capabilities?	GUI toolkit	Best use
DAP	Memory	Yes	Xforms	DSP and effects
MiXViews	Memory	Yes	InterViews	Signal analysis and resynthesis
Snd	Disk	Yes	Motif/LessTif	All-purpose for any size file
Kwave	Memory	No	Qt	All-purpose for smaller files
Broadcast2000	Disk	Yes	X11	All-purpose, with audio/video sync capabilities
Ceres	Memory	No	Motif/LessTif	Editing in frequency domain (spectral editing)

Use of the various editors is quite straightforward. The following reviews will concentrate on the unique and important features of the different profiled editors rather than give step-by-step instructions for their basic functions.

DAP

Author: Richard Kent
Version profiled: 2.0.2
Web site: http://www.cee.hw.ac.uk/~richardk/
FTP site: n/a
Maintained: Yes
Availability: Free, open-source
License: GPL
Capsule summary: Large assortment of processing modules, handy looping tools for AIFF and WAV files, most extensive editing suite

Richard Kent's Digital Audio Processor (DAP) for UNIX is an outstanding application, providing a full complement of basic and advanced file editing and signal processing tools. Based on the XForms cross-platform GUI toolkit, DAP is available in source code and binaries for SGI computers and their IRIX operating system, Sun's Solaris, and Linux. Soundfile editors depend heavily on the capabilities of their GUI toolkit, and Richard has used the XForms capabilities to their fullest. DAP's somewhat unusual interface is logically organized for quick access and ease of use.

Getting It, Building It

DAP is available as a pre-built binary or in a source code package. If you retrieve the binary, you need only place it somewhere in your system's PATH statement and you're good to go. Building DAP is a little more work: You'll need the Xforms development package and an up-to-date C++ compiler. Both are easy to obtain: The compiler should be standard in every contemporary Linux distribution, and the Xforms package is available for free from http://bragg.phys.uwm.edu/xforms. If you have the right tools in the right places, you need only follow Richard's instructions to build DAP on your own machine.

Using DAP

DAP's main window displays the soundfile's waveform. Clicking on the **Edit** button (on the right of the top menu bar) will call up a sample-level display in the main window; in this mode editing can be performed with single-sample accuracy, that is, on any single point of the soundfile data. You can use the mouse as a drawing tool during (and only during) an Edit session. The DSP (digital signal processing) button (next to the Edit button) opens a window of effects (all listed in "Special Effects" below) that can be applied to the waveform.

Editing

Special Effects

Figure 4-1 illustrates the DSP section opened to the reverb parameter edit window. The reverberation type is set to "Moorer" (many reverb types are named after their designer), and the other parameters have been left at their default values. As you can see, the reverb processor provides many controls over the effect, all of which can be set by direct numerical entry or by moving a slider.

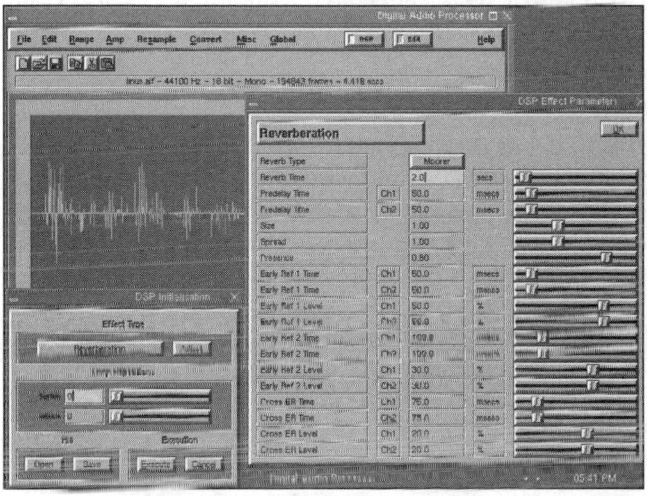

Figure 4-1: DAP in a DSP session with Reverberation feature selected

DAP's effects types and controls are more extensive than in any other Linux soundfile editor. The list includes the following processors:

- Three types of reverbs (Moorer, Schroeder, and multi-tap)

- Four types of delays (stereo, modulated, multitap, multi)

- A flanger

- A phaser

- Distortion

- Four filter types (low-pass, high-pass, band-pass, band-reject)

- A noise gate

- Auto-panning

- A compressor/limiter

After you enter or edit the parameter values with the faders (on the right side of the screen) and click Execute, another window opens running a process-meter to display time elapsed/remaining. A third post-processing window then opens automatically, and you can preview results of the added effects before "printing" them to the soundfile (though of course the ever-ready Undo can always restore the file to its pre-processed condition since the last Save).

The post-processing window also controls the mix ratio of the affected (revised) signal to the "dry" (unchanged) original, and a master fader controls the overall level of the applied effect. Click the **OK** button in the post-processing window to write the effect to the soundfile, or select **Cancel** to close the processing session without saving the results.

The Zoom Window

Figure 4-2 shows DAP opened to an Edit session. The display immediately centers and zooms in to the midpoint of the opened soundfile, where you use the cursor as a drawing tool to edit the waveform or create a new one. Because the Zoom window will focus down quite far, you can edit soundfiles in DAP at the single-sample level.

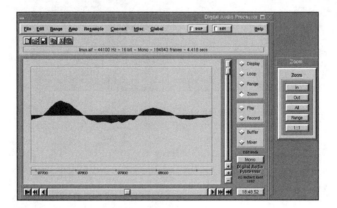

Figure 4-2: DAP in an Edit session

Looping

Because DAP works only on AIFF soundfiles (imported RAW and WAV files are converted before editing), it has excellent support for setting and editing loop points. Setting loop points is as easy as selecting a region then clicking on the **Range** button for the loop you want to create (either Sustain or Release). Loop mode can be set to Off, Forward, and Forward/Backward. On playback, the **Release** button in the Play window will cancel the loop and continue on in the file.

Figure 4-3 shows the Loop panel in operation.

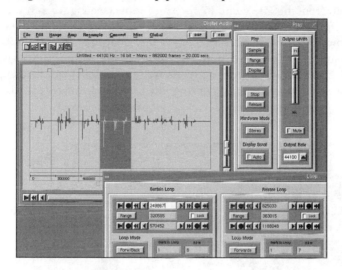

Figure 4-3: DAP's Loop panel

The Play Function

Figure 4-4 shows DAP with a soundfile loaded and the Play functions selected. The Play functions do much more than merely turn file play on and off. You can set the playback length to the length of the entire loaded file, a selected range of the file, or to only what is visible in the main display window. You can also lock the faders or instantly mute the output level. You can further control output by specifying playback sampling rates from 8 kHz to 48 kHz.

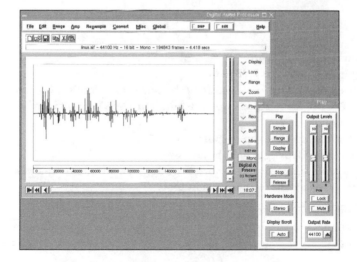

Figure 4-4: DAP with the Play functions selected

DAP can record as well as play back. Recording is straightforward: Select **New** from the **File** menu to open a window (see Figure 4-5) for setting the sampling rate, bit resolution, number of channels, and duration; the Mixer (lower right in Figure 4-5) controls the recording source and its input volume. Toggling on the Meter in the Recording panel will provide a visual monitor for the input level. Once all levels are optimal, click on the **Sample**, **Range**, or **Display** button to start recording; the threshold Trigger can also start recording (note that the Trigger can be set to voice-activate).

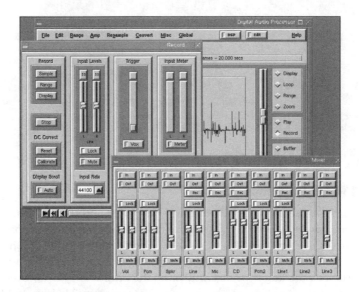

Figure 4-5: DAP's Recording window

MiXViews

Author: Doug Scott
Version profiled: 1.22 pl 00
Web site: http://www.ccmrc.ucsb.edu/~doug/htmls/MiXViews.html
FTP site: ftp://ftp.create.ucsb.edu/pub/MiXViews/binaries/
Maintained: Yes
Availability: Free, open-source
License: Copyright held by author
Capsule summary: Wide variety of data visualizations, analysis/resynthesis tools, excellent file conversion tools

Although its InterViews GUI betrays its age, MiXViews is a powerful and unique editor, particularly in the analysis and resynthesis of sound. Updates of MiXViews appear rather slowly, but the author keeps his Web page current.

I use MiXViews daily in my studio. No other Linux soundfile editor has its visualization capabilities or its analysis/resynthesis functions. Whenever I need detailed views of a soundfile's frequency content, if I want to warp a soundfile by cutting and pasting data between analysis displays, or if I just need to quickly apply a fade-in to a sound, I turn to MiXViews.

Getting It, Building It

Building MiXViews from its source code is not difficult, but it does require the InterViews toolkit libraries and header files. InterViews is not typically included in Linux distributions; directions for acquiring the toolkit can be found on the MiXViews Web page. Unless you are experienced at building Linux libraries, I suggest using the MiXViews binary provided by its author. Once you have the binary distribution, `tar xzvf mixviews-latest.tar.gz` will unpack MiXViews and create a MiXViews directory containing the application. Copy it to anywhere in your system PATH (`/usr/local/bin` is good), and you're ready to use MiXViews.

Using MiXViews

Learning to use MiXViews effectively requires some trial and error, particularly when working with its LPC (linear predictive coding) capabilities (LPC settings require some guesswork to optimize the results of the analysis). Many of its strengths, such as its phase vocoding resynthesis, require understanding some rather abstruse audio analysis and signal processing methods. However, since the InterViews toolkit allows graphic exploration and manipulation of the data files, it is easy to use and experiment with the analysis/resynthesis routines.

Editing Tools

MiXViews opens with a typical waveform display window and a smaller status display box. MiXViews is very generous with its support for various soundfile formats, loading and playing WAV, AIFF, SND, AU, RAW, and SF files. In addition to the standard editing tools, MiXViews provides splice-in/splice-out, mix, and crossfade functions as well as high-quality digital filtering, a delay line, gain, and pitch-shifting. File length, sample format, and sample rate can also be adjusted.

Unique Signal Processing Features

The Analysis menu provides tools for pitch and amplitude envelope extraction, phase vocoder analysis, linear predictive coding (LPC), and fast Fourier transform (FFT) analysis. Because the InterViews toolkit permits data exchange between different datatypes, you can mix data from the various analysis screens and resynthesize the results with either LPC or the phase vocoder. MiXViews also supports LPC formant filtering—that is, the filter is designed from the pattern of formants (resonant peaks in the overall frequency spectrum) derived from analyzing a sound.

Using the Phase Vocoder

The phase vocoder in MiXViews works well with the default settings. The process is very simple: Open a soundfile in MiXViews, select all or any part of the sound you want to analyze, then select **Phase Vocoder Analysis** from the **Analysis** menu. For this exercise, we'll accept the default settings (shown in Figure 4-6), press the **Confirm** button, and watch the Status window fly through its calculations.

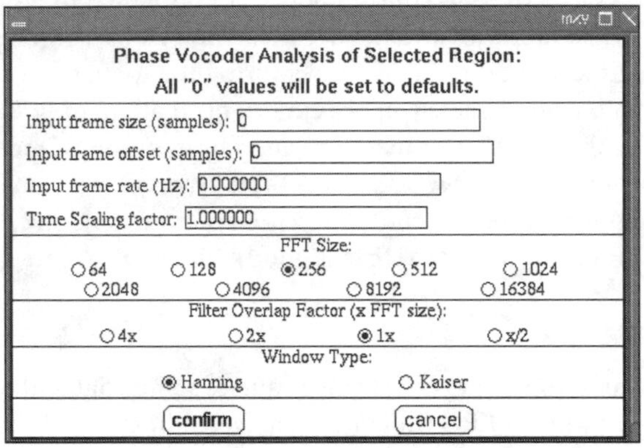

Figure 4-6: Default settings of the phase vocoder

When the status returns to Ready, a new phase vocoder window will appear. This window permits graphic modifications to the analysis data, either globally or by individual channel. For our example we'll leave everything untouched. However, for the next step we do need to select all channels of the vocoder by right-clicking the mouse anywhere within the channel display. By now the phase vocoder window should look like Figure 4-7.

Open **File • New** to create an empty soundfile with the same length and sampling rate as your original source file. A new instance of mxv will open with a blank waveform display. Select the phase vocoder from the **Sound • Synthesis** submenu, watch the Status window fly through the synthesis, and you will soon see a replica of your original file, resynthesized into the new Soundfile window.

That's all there is to it. I leave it to you to revise this example using different analysis settings and modifications in the vocoder window (which include reverse, scale, envelope, and delay functions).

Using LPC

The linear predictive coding (LPC) routines are somewhat trickier. A detailed explanation of LPC is beyond the scope of this book; interested readers should consult the relevant material in Charles Dodge's *Computer Music*.[1] Briefly, LPC

---

1 Dodge, C., and Thomas A. Jerse. *Computer Music*. New York: Schirmer 1997. ISBN 0-02-864682-7.

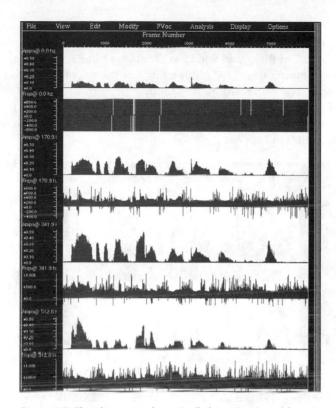

Figure 4-7: The phase vocoder with all channels selected for editing

designs an analysis-derived filter that will recreate the original waveform of the sound, retaining the formants of the sound's spectral envelope (the relative strengths of the sound's frequencies). Because formant positions and strengths indicate age and gender of a voice, the technique has been especially useful in speech synthesis.

For your first experiment with LPC, load a short (about 4- or 5-second), 16-bit, 44.1 kHz soundfile of a speaking voice, then select **LPC Analysis** from the **Analysis** menu. The window shown in Figure 4-8 will appear.

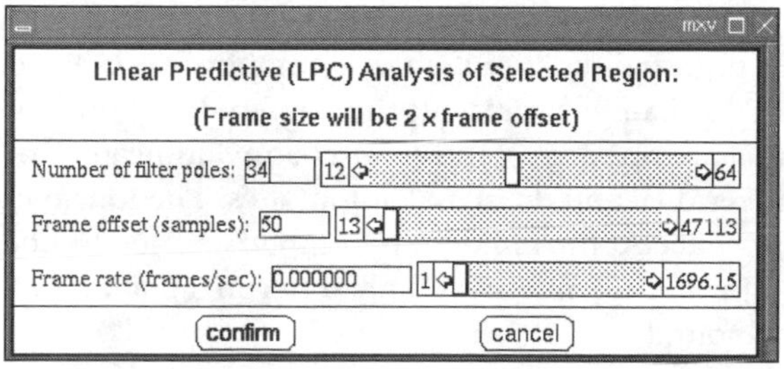

	mxv □ ✕
Linear Predictive (LPC) Analysis of Selected Region:	
(Frame size will be 2 x frame offset)	
Number of filter poles: 34   12 ◇   ◇ 64
Frame offset (samples): 50   13 ◇   ◇ 47113
Frame rate (frames/sec): 0.000000   1 ◇   ◇ 1696.15
confirm   cancel

Figure 4-8: LPC analysis parameters

Set the number of poles (peaks in the filter amplitude response) to 45, leave the frame offset at 50, and set the frame rate to 220. The analysis takes "snapshots" of the sound and casts them into frames, very much like a video is a series of frames, and each frame supplies the resynthesis with the information to recreate that part of the sound.

Press the **Confirm** button. The Status window will display the number of frames processed, then the graphic representation of the analysis data shown in Figure 4-9 will appear.

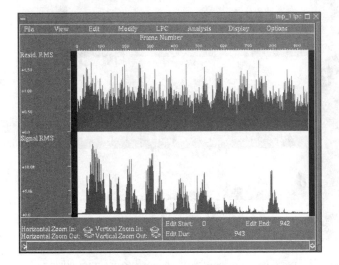

Figure 4-9: LPC data window

Before going farther with the process, select **Stabilize Frames** from the LPC menu. This will help the constructed filter keep parts of the sound from "exploding" when their amplitudes approach the upper limit of their range (a little more than 30K for 16-bit soundfiles). The frame stabilization is an automatic process without parameters. When it finishes, go to **View • Channel Display • Set Channel View** and set it to the first four channels (0 through 3). These channels contain the data you will most likely want to edit for the resynthesis. Your data display should now look like Figure 4-10.

Let's look from the top down at those four channels. The first is called the RMS (root mean squared) amplitude of the residual, a fancy way of saying that it represents the amplitudes of the noise components in the original sound. The signal RMS channel represents the amplitudes of the voiced components (the parts that are not noise); the error channel indicates the difference between the residual and the signal amplitudes. The fourth channel contains the frequency data: At the moment it's empty, so if you want to include pitch information in your resynthesis you need to run a pitch envelope detection on your original sound.

Select **Pitch Envelope Extraction** from the **Analysis** menu. A window will open, as seen in Figure 4-11.

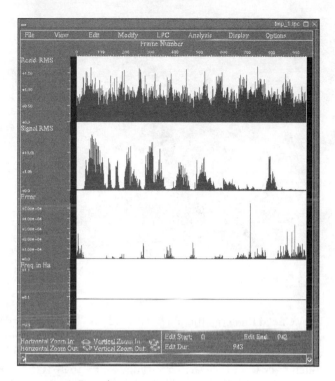

Figure 4-10: Four channels of LPC analysis data

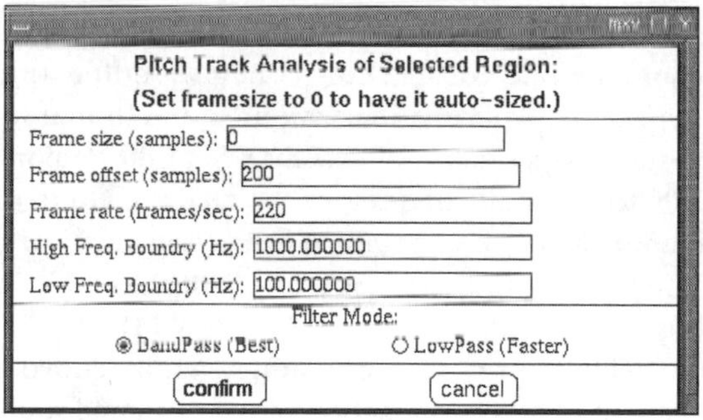

Pitch Track Analysis of Selected Region:
(Set framesize to 0 to have it auto-sized.)

Frame size (samples): 0
Frame offset (samples): 200
Frame rate (frames/sec): 220
High Freq. Boundry (Hz): 1000.000000
Low Freq. Boundry (Hz): 100.000000

Filter Mode:
◉ DandPass (Best)   ○ LowPass (Faster)

confirm   cancel

Figure 4-11: Pitch envelope analysis parameters

Set the frame size to 0 (for autosizing the frame throughout the pitch detection), set the frame rate to 220 (the same rate used in the LPC analysis), and leave the other settings at their default values. Press **Confirm**, watch the Status window whip through the detection, and the pitch track window will appear (Figure 4-12).

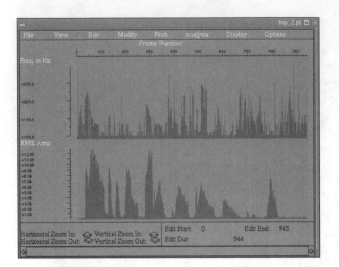

Figure 4-12: Pitch analysis data window

Now we need to merge the pitch data with the LPC analysis data. Look at the lower right corner of the Analysis window for the edit range (Edit Start, Edit End, and Duration), then set the pitch track edit range in **Edit • Set Edit Region** of the pitch track window to the same range as the analysis (for the best fit of pitch and amplitude). Return to the Analysis window and select **Merge Pitch Data** from the LPC menu. Now your analysis display should look like Figure 4-13.

At this point you are ready to resynthesize the analysis data. Select **File • New** and create an empty soundfile with the same characteristics as your original (length, sampling rate, format, etc). A new soundfile window containing no data will appear. We will resynthesize our sound in that window.

Return to the analysis data. Select **Edit • Set Edit Region** and set the last channel to 1000 to select all channels of the analysis. Go to the **Modify** menu and select **Smooth Curve**, then **Stabilize Frames** again. Now go to the new, empty soundfile window and select **Sound • Synthesis • LPC Resynthesis**. There, a dialog will appear (as shown in Figure 4-14).

Accept the defaults, press **Confirm**, and in a moment your empty soundfile will be filled with an LPC reconstruction of your original sound. The screenshot in Figure 4-15 on page 56 displays the results of running the process described above on the linus.wav file (included on this book's CD).

Going Farther

As you can see, our reconstruction needs more work, but we will go no farther now. Hints for better resynthesis include adjusting the RMS of the residual downward, boosting the signal RMS, rescaling the error channel, and stabilizing the frames after each edit (all of these adjustments are available from the Mod-

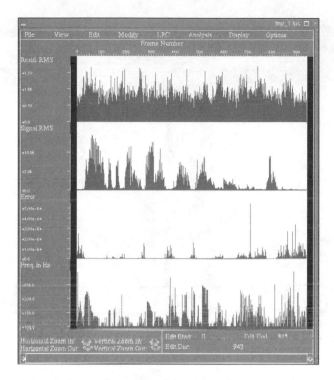

Figure 4-13: Data from pitch analysis merged into LPC analysis

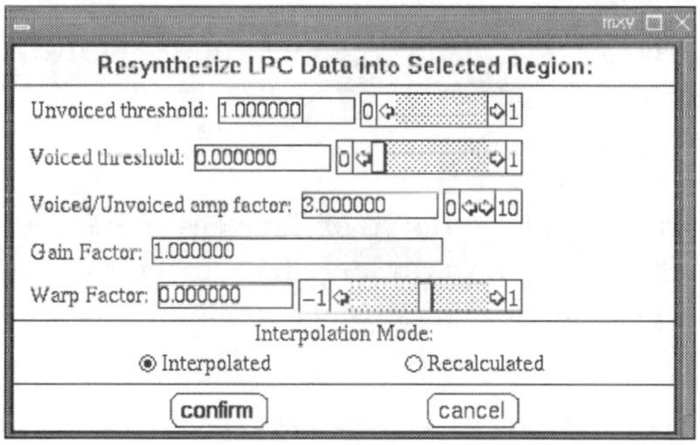

Resynthesize LPC Data into Selected Region:

Unvoiced threshold: 1.000000   0   1

Voiced threshold: 0.000000   0   1

Voiced/Unvoiced amp factor: 3.000000   0   10

Gain Factor: 1.000000

Warp Factor: 0.000000   -1   1

Interpolation Mode:
⊙ Interpolated   ○ Recalculated

(confirm)   (cancel)

Figure 4-14: Dialog showing LPC Resynthesis

ify menu in the LPC analysis data window). You will likely need to boost the gain of your new soundfile: Do this using the **Phrase** function from the soundfile's **Modify** menu. Some very interesting effects are possible using the Reverse and Apply Envelope functions found in the analysis data Modify menu. I leave the exploration of these possibilities as an exercise for the interested reader.

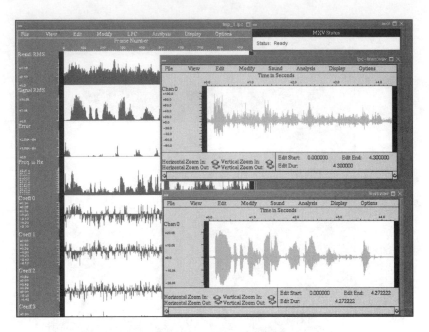

Figure 4-15: Linus.wav before and after LPC analysis/resynthesis

Snd

Author: Bill Schottstaedt
Version profiled: 3.2
Web site: http://ccrma-www.stanford.edu/CCRMA/Software/snd/snd.html
FTP site: ftp://ccrma-ftp.stanford.edu/pub/Lisp/
Maintained: Yes
Availability: Free, open-source
License: Copyright held by the Board of Trustees at Stanford University
Capsule summary: Loads arbitrarily large files, includes synthesis and process-ing capabilities of Common LISP Music, accommodates widest variety of soundfile types

Snd is a straightforward tool, easy to use, with considerable power lurking behind its simple interface. It is tightly integrated with Common LISP Music (CLM, a MusicV-type audio processing environment similar to the Csound programming language), allowing users of CLM to quickly see the results of their computations, edit the results in Snd, and send the data back to CLM for further processing. Recent evolution of Snd includes the integration of CLM's processing power directly into Snd—in other words, CLM is compiled as a normal object file and included in the build of Snd.

Getting It, Building It

The Snd distribution package includes makefiles for various machines and environments, including Linux and LessTif. If any particular makefile doesn't work, running **./configure** should create a site-specific makefile. After configuration, Snd is compiled and installed by running **make** and then (as root) **make install**.

Editing Tools

At first glance Snd seems a bit bare: No drop-down menus offer lengthy lists of DSP functions, and in fact very few functions—beyond display and cut/copy/paste operations—seem in residence. Figure 4-16 shows what Snd looks like when invoked with a filename from the command line. Not much to look at, until the Show Controls option is selected from the View menu. Figure 4-17 shows the file display with controls: The amplitude and speed controls are usable in realtime, whereas the other settings must be applied (with the Apply button) before they take effect.

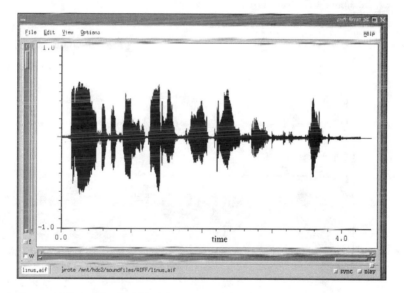

Figure 4-16: Snd invoked from the command line

The Filter control is of special interest: The window at the bottom of the figure provides a graphic envelope editor (the horizontal line), while the window immediately to the right of the "filter" label displays the graph coordinates in the proper LISP notation for use in CLM. Figure 4-18 demonstrates the use and application of the graphic filter control.

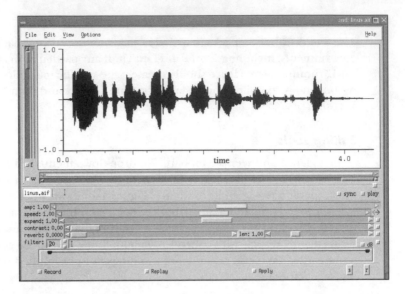

Figure 4-17: Snd's display with controls

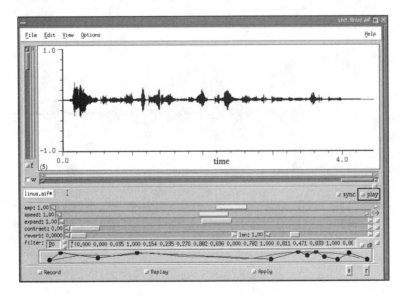

Figure 4-18: Snd's graphic filter controls applied to linus.aif

Figure 4-19 shows Snd's graphic envelope editor. The example illustrates an envelope applied to the amplitude of the selected soundfile, but the envelope drawn may also be applied to the file's spectrum or its sampling rate. You can save envelopes and recall them for later use, thus creating personal libraries of specialized envelope functions.

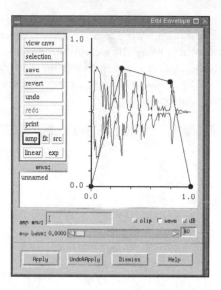

Figure 4-19: Snd's graphic envelope editor

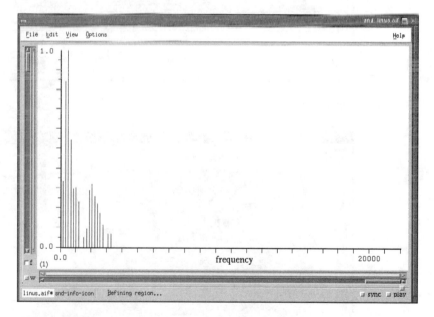

Figure 4-20: Snd's spectral display

Like many other editors, Snd offers spectral displays as well as the typical display of the waveform amplitude. Snd excels here: Numerous controls help you calculate and display a soundfile's spectral components. Figure 4-20 shows our test soundfile in its default spectral display, a 256-point FFT using a Blackman window and represented as a normal FFT.

Figure 4-21 illustrates a 2048-point FFT performed on the soundfile, using a Hanning window and represented as a sonogram. Figure 4-22 shows the results of a wavelet transform using the default settings and displayed as a spectrogram (drawn with the Dots & Lines option from the Graph Styles in the View menu). Figure 4-22 also shows the Transform Options dialog box and the Help box for those options.

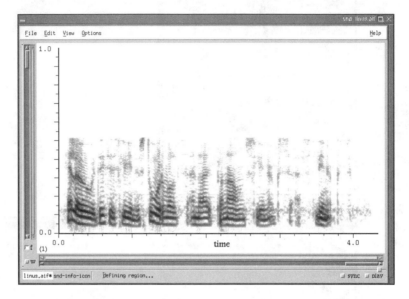

Figure 4-21: Snd's sonogram display

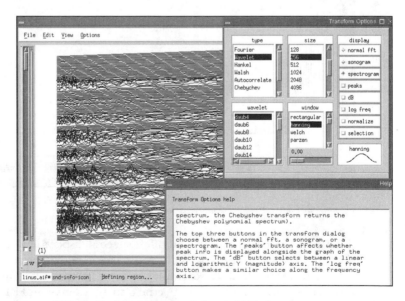

Figure 4-22: The Transform Options dialog and Help boxes

Recording and Playback

Snd records and plays soundfiles in a variety of formats, including some unusual types such as NIST/SPHERE and AFsp. It can even read formats from popular samplers and hybrid synthesizers (such as the Kurzweil K2000, Yamaha SY85 and SY99, and Yamaha TX16W) and from other soundfile editing and processing applications (such as Sound Tools, Sound Designer I and II, Sonic Foundry's Sound Forge, and Turtle Beach's Wave).

Playback in Snd is straightforward: Simply click on the **Play** button, and the file will begin playing (hold the CTRL key down when you click on **Play**, and you'll see a tracking cursor move through the file as the file sounds). If you have opened Snd's performance controls (seen in Figure 4-17) you can add reverberation and make adjustments to the sound's amplitude and pitch in real time. Click on the **Play** button again to stop playback.

Selecting the **Record** function from the **File** menu opens Snd's recording console (Figure 4-23), which provides a mixer (or mixers in the case of multiple soundcards) and input/output level meters. You can specify the recorded file's name, sampling rate, data format, number of channels, duration, buffer size, and I/O sources; if the file format permits comments, an entry box is provided so you can add them to the soundfile header. As Figure 4-23 indicates, Snd can determine how many cards are present in the system and configure itself to reflect the available controls for those cards. As seen in the figure, my cards have different mixer capabilities, which Snd accurately displays (the upper meters and mixer represent the PCI128, and the second row applies to the AWE64).

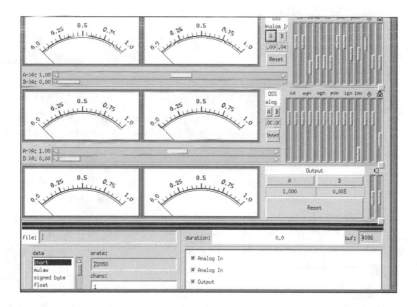

Figure 4-23: Snd's recording console

Advanced Uses of Snd

The Listener window is Snd's interface to the powerful synthesis and signal processing options of Common LISP Music, a dynamic plug-in architecture, and full customization of the Snd GUI. However, I must remind the reader that what follows requires a healthy measure of the hacker spirit. If you already program in another language, you should have no undue difficulties with this material. If you're new and willing, just follow the instructions closely, think about what you're doing, and try again if things fail. Don't be shy about asking questions on newsgroups and mail lists!

The Listener creates or transforms sound by interpreting commands and routines written in Guile, a LISP-like programming language. Files with the scm extension are packages of Guile code. These packages can be loaded from the command line, the HOME/.snd resource file, or dynamically in the Listener. Study examp.scm, mix.scm, and snd-test.scm (all in HOME/snd-3) for examples.

To use the Listener, Snd must be compiled with support for Guile. If Guile is not included with your distribution, see the Guile Web site at www.gnu.ai.mit.edu/software/guile/guile.html for information about downloading and building the latest version.

LessTif is a fine free replacement for the Motif GUI toolkit, but the Listener will not work with the default LessTif installation. In LESSTIF_SRC/lib/Xm/TextIn.c, comment out the block starting at line 826 (LessTif version 0.89):

```
#if 0                   /* add this */
    if (Text_EditMode(tw) != XmSINGLE_LINE_EDIT)
    {
        return;
    }
#endif    /* and add this */
```

Recompile and reinstall LessTif, then compile Snd. The Listener will now work, but you will need to click the mouse in the window after each time you press the ENTER key.

From the Snd home directory, run **snd -l examp.scm** to load an example set of signal processing routines and functions. When Snd starts, load a sound-file and open the **Listener** from the **View** menu. Snd should now appear as shown in Figure 4-24.

Now you can experiment with the Guile/Scheme examples you loaded when you invoked Snd. For a quick demonstration, enter this line at the Listener prompt:

```
(jc-reverb 2.0 #f .1 #f)
```

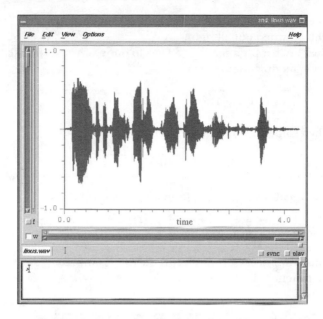

Figure 4-24: Snd's waveform display and Listener window

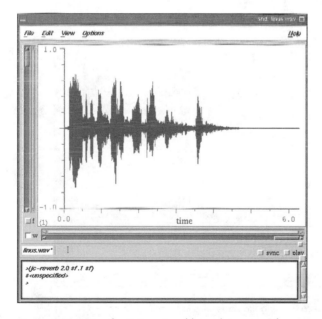

Figure 4-25: Using the Listener to add reverb to a sound

A small hourglass will appear beside the file name (`linus.wav` in the screenshot) and will remain until the reverb process finishes. Now your display should look like Figure 4-25.

The #<unspecified> message at the prompt is Snd's way of telling you everything turned out all right.

Next we'll apply a series of effects to our newly reverberated sound. First, some ring modulation:

```
(map-chan (ring-mod 100 '(0 0 1 0)))
```

Then some chordal comb filtering:

```
(map-chan (comb-chord .95 40 .3))
```

And finally some moving formant filtering:

```
(map-chan (moving-formant .01 '(0 200 .5 400 1 100)))
```

This last process significantly reduces the amplitude of the output. Let's use the Listener one last time to call a scale plug-in.

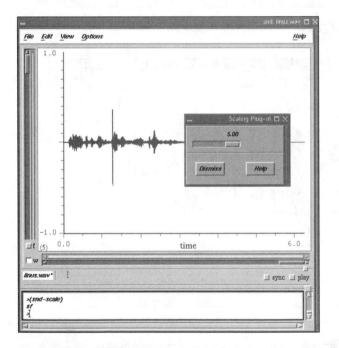

Figure 4-26: Calling the scale plug-in from the Listener

In the Snd And Motif section of the extsnd.html file you will find the C code for building a plug-in to scale amplitude up or down. Follow the directions, build the plug-in, and update Snd by entering these commands in the Listener:

```
(define lib (dynamic-link "HOME/snd-3/scale.so"))
    (dynamic-call "init_snd_scale" lib)
```

Enter (snd-scale) in the Listener and set the slider in the plug-in window as shown in Figure 4-26.

Save your work.

Details of these and other interesting transformations can be found in the examp.scm file. For more plug-ins, see the Web page at www.sci.fi/~mjkoskin/ for Matti Koskinen's soundfile denoising utilities. More information about extending Snd is available in the extsnd.html file.

The Listener opens Snd's entire tool chest for defining its interface components, audio I/O settings, and signal processing parameters, but you must have the desire to hack the system. Study the examples, read the fine manual, explore and experiment.

Kwave

Author: Martin Wilz
Version profiled: 0.29.7
Web site: http://fs.spinfo.uni-koeln.de/~kwave/
FTP site: n/a
Maintained: No
Availability: Free, open-source
License: GPL
Capsule summary: Graphic additive synthesizer, fast graphic envelope editing, good basic editor

Kwave is a newer editor based on the Qt GUI and the KDE libraries. It presents a modern interface that takes advantage of Qt's graphics and Linux threads, presenting the possibility of interactive editing.

Getting It, Building It

If your Linux distribution bundles the Qt GUI toolkit and the KDE desktop environment and its development packages, you should be able to compile Kwave with the by-now familiar command sequence of ./configure, then make, then make install.

If not, you will need to acquire the Qt and KDE development packages before you can build Kwave. You don't need the entire KDE desktop environment, only the development libraries and headers (complete instructions for these components are included with the packages).

Qt is available from www.trolltech.com, and KDE is available from www.kde.org.

Using Kwave

Kwave's waveform display occupies the bulk of the main window, with a continuously updated status display across the bottom.

Editing Tools

Kwave's feature list is impressive. It is capable of

- Importing ASCII text files and converting them to WAV format (and vice versa)

- Calculating a variety of generated sounds (besides the additive synthesis it can create silence, noise, or a pulse train)

- Undoing your mistakes with the Revert function

  Upon opening, Kwave offers few amenities—as shown in Figure 4-27.

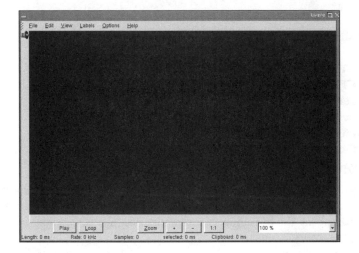

Figure 4-27: Kwave opening screen

However, when a soundfile has been loaded, the top menu expands, as shown in Figure 4-28.

Kwave makes excellent use of the Qt graphics toolkit. Figure 4-29 shows an example from the Create item under the Fx-Filters menu. The soundfile seen in Figure 4-28 has been normalized (its overall volume has been maximized relative to the sound's peak volume) and the Create Filter window is open for tweaking.

The graph updates in realtime as the sliders are moved, giving immediate visual feedback to the filter design.

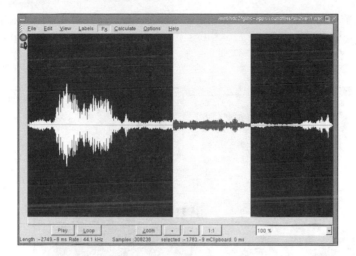

Figure 4-28: Kwave with a loaded soundfile

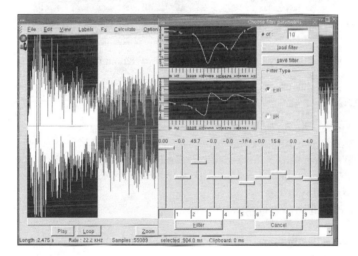

Figure 4-29: Kwave's filter designer at work

Recording and Playback

Kwave provides only Play and Loop-play—it doesn't yet record soundfiles.

Special Effects: Sounds from Scratch

Kwave can also create sounds from scratch. Figure 4-30 shows Kwave's Additive Synthesis editor (upper right) opened along with the main display (bottom) and the synthesis parameter (upper left) windows.

Similar to the sample generator in Figure 4-30, the synthesis graph updates in realtime with slider (fader) movements. The Sweep envelope editor is similarly interactive.

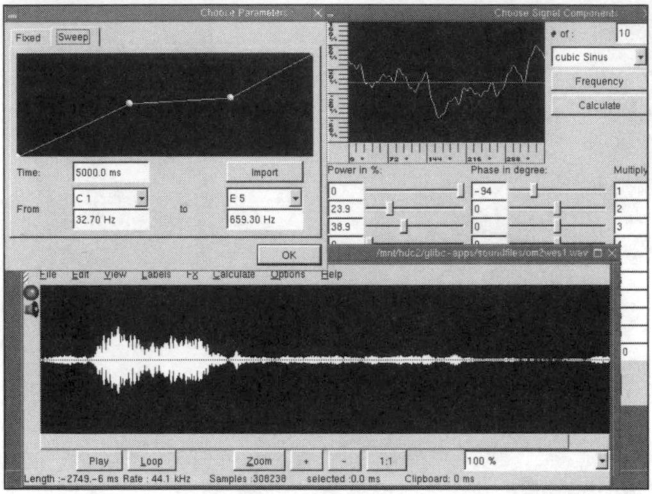

Figure 4-30: Kwave's Additive Synthesis editor (upper right)

Broadcast 2000

Author: Adam Williams
Version profiled: Final
Web site: http://heroine.linuxave.net/bcast2000.html
FTP site: n/a
Maintained: Yes
Availability: Free, open-source
License: GPL
Capsule summary: Non-destructive edits, handles very large files, synchronized audio/video editing

Broadcast 2000 has the distinction of being the first free non-linear realtime audio/video editor available for Linux. It also functions as an a/v recorder and player, but as author Adam Williams writes, "Broadcast 2000 is first and foremost an editor."

For audio purposes, you can use Broadcast 2000 (from here on referred to as BC2) as a standalone sound editor, recorder, processor, and mixer. Noteworthy recording and playback features include:

Unlimited tracks

Floating-point audio processing

64-bit effects

Realtime effect plug-ins

Full-duplex recording

Variable speed, bidirectional playback

5:1 channel 24 bit 196 kHz audio output

Batch rendering

Track concatenation

Signal processing functions include this list of audio effects:

CD ripper	Gain	Spectrogram
DC offset	Synthesizer	Time stretch
Delay	Invert	Pitch shift
Denoise	Limit/expand	Resample
EQ graphic	Normalize	Reverb
EQ parametric	Reverse	

Although this profile will focus only on BC2's audio editing capabilities, I must mention that the video capabilities of BC2 are also impressive. According to its Web page, it can ". . . strip commercials in an instant, perform image enhancement, copy without generation loss, play back hours of edited movies without copying back to a second tape . . . record TV shows and watch them when you want in the original broadcast quality . . . "

All of this and more, for free, with open source code. Definitely a "Most Recommended" Linux audio package.

Getting It, Building It

BC2 is available in source code and as a "trial" binary. The author suggests downloading the binary and testing it on your system before you decide to retrieve the sources and build it yourself. If you decide to build your own binary, download the latest source package from the BC2 Web site, unpack it in your /home directory, and enter the newly created bcast2000_final_source directory. Compiling BC2 requires only common X libraries included with almost every Linux distribution. If you have any doubts about the compatibility of your libraries, you can download a pre-packaged set from the BC2 Web page. Finally, run **make** and (as root) **make install**. Your new build of BC2 is complete.

Using BC2

You can start BC2 by entering **bcast2000** in the BCHOME/newbc/bcast directory. You can also edit the bcast2000.sh script (in the BCHOME top directory) for the location of the bcast2000 binary and libbcbase.so library, then copy the script to /usr/local/bin. Now you can start BC2 from any directory.

But First . . .

Before doing anything else, you should read the BC2 HTML documentation (in /docs under the top BC2 directory) for clear descriptions of all the program's features and tools. This documentation is not called from within BC2 itself, so you'll need to keep a Web browser open in order to read it while you're working.

Start the program from an xterm by entering **bcast2000.sh** at the prompt. The default configuration will open a main window with three smaller panels, as seen in Figure 4-31. If your screen feels cluttered you can freely open and close the console, level indicator, and video windows.

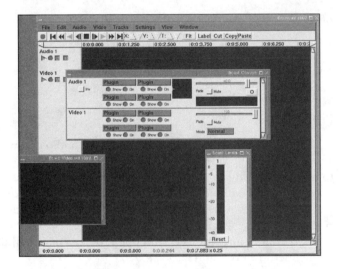

Figure 4-31: Broadcast 2000's opening appearance

From the menu bar at the top of the main window, open **Settings • Preferences** and edit the information (if necessary) in this panel as shown in Figure 4-32. If you are unsure about what to change, simply use the default settings.

Assets and the Edit Decision List

Unlike the other editors profiled in this chapter, BC2 organizes all of your loaded soundfiles into a set of assets. Assets are then referenced to build what is called an edit decision list (EDL). Using the assets manager (available in Files • Assets . . .) you can delete soundfiles from your disk or project, append files to new tracks, retrieve soundfile information, and rebuild the EDL index.

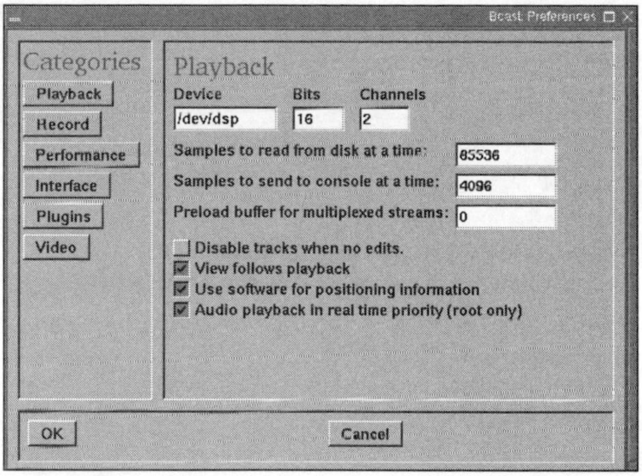

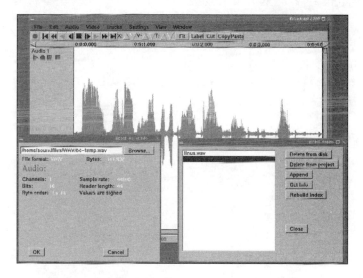

Figure 4-32: The global Preferences window

Figure 4-33: Waveform display and asset manager windows

Figure 4-33 shows the asset manager for the project below, with the Get Info panel opened for the edited portion (bc-temp.wav).

When you select **File • Save** or **File • Save As**, you will be saving the EDL. This point is very important: You are not saving soundfile data with those save functions, you are saving a text file composed in BC2's Hypertext Audio Language (HTAL).

WARNING *Don't make the mistake of giving your saved EDL file the same name as your soundfile: It is not a soundfile and you will overwrite your sound data!*

Here's an example edit decision list written and saved in the HTAL format:

```
<HTAL>

<ASSETS>
<ASSET SRC=/home/soundfiles/WAV/linus.wav>
<FORMAT TYPE=WAV>
<AUDIO CHANNELS=1 RATE=44100 BITS=16 BYTE_ORDER=1 SIGNED=0 HEADER=44>
</ASSET>
</ASSETS>

<LABELS>
<LABEL SAMPLE=24320><LABEL SAMPLE=79104>
</LABELS>

<VIDEO FRAMERATE=10.000000 FRAMES_PER_FOOT=16.000000 TRACKW=240 TRACKH=120 OUTPUTW=240
OUTPUTH=120 ASPECTW=4.000000 ASPECTH=3.000000>

<AUDIO SAMPLERATE=44100 OUTCHANNELS=1 CHPOSITION0=270>

<TRACK TYPE=AUDIO>
<PATCH><PLAY><RECORD><AUTO><DRAW><TITLE>Audio 1</TITLE></PATCH>
<MODULE>
<TITLE>Audio 1</TITLE>
<PLUGIN TYPE=0>
<SHOW><ON>
</PLUGIN>
<PLUGIN TYPE=0>
<SHOW><ON>
</PLUGIN>
<PLUGIN TYPE=0>
<SHOW><ON>
</PLUGIN>
<PLUGIN TYPE=0>
<SHOW><ON>
</PLUGIN>
<PAN X=1 Y=150 PAN0=1.000000><FADE VALUE=0.000000>
</MODULE>
<EDITS>
<EDIT STARTSOURCE=0 FEATHERLEFT=0 FEATHERRIGHT=0 SAMPLES=188405 CHANNEL=0>
<FILE SRC=/home/soundfiles/WAV/linus.wav></EDIT>
</EDITS>
</TRACK>

</HTAL>
```

You can edit the EDL in any text editor. The HTAL tags surround a list of Assets, Labels, Settings, and Track information, and from there the content is self-explanatory.

Basic Editing

BC2's main window is designed for synchronizing video and audio streams. Some of its terms and tools may confuse you at first, but once you learn the basic interface controls you'll fly through your edits. Let's take a closer look at the main window interface.

Directly beneath the top menu bar, you see three groups of controls: the transport controls (for starting and stopping play and record functions), the display controls (for resizing the waveform x/y axes and the track displays), and the Fit/Label/Cut/Copy/Paste buttons. The Fit button fits the entire soundfile to the main window; the Label button adds a marker at the current location of the cursor. Cut/Copy/Paste do just as they indicate.

Beneath the control strip, you can see the time line. The end points of the time line serve as autolocators for moving the cursor quickly to the next label in the pointer's direction.

To the left of the large waveform display window, you see the track label (Audio 1 by default) and four track controls. From left to right, those controls are toggles for play, edit, automation, and display. By default they are all toggled on.

At the bottom of the main window, you see five time displays indicating selection start time, selection length, selection end time, current cursor position, and total length.

Close the **Preferences** window, then select **File • Load** to open an audio file. You will see the waveform amplitude display, along with the soundfile name and the edit handles (the small arrows) at the beginning and end of the file as shown in Figure 4-34.

Let's perform some simple edits on this file.

NOTE *For audio-only edit sessions, turn off **Settings • Align cursor on frames**. Otherwise, the track cursor will place itself on the nearest video frame boundary instead of the mouse pointer location.*

An area can be selected by simply left-clicking and dragging the mouse pointer over the desired span. You can make extremely precise selections by using the markers with the autolocators. Place two labels in your soundfile, then click on the right locator to position the cursor. Now hold the SHIFT key down and click on the left locator, and the area between your markers will be selected automatically, as shown in Figure 4-35.

Now let's apply a simple effect. Select **Audio • Effects** . . . from the menu bar, click on the **Reverse Audio** entry, and set the options for bit resolution (8, 16, and 24) and dithering (a "smoothing" effect, useful when lowering a selection's sample rate). Figure 4-36 shows this process.

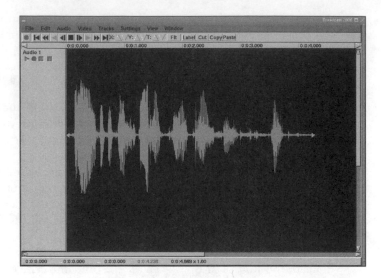

Figure 4-34: Broadcast 2000's waveform display

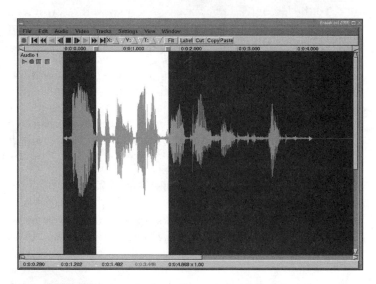

Figure 4-35: Waveform display with area selected for edits

Click on the **OK** buttons for the **Options** and the **Effects** windows. A progress bar will appear, and finally the waveform display will be redrawn and relabeled, as shown in Figure 4-37.

Look carefully at Figure 4-37. Note that the reversed section is labeled bc-temp.wav: Remember that BC2 stores its data in an edit decision list, leav-

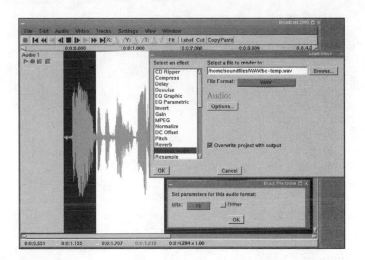

Figure 4-36: Broadcast 2000's Effects panel

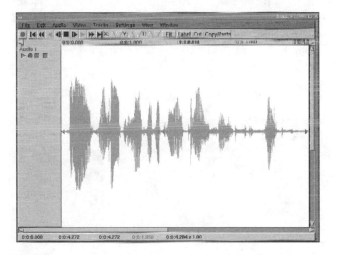

Figure 4-37: Waveform (from Fig. 4-35) after reversal

ing your original files untouched. Your newly affected section will play backward, just as it should, but the original soundfile is unchanged. Choose **File • Render** (see Figure 4-38) when you're ready to commit your edited file to disk as a soundfile and not an EDL.

With these basic maneuvers, you can now experiment freely with BC2's other effects. If you don't like anything you've done, the handy Undo function is available in the Edit menu.

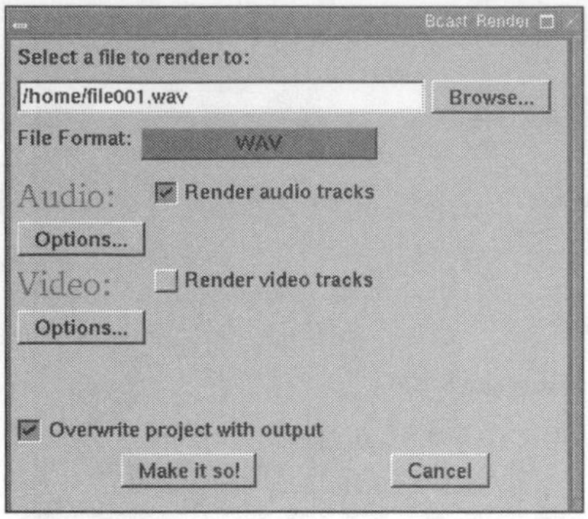

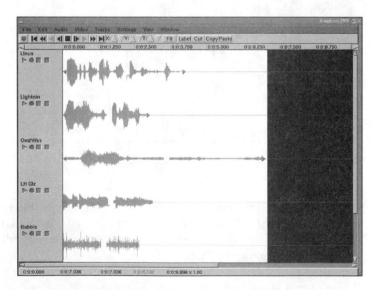

Figure 4-38: Broadcast 2000 rendering options

Advanced Editing

Now we'll try some larger-scale editing, this time treating BC2 as a soundfile mixer. Select **File • Load** . . . from the menu bar and add a soundfile to the first audio track. Next, use **File • Append** . . . to add soundfiles until you have four or five audio tracks. Your main window should now look something like the display in Figure 4-39 (the soundfiles are selected to show the labels and edit handles more clearly). You can turn off the edit handles and the labels in the View menu.

Figure 4-39: Multiple soundfiles in the waveform display

Now we want to move some of these soundfiles around in the main window. Let's start by moving the first and last files 2 seconds forward in their tracks. First, deactivate the other tracks for editing by clicking on the round red button under each track name. The button will turn gray, indicating that the edits will not affect that track. Next, locate the tracking cursor at the 2-second point: This is easily accomplished simply by moving the mouse pointer until the red time display (at the bottom of the screen) shows 2.000. Alternately, you can type the value directly into the selection end time display and hit ENTER; the cursor will autolocate to the indicated time. Next, either click and drag the mouse pointer to the zero point or enter the time point value directly. Your main window should now look like Figure 4-40. (Note that the labels and edit handles have been turned off.)

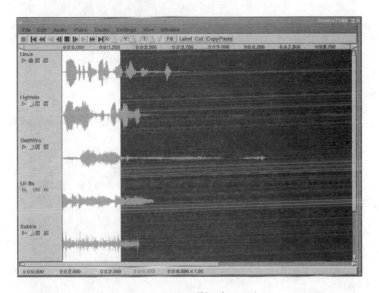

Figure 4-40: Ready to move two soundfiles forward

Now go to the **Edit** menu and select **Paste Silence**. Your two active tracks will be moved forward exactly 2 seconds, resulting in the display shown in Figure 4-41.

Repeat this procedure until the soundfiles are placed precisely where you want them. When you have finished moving your sounds, save the EDL and render the mix to a WAV or RAW soundfile.

For your final step in this session, add some reverb to the other tracks. Follow the track and area selection methods already outlined, but this time use the markers to select an area from 1 second to 2. Then go to **Audio •** **Effects** . . . and choose the **Reverb**. Adjust the effect's parameters in the pop-up Reverb control panel, then press the **Do It** button in the **Prompt** box. Your main window should closely resemble the display in Figure 4-42.

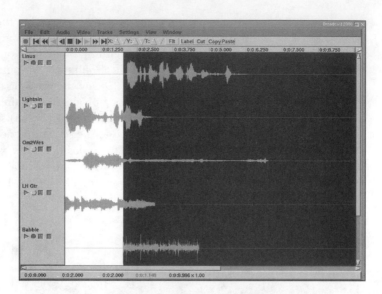

Figure 4-41: Arrangement in Fig. 4-39 with two files moved forward

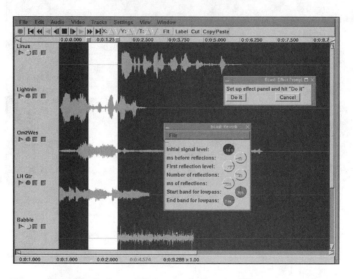

Figure 4-42: Applying an effect to multiple soundfiles

When the status bar indicates that the processing is complete, press the **Rewind transport** button (beside the red Record control) to move the cursor to the start of your mix, then press the **Play** button (the green arrow pointing to the right) to hear your mix. Save your work.

Going Farther

BC2 contains an embarrassment of riches, and I have barely indicated its possibilities. With the practical uses demonstrated in this profile, you can start discovering those riches and possibilities. The documentation will reveal more of the program's depth, and practice will perfect your use of BC2. Enjoy!

Ceres

Author: Oyvind Hammer
Version profiled: 0.13
Web site: http://www.notam.uio.no/notam/ceres-e.html
FTP site: ftp://mustec.bgsu.edu/pub/linux
Maintained: Yes
Availability: Free, open-source
License: Copyright held by author
Capsule summary: Graphic spectral editing, very unusual processing options (Transforms)

Ceres was originally written for SGI computers by Oyvind Hammer, of the Norwegian Network for Technology, Acoustics, and Music Research (NoTAM). In 1997, I ported Ceres to Linux with the help of Richard Kent's libraries written for his DAP editor. Both the SGI and Linux versions of Ceres have the same functions and documentation, so Dr. Hammer's invaluable instructions for the original Ceres, which clearly explain its various operations and functions, are a great help for the Linux version too.

Getting It, Building It

The latest package is always available at ftp://mustec.bgsu.edu/pub/linux/ceres-linux.tar.gz. Download it to your /home directory, unpack it with **tar xzvf ceres-linux-latest.tar.gz**, and enter your new Ceres directory.

Before building Ceres you must install Motif 1.2 or the equivalent LessTif libraries and headers. Motif is a commercial product available from many vendors (such as Red Hat and Metro Link). LessTif is a free replacement for Motif: It is usually bundled with Linux distributions, but you can always find the latest version at www.lesstif.org. Motif (or LessTif) will provide the GUI for Ceres.

The Ceres package also requires and includes Richard Kent's audio libraries. Enter the Ceres/tich directory and run **make**. When you build Ceres its makefile will access this directory for the needed files. Now return to the Ceres home directory and run **make** and then (as root, of course) **make install** to compile and install the program.

Using Ceres

Enter **ceres** in an xterm window and the program will open to a single empty window. Select **File • Load & Analyze** to load an AIFF soundfile (Ceres will currently only load AIFF files). An FFT analysis will be automatically performed on the selected soundfile and rendered as a graphic display of the sound's frequency content over its length (in seconds).

Editing Tools

By default, edits and transforms apply to the entire soundfile, but you can make highly detailed alterations by using area selection, a control function, and the paintbrush.

Area selection   Clicking and dragging the right mouse button selects an area by drawing a box around the area to be affected by the transform. You can then create a control function curve point-by-point.

NOTE   *Area selection works only on the Sieve, Frequency-shift, Mirror, Pitch-shift, Gain, and Convolve transforms.*

Control functions   The Extract function, which derives the amplitude, pitch, and centroid (brightness) curves from the soundfile, offers another method of transforming a soundfile. If you select one of these curves from the Extract menu, that curve becomes the default control function.

The paintbrush   The paintbrush is a simple editing tool. If the paintbrush is turned on in the display settings, clicking and dragging the right mouse button will paint over an area. The painted area can then be removed, or the painting can be rejected to start again.

Figure 4-43 shows Ceres' centroid graph displayed and an edit area selected:

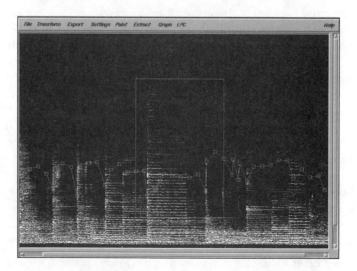

Figure 4-43: Centroid graph with selected area displayed in Ceres

What's Special about Ceres?

The editing capabilities of the NoTAM software, originally written for SGI computers but ported into Linux, offer something other Linux editors don't: They perform edits on the graphic results of a Fast Fourier Transform (FFT) analysis of a soundfile. It is beyond the scope of this book to explain the FFT (see Dr. Hammer's Ceres documentation for a brief explanation), but the results of the transform are depicted in what is known as a "spectral representation," or a representation of a sound's frequencies (as opposed to its amplitudes) against time. Through the graphic spectral representation, the NoTAM software lets you directly edit the frequency content of a sound wave. Before Ceres, Linux had no software with such capabilities.

Resynthesis

After Ceres renders the FFT results of its analysis of a wave into a graphic display, you can subject those results to several interesting transformations. The Resynthesis window lets you control the final pitch and duration after you've run the transforms. Select **File • Synth & Save** to apply these transformations to the original sound wave—and you've created (resynthesized) a new sound.

The example soundfile used in Figures 4-44 and 4-45 is a 6.82-second long, 44.1 kHz, 16-bit monaural AIFF file of me saying "Hello, my name is David Phillips, and I pronounce Linux as Linux." Figure 4-44 shows the results of a default FFT analysis of hello.aif. The vertical scale measures the frequencies in kHz, and the horizontal scale measures the time of the file.

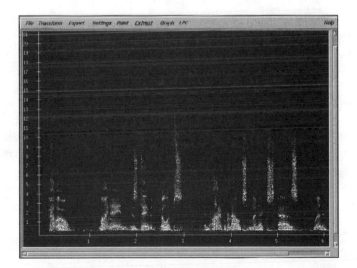

Figure 4-44: Default FFT analysis of hello.aif

Figure 4-45 illustrates an extensive warping of our original soundfile. I edited the soundfile with familiar transforms, such as pitch-shifting and gain adjustment, as well as more exotic alterations, such as spreading and blurring effects. Resynthesizing performed the final transformation (an extended file length and slightly lowered pitch).

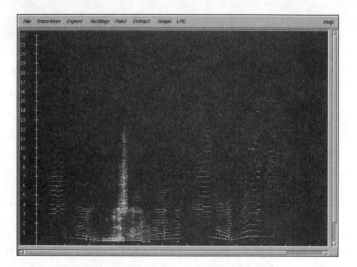

Figure 4-45: FFT analysis of the processed hello.aif file

LPC in Ceres

The primary analysis method in Ceres is the FFT-based phase vocoder. However, the program also includes an implementation of LPC analysis and resynthesis. Although the LPC in Ceres is not as detailed as that in MiXViews, it is still quite useful. A spectral envelope derived from LPC can be used to modify another soundfile's formants, and Ceres can apply the derived formant filter envelope in the synthesis of a new soundfile. This means you can shift pitch while retaining aural signatures such as age and gender of a voice, and create cross-synthesis effects such as the "talking orchestra."

Using LPC in Ceres

Let's create our own talking orchestra. Go to **Settings • Analysis** and set a relatively low number of poles (20 should be good). Select **File • Load & Analyze** for your orchestra sound using both FFT and LPC loads (in other words, you will load and analyze the same file twice). Figure 4-46 shows our original sound in the default FFT spectral display. (The LPC results are not displayed.)

From the LPC menu, run the inverse filter to flatten the spectrum. The display will change to something like the screenshot in Figure 4-47.

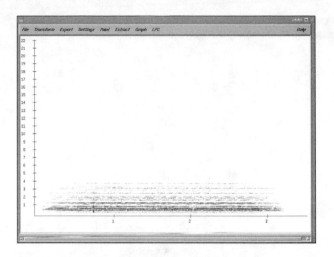

Figure 4-46: FFT display before LPC resynthesis

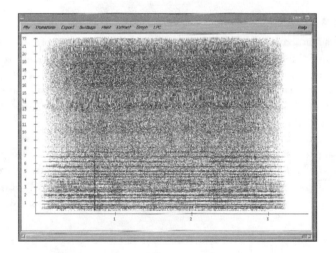

Figure 4-47: FFT display with "flattened" spectrum

Now run a new LPC analysis on your filter sound (for this example we want a speaking voice) using a higher number of poles (60 is recommended). Select **Filter Current Spectrum** from the LPC menu and increase the gain (in the **Transform** menu) if needed. Run **Synth & Save** from the **File** menu, then use **File • Play** to audition your new sound as shown in Figure 4-48. Voilá—the orchestra speaks!

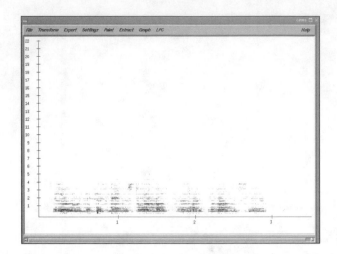

Figure 4-48: Spectral display after LPC resynthesis

Ceres Development

Ceres has spawned a small family of versions: Johnathan Lee's Ceres2 greatly expands the number of control and editing functions, and Reine Jonsson's Ceres2w is Johnathan's version with WAV support. Guenter Geiger recently joined the list of developers lending their efforts to extend and expand the program and has already improved the FFT analysis code and added a microphone input record function.

Ceres grows slowly, but its feature list has become noteworthy, offering signal processing and transformation options found in no other program. Further, the ability to directly edit the spectral display of a sound wave makes Ceres a unique and indispensable tool for the Linux musician and sound researcher. I consider it a "Most Recommended" piece of Linux audio software.

5

MOD FILES AND LINUX

The Mod (from "module") digital music file is created using tracker software, which is essentially a sequencer for a set of sound samples and the patterns they fill. You can add optional effects such as vibrato, filters, and panning to the basic samples, and all of this information (soundfiles, sample number, effects, sequence position), along with the song structure, is contained in the module itself. The format is compact and usable across a wide variety of platforms with minimal system requirements: Even the lowliest 8-bit soundcard will work with most trackers. However, Mods are a digital audio format, so it's always better to have support for higher sampling rates and bit resolution when working with Mod files.

Comparing the MIDI and MP3 formats (see Chapters 6 and 7) to Mod files, a MIDI file is smaller, but it contains no sound data and must rely on the soundcard or an external synthesizer for the actual sounds. MP3 *is* a digital audio format, but MP3 file sizes are typically much larger than Mods, and there are no direct composition tools like MIDI sequencers or Mod trackers for creating MP3 files. If you want to compose using sampled sounds, and you want listeners to hear your music with those same sounds, then the Mod format is the way to go.

Preparing Your Mod File

Creating a Mod file is quite easy. The composition model is similar to a pattern/track-oriented MIDI sequencer or drum machine: Simply lay samples out in tracks, organize your tracks into larger patterns, and then link these larger patterns together to create a song. You can play numerous tracks simultaneously, and you can easily direct patterns to repeat, permitting the quick composition of complex multi-voice music.

Remember to prepare your sample well. Tuning and looping are basic considerations, and some trackers support extensive editing of a sample's volume and *panning*. "Pan" is short for "panorama" and refers to the placement of a sound in the auditory space. So, for example, a sound that is panned "hard left" will sound only from the speaker on your left. Although a sample editor is included in the design of almost every tracker, you will need a more powerful soundfile editor such as Snd or DAP (see Chapter 4) for finer editing. These dedicated editors provide greater resolution, more effects processing, and file conversion routines not available in the editors included with trackers.

Tracker and Player Mod File Compatibility

There are many types of modules, including the MOD, IT, S3M, XM, and 669 formats. Most players support a variety of mod file types, whereas trackers create only one or two (the other mod file types come from trackers available on other platforms). The various module formats differ in the number of tracks allowed, the number of samples supported, and the permissible bit resolution of the samples. Fortunately for Linux users, the most popular Mod formats are supported by most of the available trackers and players (see Tables 5-1 and 5-2).

Other Trackers and Players

Linux Mod trackers and players are surprisingly numerous. Which ones you prefer will be determined mainly by your machine's graphics capabilities: For X users, SoundTracker and Voodoo Tracker are good trackers designed with the Gtk interface, while Xsoundtrack requires only the basic X11 libraries. If you want to do your tracking from the Linux console, try FunktrackerGOLD. Mod players for X are available in nearly every flavor of Linux graphics toolkits, including Gtk (Gmodplay), Qt (Kmodbox), and Xforms (Mod4Xwin). Console-based players include MikMod and the Falcon Module Player.

I've chosen to profile the SoundTracker Mod tracker and the MikMod player. Both applications are easy to set up and use, and they are steadily and consistently maintained. I especially like SoundTracker's user interface. MikMod has also been selected for its availability: It is included as a standard component in all mainstream Linux distributions.

Table 5-1: Tracker support for the various mod formats

Tracker	Supported Modules
FunktrackerGOLD	MOD
Keg Tracker	MOD, XM
SoundTracker	MOD, XM
Voodoo Tracker	MOD, XM
Xsoundtrack	XM

Table 5-2: Player support for the various mod formats

Player	Supported Modules
Falcon Module Player	MOD, S3M, XM
Gmodplay	MOD, S3M, XM, IT, 669, MTM, STM, FAR, ULT, AMS, DBM, MDL, OKT
KmodBox	MOD, S3M, XM, IT, 669, MTM, STM, FAR, ULT, MED, IMF, STX, AFM, DSM, GDM, UNI, M15
MikIT	MOD, S3M, XM, IT
MikMod	MOD, S3M, XM, IT, 669, MTM, STM, FAR, ULT, MED, IMF, STX, AFM, DSM, GDM
Mod4Xwin	MOD, S3M, 669, MTM, STM

The Tracker: SoundTracker

Author: Michael Krause
Version profiled: 0.1.9
Web site: http://www.soundtracker.org/
FTP site: n/a
Maintained: Yes
Availability: Free, open-source
License: GPL
Capsule summary: Fast, stable, and easy-to-use MOD/XM tracker with an excellent Gtk interface in X

SoundTracker is the most feature-packed of all the trackers I've used in Linux. Its interface presents all the program's tools in a single screen, making it easy to understand and a joy to use. As you'll see, tracking with SoundTracker is a simple process and great fun.

Getting It, Building It

Before you build SoundTracker, verify that you have all the necessary libraries and development tools. SoundTracker runs in the X window system, and most of what you will need should be included in any modern Linux distribution. However, you may need to acquire the most recent packages to build and utilize all of SoundTracker's features. In particular, SoundTracker uses the latest GNOME development libraries and headers, so you may need to visit the GNOME project Web site (www.gnome.org) and pick up the newest packages. You will also need Michael Pruett's libaudiofile, available from his Web site at http://www.68k.org/~michael/audiofile. SoundTracker's installation documentation specifies what you will need to build the program, so be sure to read it before you compile the application.

After you have downloaded SoundTracker and acquired the necessary support software, building SoundTracker is easy. Typing **./configure –help** will result in a list of options you can select for customizing the build process, and running **./configure** will create the makefiles needed to compile Sound-Tracker. If no errors were reported by the configuration procedure, you can then type **make** and watch the compilation take place. If no errors were reported by the make process, become the superuser by typing **su root** and entering your root password, then type **make install** and SoundTracker will install itself. The tracker is now ready to use; start it by simply typing **soundtracker** in an xterm window.

Using SoundTracker

As shown in Figure 5-1 (page 90), SoundTracker's global organizing controls are at the top left, and the tracker and other editors at the bottom of the screen. Event entry is simple: Use the QWERTY keyboard to audition, insert, and delete the instruments along the tracks. A two-octave span of notes is laid out in piano keyboard order. The keys Z S X D C V G B H N J M correspond to the notes C C# D D# E F F# G G# A A# B. The keys Q 2 W 3 E R 5 T 6 Y 7 U repeat that pitch sequence one octave higher.

C	C#	D	D#	E	F	F#	G	G#	A	A#	B	
Z	S	X	D	C	V	G	B	H	N	J	M	Plays notes
Q	2	W	3	E	R	5	T	6	Y	7	U	Plays one octave higher

You can use the computer keyboard in other ways as well. Controls are available for song, pattern play, and nearly all of the editing functions. The combined keyboard/mouse interface is easy to master—you'll quickly be able to compose and audition with ease.

Tracking a Module

General Instructions

As of version 0.1.9, the documentation for SoundTracker consists of a single README file, but little more is really needed. Trackers all follow a similar design, and the reference materials found on Kristian Grundstrom's United Trackers site (www.united-trackers.org) will help you understand the basic use of almost any tracker.

Creating Sound Patterns

Tracking (i.e., creating a module) in SoundTracker is a simple four-step process:

1. Click on the **Edit Mode** radio button and select **Instrument 1** in the global section.

2. Click on the **Sample Editor** tab to load the sample you want for that instrument.

3. Click on the **Tracker** tab, position the cursor box over the first event entry space for Instrument 1, and select the note desired from the QWERTY keyboard. If you select a note you later decide you don't want, it can be deleted simply by selecting it again and pressing DELETE.

4. Repeat this process for each instrument until you have the pattern and instrumentation desired. The pattern can be played at any time, a feature that greatly speeds up the composition process.

Event Details

The event entry line has four fields, shown as columns of numbers in Figures 5-1 and 5-2. The first indicates the pitch chosen for the sample playback, the second displays the instrument number, the third indicates the volume, and the fourth combines the effects command and parameter value into one three-digit entry. Only the pitch indicator follows the traditional pitch/octave notation; all other values are represented in decimal or hex numbering (you can select the representation you prefer).

The effects command not only adds typical effects such as vibrato, tremolo, LFO, and filtering—it provides signals to start the subsequent pattern, jump to a new position in the event list, and even jump to a new position and loop from that point for a specified time. The fine-tuning parameter will give you more accurate intonation of a sample at a particular pitch level.

The highlighted line in Figure 5-1 shows a typical tracker event entry: a bass instrument with a pitch of C5 (in octave 5, selected in the global area in the upper left corner) and the defaults for volume and effects. The entry is located on the first beat of a 4-beat pattern. Figure 5-2 shows the procedure carried out to create a C major scale, rising over a period of 16 beats, from C5 to C6 (the

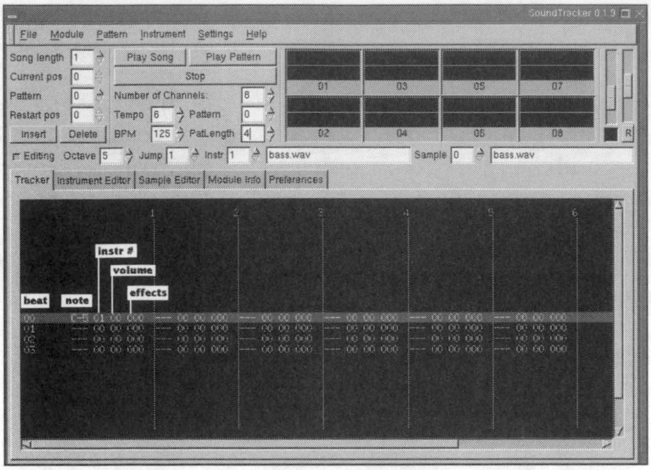

Figure 5-1: The SoundTracker screen

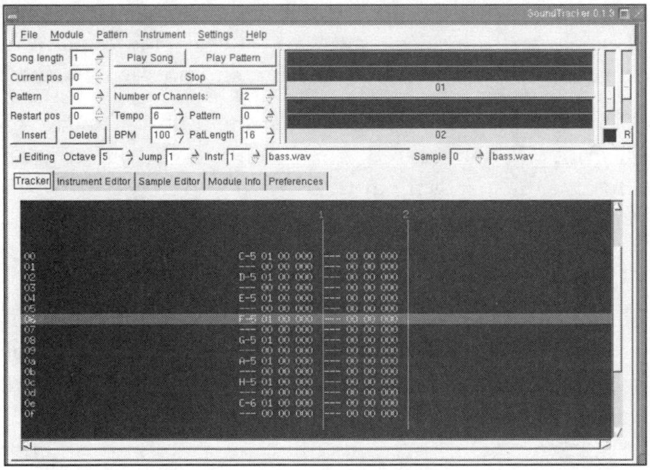

Figure 5-2: The updated SoundTracker screen

highlighted line is mid-scale at F5). The tempo has been set to 100 BPM (beats per minute), and only two channels are represented (with nothing in channel 2 yet). The pattern length and number of channels can be varied at will in the global section. Changing the pattern length or the number of channels in the global section immediately updates both the global and tabbed sections.

Figure 5-3 shows a more complete pattern: This screenshot was taken while looping pattern 5, so you can see the activity of the individual instruments in the oscilloscopes at the upper right. The pattern is set to 16 beats (4/4 time)

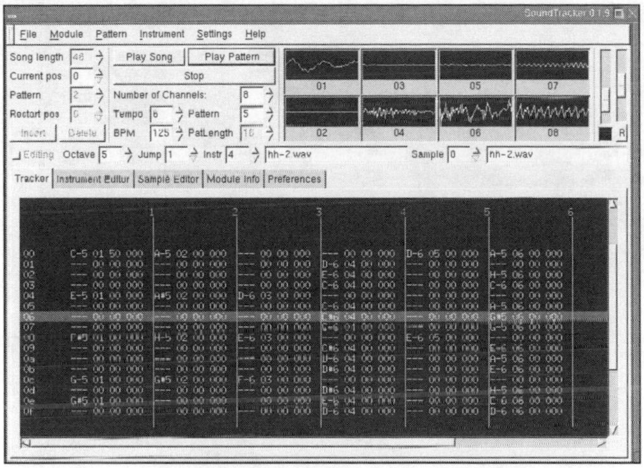

Figure 5-3: SoundTracker screen from the example XM file

with events added for bass guitar, bass drum, snare, hi-hat, cymbal, and guitar. Trackers are especially well suited to beat-oriented music, such as techno and other dance music, but because any sort of sample can be used by the software, it is not limited to any particular style.

Stringing Patterns Together into a Song

After creating patterns, you string them together to create a completed song. This procedure is also easy: In the upper left corner, set the song length desired (the Insert/Delete buttons can also dynamically control song length), use the **Current Position** box to indicate song measure location, and then use the **Pattern** box to select which pattern will play at that location. In the example shown in Figure 5-3, the song length is set to 46 patterns. The display can show only one pattern at a time, but scrolling the **Current Position** box would reveal that positions 0 through 3 are taken by pattern 2, positions 4 through 6 are occupied by pattern 1, position 7 belongs to pattern 11, and so forth. When completed, files can be saved in the common MOD or XM formats.

Additional SoundTracker Features

Sample Editor

Figure 5-4 shows the `bass.wav` file loaded in the Sample Editor. SoundTracker's editor is not intended to be a full-fledged soundfile editing environment, but it does provide basic cut/copy/paste operations along with the more significant loop mode setting and initial volume, pan, and fine-tune controls. It also has the option to load 8-bit soundfiles.

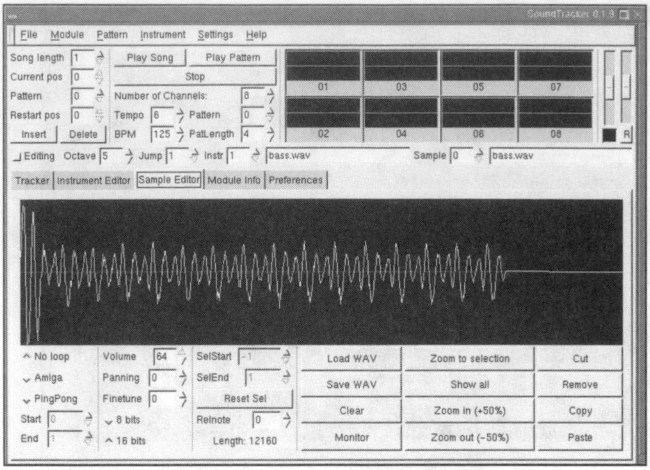

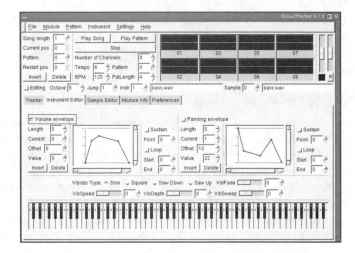

Figure 5-4: The Sample Editor

Figure 5-5: SoundTracker's Instrument Editor

Instrument Editor

Figure 5-5 displays the Instrument Editor, which lets you edit the volume and pan envelopes on the sample while the song or pattern is playing. This editor also provides a keyboard for mapping your samples across an instrument's range.

Closing Remarks

SoundTracker continues to grow in power and flexibility. It is consistently maintained by its author, often incorporating features and fixes submitted by users. Performance is quite stable, and as you have seen, the program is easy to use. Whether you're a seasoned pro or a complete newbie to tracking, Sound-Tracker is the tool you need to create your own Mod masterpieces in Linux.

After you've composed or collected some Mods, you might want to show them off to your friends. You could open your files one by one in SoundTracker, but SoundTracker is optimized as a Mod tracker, and its file support is limited to MOD and XM formats. A Mod player is a playback-only application, providing amenities such as support for playlists and a wide variety of mod file formats. In the next section we'll look at MikMod, my mod player of choice.

The Player: MikMod

Authors: Jean-Paul Mikkers, Steve McIntyre, Peter Amstutz, Miodrag Vallat, many others
Version profiled: 3.1.6
Web site: http://mikmod.darkorb.net/index.html
FTP site: n/a
Maintained: Yes
Availability: Free, open-source
License: GPL

MikMod is a powerful yet straightforward command line Mod player that requires only a Linux console and an audio-ready system. Originally a project designed by one man (Jean-Paul Mikkers), MikMod has evolved into a distributed development project with code contributed by programmers from around the world, and it is now included in every major Linux distribution. MikMod is heartily recommended: It supports a wide variety of module file formats, several graphic interfaces are available for it, and it is in continuous development and maintenance.

Getting It, Building It

MikMod is easy to build and install from sources, requiring only the ncurses (a screen manipulation library for displays not running the X window system) and C libraries included in every Linux distribution. Versions of MikMod with GUIs (see Figure 5-9 on page 96) will of course require their own libraries and headers (see each package's installation instructions for details of obtaining the necessary interface toolkits).

After retrieving the latest source package from the MikMod Web site, unpack it by typing `tar xzvf mikmod-latest-tar.gz`. A directory will be created containing the source code and documentation: *Be sure to read the docs for any late-breaking news about the compilation process!*

Switch into your new MikMod directory and type `./configure --help` to see what options are available during the configuration process, and then type `./configure` (including any selected options) to create the Makefile needed to build the program. Then just type `make` and grab a cup of coffee while the build process finishes. If no errors are reported, enter `su root` to become super-user, type `make install`, and your new version of MikMod is now ready to use.

Using MikMod

To play a Mod file with MikMod you need only type `mikmod my_song.xm` (substituting your song name and its appropriate Mod file extension) and the program will do the rest. The command `mikmod -h` displays the available options, which include:

- Device selection

- Panning, reverb, and volume effects

- Output to mono and/or 8-bit resolution

- Support for playlists, including random selection

Figure 5-6 shows the Help options, Figure 5-7 shows MikMod's Configuration menus, and Figure 5-8 lists the samples/instruments used in the XM module. (The screen shots in this section were all captured while running MikMod in an xterm window and playing the example XM file from this book's CD.)

MikMod makes good use of ncurses, and, as noted earlier, it is also available in versions for Gtk, Java, Qt, and XForms. The Java version is a command-line application that does not make use of the Java graphic user interface classes. However, in Figure 5-9 on page 96 you can see MikMod in its glorious GUI incarnations as KMikMod (Qt), Mod4XWin (XForms), and GtkMikMod. Note that the playlists indicate MikMod's versatility with Mod file formats—they can freely combine any of the supported file types.

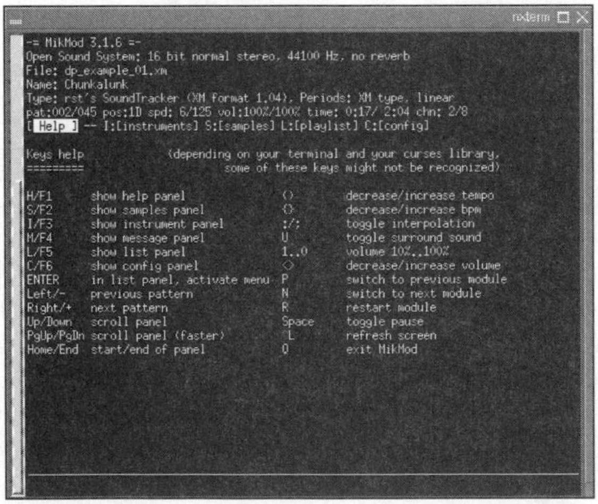

Figure 5-6: MikMod Help options

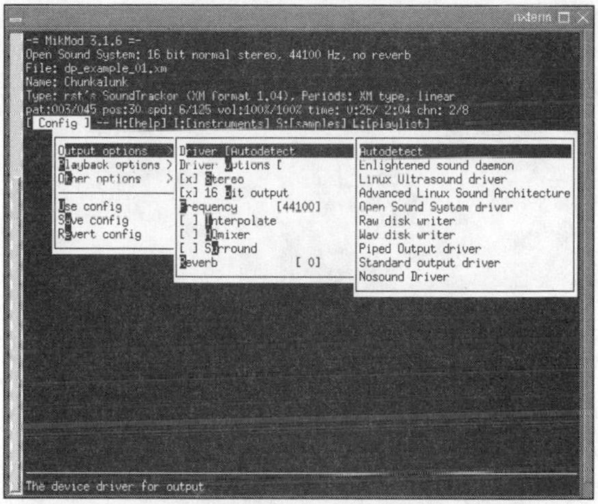

Figure 5-7: MikMod Configuration menus

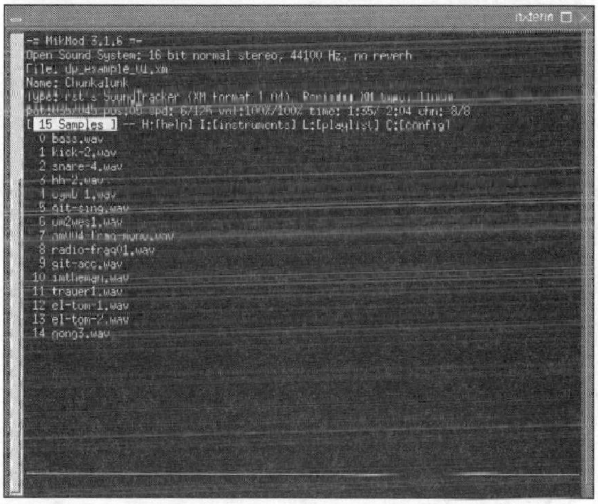

Figure 5-8: MikMod samples/instruments screen

Mod Conversion Tools

You may choose among several useful conversion utilities to work with mod files. The mod2text and text2mod tools, for example, convert Amiga Protracker modules (files with the MOD extension) to and from a text file. The author of these tools has remarked that they essentially let you "turn Emacs into a tracker!" If you want to convert your MIDI files into Mods, you'll want Guy Thornley's GMid2Mod, a very useful tool that converts a Standard MIDI file to an XM-format module file. These utilities and others are listed in the section on Mods in the Linux soundapps pages at http://sound.condorow.net/mod.html.

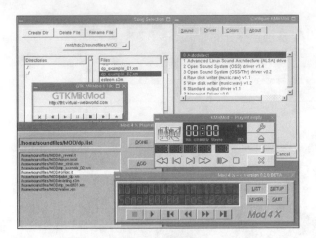

Figure 5-9: MikMod in different windowed environments

MikMod and the Linux Demo Scene

Because the MikMod library is central to many Linux audio and multimedia projects (including the ClanLib, Crystal Space, and MAM graphics/gaming projects) and is easily integrated into other applications, it has become the sound engine of choice for many Linux demo artists. A *demo,* or demonstration program, shows off some neat graphics or animation with text and music. The demo scene is mainly populated by Amiga users and DOS hackers, but some very good demos exist for UNIX/Linux. I have included some examples on this book's CD. Check them out—they show how Linux can be a powerful multimedia presentation platform. And be sure to visit the Linux Demo Scene site (http://linux.scene.org) for up-to-date news of demo-related events as well as links to tools, utilities, and documentation.

Learning More about Things Mod

Interested readers should check out all Internet resources listed in this chapter. The United Trackers page (www.united-trackers.org) is an excellent guide to finding trackers and players, sample archives, links to Mod collections (an incredible number of modules are available over the Internet), and tutorials. You may also want to keep up with the alt.binaries.sounds.mods and alt.binaries.sounds.mods.techno newsgroups, where many independent musicians post their creations, questions, and information regarding the very active Mod tracking scene.

6

THE LINUX MIDI STUDIO

MIDI History

In 1981, Sequential Circuits engineer Dave Smith drafted a specification for a digital musical instrument interface that would allow
communication between synthesizers built by different manufacturers. This communications protocol was presented to and widely adopted
by the various synthesizer companies such as Roland, Yamaha, Oberheim, and
Sequential Circuits. A manufacturers consortium was organized, the protocol
was established as a specification, and by 1985 MIDI (Musical Instrument Digital Interface) had become one of the most important advances in 20th-century
music technology.

MIDI Advantages

By placing inexpensive and powerful tools for composition, arrangement, and
recording on the composer's desktop, MIDI quickly revolutionized the music
industry and is now a ubiquitous music technology. The MIDI interface is a
standard device on every modern synthesizer and soundcard, and its compact
file format is probably the most widely used format for digital music data.
MIDI's design favors keyboard controllers, but pitch-to-MIDI converters have
made it possible to implement the interface on wind instruments, percussion,
and even plucked and bowed string instruments. Its utility has spread to the

control of professional mixing boards, lighting consoles, signal processors, and recording devices such as analog tape decks and hard-disk recorders.

MIDI has a great advantage over audio formats such as WAV, MOD, or MP3 files: It is extremely compact, because no audio data is included in a MIDI file. Transferring MIDI files over a network is much faster than transferring digital audio, and the development of the General MIDI sound set (found on virtually every modern soundcard) ensures that what is heard on my system will be heard with the same sounds on my friend's system (with some caveats; see below).

How MIDI Works

MIDI is a simple control protocol or a convention for sending messages; it is not encoded sound data (i.e., it is not data of a sound wave). The MIDI protocol switches machine functions between on/off states and can provide control streams for continuous controllers such as MIDI volume, pitch bend, modulation, and aftertouch. These functions and control streams are sent back and forth over a MIDI cable, in a digital data format called MIDI messages.

The MIDI Message

A MIDI music file (also known as a sequence) is a very compact series of on/off messages, with no concern for what device is sending or receiving the messages. When a MIDI file sends a message to a MIDI instrument (an instrument that can understand MIDI messages), the message gives the instrument instructions such as which note to play on what channel and with which effects. Similarly, a MIDI instrument can record to a MIDI file by sending messages to a MIDI recorder capable of saving performances in the Standard MIDI File format. Here is a brief series of MIDI messages, typically represented in hex (hexadecimal) numbering:

```
90 3C 40
90 3C 00
C0 00
```

The first and second messages are each three bytes long and together compose a note-on (first message)/note-off (second message) pair.

The first byte (90) indicates the message status (9x, a note-on) occurring on channel 1 (x0). The original MIDI specification allowed transmission and reception on 16 channels, numbered from 0 to 15 (or 00 to 0F in hexadecimal).

The next byte (3C) in the note-on message is reserved for the value of a MIDI note-number, in this instance number 64 (middle C on the keyboard).

The last byte (40) is the attack velocity of the note-on. Velocity is sometimes confused with MIDI volume: Whereas velocity does indeed relate to loudness (a hard-struck note is louder than one softly played), it is also related to a sound's tone color (the hard-struck note sounds brighter). The velocity value for the first message is 64, about a mezzoforte in musical terminology.

The second message is identical to the first except for its velocity data. The zero velocity value ends the sound turned on by the first message.

The third message is a program change (instrument designator) message. Again, the first byte identifies the message status, this time as a program change (Cx) on channel 1 (x0). The second byte is the number of the requested patch (program), here with a value of 1 (00 in hex). Note that, for these simple messages, the range of data values is restricted to integers (whole numbers) between 0 and 127. Other MIDI messages (such as pitch bend) have much greater available ranges for a more fine-grained resolution.

You may notice that a single MIDI message (i.e., one of the lines above) does not indicate the duration of the note played because there is no way to predict when a player might hold or release a key-press. Notes are assumed active until a MIDI note-off message (or a note-on with a velocity value of 0) is received. In a MIDI file, messages are stored in the sequence of their occurrence, and duration is determined by the combination of note-on and note-off (or zero-value note-on) messages.

Step Recording

This special method of note entry lets the user add notes to a MIDI track with the sequencer in record mode, but moving forward only after a note or rest has been entered, then waiting until the next event is entered before moving forward again. Step recording is especially valuable to those of us with minimal keyboard skills, permitting the creation of complex music without the need for high-level instrumental ability.

Enhancing Your Sounds

Following are several ways to enhance different aspects of your sounds with MIDI.

Velocity Value

The velocity value of a MIDI note-on message can add a sense of liveliness and animation to the note played.

Aftertouch

Most MIDI synthesizers respond to aftertouch, the amount of pressure placed on a key after the note is struck.

Continuous Controllers

More expression can be added to MIDI data by using the continuous controllers, such as the mod (modulation) wheel, volume pedal, and pitch-bend wheel. Unlike the simple on/off nature of MIDI note data, most continuous controllers on synthesizer keyboards produce streams of data that affect some aspect of the sound. For instance, the mod wheel typically controls the addition of a vibrato to the sound. When the wheel is in its bottom position, the vibrato will be set to 0, and the wheel's top position will apply the maximum amount (127). Because the wheel is a continuous controller, the vibrato effect can be added in a smooth curve instead of as an abrupt off/on, allowing the player to determine how much is enough.

NOTE *Many continuous controllers can be routed to affect different aspects of the sound, though exactly what can be modulated depends on the particular device. On my DX7II, the mod wheel not only sets the vibrato rate, but can also be routed to affect filter cutoff, letting me control the brightness of the sound while performing. Most commercial performance-grade synthesizers are designed to permit a broad range of effects controllable in real time by various wheels, pedals, and sliders.*

System-Exclusive MIDI Messages

A special type of MIDI system-exclusive (or sys-ex) message delivers and receives machine-specific data, usually to transfer synthesizer patch settings between identical synthesizers or between a computer and a synthesizer. For example, if you wanted to save a set of patches you designed for your MIDI synthesizer, you could initiate a patch data bulk dump to your computer. Later you could send it back to your synth with a bulk send message. You can build and save libraries of your own patches this way.

System-exclusive messages also let you dynamically control a device's parameters that may not be controlled by any other MIDI data format. For example, if you wanted to change a single parameter within one synthesizer patch, you could place the appropriate sys-ex message into the sequence data stream to make the adjustment in realtime performance.

A sys-ex message begins with a single byte with the value of F0H, followed by a header of information including the manufacturer identification number and the identity of the machine (or machines) that can respond to the message. The machine-specific data comes next, arranged in whatever manner suits the manufacturer, and the system-exclusive message ends with another single byte, this time with the value of F7 (remember, the values are in hexadecimal notation). Here is a simple sys-ex message:

F0 43 10 01 06 00 F7

And here is its breakdown:

F0	Begin sys-ex message
43	Yamaha manufacturer ID
10	Device number (variable)
01	Parameter group/subgroup number
06	Parameter number for algorithm selector
00	Value for algorithm #1
F7	End sys-ex

NOTE *Because MIDI sys-ex message length is unconstrained, you could disrupt the MIDI data flow during recording or playback by inserting a large sys-ex packet into a flow of MIDI note-ons or in the middle of a held note. Embedding sys-ex messages within MIDI sequences can provide unique control of an instrument, but you should place the messages at points where the overall data flow is relatively light. When placing small sys-ex packets, look for inactive areas between MIDI events. A large sys-ex message (such as a bulk send) should be placed one or more measures before the music actually begins, giving the sequencer time to send the entire packet without disturbing other data flow.*

The General MIDI Specification

Because the protocol (i.e., the MIDI message) doesn't care about the actual instruments involved, there was originally only one way to ensure that a MIDI composition would be played with its intended sounds: The same instruments were needed for playback as were used for the composition. However, a later development standardized a set of instruments now known as the General MIDI (GM) specification. GM is a patch layout that has been agreed upon by the MIDI standards organizations. Now, when I send a composition to a friend overseas, I can be relatively assured that she will hear it as I intended it to be heard, as long as we are both using devices that support the GM patch set. Most contemporary soundcards support the General MIDI set, and many external synth modules also support the layout. General MIDI isn't a perfect solution: My friend's card uses the Yamaha OPL3 FM chip for its GM patches, whereas I use the ROM samples on a Sound Blaster AWE64. The difference between her Bright Piano and mine is remarkable, but at least I can send my file knowing she has something like a Bright Piano at program location #1 or a standardized drum set on MIDI channel 10.

Additional MIDI Specifications

Other notable extensions to the original MIDI specification include the MIDI Sample Dump Standard (which provides a common format for transfer of soundfile data between MIDI-capable samplers), MIDI Machine Control (for remote operation of various studio and performance machinery, such as mixers and light-show controls), Bank Select (for soundcards and synthesizers with multiple banks of patch data), MIDI Time Code (for synchronizing the actions of MIDI-linked devices), and support for multi-port interfaces with more than sixteen discrete channels.

NOTE *Not all MIDI-capable devices support the full set of MIDI messages. Some types of data may not be applicable to a device, and the manufacturer might simply ignore others in order to reduce costs. Most MIDI devices have a MIDI implementation chart that specifies the data types accepted and transmitted by the device. You should consult that chart to learn the particular MIDI capabilities of your instrument.*

MIDI Software

A plethora of software programs allows users to compose, edit, and arrange MIDI data on a computer. The most basic of these programs is the MIDI sequencer.

The MIDI Sequencer

The MIDI sequencer, certainly the most commonly encountered MIDI software, is so called because it can record MIDI data as it arrives in sequence and reorganize the sequenced events for later playback. The sequencer provides the tools for quick and easy manipulation of recorded MIDI data by setting up a cycle of recording and editing a musical performance until it is tweaked to perfection. Indeed, the sequencer might be called the very heart of your MIDI studio.

Other MIDI Software

Other useful MIDI software packages include patch editors for synthesizers, rhythm composers for controlling drum machines, music notation editors, and experimental composition environments. Many popular sequencers for Windows and the Mac (such as Steinberg's Cubase and Opcode's Vision) have incorporated all of these functions into one huge package, usually including support for sequencing digital audio as well as MIDI data. Choosing between the large or small packages depends on your requirements: The large packages may seem to provide convenience, but they may lack fine control of some processes; if you need fine control of a process, use a smaller program that specializes in that process.

MIDI File

In the beginning of MIDI, the major sequencer developers saved their sequence data in incompatible formats, and eventually it was agreed that a file system standard was desirable. Thus the Standard MIDI File format was born. Popularly known as the MIDI file, this format has enabled users of different sequencing packages to share compositions without the need for external format converters.

Linux Support for MIDI

Standard kernel support for MIDI devices includes the hardware interfaces implemented on most soundcards (the UART 16450/16550) and standalone interface cards (MIDI-only cards) such as the Roland MPU-401 and the Music Quest MQX16. When you compile a kernel with MIDI support (see Chapter 2), closely follow the configuration instructions and that should keep everything straight. As always, make sure your configuration selections actually match your hardware and be sure to have your documentation nearby.

Soundcards

Most soundcards provide a MIDI interface as well as a MIDI-controllable on-board synthesizer. If you have external MIDI devices, you can utilize the hardware port, but if the soundcard synth is all you have, you can still enjoy making and listening to MIDI music. And as we shall see, some ways of using your soundcard for MIDI playback will obtain much better sound than the card's synth will create (see the profile on TiMidity++ below).

For most desktop and small-scale studio use of MIDI, your soundcard's MIDI port will work well. However, if you need services not provided by the UART mode (such as SMPTE time code or more than sixteen MIDI channels), you will require a standalone MIDI interface. Popular models include the Roland MPU-401, the Music Quest MQX32M, and the MOTU MIDI TimePiece/AV. Support for these cards varies in each driver package: Read the latest documentation for your selected driver to find the extent of support for the capabilities of your standalone interface.

Soundcard Drivers

The Linux kernel source code includes a set of soundcard drivers known as OSS/Free (or OSS/Lite). Linux distributions with installable sound modules (such as Red Hat or Mandrake) typically use the OSS/Free drivers. If your soundcard is supported and your MIDI needs are basic, the kernel drivers should work well for you.

The commercially available OSS/Linux drivers from 4Front Technologies (see Chapter 2) offer MIDI support for various soundcards as well as for a variety of standalone MIDI interface cards. During installation of the driver, simply select the appropriate card from the menu of supported cards. If desired, various options such as IRQ and the interface's base address can be manually configured.

The ALSA drivers (see Chapter 2) currently supply limited MIDI resources, but a very comprehensive API (applications programming interface) has been designed that will eventually provide powerful MIDI capability, including support for SMPTE time code, multi-port MIDI interfaces, and direct control of more soundcard synths. At present, ALSA supports only a few on-board synthesizers.

MIDI Software for Linux

Once MIDI support is installed, its use is transparent. You can reconfigure the interface device on most MIDI applications, and with some you can send MIDI output to any or all active devices. Typically, you can choose the interface device from a program's menu and freely switch between selections.

In this section I will profile several solid Linux MIDI applications, including sequencers (Brahms and Jazz++), MIDI file players (TiMidity++ and playmidi), an experimental MIDI composition environment (KeyKit), and a software fader box (xphat). Armed with the information given below, you will be well prepared to explore the MIDI side of Linux music and sound applications.

Brahms	MIDI sequencing with interfacing to external software synths. Most useful when combined with the aRts synthesizer.
Jazz++	A professional-grade MIDI/digital audio recorder and editor, suitable for nearly any MIDI demands.
TiMidity++	High-quality MIDI-to-WAV rendering, especially useful if your soundcard has no on-board synthesizer.
playmidi	Command-line MIDI player with extensive playback options; can be configured for any Linux machine (including extremely low-end boxes).
KeyKit	An environment for experimenting with MIDI with a GUI and a command-line language; exceptional for generating MIDI data and processing it in often-unusual ways.
xphat	A MIDI fader box; provides controllers for machines without them. Very useful for adjusting sound parameters via system-exclusive messages.

Brahms

Authors: Jan Würthner and Fabian Wenzel
Version profiled: 0.97.2
Web site: http://lienhard.desy.de/mackag/homepages/jan/Brahms/
FTP site: n/a
Maintained: Yes
Availability: Free, open-source
License: GPL
Capsule summary: Solid MIDI sequencing environment, interfaces and cooperates with aRts realtime software synthesizer

The Brahms specification file describes the program as a "MIDI sequencer with extensive editing facilities." That's putting it mildly. Originally inspired by the popular Cubase MIDI sequencer for Windows, Brahms has found its own design path and has rapidly become a powerful addition to the Linux MIDI studio. It supports several MIDI data input methods using standard music notation, drum grid, and piano-roll editors, and it imports and exports Standard MIDI files. It also supports various track types, including MIDI note data, MIDI tempo data, and WAV soundfiles. But Brahms goes beyond these amenities to offer a unique feature: the ability to work with the aRts realtime synthesizer (profiled in Chapter 10), providing MIDI data to drive the synth by way of a CORBA link between the two programs. CORBA (Common Object Request Broker Application) is a means for applications to share data and pass messages to each other, allowing well-managed interprocess communication. This feature is important if you would like to run concurrent applications that might have something to say to one another, such as a MIDI sequencer and a MIDI-controllable synthesizer.

Figure 6-1 displays Brahms with its various editors opened.

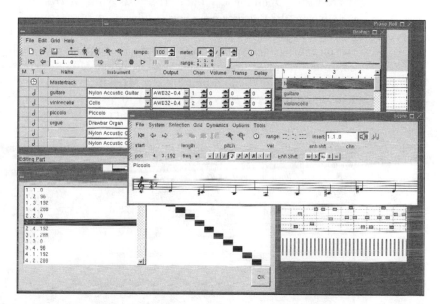

Figure 6-1: Brahms and its editors

Getting It, Building It

Retrieve Brahms from the Web site or this book's CD-ROM and unpack the distribution with **tar xzvf brahms-latest.tar.gz**. Change to the Brahms directory and read the build instructions carefully. Brahms requires the Qt (www.troll-tech.com) and KDE (www.kde.org) development packages that are included with most modern Linux distributions, as well as the standard complement of X libraries and headers. Run **./configure –help** for a list of configuration options, and then run **./configure**, **make**, and (as root!) **make install**.

NOTE *If you choose to build Brahms with an interface to the aRts synthesizer, you will need aRts installed first (see Chapter 10). Because I've profiled Brahms with the aRts interface, you'll need a working aRts installation to follow the example in this section. And, of course, you'll need a MIDI device, either a soundcard or external synthesizer.*

Running Brahms with aRts

After starting the artsserver (an application running behind the scenes that makes the aRts synthesizer available to other aRts-aware programs) in one window, type **Brahms** in another xterm window. When the program appears, open the **File** menu, select **Import/Export MIDI File**, and load a file into Brahms. From the **Output** selector, choose which synthesizer device you want to use. For our example, select **MidiBus**.

Now you will need to complete a setup of the aRts synthesizer. Fortunately, the aRts authors have provided excellent documentation on just what to do, and it's very easy. Open the artsbuilder (the aRts synth GUI), select a MIDI mapping system from the **Retrieve from Server Files** menu item (one of the mixers will do fine), then click on **Execute Structure** in the same menu. At this point aRts will turn into a pleasant-looking synthesizer, complete with knobs and other controls. Brahms will play this instrument via the MidiBus. You can now return to Brahms and hit the **Play** button; your MIDI file will use the aRts synthesizer as its sound source. You can edit the aRts synth parameters while Brahms plays.

Figure 6-2 shows Brahms opened along with the aRts synthesizer.

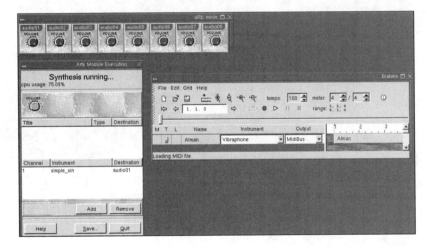

Figure 6-2: Brahms with the aRts synthesizer

Summary

Brahms is evolving into a wonderful Linux MIDI tool. It is already a stable and usable sequencer, but its authors have great plans for the program. Their alliance with aRts is a step toward making Brahms into a complete hard-disk recording solution, requiring no hardware beyond your computer and your soundcard. The authors are committed to the program's development, and I look forward to seeing where they will take it next.

Jazz++

Authors: Per Sigmond and Andreas Voss
Version profiled: 3.2
Web site: http://www.jazzware.com
FTP site: n/a
Maintained: Yes
Availability: Open-source, free
License: GPL
Capsule summary: Integrated audio/MIDI sequencer with rich selection of editing and randomization tools

Jazzware's Jazz++ is a professional-grade tool for recording, editing, and playing MIDI data and has the distinction of being the first Linux sequencer with integrated MIDI and digital audio sequencing. It provides a wide assortment of tools for the manipulation of recorded MIDI data, including a full complement of the basic tools (cut/copy/paste, mute/solo, track quantization and transposition, and so on), a variety of interesting and useful MIDI event generators and modifiers, and an editor and other tools for digital audio tracks.

Jazz++ is powerful and easy to learn. It has been available since 1993 and is a well tested, stable sequencer. The authors are committed to its development and have planned a complete overhaul of the user interface, switching it from Motif to the more modern GTK, and support for the ALSA sequencer API was added early in 2000. Jazz++ is an excellent program for any Linux MIDI music-maker, whether newbie or professional. Consider it highly recommended.

Getting It, Building It

Jazz++ is available on this book's CD or online from Jazzware's Web site. Formerly a commercial product, in February 2000 Jazzware licensed Jazz++ under the GNU Public License and now freely distributes the application's source code and pre-built binaries. Source and binaries are available at the Jazzware Web site.

If you're relatively new to building applications in Linux, I recommend downloading a prebuilt binary package. The authors have prepared packages in the Unix standard tarball (a compressed file with the .tar.gz or .tgz extension) and the Red Hat RPM formats. Most mainstream Linux distributions can handle either format: The RPM is easier for novices (more automated installation), but more experienced users may prefer the older Unix packaging for a more "hands-on" installation.

After retrieving Jazz++, place it in your /home or /usr/local directory. If you downloaded the RPM file, simply run **rpm -iv jazz-bin-latest.rpm** and you'll be ready to go. If you got the tarball, unpack it with **tar xzvf jazz-bin-latest.tar.gz**, then go into the new Jazz++ directory and read the installation instructions. Follow those directions, run **./install-jazz**, and let the installation complete itself.

If you have opted for building Jazz++ yourself, follow the directions above, substituting **jazz-src-latest** for the binary package name. However, before you can build Jazz++ you must install the wxWindows GUI toolkit, available from http://www.wxwindows.org. With wxWindows installed, follow the build instructions in the Jazz++ package to make and install Jazz++.

Drivers

Give some extra consideration to your choice of drivers, because Jazz++ includes code for its own driver (`mpu.o`, installed as a kernel-loadable module) for a true Roland MPU-401 MIDI interface card. That driver supports only MIDI, with no support for the digital audio side of Jazz++, but it provides synchronization capabilities not found in the kernel (OSS/Free) driver. It also provides a network daemon (`midinetd`) that lets Jazz++ act as a client application over a TCP/IP network, allowing the sequencer and the MIDI driver to run on separate machines. The `mpu.o` driver can be either selected at runtime or indicated in the `~/.jazz resource` file.

If you intend to sequence MIDI tracks and audio tracks, you can use the OSS/Free kernel drivers or the commercial OSS/Linux drivers. Any of those packages can be used for MIDI-only work.

Recording with Jazz++

You can put data into Jazz++ either by loading a MIDI file (one with the `.mid` extension) or by recording from an external MIDI instrument. Let's first record into the sequencer and then edit the recorded data.

Opening the program brings up the Track window. Select a track to record into, name it, click on the **Record** button, and play away. When you've finished recording the track, click on the **Stop** button, and Jazz++ will prompt you to save or discard the recorded data. Figure 6-3 shows the Track window of `noname.mid` (the default file name) with one track recorded.

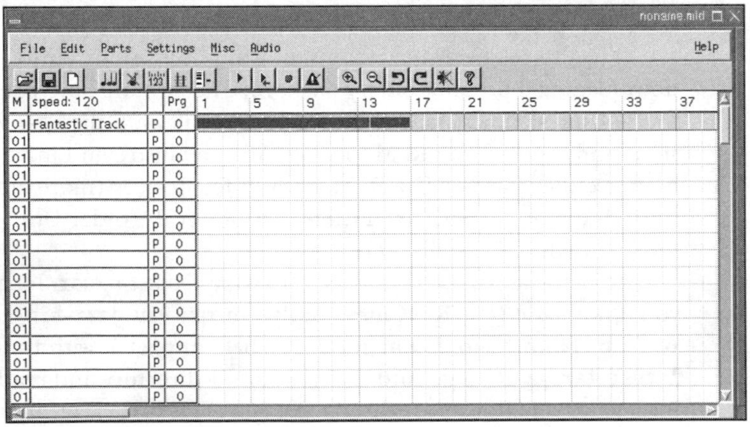

Figure 6-3: Jazz++ with one track recorded

Editing with Jazz++

After recording a track, you can look closely at its contents in the piano roll editor by double-clicking anywhere within the recorded track display. Figure 6-4 displays some measures from our newly recorded Fantastic track, with a small area selected for processing. Note that each column in the grid represents one beat in a four-beat measure.

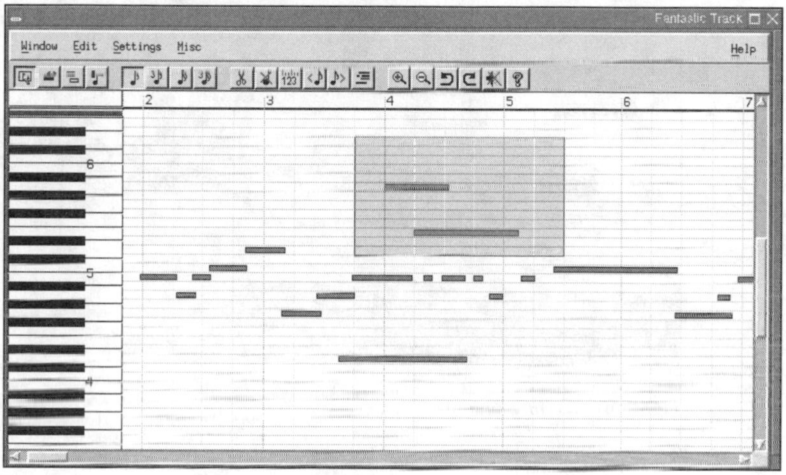

Figure 6-4: Jazz++'s piano roll editor

We can now decide to edit the recorded notes, record another track, or apply a randomization process. If we want to edit our new track, we have an assortment of tools for the job, including quantization (setting note start-times and lengths to a specified value), MIDI channel assignment, transposition, and so forth. Figure 6-5 shows some of the editing windows available from the Edit menus in the main track window and the piano roll editor.

Jazz++ also includes a multiple Undo function, certainly one of the most important features of any modern sequencer, so you can edit and undo until you have just what you want.

MIDI Features Unique to Jazz++

So far we've looked at Jazz++ features offered on most sequencers available today. Now let's look at some of the features unique to Jazz++.

Randomization functions are not new to contemporary sequencers, but few sequencers have as extensive a collection as Jazz++ nor are they as easy and intuitive to use. Pulling down the **Misc** menu in the **Track** window, we see randomization routines for rhythm, melody, track shuffling, and arpeggiation (breaking block chords into single-note sequences). Let's play with some of these routines and see what happens.

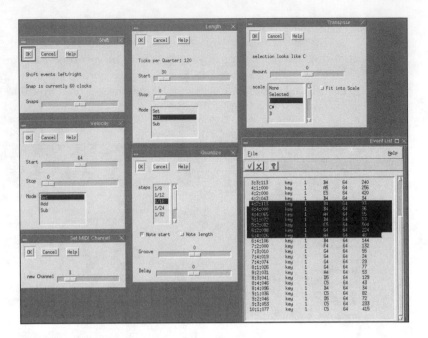

Figure 6-5: Editing options in Jazz++

Random Shuffle

First, copy your recorded track by selecting **Replicate** from the **Edit** menu in the **Track** window. This creates a copy of Track 1 on Track 2. Next, click and drag the mouse over **Track 2** to select the entire track for randomization, then choose **Random Shuffle** from the **Misc** menu. (Incidentally, if you're completely mystified by the randomization windows or any other aspect of Jazz++, have no fear. The authors have provided excellent online help that explains the purpose and usage of every function in the program.) Figure 6-6 demonstrates the Random Shuffle process parameters (the values applied by the particular function) and the effect they have on our new Track 2 (Replicant), along with the Help window for the Random Shuffle option.

Random Rhythm Generator

As the Help file states and as you can see in Figure 6-6, the Random Shuffle chopped and shuffled our track into quite a new arrangement. Now we'll apply the **Random Rhythm Generator** (also from the **Misc** menu in the main track window) to Track 2 to give the recorded notes randomly selected start and end times. Figure 6-7 again shows the altered track along with the function dialog box and the appropriate Help window.

Once again we can see the effect on the track, but to get a better idea of what happened, we need to look at the data in the **Note editor**. We started with measures that looked like those in Figure 6-8.

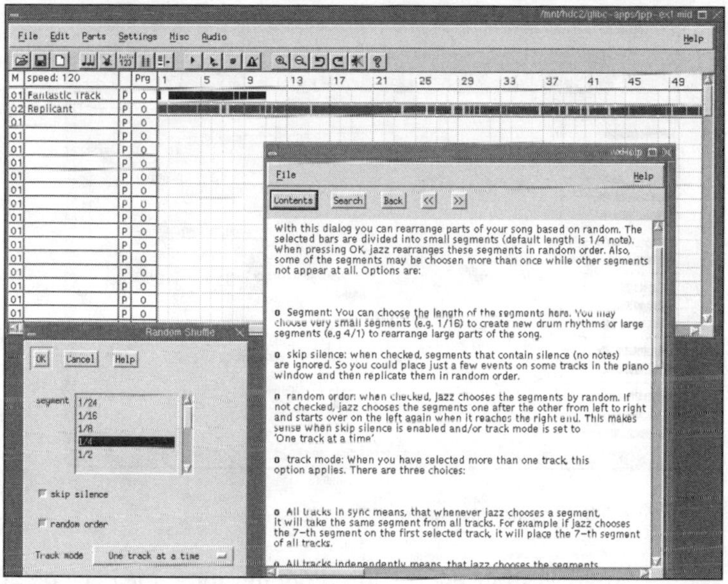

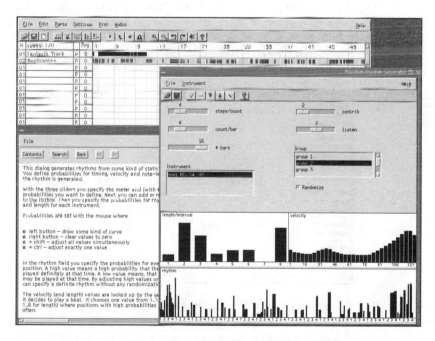

Figure 6-6: Randomizing a track in Jazz++

Figure 6-7: The Random Rhythm Generator with function dialog box and Help window

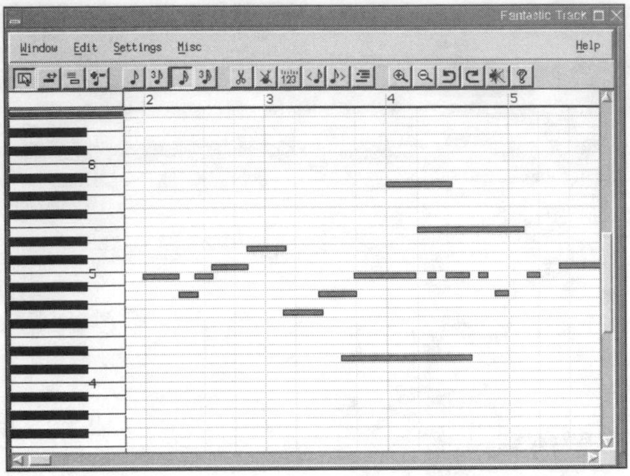

Figure 6-8: Original recording

After we apply the rhythm randomization, the data look like those in Figure 6-9. Note that the pitch content of the track has been reduced to only two notes: This is because the Random Rhythm Generator only creates a random rhythm sequence. To further massage Track 2, we want to give it some pitch movement, which is where the Random Melody Generator comes in.

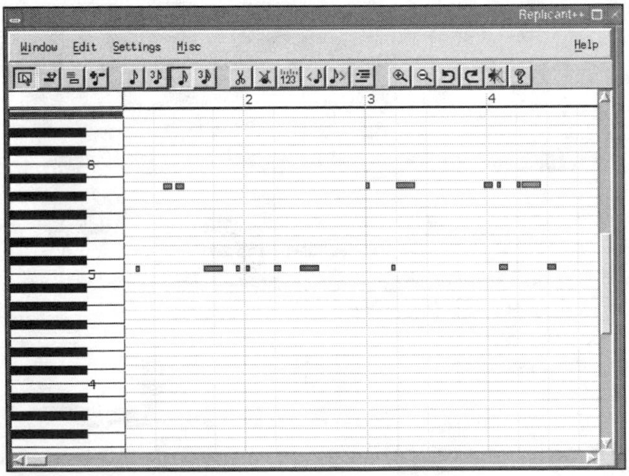

Figure 6-9: Recording after randomizations

Random Melody Generator

Our rhythm transformer reduced the pitch content to only two notes. We can now Undo the action and try something else, or we can push further and see what happens when we subject the track to a Random Melody routine. Figure

6-10 shows the transformed track along with the function window, the relevant Help file, and the Note editor. The Random Melody track has added melodic movement, and now the track is starting to sound like real music.

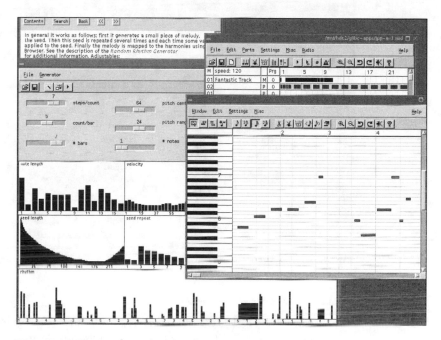

Figure 6-10: The transformed track with various windows

Harmony Browser

As a final flourish to our random manipulations, we will employ the unique Harmony Browser. Using this tool, you can drop chords anywhere into the music: Simply select a starting note and associated chord in the Harmony Browser's chord selector box, then click in the **Note editor** window at the point you want to drop the chord. Complex harmonic passages can be quickly arranged this way. Figure 6-11 shows the chord selector (with an Am7 chord highlighted), the Harmony Browser Help page, and piano roll editor with the results of adding three chords into the track.

Chords can be auditioned in the Browser window and pasted anywhere in the piano-roll editor, making a simple task out of the work of harmonizing a melody line. Like the other generators and randomizers, the Harmony Browser has other options, too many to investigate here, that modify its effect on tracks; the well-planned graphic interfaces and the online help encourage experimentation.

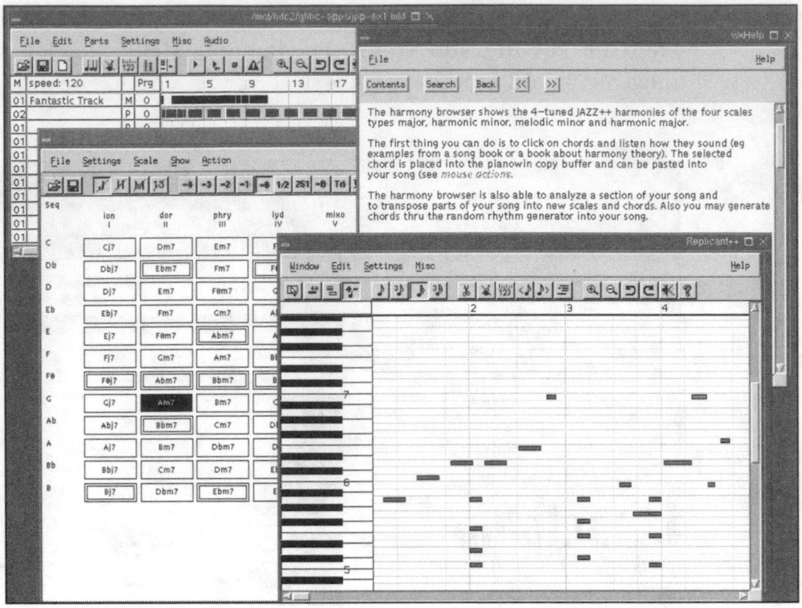

Figure 6-11: The Harmony Browser

Graphic Controller Edit Windows

Before leaving the MIDI side of Jazz++, we should look at the graphic controller edit windows. These functions will be immediately familiar to anyone who has used sequencers in Windows or on a Mac. Editing controller data by drawing curves with the mouse is very intuitive, and Jazz++ provides graphic editing for pitch bend, mod wheel, and other continuous controllers. The program also provides graphic editing for aftertouch, velocity, and song tempo. Figure 6-12 gives us a view of the graphic editor for MIDI Volume (continuous controller #7), applied to the starting measures of Track 2 in our example.

Jazz++'s Digital Audio Features

Jazz++ provides extensive support for digital audio, as our next edits will demonstrate. The combination of MIDI and digital audio features is useful if you want to add vocals or acoustic instruments to your recorded MIDI tracks. But before we can use the audio features of Jazz++, we must first select a track and declare it an audio track. From the **Audio** menu we select **Global Settings** to enable audio support and set the parameters for audio recording and playback. Figure 6-13 shows the track definition window and the global audio settings.

Now open the **Sample Settings** dialog from the **Audio** menu and attach some soundfiles to MIDI note numbers. If any of those numbers are encountered in the audio track, the corresponding sample will be played. Figure 6-14 displays a typical arrangement, with soundfiles attached to MIDI note numbers

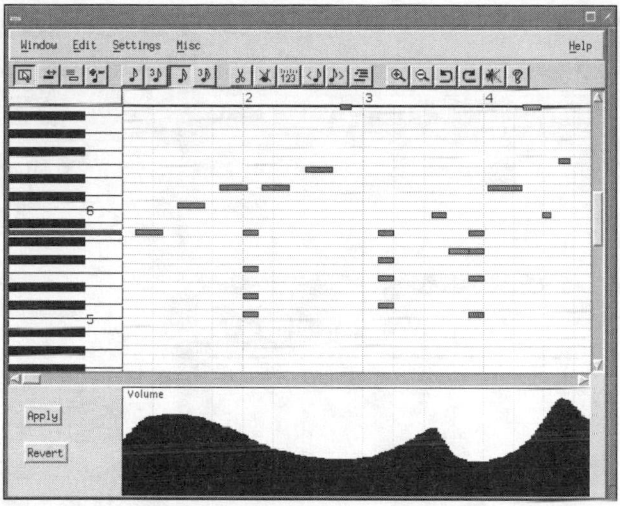

Figure 6-12: The graphic editor for MIDI Volume

64 through 67 (in the Sample Settings window). When the piano-roll editor is opened in an audio track, the keys of the piano keyboard are replaced by names of the soundfiles associated with the MIDI notes. When played, those notes will then trigger their attached soundfile (shown in list at right).

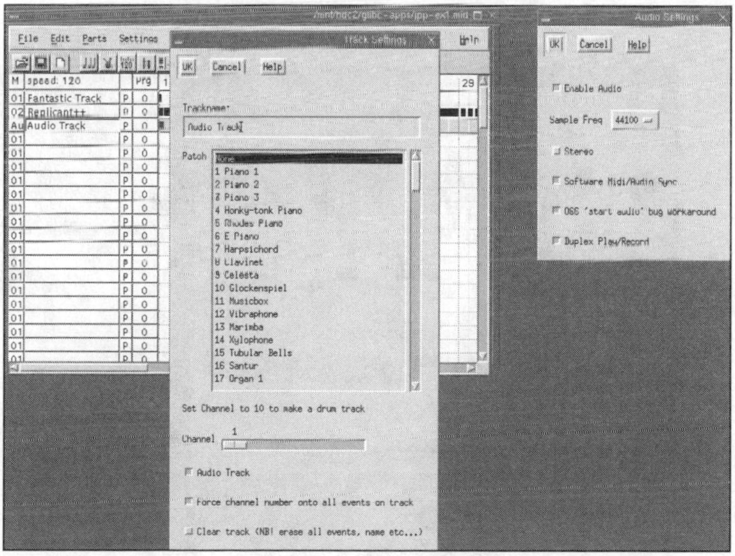

Figure 6-13: The track definition window

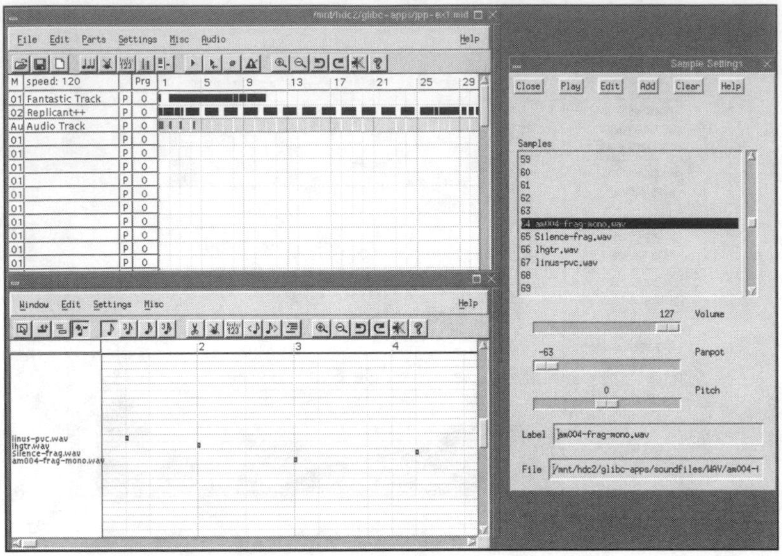

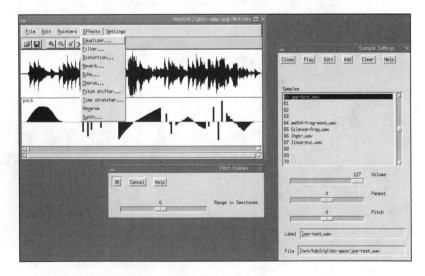

Figure 6-14: Assigning audio files to different MIDI notes

If your soundcard supports full duplex, you can record a new audio track while playing the combined MIDI and audio data already present in your song.

Jazz++ also has an audio file editor and a variety of processing options, including reverb and echo effects, time-stretching, pitch-shifting, and distortion. Figure 6-15 shows the wave editor at work.

Figure 6-15: Jazz++'s audio wave editor

In Figure 6-15, the wave editor is opened to the recorded soundfile, and the Equalizer has been selected from the Effects menu. The "painter" (graphic editor) for pitch has also been opened and applied to the soundfile. Painters are available for drawing curves for pitch, volume, panning, and filtering.

Jazz++ has a general features list too extensive to explore completely here. Other noteworthy tools and functions include a generator for drum grooves, support for synchronization to an external time-code source, a metronome, a MIDI event list editor, a sys-ex editor, and support for the General MIDI patch layouts.

TiMidity++

Authors: Tuuka Toivonen, Masanao Isumo
Version profiled: 2.7.0
Web site: http://www.goice.co.jp/member/mo/timidity/
FTP site: n/a
Maintained: Yes
Availability: Free, open-source
License: GPL
Capsule summary: Renders MIDI file to audio in realtime, with wide range of controls for effects and other playback options

Because many soundcards do not have on-board synthesizers or have only a low quality hardware device for use with MIDI files, getting good MIDI output can be a problem. TiMidity, a MIDI-to-WAV converter that currently runs on Linux, FreeBSD, HP-UX, SunOS, and Win32 systems, solves this problem. By using the audio device of a soundcard to play MIDI files (i.e., by converting a MIDI file to a PCM stream and playing it through a soundcard's audio device), TiMidity enables even a lower-quality card to render high-quality audio for MIDI file playback.

TiMidity utilizes patches in the Gravis Ultrasound (GUS) patch format for its sound sources. Conversion with TiMidity is very fast, and its sound output is excellent. Since Tuuka Toivonen ceased developing TiMidity, it has been superseded by TiMidity++, a distributed development project led by programmer Masanao Isumo. TiMidity++ is a great advance over the original program.

TiMidity++, included with many popular Linux distributions, is in continuous development and improves with each release. It can be used on almost any Linux machine, from a 386SX to the latest screamer, requiring only a soundcard capable of PCM audio. I consider TiMidity++ an essential piece of Linux sound software.

Getting It, Building It

After retrieving the package from this book's CD or the TiMidity++ Web site, unpack it with **tar xzvf TiMidity++-latest.tar.gz**.

Unpacking it in /home will create the TiMidity-latest directory. Following the instructions in the INSTALL text file, you can run the familiar **./configure**; **make**; **make install** command sequence to build and install TiMidity++. However, you will want to run **./configure --help** first: TiMidity++ has many options for the build process, including interface selection (ncurses, X11/Motif, Xaw, Tcl/Tk, and Gtk), choice of sound drivers (OSS, ALSA, ESD), and whether to include support for network audio. Of course, the necessary libraries and headers must be present to compile the desired interface selections into the application.

Once the program is installed, type **timidity -h** to bring up lists with the various command-line options for running TiMidity; type **man timidity** for a more leisurely look at those options presented in a UNIX "man" (manual) page. The man pages are viewable in an X window or at the Linux console, so help for TiMidity++ is always easily available.

What All Does It Do?

TiMidity++ has an impressive feature list. It

- Plays MIDI files without using an external MIDI synthesizer by rapidly converting a MIDI file to a WAV file and playing it through the soundcard DACs

- Places a very low load on the CPU

- Converts a MIDI or a MOD file to various audio file formats (WAV, AU, RAW, AIFF)

- Plays MIDI files over a network

- Handles MIDI files that utilize a 32-channel format

- Automatically detects the drum channel and patch layout mode of MIDI files (General MIDI, Roland GS, Yamaha XG)

- Has a sound spectrogram display and support for almost all common MIDI messages as well as for some uncommon ones (particularly some karaoke display functions)

- Supports playlists

- Plays files contained within archived files, including tarballs, zipfiles, and lzh-compressed files

- Accesses and plays files (including archived files) over a network, including the HTTP (e.g., http://foo.mid), FTP (e.g., ftp://foo.mid), and NNTP (e.g., news://foo.mid) protocols

TiMidity++ uses the same GUS-compatible patches as the original TiMidity and can now employ SoundFonts (a soundfile format for the Sound Blaster AWE32/64 cards). If neither format is available, you can use a GUS2WAV conversion utility to create Gravis Ultrasound PAT files from WAV files. With the

GUS patches, TiMidity++ renders MIDI files to disk or to a realtime audio stream. It supports 8-bit and 16-bit rendering at variable sampling rates—though, of course, the higher sound quality will demand fast CPU and disk resources.

Using TiMidity++

Launching TiMidity++ in X is as simple as opening an xterm window and entering `timidity -im foo.mid`, where -i selects the interface (the m stands for Motif) and foo.mid is the MIDI file to be rendered. TiMidity++ has an impressive list of command-line flags, including switches for output modes, interface selection, format options, and added effects. Here is an example of a more complex command line for starting TiMidity++:

```
timidity -ik -s 22050 -R 450 -Ow1S alman.mid
```

This will start TiMidity++ with a Tcl/Tk interface, setting the sampling frequency to 22,050 Hz, adding a reverb with a 450-ms release, and sending the output to a 16-bit stereo WAV file. Figure 6-16 shows what it looks like.

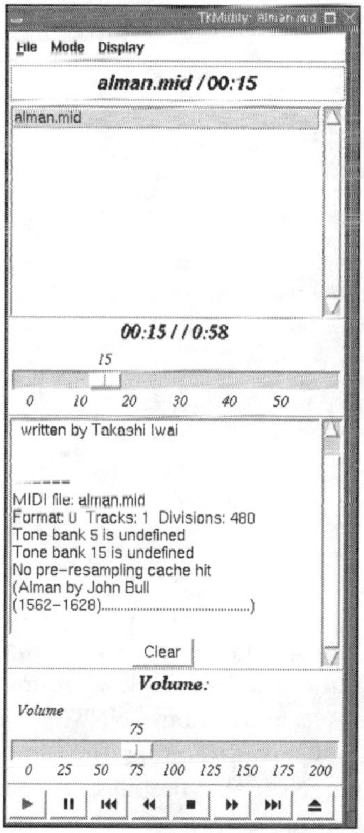

Figure 6-16: TiMidity++ in the Tcl/Tk interface

Figures 6-17, 6-18, and 6-19 show TiMidity++ with its X11/Motif, Xaw, and Gtk interfaces.

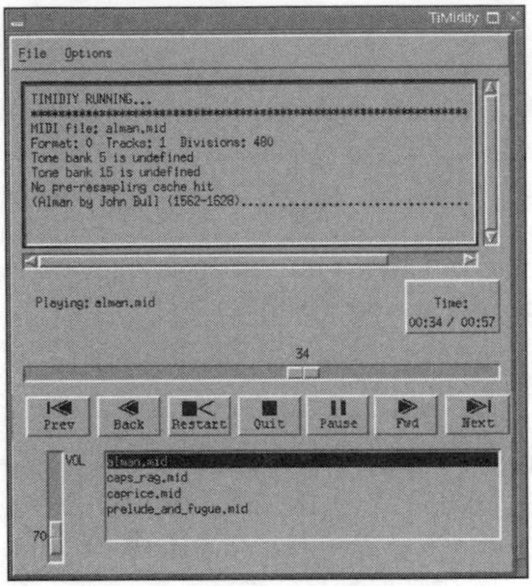

Figure 6-17: TiMidity++ in X11/Motif

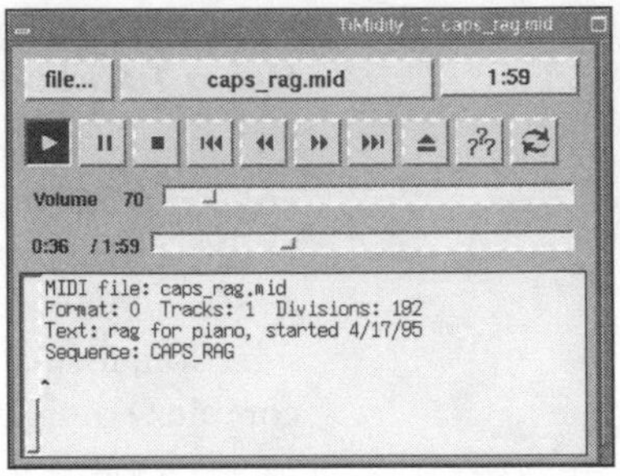

Figure 6-18: TiMidity++ in Xaw

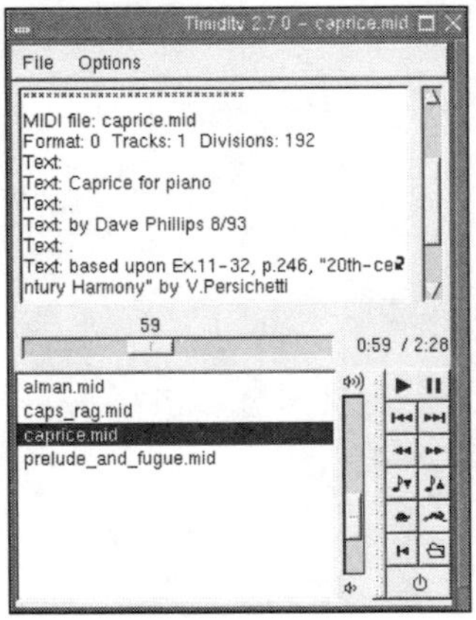

Figure 6-19: TiMidity++ in Gtk

NNTP is the network news transport protocol, the software responsible for moving all the news in and out of the Usenet newsgroups. One of TiMidity++'s most interesting features is its ability to use NNTP to retrieve all the MIDI files posted in a specified newsgroup, adding them to a playlist for immediate play or later rendering. Note that the files in the newsgroup must be uuencoded (the .uue extension indicates a uuencoded file). Enter **man timidity** at the command prompt for specific instructions on how to use this feature (enter **man uuencode** for more information about that Linux utility).

UMP

TiMidity++ is also the rendering engine in the UMP plug-in for Netscape. This application provides a simple interface for playing MIDI files found on Web pages. UMP's supported actions are Start, Pause/Restart, and Stop, and it is simple to install and use. With TiMidity++ as its engine, UMP can render high-quality sound for Web-based MIDI files. UMP binaries, sources, and instructions are available at http://pubweb.bnl.gov/people/hoff/.

playmidi

Authors: Nathan Laredo, Takashi Iwai (support for AWE32)
Version profiled: 2.4
Web site: http://playmidi.openprojects.net/
FTP site: n/a
Maintained: Yes
Availability: Free, open-source
License: GPL
Capsule summary: Excellent MIDI file player for virtually any soundcard; can be used in simple console-only mode or in a variety of GUI modes

playmidi can play MIDI files through the synthesizer on your soundcard (such as the OPL3 on most cards or the EMU8000 on the Sound Blaster AWE32/64 cards), or it can direct its output through a MIDI port to an external synthesizer. Like TiMidity, playmidi has spawned a family of versions based on the original software. It is found in almost every mainstream Linux distribution, and it is now an official GNU project.

playmidi is my command-line MIDI file player of choice. It is powerful and versatile, yet requires only the ncurses library for use on a Linux console without graphics. Thanks to the low demands placed on the CPU by the MIDI data stream, playmidi (in command-line form) is perfect for playing MIDI music files on console-only systems or on slower machines such as legacy 486s and old Pentiums, whereas more modern machines can take advantage of its various versions for X. If I want to listen to my MIDI file collection while working at the Linux command-line, with or without X, I turn to playmidi.

playmidi provides a rich set of options for playing MIDI files, including the ability to force or exclude playback on specific MIDI channels, redefine the synth device and MIDI output port, force or exclude percussion channels, control the synthesizer, and enable realtime graphics. In addition, playmidi does things big sequencer packages like Jazz++ can't do: It provides support for playlists and controls for the effects processing on some popular soundcards (e.g., AEW32/64 cards).

The Setup

After unpacking the source code with **tar xzvf playmidi-latest.tar.gz**, change directories to your new playmidi directory. Run the playmidi Configure utility and step through the configuration sequence, selecting your default synth device (external, OPL3, AWE 32/64, Gravis Ultrasound) and MIDI output device (if more than one exists). Run **make** and (as root, of course) **make install**, and if all goes well you will have a fresh binary of playmidi ready to play your MIDI files. If your system has the Xaw libraries (also called the Athena widget set), then the compile process will also build xplaymidi, a simple X interface for playmidi.

Using playmidi

Here's an example of a playmidi command sequence:

```
playmidi -e -D /dev/midi -p 63 -r -V 75 myfoo.mid
```

This command enables a realtime display of MIDI activity, sets the playback volume, and sends a program change message (63) and the file data (myfoo.mid) to an external synthesizer connected to the default MIDI interface (/dev/midi). With the appropriate hardware, even more complex commands can be prepared for file play and synthesizer control.

Here is a more elaborate command for playback with a Sound Blaster AWE64:

```
playmidi -a -p 1,41 -R 48 -C 24 -V 1,80 -r myfoo.mid
```

where -a tells playmidi to use the AWE32/64 internal synthesizer and -p sends a General MIDI patch number (41) to it on MIDI channel 1. -R sets an initial reverb value, -C sets an initial value for a chorus effect, and -V sets the volume for MIDI channel 1. Reverb, chorus, and volume each have a range of values from 0 to 127. The -r option activates a realtime display of MIDI activity: Instru-

Figure 6-20: fXPlayMidi

ment names are listed per MIDI channel, and labels for the notes played in a channel flash on and off in the display in an animated bouncing-ball effect.

Various playmidi Incarnations

In keeping with the nature of open-source projects, programmers around the world have taken on the development of playmidi. Kevin L. McWhirter's fXPlay-Midi (Figure 6-20) adds an XForms interface and support for album playlists, and Satoshi Kuramochi's Eplaymidi (Figure 6-21) adds an X11 interface to the player and file selector, along with a MIDI status display and a player for WRD files (a format that synchronizes animation, music, and a lyrics display). Figure 6-22 displays XPlaymidi, the default X interface in the playmidi package.

See the listing at http://sound.condorow.net for links to all of these GUIs.

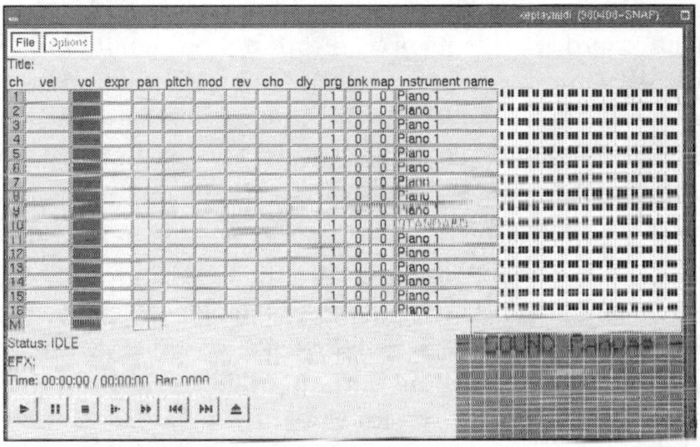

Figure 6-21: xeplaymidi

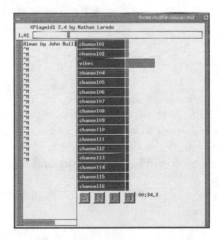

Figure 6-22: XPlaymidi

KeyKit

Author: Tim Thompson
Version profiled: 6.5a
Web site: http://209.233.20.72/keykit/index.html
FTP site: n/a
Maintained: Yes
Availability: Free, open-source
License: Held by the author and AT&T
Capsule summary: Environment for exploring algorithmic MIDI composition, with an excellent GUI and extensive features list

KeyKit is a MIDI composition environment with abundant tools and features—its toolkit far outstrips that of Jazz++. It includes a graphic user interface for X displays, a powerful MIDI process control language, and an incredible array of functions and routines for interactive composition. KeyKit can be used as a straightforward MIDI sequencer, recording your input from a MIDI device (keyboard, MIDI guitar, wind controller), but no MIDI input device is required. The program will also load, play, and manipulate Standard MIDI files. In our examples we'll see how it excels at the creation and permutation of MIDI data.

Getting It, Building It

KeyKit is available only from the Web site listed above. KeyKit can be obtained as a pre-compiled binary or as source code. If you retrieve the binary, you need only place it in your system PATH and type **keykit** in an xterm window—the application will start up. Building KeyKit is also simple: Just unpack the source package with **tar xzvf keykit-src-latest.tar.gz** and follow the directions in the author's installation documentation.

NOTE *The Linux version of KeyKit currently supports only external MIDI (/dev/midi), so you must have an external synthesizer to use KeyKit. It will not access a soundcard's onboard synth.*

Using KeyKit

KeyKit has far too many interesting features to illustrate or even list here. We will look at two examples: The first will show how to load a MIDI file and play it, and the second will demonstrate how to record and manipulate MIDI data with one of KeyKit's randomization tools. For a full list of the program's features and how to use them, go to the KeyKit Web site and follow the links to the online documentation.

When you first open KeyKit, you will see a blank display and the key> prompt in the KeyKit language command Interpreter window. Left-click the mouse anywhere outside the Interpreter to pop up a menu of KeyKit's various tools and functions (Figure 6-23).

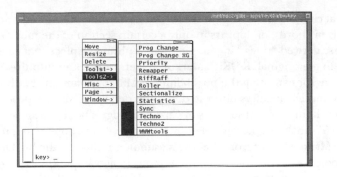

Figure 6-23: The KeyKit menu

Now select **Tools2** from the pop-up menu and click on the **RiffRaff** tool. A small "sweep" icon will appear; click and drag the icon to open and size the RiffRaff window. Clicking on **More** in the **RiffRaff** tool lets you choose between recording new notes into the tool or loading a MIDI file into it. Click on the **On** button or anywhere within the graphic note display to audition the MIDI file or recorded events. You can also trigger playback (of RiffRaff and most of KeyKit's other tools) by using the **Bang** tool. Bang is especially useful in complex KeyKit structures where you want to manually trigger a process or processes at random. To use it, open the pop-up menu and select **Bang** from the **Tools2** submenu. Click on the **Add** button on the **Bang** tool, and a line will appear. Drag this line into the **RiffRaff** tool. Release the mouse button, and you can now switch the tool on or off by using the **Bang** tool. Figure 6-24 shows the Bang tool ready to get wired to the On button of the RiffRaff processor.

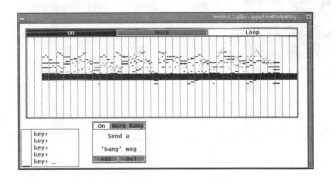

Figure 6-24: KeyKit's Bang tool

Example 1: Generating MIDI Files with the Markov Maker

The Markov Maker utilizes a randomization process known as a Markov chain. The Markov Maker will analyze a piece of music, calculate its note-order probabilities from existing music, and tabulate how often each note occurs and in what circumstances (e.g., whether it follows only certain other notes, appears only in chords, or appears in only a certain section of the music). By applying these derived "rules," it generates a new phrase or piece that can be quite similar to the original. KeyKit's Markov Maker provides an intuitive, interactive means for exploring the possibilities of Markov chains, instantly turning theory into music. (Readers interested in more details on Markov processes should consult the relevant sections in Charles Dodge's book, *Computer Music.*[1])

To analyze a file with Markov Maker, open the pop-up menu again, choose the **Markov Maker** from the **Tools2** submenu, click on the big **Orig** button, and choose **Read File** from its menu. For our first example (following the suggestions given in the tools.pdf file included with the distribution), we'll select the Bach prelude (`prelude.mid`) from the MIDI files in the KeyKit music directory.

Next, set the permutation probabilities by pressing **Orig** again, this time selecting the **Set Sim** item to set the similarity parameters and choosing **Win 1b/2** and **Inc 1b/4**. The Win value signifies the size of the analysis window, and the Inc value is its increment as it moves across the analyzed music. Figure 6-25 shows `prelude.mid` loaded into the Orig area of the tool. As with most of KeyKit's windows, clicking anywhere within the tool will start and stop playback of the MIDI data.

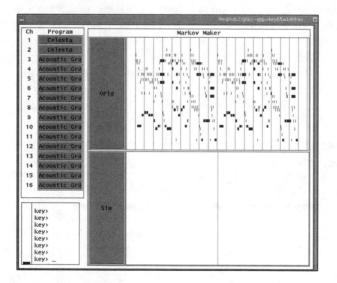

Figure 6-25: KeyKit's Markov Maker

Now you can generate a phrase of a few bars or an entire piece out of the data loaded in the Orig area. Click on the big **Sim** button, select **Make Sim**, and choose the length of output you desire. In Figure 6-26 we see the results of choosing Make Sim • 256.

1 Dodge, C. and Thomas A. Jerse. *Computer Music: Synthesis, Composition, and Performance.* 2nd ed. New York: Schirmer Books, 1997.

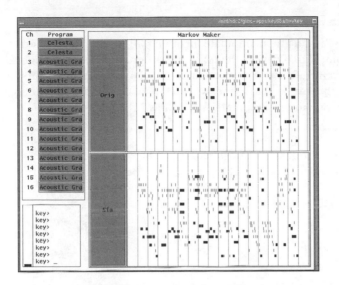

Figure 6-26: The results of KeyKit's Make Sim feature

Using the oddly named **Snarf** tool from the **Sim** menu, you can now save your generated music for processing in other KeyKit modules. For instance, you could click on **Orig** again, choose **Read • Snarf** to place your newly generated music into the Orig area, and run the entire process again.

Other KeyKit Features

KeyKit has a tool for every MIDI data type, including note events, controller data, program changes, system-exclusive messages, and MIDI time code. We have already seen the Program Change tool in Figures 6-25 and 6-26. In those figures, the Celesta instrument is selected for channels 1 and 2. The General MIDI instrument order is the default layout, and the remaining channels have been left at Acoustic Grand Piano, the default program selection.

KeyKit is also a powerful MIDI command language. It is an object-oriented language, with full support for modern programming methods, including arrays, functions, and conditional evaluations such as "if/else" statements and "for" loops. Here is a very simple example of KeyKit as a MIDI command language:

```
key> realtime ('c e g b, f a c e, g b d f, c e g b')
```

The realtime function will send MIDI data immediately out the MIDI interface to any connected MIDI devices. In this example, four chords are sent in sequence: a Cmaj7 (c e g b), followed by an Fmaj7 (f a c e) and a G7 (g b d f), then resolved back to the Cmaj7 (c e g b).

See the program documentation for more details about KeyKit's programming language.

Example 2: Working with MIDI Input

KeyKit can also manipulate incoming MIDI data. When KeyKit receives data from a MIDI device, the following program cycles it through four MIDI channels (i.e., four separate instruments). To perform this example, your external synth must be able to receive MIDI data on multiple channels, so be sure to set it up to receive on MIDI channels 1 through 4.

```
#
# This is an example program that takes MIDI input and
# maps it to different channels, cycling through them for each note.
#
# This code was written by Tim Thompson.
#

function example5() {

    # Turn Merge off so that the notes you play on the external
    # keyboard aren't actually echoed (this assumes that you don't have
    # the external keyboard directly driving your MIDI synths).
    print("Turning Merge off...")
    Merge = 0

    # spawn the task that will monitor MIDI input
    t = task task_example5()

    Root.waitforconsolekey()

    print("Turning Merge back on...")
    kill(t)
    Merge = 1;
}

function task_example5() {

    Midiin[$] = f = open()
    onexit(closemidi,$)

    lowchan = 1
    highchan = 4
    ch = lowchan
    while ( (n=get(f)) != Eof ) {
            if ( n.type == NOTEON
                    || n.type == NOTEOFF
                    || n.type == CHANPRESSURE
                    || n.type == CONTROLLER
                    || n.type == PITCHBEND ) {
```

```
                n.chan = ch
        }
        if ( n.type -- NOTEOFF && sizeof(Current) == 0 ) {
                # Cycle from lowchan to highchan
                if ( ch < highchan )
                        ch++
                else
                        ch = lowchan
        }
        realtime(n,0)     # play it
    }
}
```

The above function is included in a KeyKit library file called example5.k. Load and run it by typing the following commands at the key> prompt in the Interpreter window:

```
key> #include "example5.k"
key> example5()
```

As you play your MIDI instrument, you will hear the notes played through MIDI channels 1 through 4, rotating through whatever sounds you've selected for those channels.

Summing Up

I've barely scratched the surface of KeyKit. Fortunately, the program invites and encourages experimentation with its array of tools. As I wrote this profile, I kept finding one interesting tool after another, and it was difficult to stop playing with KeyKit and get back to writing. But KeyKit is far more than a diversion and it is certainly not a toy: It is a well-designed toolkit for the creation and transformation of virtually any kind of MIDI data. Because it is so powerful, unique, and enjoyable, I consider it necessary software for the complete Linux MIDI studio.

xphat

Author: Paul Barton-Davis
Version profiled: "preliminary pre-alpha"
Web site: http://www.op.net/~pbd/xphat/xphat.html
FTP site: n/a
Maintained: No
Availability: Free, open-source
License: GPL
Capsule summary: One of a kind "virtual MIDI fader box," uncomplicated and simple to use

xphat is a software emulation of a MIDI fader box. A hardware fader box is a control interface that provides sliders, buttons, and wheels to send MIDI messages to another hardware device, typically a MIDI synthesizer, allowing you to assign controllers that may not exist on your hardware. xphat is a wonderful tool because it works in the same manner as the hardware fader box and thus saves you from having to buy one. xphat's controls can be assigned to any MIDI message type.

Getting It, Building It

Unpack the source code (from the Web site or this book's CD-ROM) with **tar xzvf xphat.tar.gz** and change to the new xphat directory. xphat requires the XForms library (available at http://bragg.phys.uwm.edu/xforms) and the X libraries included with most Linux distributions. After editing the Makefile to indicate the location of your XForms library, simply type **make**, and in a few minutes you will have your new xphat. Type **./xphat** to try it out. Copy it to a directory in your system PATH (/usr/local/bin is a good choice) and you can then run it anywhere simply by typing **xphat** in an xterm window.

Using xphat

A simple use for xphat is as a transmission device for MIDI controller messages. However, the sliders can be programmed to send any type of MIDI message, including system-exclusive data (for editing external synthesizer sound parameters) and MIDI note-ons and note-offs.

On start-up, xphat looks for a file named xphat.sysex, a user-configurable file that specifies a list of system-exclusive messages that can be controlled by the sliders. I wrote the following file for my Yamaha TX802 (an external FM synthesis module):

```
#
# Sysex Info File for xphat
#

Yamaha TX802
   algorithm select = f0 43 10 01 06 P f7
   feedback level = f0 43 10 01 07 P f7
   transpose = f0 43 10 01 10 P f7
   pitch EG scaling = f0 43 10 60 26 P f7
   oscillator fine = f0 43 10 00 13 P f7
```

NOTE *The* xphat.sysex *file is not necessary for any other xphat operations. The program will launch and run perfectly without it.*

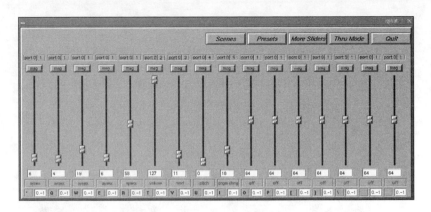

Figure 6-27: xphat

Figure 6-27 shows xphat with the first five sliders configured as sys-ex controllers on MIDI channel 1 for the parameters included in my `xphat.sysex` file. The next four sliders are configured for controlling MIDI volume, modulation wheel amount, pitch bend, and program change on MIDI channels 2 through 5; the remaining seven sliders are currently not in use.

Summary

That's all there is to xphat. It performs its tasks well, and there's no other program like it for Linux. I especially like to use it for editing my synthesizers: They all have displays that are too small, and xphat provides a much more usable interface. I highly recommend it for any Linux MIDI studio.

MIDI revolutionized the world of commercial music-making. By placing powerful and affordable composition, recording, and editing tools in the hands of musicians everywhere, MIDI has made it possible for one person with a home studio to create and record music as complex and polished as that coming from a major recording label. However, MIDI is not perfect for everyone, and the original specification is showing its age. But even though various schemes have been devised for replacing MIDI, none have been widely accepted and it is generally agreed that MIDI is here to stay. If you're planning a full-featured Linux music studio, don't forget about MIDI!

LINUX DOES MP3

All soundfile formats have limitations. CD-quality audio in the WAV soundfile format requires 10 MB of disk storage per stereo minute. Furthermore, Internet bandwidth and transmission rates do not favor CD-quality WAV or AIFF audio files streamed to your computer in realtime over the Net. The MP3 audio file format, however, overcomes these limitations by significantly reducing storage and network transmission requirements while maintaining high-resolution (at least 16-bit) sound quality. Not surprisingly, the MP3 audio file format is commonly encountered on Web pages and is a popular Internet broadcasting medium.

What Is MP3?

MP3 is the popular name for soundfiles in the MPEG Layer 3 Audio file format. MPEG, the Motion Pictures Experts Group, is an organization that defines data compression standards for digital audio and digital video. In addition to being used to distribute and broadcast high-quality compressed audio over the Internet, the MP3 audio format is used by HDTV (high-definition television) and DVD (digital video disc). MP3 technical details are beyond the scope of this book, and I refer the reader to the excellent MP3 Tech Web site at http://www.mp3-tech.org for the format's history, technical specifications, and terminology.

MP3 is the preferred format for distributing and promoting music on the Net, yielding near-CD sound fidelity with 16-bit resolution in file sizes friendly to modem transfers (a 50-MB WAV file can be reduced to a 5-MB MP3 file). MP3-encoded music can also be broadcast over the Internet as streaming audio (compressed data formats suitable for realtime transmission over a network), allowing you to listen to MP3 files as they download to your computer.

Hardware MP3 players, such as Diamond's Rio (which lets you save and play downloaded MP3 files on their portable player), combined with faster Internet connections, have helped to turn MP3 into an effective way to distribute music over the Internet. Web sites like MP3.com (www.mp3.com) and the Internet Underground Music Archive (www.iuma.com) are essentially huge collections of all types of MP3 files that have brought a wide range of music to the Web almost overnight (along with all sorts of copyright issues). You can listen to selections over the Internet in streaming audio, download the music you like, organize it into customized playlists, and fire it through the computer's parallel port into your portable MP3 player.

Bitstreams and Bitrates

Whereas the audio quality of a WAV file depends on its sampling rate and bit resolution, the audio quality of an MP3 file depends on its bitrate. The bitrate is the number of kilobits (kbits) per second at which an MP3-compressed bitstream flows from storage (disk or RAM) to the decoder input. A bitstream is simply the series of bits representing the encoded data. The standard bitrate for near-CD audio quality stereo MP3 files is 128 kbits. Higher bitrates improve the audio quality, but at the cost of a correspondingly larger file size.

Linux MP3 Applications

Linux MP3 applications include encoders and decoders, MP3 file servers for network audio broadcasting (see Chapter 12), file identification tag editors, database management software for large collections of MP3 files, and file transfer utilities for hardware players like the Rio. Versions of these tools are available for the Linux console and the X window system.

The Encoder

An MP3 encoder compresses soundfile data. MP3 data compression (or "encoding") is the process of reducing the size of a file by applying sophisticated algorithms to recognize and compress redundant data. The popular PKZIP compression utility for DOS/Windows works with a plain text file in this way, removing the redundant white-space data and marking its location for decompressing later. For text files and many other file formats, the compression algorithms in programs such as PKZIP and GZIP can yield greatly reduced file sizes, facilitating archive maintenance, conserving storage space, and reducing the burden on network transfers. High-resolution digital graphics, video, and audio also require large amounts of disk storage, but the data compression and reduction routines of the ZIP-style utilities will not significantly reduce their file sizes. A five-minute WAV-format stereo soundfile contains 40 million bytes, and very few of them are absolutely identical values. Data compression for text files is called a "lossless" compression; that is, when the compressed file is uncompressed, the data is restored to its original condition. "Lossy" compression schemes can provide greater soundfile size reduction, but they do so by sacrificing data considered irrelevant or unnoticeable. Specialized lossy data compression schemes (such as MP3) have been devised for soundfile formats. One of the best-known implementations of an MP3 compressor is the BladeEnc encoder.

The BladeEnc MP3 Encoder

Author: Tord Jansson
Version profiled: 0.76
Web site: http://bladeenc.mp3.no/
FTP site: n/a
Maintained: Yes
Availability: Free, open-source
License: LGPL
Capsule summary: Fast, stable, open-source encoder with broad range of bitrates.

Among the several Linux encoders (including the Hannover MPEG Encoder and MP3ENC from Frauenhofer IIS), my first choice is BladeEnc. A freely available encoder that reads WAV and AIFF soundfiles, BladeEnc supports bitrates from 32 to 320 kbits per second. It will accept 8-bit and 16-bit stereo or mono soundfiles with sampling rates of 32, 44.1, or 48 kHz. BladeEnc is a command-line utility, but graphic front-ends are available in Gtk and Qt interfaces.

Getting It, Building It

After copying the package from this book's CD or downloading it from the BladeEnc Web site, move it to wherever you keep new packages (either your /home or /usr/local directory is a good choice, depending which has more space). Unpack it with **tar xzvf bladeenc-latest.tar.gz**, then switch to your new BladeEnc directory and follow the instructions there to build and install the program. A simple **./configure** and **make** will build it. Become superuser with **su root** and enter **make install** to put a working copy of BladeEnc in your system path, and you are now ready to run the encoder.

Using BladeEnc

Running BladeEnc with no command-line argument or options yields the display in Figure 7-1.

Running BladeEnc with its defaults yields the display in Figure 7-2.

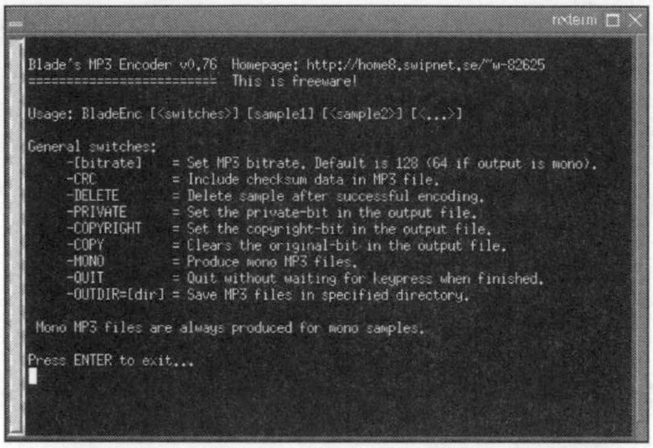

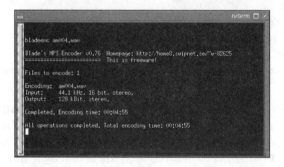

Figure 7-1: BladeEnc help screen

Figure 7-2: BladeEnc run with its defaults

In the example shown in Figure 7-2, the original 76.65-second-long file was reduced from 14 MB to less than 1.3 MB on my Pentium 166 in just under five minutes with the command **bladeenc am004.wav** (am004.wav is the name of the file that was encoded).

GUIs for BladeEnc

KBlade and Grip, shown in Figure 7-3, are two of BladeEnc's GUI front ends.

KBlade presents simple, command-line options in a pleasant Qt frame. It runs as fast as BladeEnc and is very convenient in an X session. Mike Oliphant's Grip is more complex: Like KBlade, it provides a nice interface to BladeEnc (and other encoders), but it also has a user-definable CD ripper and Mike's GCD player. (Grip is described at greater length later in this chapter.)

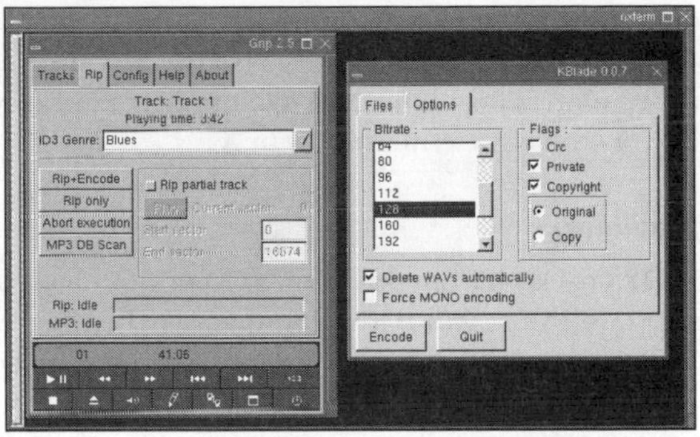

Figure 7-3: KBlade and Grip, two of BladeEnc's GUI front ends

Why Choose BladeEnc?

BladeEnc appeals to me (over the other encoders mentioned above) for several reasons: It is an open-source project licensed under the LGPL (a version of the GNU Public License specifically for the use of GPL-protected library components in non-GPL'd software), it supports the widest range of bitrates (with excellent results at 192 kbits), it will run in "batch" mode for automatically processing multiple files, and it can mix a stereo file to mono while encoding (no prior conversion is necessary).

Tord Jansson has kept BladeEnc in continuous development, and it is widely regarded as one of the fastest MP3 encoders. I've used it to create MP3s from dozens of WAV files, and I recommend it to anyone looking for a fast, flexible, and freely available MP3 encoder.

The Decoder and the Player

Before an MP3 file can be played, it must be decoded. A decoding engine powers every MP3 player: many players (such as XMMS) use the mpg123 decoder, but some prefer to employ their own decoders. Decoders vary in their support of the MPEG audio format series (there are currently four commonly encountered formats), range of supported bitrates, and decoding speed.

mpg123: The Decoder

Author: Michael Hipp
Version profiled: 0.59k (beta)
Web site: http://www.mpg123.de/
FTP site: n/a
Maintained: Yes
Availability: Free, open-source
License: All rights held by the author

Michael Hipp's mpg123 (shown in Figure 7-4) is the default MP3 decoder used by XMMS (see section below) and is also the decoding engine inside many other MP3 players for Linux. You can use mpg123 easily at the console command-line or from an xterm window in X.

Getting It, Building It

Copy the mpg123 package from this book's CD or download the latest version from the mpg123 Web site. Move it to your package holding area, then unpack it with **tar xzvf mpg123-latest.tar.gz**. Enter your newly created mpg123 directory and read the instructions on building and installing the program. Once again, a simple **./configure** followed by **make** and (as root) **make install** is all you have to do.

Using mpg123

Running it with no arguments brings up the help screen shown in Figure 7-4.

```
                                                              rxterm
High Performance MPEG 1.0/2.0/2.5 Audio Player for Layer 1, 2 and 3.
Version 0.59q (1999/Jan/26). Written and copyrights by Michael Hipp.
Uses code from various people. See 'README' for more!
THIS SOFTWARE COMES WITH ABSOLUTELY NO WARRANTY! USE AT YOUR OWN RISK!

usage: mpg123 [option(s)] [file(s) | URL(s) | -]
supported options [defaults in brackets]:
    -v    increase verbosity level        -q    quiet (don't print title)
    -t    testmode (no output)            -s    write to stdout
    -w <filename> write Output as WAV file
    -k n  skip first n frames [0]         -n n  decode only n frames [all]
    -c    check range violations          -y    DISABLE resync on errors
    -b n  output buffer: n Kbytes [0]     -f n  change scalefactor [32768]
    -r n  set/force samplerate [auto]     -g n  set audio hardware output gain
    -os,-ol,-oh  output to built-in speaker,line-out connector,headphones
                                          -a d  set audio device
    -2    downsample 1:2 (22 kHz)         -4    downsample 1:4 (11 kHz)
    -d n  play every n'th frame only      -h n  play every frame n times
    -0    decode channel 0 (left) only    -1    decode channel 1 (right) only
    -m    mix both channels (mono)        -p p  use HTTP proxy p [$HTTP_PROXY]
    -@ f  read filenames/URLs from f
    -z    shuffle play (with wildcards)   -Z    random play
    -u a  HTTP authentication string      -E f  Equalizer, data from file
See the manpage mpg123(1) or call mpg123 with --longhelp for more information.
```

Figure 7-4: Running mpg123 with no arguments

As you can see in Figure 7-4, mpg123 offers a broad range of options, including output specifications, decoding instructions, and playlist manipulation. I especially enjoy the ability to play MP3 files from a URL. For example, the command sequence

```
mpg123 http://www.bright.net/~dlphilp/mpieces2a.mp3
```

will retrieve my MP3 masterpiece (the `mpieces2a.mp3` file) from the designated Web address, load it into mpg123, and play it once it's downloaded.

A popular decoder, mpg123 has front-end interfaces in Tcl/Tk, Gtk, ncurses, and Python. Figure 7-5 shows a screenshot of Tk3Play, a Tcl/Tk incarnation.

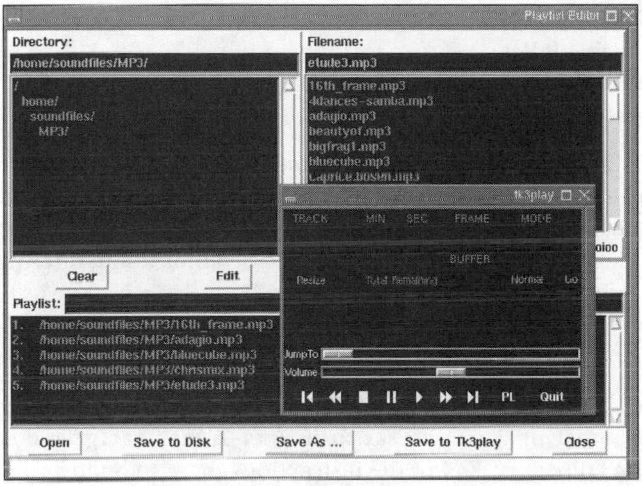

Figure 7-5. Tk3Play

Figure 7-6 shows Andy Lo A Foe's Alsaplayer, another fine multimedia player that uses mpg123 for its decoding engine and the Gtk (GIMP Toolkit) for its graphic user interface, and supports the most current ALSA sound drivers (see Chapter 2 for more information regarding ALSA).

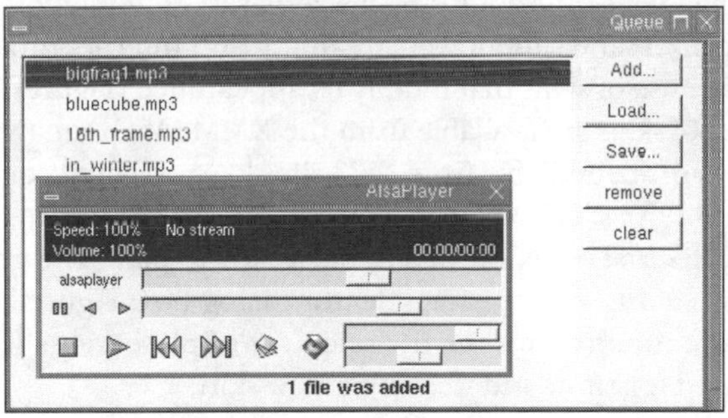

Figure 7-6: Andy Lo A Foe's Alsaplayer

Tk3Play and Alsaplayer are fine front-ends for mpg123, as is XMMS. However, XMMS includes support for a wider range of multimedia file types (video, audio, animations), whereas Tk3Play and Alsaplayer work for soundfiles only.

XMMS: The Linux Multimedia Player

Authors: Peter and Mikael Alm
Version profiled: 0.9.1
Web site: http://www.xmms.org
FTP site: n/a
Maintained: Yes
Availability: Free, open-source
License: GPL

XMMS (X Multimedia System) is one of the most popular MP3 players for Linux. Formerly known as X11amp, XMMS began as a Linux emulation of the popular WinAmp (an MP3 player for Windows 95/98). It has since been developed into a powerful Linux-specific application, offering support for various window managers and the GNOME desktop.

Getting It, Building It

After downloading the latest package, move it to your /home or /usr/local directory. Unpack it with **tar xzvf xmms-latest.tar.gz** and enter your new XMMS directory. Follow the instructions there to build and install XMMS. It's as simple as **./configure**, **make**, and (as root again) **make install**, after which you need only type **xmms** in an xterm window to begin using XMMS.

Using XMMS

XMMS, an excellent soundfile player, can handle MPEG audio layers 1, 2, and 3 (the numbers refer to format series), WAV and AU soundfile formats, all mod music formats supported by the MikMod library, and standard CD audio. Its features list extends far beyond the expected controls for playing files, including a spectrum analyzer, support for plug-ins, a playlist editor, an oscilloscope mode, a graphic equalizer, and support for streaming and Internet broadcast audio. It can also make use of skins that modify its appearance (Figures 7-7 and 7-8). Some very cool skins are available from the XMMS Web site (www.xmms.org), and many more are available from MP3 sites like www.mp3.com.

Figure 7-7 shows XMMS in its disconnected appearance, with a playlist loaded and the first selection (a Samba) ready to play. The graphic equalizer is also shown, along with the file selector dialog box. Figure 7-8 shows the same configuration (minus the file selector) of player, equalizer, and playlist, but connected together and wearing a new skin.

XMMS is a versatile multimedia player that supports a number of media file types, including MIDI and video streams. It also provides a system for installing plug-ins (loadable software modules that extend the program's capabilities). Visualization (like spectrograph displays) and effects (like chorus or reverb) plug-ins can be added, as well as plug-ins for output destination (XMMS can send its audio to the standard OSS/Free and OSS/Linux drivers, to the EsounD audio daemon [a small program that runs as a background process and

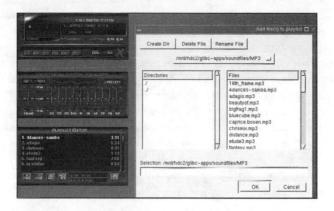

Figure 7-7: XMMS at work in a typical session with its default appearance

Figure 7-8: XMMS dressed in J. Mayled's "Ultrafina" skin

allows several audio streams to use one device], and direct-to-disk). By the time this book is published, XMMS will likely also support the ALSA drivers.

XMMS is also a superb Shoutcast player. Shoutcast is a streaming MP3 audio protocol used by many Internet broadcasting stations. In order to listen to Shoutcast programs from the Netscape browser (similar steps can be taken for other browsers), enter the following information into the **Edit • Preferences • Navigator • Applications . . .** window:

Description:	Shoutcast streaming audio
MIMEtype:	audio-xscpls
Application:	xmms %s
Suffix:	(none required)

After you've done this, log into the Shoutcast page at www.shoutcast.com and look over the various station addresses and descriptions. Find one that looks interesting (you'll see all sorts of music, news, and talk programs to choose from), click on its Web address, and XMMS will pop up to play the streaming broadcast. A word of warning, though: You will need to determine if your Internet connection is fast enough for your selection, which means that transmissions at higher bitrates will require higher-speed connections. If you're fortunate enough to have an ADSL or cable modem connection, you can try out any of the stations listed on the Shoutcast page, but a 56K modem will dependably deliver streaming MP3 audio at bitrates of 24 kbps or lower. High-bitrate MP3 streaming audio will suffer annoying break-ups and discontinuities on a comparatively low-speed connection.

Why Choose XMMS?

XMMS is my hands-down recommendation for an MP3 player for X. I confess that I was attracted by the XMMS "eye candy"—its attractive GUI and support for easily reconfiguring the GUI with skins—but XMMS is more than that: Its controls are intuitive, the equalizer is handy, and its support for a very broad range of soundfile types makes it useful as a general-purpose soundfile player. Further, its plug-in architecture will soon allow XMMS to accommodate video files. Finally, it is an open-source project, which appeals to the Linux audio hacker in me, and is licensed under the GPL.

The Ripper

To convert an audio track from a CD to an MP3 file, you must "rip" or "grab" the file, which means that the file is copied from a compact disk, converted into an intermediate format (WAV or sometimes RAW), and then converted to an MP3 file. With compression ratios of up to 10:1 not uncommon, an entire audio CD of over 600 MB can be reduced to less than 100 MB—the size of a Zip disk.

Grip

Author: Mike Oliphant
Version profiled: 2.5
Web site: http://www.nostatic.org/grip/
FTP site: n/a
Maintained: Yes
Availability: Free, open-source
License: GPL

Grip is a front-end for a number of CD and MP3 utilities, including a ripper, an encoder, a tag editor, a CD player, and other tools. Creating MP3 soundfiles from CD audio tracks is a simple process using Grip.

Getting It, Building It

After downloading the latest package from the Grip Web site (or copying it from this book's CD), move it to your /home directory. Unpack it with **tar xzvf grip-latest.tar.gz** and enter the new Grip directory. Read the instructions to build and install the program. Once again, it's as easy as **./configure**, **make**, and **make install** (this last step as root, of course). You are now ready to run Grip.

Using Grip

First open an xterm window and invoke Grip with the following command:

```
grip -d /dev/hdd
```

The -d option selects the CD drive, in this instance an IDE drive (though SCSI drives work just fine with Grip, too).

One of Grip's coolest features is its support for the CDDB (compact disc database) service. CDDB is a project with two primary aims: to build an on-line database of CD titles and track lists, and to supply those lists to any CDDB-aware CD player. For instance, when I'm surfing the Web I can start the Grip GCD player and it will find and search my preferred CDDB databases (specified in Grip's Options menu for CDDB), automatically listing the track titles on the disk I currently have in the player.

NOTE *Do not mount the CD drive before using Grip. The program will politely fail.*

In Figures 7-9 through 7-12, you can see how I selected an audio track from my CD (Figure 7-9), defined what part I would convert (Figure 7-10, page 144), ripped (Figure 7-11, page 144) and encoded (Figure 7-12, page 145) the partial track, and defined an ID3 tag for the resulting MP3 file.

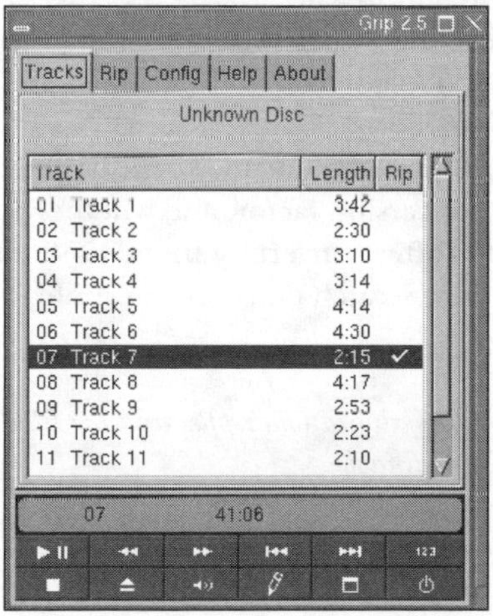

Figure 7-9: Selecting CD track 7 from the listing in Grip

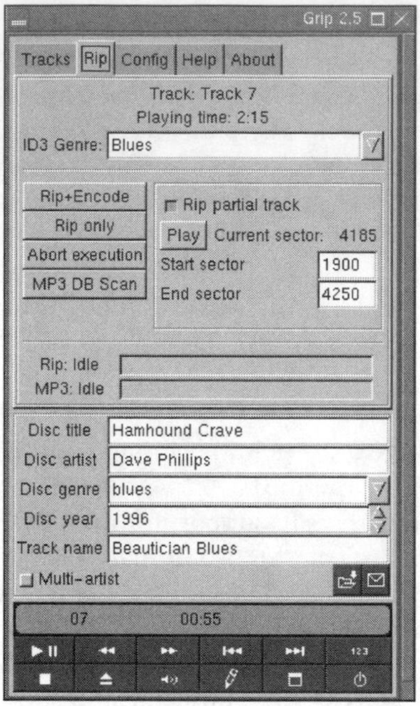

Tracks | Rip | Config | Help | About |

Track: Track 7
Playing time: 2:15

ID3 Genre: Blues

Rip+Encode | ☐ Rip partial track
Rip only | Play | Current sector: 4185
Abort execution | Start sector | 1900
MP3 DB Scan | End sector | 4250

Rip: Idle
MP3: Idle

Disc title | Hamhound Crave
Disc artist | Dave Phillips
Disc genre | blues
Disc year | 1996
Track name | Beautician Blues
☐ Multi–artist

07 | 00:55

Figure 7-10: Ripping setup under Grip

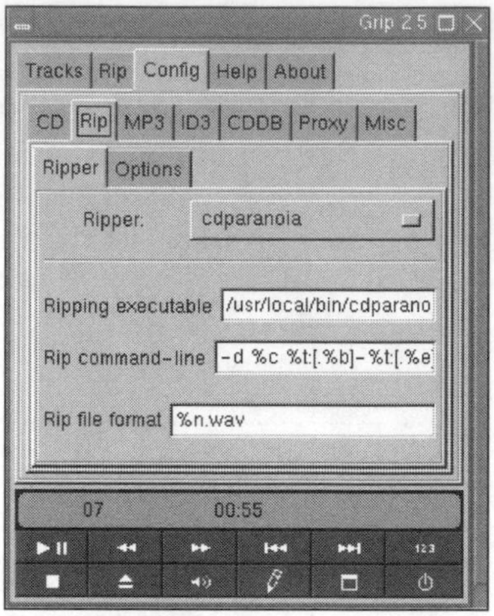

Tracks | Rip | Config | Help | About |

CD | Rip | MP3 | ID3 | CDDB | Proxy | Misc |

Ripper | Options |

Ripper: cdparanoia

Ripping executable /usr/local/bin/cdparano

Rip command–line -d %c %t:[.%b]–%t:[.%e

Rip file format %n.wav

07 | 00:55

Figure 7-11: The ripper under Grip

If the CD drive is recognized by Grip, you can begin building a collection of favorite tracks as MP3 files. Figure 7-9 shows the CD track listing.

Right-clicking over the selected track will tag it for conversion.

Figure 7-10 shows the setup for ripping 30 seconds—from sector 1900 to 4250—of audio from Track 7.

Pressing the **Rip+Encode** button will start the process. Because Grip is a front-end for a variety of tools, the results will be conditioned by the configuration options for each utility. Figures 7-11 and 7-12 show the configuration tabs for the ripper and the encoder.

Configuration options for the MP3 encoder include the output file name and destination, the bitrate conversion factor, and whether converted WAV files are to be saved or deleted after converting them. Options for the ripper include which ripper to employ, scratch detection, and file format and path for the ripped audio.

NOTE *Grip provides explicit support for the cdparanoia ripper and the BladeEnc encoder, but all the supported utilities are user-definable.*

In the above example, each action required its own application: cdparanoia did the ripping, BladeEnc did the encoding, and Grip provided the ID3 tag editor. If title and track information for the ripped CD were in a CDDB

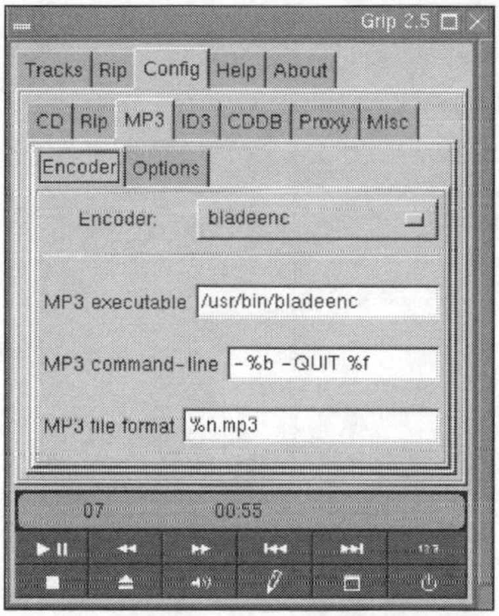

Figure 7-12: The encoder under Grip

database, Grip would have found it and provided a complete track list. By bringing together all the tools necessary for auditioning, converting, and managing CD and MP3 files, Grip's flexibility and organization make it an outstanding Linux audio utility.

Other MP3 Software

Support software for MP3 file creation and maintenance includes the following:

ID tag editors create, edit, or delete the ID3 tags that identify MP3 files with the name of the song, the artist, the source, the year it was recorded, and a comment.

Renamers rewrite ID3 tags in a batch mode, enabling quick renaming of any of the identification fields.

Playlist editors prepare lists of MP3 files in HTML and other formats, including SQL database formats.

MP3tools bundles an ID tag reader/editor, a file information viewer, and an indexing utility for playlists all in one program. The tools can be run as separate applications from a command line, or they can be accessed through a nice Perl/Tk GUI. Figure 7-13 on page 146 shows MP3tools' graphic interface in action.

Kmp3te, shown in Figure 7-14 on page 146 is another graphic interface to MP3 file information and tag data.

Kyle Smith's Krio (Figure 7-15, page 147) is an easy-to-use interface for uploading and downloading files for the Diamond Rio player.

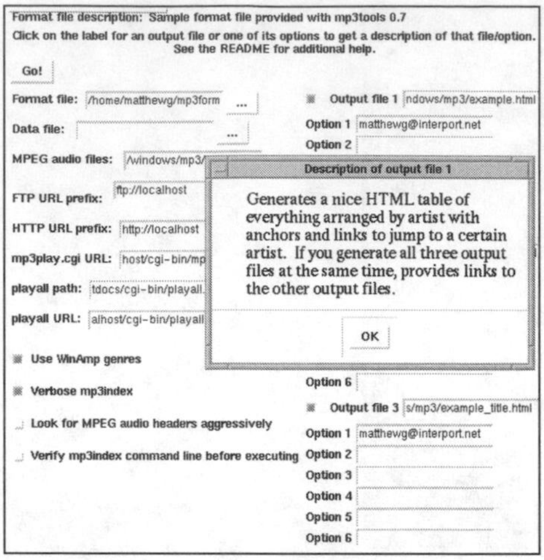

Format file description: Sample format file provided with mp3tools 0.7

Click on the label for an output file or one of its options to get a description of that file/option.
See the README for additional help.

Go!

Format file: /home/matthewg/mp3form   ...   Output file 1 ndows/mp3/example.html

Data file: ...   Option 1 matthewg@interport.net

   Option 2

MPEG audio files: /windows/mp3/

FTP URL prefix: ftp://localhost

HTTP URL prefix: http://localhost

mp3play.cgi URL: host/cgi-bin/mp

playall path: tdocs/cgi-bin/playall

playall URL: alhost/cgi-bin/playall

☒ Use WinAmp genres

☒ Verbose mp3index   Option 6

☐ Look for MPEG audio headers aggressively   ☒ Output file 3 s/mp3/example_title.html

☐ Verify mp3index command line before executing   Option 1 matthewg@interport.net

   Option 2

   Option 3

   Option 4

   Option 5

   Option 6

Description of output file 1

Generates a nice HTML table of everything arranged by artist with anchors and links to jump to a certain artist. If you generate all three output files at the same time, provides links to the other output files.

OK

Figure 7-13: The MP3tools interface

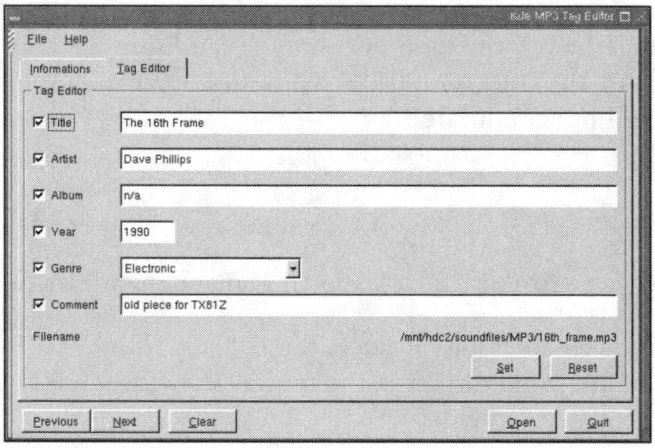

Kde MP3 Tag Editor

File   Help

Informations   Tag Editor

Tag Editor

☑ Title   The 16th Frame

☑ Artist   Dave Phillips

☑ Album   n/a

☑ Year   1990

☑ Genre   Electronic

☑ Comment   old piece for TX81Z

Filename   /mnt/hdc2/soundfiles/MP3/16th_frame.mp3

Set   Reset

Previous   Next   Clear   Open   Quit

Figure 7-14: The Kmp3te interface

NOTE   *As noted earlier in this chapter, MP3 also exists as a streaming audio format for Internet broadcasting. Specific MP3 servers and database managers available for Linux are detailed in Chapter 12, "Network Audio Software."*

Links to these utilities and many others can be found at http://sound.condorow.net/cd.html or Damien Morel's excellent DAM's MP3 Pages at http://www.multimania.com/damsmp3.

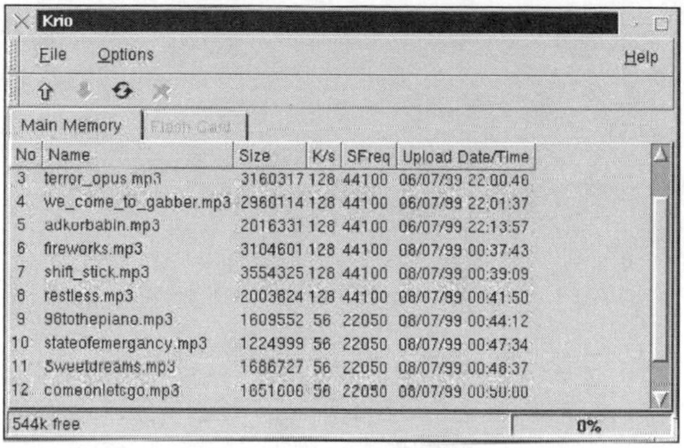

Figure 7-15: Krio's interface (image courtesy of Kyle Smith)

MP3 Politics

Music distribution using the MP3 format is a rather hot topic because MP3's compression scheme and its high audio quality made it a natural for distribution of both legal and pirated music over the Internet. The Recording Industry Association of America (RIAA) has targeted MP3 as promoting music piracy (given that there is currently no way to prevent the illegal copying of MP3 files) and even sued Diamond Multimedia in October 1998 in an attempt to halt the sale of their Rio MP3 player. The suit failed.

In late 1999 the MP3 format was embroiled in more legal hot water, thanks to the Napster (www.napster.com) MP3 server software. Napster lets users register their MP3 collections online, making the contents freely available to anyone with a Napster client (see the Web sites listed above for Linux versions of Napster client and server software). Consequently, the RIAA has sued Napster's authors.

Whether the MP3 proves to be bane or boon to the recording industry remains to be seen. On the consumer's side, the format's audio quality, ease of reproducibility, and ease of transfer have made it an enormously popular soundfile format for legitimate (and not so legitimate) Internet music distribution, and it shows no signs of disappearing anytime soon. On the industry's side, it understandably wants to protect its interests. Music piracy and the theft of copyrighted material cannot be condoned, but MP3's very strengths have raised some difficult issues regarding the consumer's de facto freedoms and the industry's rights. Until those issues are resolved legally, we will each have to resolve them with our own set of personal ethics.

8

MULTITRACK HARD-DISK RECORDING AND MIXING

A multitrack hard-disk recording system facilitates the recording and mixing of multiple tracks of digital audio on a computer's hard disk. Recording to disk has many advantages over the older method of multitrack recording to analog tape: CD-quality digital audio is cleaner than tape, with much greater dynamic response (better recording of very soft and very loud signals), and random access allows immediate record and play from any point in your songfile. And the hardware required for multitrack hard-disk recording is not inaccessible: Large, fast hard disks (10 gigabytes and larger) are inexpensive these days, as are fast CPUs. Linux can claim a number of excellent hard-disk recording systems to take advantage of this hardware bounty. In this chapter we will look at three of those systems: SLab, Multitrack, and Mix.

Which Program Should I Use?

Selecting the multitrack recorder/mixer that works best for you depends on your specific background and needs. Of course, considering that they are priced at $0.00 each, you could just try them all and decide which one you like best—but you may not have the time to do so. Each one of these programs is strong in particular ways: SLab will appeal immediately to users familiar with recording in a tape-based studio, Mix is best suited to complex arrangements of pre-recorded soundfiles, and Multitrack is best suited to quick, small-scale recording sessions (such as a four-piece band or a single performer).

SLab

Author: Nick Copeland
Version profiled: 3.10-3b
Web site: http://dutw1288.wbmt.tudelft.nl
FTP site: ftp://dutw1288.wbmt.tudelft.nl/pub/audio/
Maintained: Yes
Availability: Free, binary-only
License: Held by the author
Capsule summary: **Feature-rich system excellent for medium- to large-scale recording projects**

SLab is a direct-to-hard-disk recording studio with an amazing set of features, including a 64-track mixing console (with selectable 64/16/8/4/2 track configuration), a large variety of per-track processing options (including DSP effects, dynamics processing, and digital filters), a handy soundfile editor, and the ability to record up to 16 simultaneous tracks. No other multitrack system for Linux offers SLab's variety of options and features.

SLab is easy to use, even for the complete beginner, but its features set should meet the needs of a professional digital audio recording and mixing studio. If you're looking for a multitrack hard-disk recording suite that has a flexible user interface, is capable of handling up to 64 tracks, and offers modular effects processing and support for advanced soundcards such as the SBLive!, then SLab is definitely for you.

NOTE *Various configuration resources optimize SLab's performance for a wide range of CPUs, and it is flexible enough to work well on relatively low-powered machines (it was originally developed on a Pentium 133).*

Getting It, Building It

Because the SLab package is a binary-only distribution, all you need to do is unpack it with **tar xzvf slab-latest-tar.gz**, enter the newly created slab directory, and follow the installation instructions there. The default installation directory is /usr/slab. After unpacking the distribution, change directories to **/usr/slab/bin**. You can now launch SLab by running the **startSLab.bash** or **startSLab** script, depending on whether you have the bash or C shell installed. If you don't know which shell is installed, try each script.

Configuring SLab

SLab opens to the display shown in Figure 8-1.

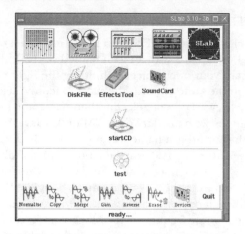

Figure 8-1: SLab's opening display

Start basic use of SLab by selecting SoundCard and then setting the audio mode. SLab supports a variety of recording modes for soundcards, including half-duplex (record or play), full-duplex (record and play), and a false-duplex (low-quality record and play). To set the audio mode for your first recording, simply left-click on the **SoundCard** icon, then left-click on the appropriate card-type icon (Sound Blaster, Gravis, Generic). When the card-model panel opens, you can drag and drop your selected model's icon onto the **Devices** icon next to the Quit button. (Drag-and-drop in SLab is accomplished using the middle button of a three-button mouse, or by simultaneously clicking the left and right buttons of a two-button mouse.) Figure 8-2 shows SLab's main window opened for the card selection procedure, along with the configuration page for a Sound Blaster PCI128:

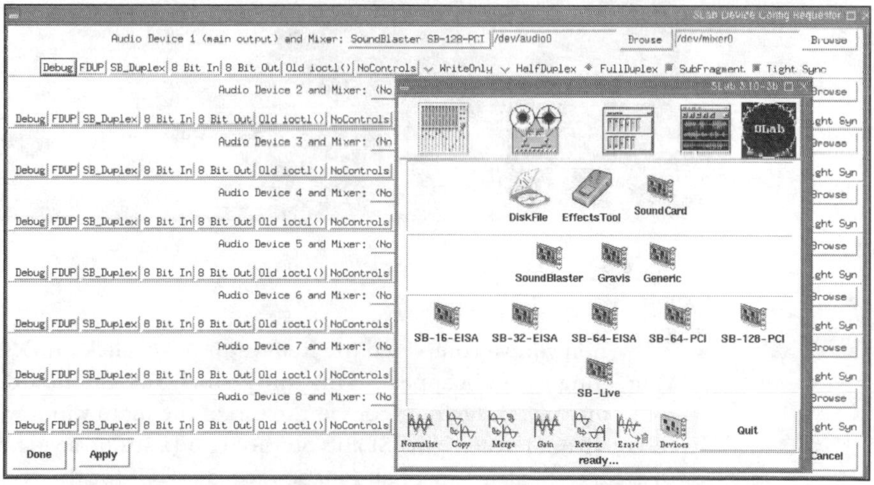

Figure 8-2: Soundcard selection with SLab

Creating Files and Using SLab

To create a file, left-click on the **DiskFile** icon in the top panel of the main window. A new panel will appear with an icon named startCD, the default project name. You can start your own project by holding the right mouse button down anywhere within the same panel as the startCD icon. A tear-off menu will appear with only "New CD" in it. Select it, then name and save your new project (for this example, we named it Your_CD) in the **Save As** dialog box. A new project icon with your project name will appear beside the default startCD icon. Left-click over the new icon, and a third panel will appear with only the word "Empty" in it. Right-click anywhere within the **Empty** panel and select the **New Song** item from the tear-off menu. A SongFile Requestor page will appear, in which you'll name your song, select the number of tracks you want to use, the sampling rate frequency, the block sample count (for managing the soundcard I/O buffers), and what compression value to use. Figure 8-3 shows the main window opened to the third panel and the SongFile Requestor page (where we've named the song Your_Song).

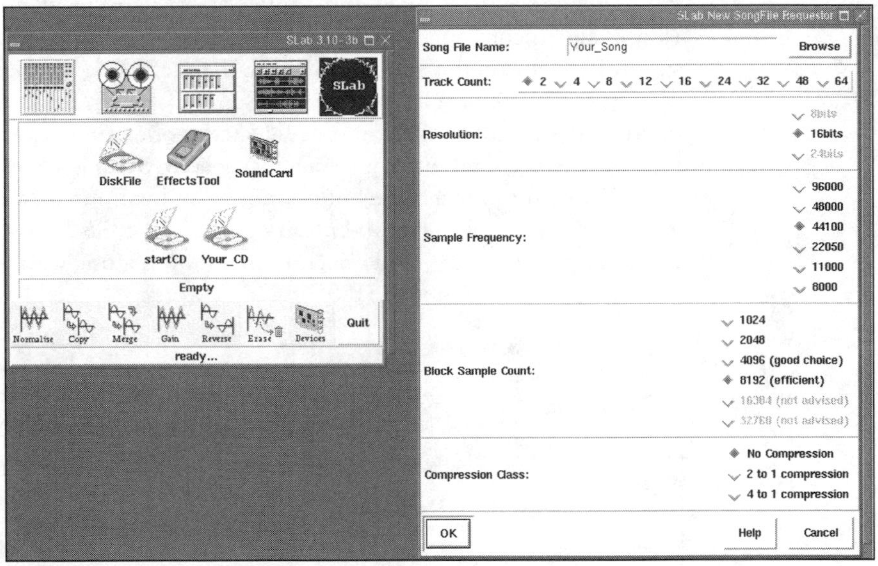

Figure 8-3: SLab's SongFile Requestor page

When you've completed the Requestor page, click on **OK**, and the Your_Song icon will appear in the third panel. You can now drag and drop that icon onto any of the four icons at the top of the main window. Those icons represent (from left to right) SLab's StudioSLab (a studio-style mixer also referred to as MixerSLab), TapeSLab (a tape-recorder GUI for the record/play functions), DeviceSLab (the soundcard mixer), and WaveSLab (a wave editor). For our first look at SLab, we'll drop the Your_Song CD onto the MixerSLab icon (each icon has a text identifier that pops up when the cursor is moved over it). SLab will go through some transformations, finally settling into a display like that shown in Figure 8-4.

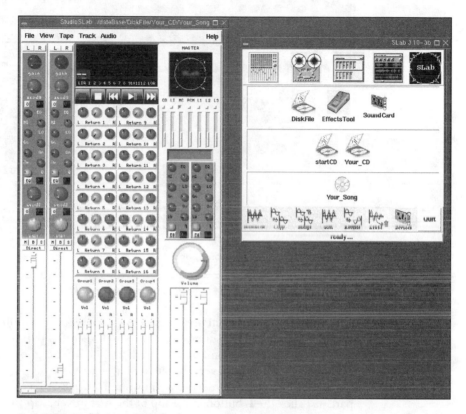

Figure 8-4: SLab's MixerSLab display

SLab's design intentionally duplicates many functions in its various windows. For example, in addition to mixing, the StudioSLab studio mixer you have just opened can also record and play back, using either the transport controls beneath the meter display or items selected from the Tape menu. You can also open any of the devices along with any others. Changes made in one of the devices will register on the corresponding displays of the other devices, so that when you move the sliders of StudioSLab's mini-mixer, for example, the corresponding sliders of DeviceSLab also move. Figure 8-5 shows the StudioSLab, the TapeSLab, and the DeviceSLab all opened and interoperable.

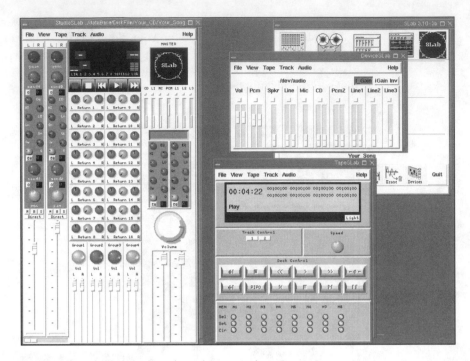

Figure 8-5: StudioSLab, TapeSLab, and DeviceSLab

Recording

Your first SLab project will be a simple two-track recording, utilizing the full-duplex capability of the soundcard. First you'll record a part on track 1, and then you'll record a second part on track 2 while listening to your first recorded part. This is all very simple in SLab.

First, open the three devices as shown in Figure 8-5. To record your first part, just click the **L** button at the top of the first mixer strip (in the top left corner of the mixer window in the StudioSLab display). This activates the track for recording. Now use the mini-mixer for your audio device (located in the upper right corner of the StudioSLab display) to raise the microphone (MC) input level, testing it by speaking into the mic and watching the meter levels for the track selected for recording. When you're satisfied with the input level, begin recording by pressing the **Record** [❏] button under the StudioSLab meter display, then pressing the **Play** [>||] button. Play your music and click on the **Stop** [■] button when you're finished. You can listen to your recording by raising the mini-mixer PCM (pulse-code modulation) channel level, pressing the **Rewind** [|<<] control and clicking on **Play** [>||] again.

To record track 2 while listening to track 1, simply repeat the process above, this time using the second mixer strip for recording. Keep the PCM channel level up, set the playback level of track 1 using the slider in the first (leftmost) strip, bring up the slider in the second strip, and repeat the recording and playback process. You should hear the first recorded track playing as you add your new track.

Adding Effects

To add an effect to your newly recorded track, you'll need to open your **Effects** toolbox and assign each effect you want to its own **Return** panel in the StudioSLab mixer. Following a standard studio recording method, the sound from your recorded track is sent to the effects panel, mixed with a specified amount of the selected effect, and returned to the audio output bus (hence the significance of the Send and Return terms).

Click on the **EffectsTool** icon in the top panel of the main window (visible in Figure 8-4). The second (project) panel will be replaced by a panel containing a variety of effects types, and clicking on any of these icons will replace your third (songfile) panel with a panel of specific effect modules. You can now drag and drop any of the effects into one of the effects Return panels located directly beneath the transport controls in the StudioSLab mixer. For example, to add a reverb effect to the first Return panel, simply drag the **Reverb** icon over the **Return** panel and drop it to assign the reverb effect to Return 1. A new window will appear, as shown in the lower right corner of Figure 8-6, representing the effect as a rack-mount effects box. To apply the effect to, for example, track 2, click on the small **I/O** button just under the **Send** (send0) rotary knob (the second knob from the top of the mixer strip). Double-click in the small box below and to the right of the I/O button, then enter the number of the effects Return panel you want to apply to the track. Adjust the **Send** control knob and the **Return** panel level until you have the exact amount of the effect you want. Figure 8-6 shows the Reverb module that was dropped into Return panel 1 and applied to track 2.

The Reverb module's controls are adjustable in realtime, as are most of SLab's controls. You can continue dropping effects modules into the **Return** panels, selecting only the ones you need for your tracks. You can build complex arrangements of effects modules, as seen in Figure 8-7.

In Figure 8-7, the two Send controls for both tracks have been activated (there are two Sends per track), and each rack-mounted module is specified beneath the appropriate Send knob. The Return panel levels are up (for panels one through four), which will allow the modules to actually process the tracks, and the rack-mount display (the window in the bottom right of Figure 8-7) shows the effects modules with their default values.

You can save your work at any time by selecting **BaseLines/Save Mix** or **Sessions/Save Session**. **Save Mix** will save all the parameters of your mix, including all volume, pan, and effect settings. If you enable **sessRec** in Tape-SLab, you can record any movements you make with the user interface, such as a fade-out with a track volume slider. **Save Session** will save those movements along with the rest of the mix and, when sessPlay is chosen in TapeSLab, the playback mix will include your recorded fade-out.

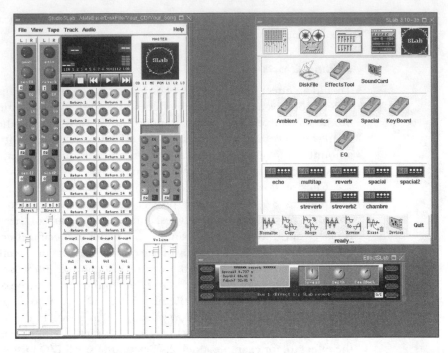

Figure 8-6: SLab with effects rack

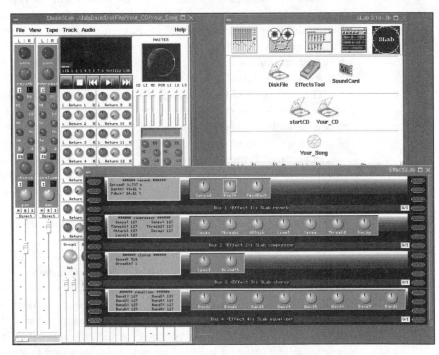

Figure 8-7: A complex arrangement of effects modules in SLab

Editing with SLab

WaveSLab is SLab's soundfile editor. It provides basic services such as cut/copy/paste routines, as well as normalize (which raises peak volume to maximum with all other amplitudes raised proportionally), gain adjust (which raises or lowers volumes by a factor), and fade functions for volume control. To edit a soundfile, open WaveSLab with your recorded tracks by simply dragging your song CD icon and dropping it on the WaveSLab icon. WaveSLab will open with the display shown in Figure 8-8.

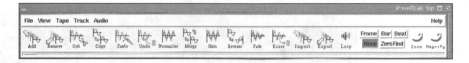

Figure 8-8: WaveSLab

Click on the **Add** icon (on the left) to select which tracks you want to add to the display. Choosing both of your recorded tracks will produce the display shown in Figure 8-9.

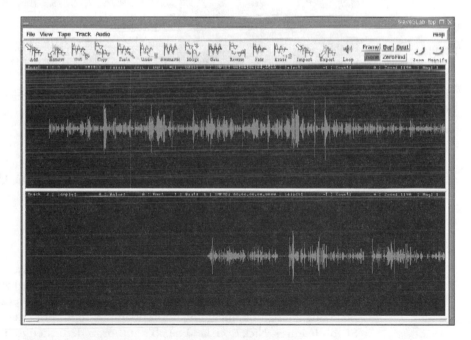

Figure 8-9: WaveSLab with two tracks

When the cursor is in the waveform display window, it appears as a cross-hair cursor. To edit a track, hold the left mouse button and drag the cursor to select the area you want to revise. Release the mouse button, then choose the appropriate edit icon and drag it into the waveform window. Figure 8-10 shows WaveSLab with one track opened, an area selected for editing, and the dialog window that opens after dropping the Cut icon into the waveform display.

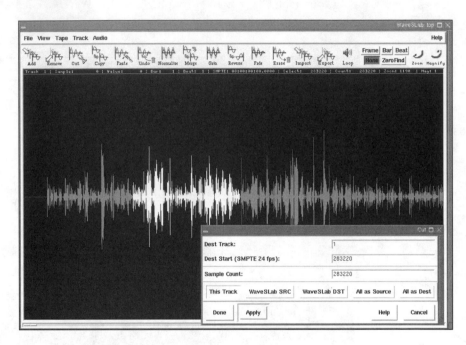

Figure 8-10: WaveSLab with the Cut dialog box opened

Accepting the default values in the Cut window will leave a blank space in the selected area. If you wish to undo any edit, just click on the **Undo** button (sixth from left at top) to undo the last edit or view the edit history and undo operations listed there.

Leaving SLab

This profile has barely scratched the surface of SLab. SLab is a very deep application, rich in professional-level capabilities, and it is well worth the effort to learn how to get around in it. Fortunately, SLab comes with very complete documentation, including tutorials and in-depth presentations of all of SLab's features. Nick Copeland, SLab's author, is dedicated to improving SLab, and he is very responsive to bug reports and users' suggestions. I heartily recommend this program to any serious Linux audio enthusiast.

Multitrack

Author: Boris Nagels
Version profiled: 2.2
Web site: n/a
FTP site: ftp://mustec.bgsu.edu/pub/linux/multitrack-2.2.tar.gz
Maintained: No
Availability: Free, binary-only
License: Copyright held by author
Capsule summary: **Good light-weight solution for small-scale projects**

Multitrack is the only multitrack hard-disk recorder available for the Linux console running in the SVGA graphics mode. It will also run under X, but for users who can't or don't use X, it is an excellent direct-to-disk recorder and soundfile editor with a graphic user interface.

Multitrack includes a variety of useful tools, including an oscilloscope and a guitar tuner not found in any other Linux multitrack recorder.

Getting It, Building It

Installation is simple. After you acquire the package, run **make install** to place the binary in the proper location. The program can then be called anywhere from the command line. If you're running it in X, you'll need to invoke it with the **-x** switch; if you have the SVGA libraries installed, you need only type in **multitrack** at the console and your session will begin in a very nice full-color Super VGA graphics mode.

An options file named "prefs" will be placed in $(HOME)/. multitrack. It is fairly straightforward, but you may need to make some adjustments in that file in order to get Multitrack working properly. In particular, be sure to set the i_nr_buffers and o_nr_buffers to a value of 1 or higher (I set mine to 10).

If you experience display or mouse problems in Multitrack's console mode (e.g., Multitrack won't open or you can't control the mouse), you may need to look into your /etc/libvga.conf file. Make sure that the settings indicated in that file actually match your configuration.

NOTE *Multitrack's use of the SVGA library may be a security concern to network administrators because the program must be run* suid root *(which means that it requires root permissions). Just to be safe, take your machine off any network when using Multitrack.*

Recording Session

Your first session in Multitrack will demonstrate a simple two-track recording. Let's assume you have a soundcard capable of full-duplex operation, so you can simultaneously record one track while playing another.

Before recording or playing anything in Multitrack, you have to create a new song file. First, select a directory for your project track information, as shown in Figure 8-11.

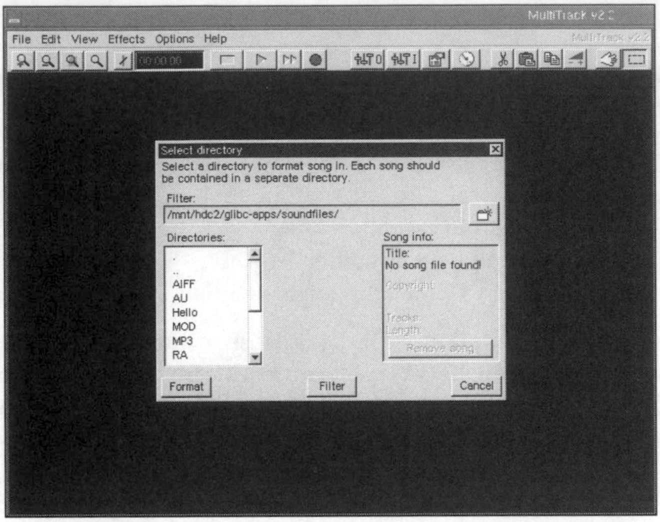

Figure 8-11: The Select Directory window in Multitrack

Clicking on the **Format** button will take you to the box shown in Figure 8-12.

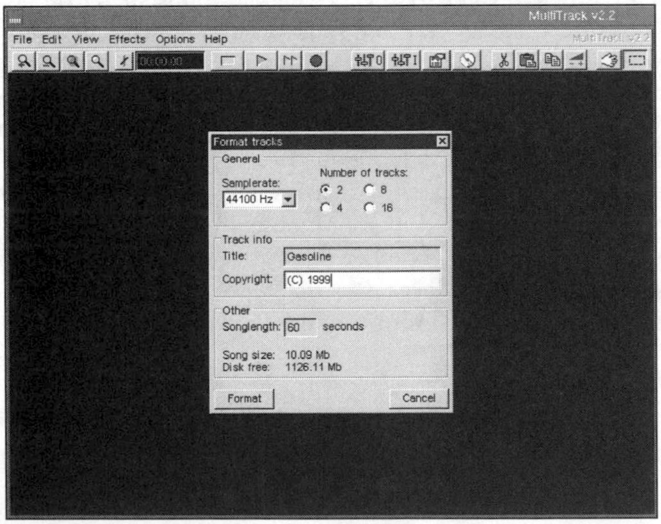

Figure 8-12: Multitrack's Format window

Here you indicate the number of tracks, the sampling rate for recording and playback, a title and copyright date, and the track length. All of these settings can be edited within Multitrack after a session is in progress.

Once you've formatted the tracks, Multitrack opens to the display shown in Figure 8-13.

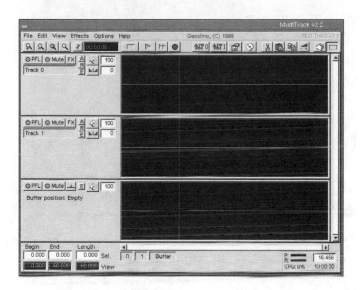

Figure 8-13: Multitrack after tracks are formatted

You can now record new tracks, import and export WAV files, perform basic edits, and add effects to your tracks. For this demonstration, you will record one track and then a second while listening to the first. To record the initial track, open the mixer (seen to the right of the transport controls at the top of the screen), select the input channel and set its level, and click on the **R** button in the Track 0 control panel. You can also rename the track by placing the mouse cursor in the name box (where it says Track 0) and entering a new name. Now press the round, red **Record** button in the transport controls (in the center above the track displays), and the dialog box shown in Figure 8-14 should appear.

This dialog box is a summary of your recording devices; the active track's name; and toggles for displaying a VU meter, disabling playback during recording (cancels duplex recording), and specifying the time for an introduction. Clicking on **Record** will immediately start recording. When you've finished, press the **Stop** button and you should see something like the display in Figure 8-15.

To set up Multitrack for simultaneous record and play, open the mixer again and set the level for the playback channel. For full-duplex operation on my PCI128 soundcard, the pre-recorded track plays through the Pcm2 channel (see Figure 8-16 on page 163). Check the output of **cat /dev/sndstat** (for OSS drivers) or **cat /proc/asound** (for ALSA drivers) to see the full-duplex capability of your soundcard.

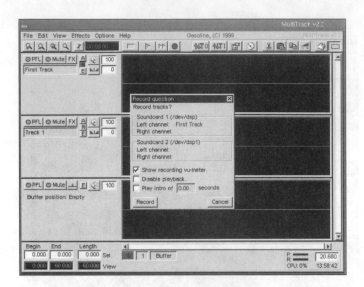

Figure 8-14: The Record question dialog box

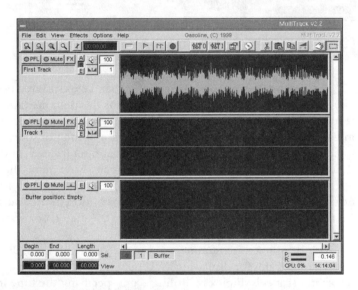

Figure 8-15: Multitrack after recording

From here the recording process is identical to the previous steps, except that you should hear the first track as you record the new one.

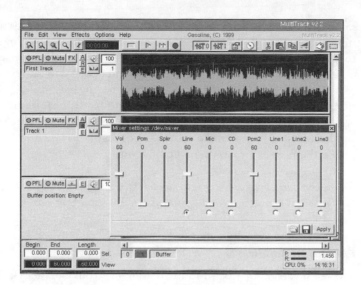

Figure 8-16: Setting up Multitrack for full-duplex recording

Summary

Its program documentation is brief, but Multitrack is very easy to learn and operate. Its X interface is clean and uncluttered, and Multitrack is the only Linux hard-disk recorder with a mouse-operated Super VGA graphic interface for users who prefer working without X. If you need a simple recording and mixing system for up to sixteen tracks of audio, Multitrack is just what you're looking for.

Mix

Author: Oyvind Hammer, Linux version by Guenter Geiger
Version profiled: 0.56
Web site: http://gige.xdv.org/mix.html
FTP site: n/a
Maintained: Yes
Availability: Free, open-source
License: GPL
Capsule summary: Best suited for arranging pre-recorded soundfiles into complex mixes

The Linux version of Mix is a powerful program that allows you to combine different soundfiles and file formats into one mix. Mix accepts WAV, AIFF, and AIFC formats, all of which can be freely mingled throughout the tracks. Mix will also let you put mono and stereo files in the same track—even in the same space on a track. You can mix all these different file types using up to nine channels, and each channel has its own volume control, mute and solo toggles, and slider to resize the waveform display. Graphic displays of the channel volume, panning, and auxiliary send curves can also be toggled.

Mix's effects processors include echo, chorus, harmonizer, ring modulation, filters (lowpass, highpass, bandpass, and bandstop), reverb, compression, and an octave divider. Most of the effects have parameter value sliders that can be adjusted in realtime playback. And, thanks to Guenter Geiger, the effects themselves are now separate plug-ins.

NOTE *The applications programming interface for Mix plug-ins is still under development, but the code is open-source, and the specification is straightforward and effective.*

Getting It, Building It

The latest version of Mix for Linux is available from Guenter Geiger's Mix page on the Web. The package is source-only, but building Mix is easy. It requires either Motif 1.2 or the equivalent libraries (available from the LessTif group at www.lesstif.org). After unpacking the **mix-latest.tar.gz** file, you need only run **./configure**, **make**, and (as root) **make install** in the Mix directory.

Give special attention to the Mix resource file: From there you can specify various helper applications that will be called during a Mix session, such as your preferred soundfile editor and your browser of choice for reading the HTML help files. Many details of the program's appearance can be customized in the resource file, including button placement, scrollbar implementation, screen size, and colors.

Loading and Recording Files

You can begin a session in Mix by opening the **File** menu and loading existing soundfiles into arbitrary positions anywhere in the nine tracks or by choosing **Record** from the **Settings** menu.

Loading Files

Figure 8-17, illustrating the first method, shows Mix with the Add Soundfile box open and loading files.

Track number and start time are selectable, and a preview play button lets you hear your samples before placing them in a track. After selecting your sounds, click **Cancel** in the selector box to close your loading process, and you should see something like Figure 8-18.

Recording Files

To record directly into Mix, open the **Settings** menu and select **Record**. Figure 8-19 on page 166 shows the Record File window opened and set to record a

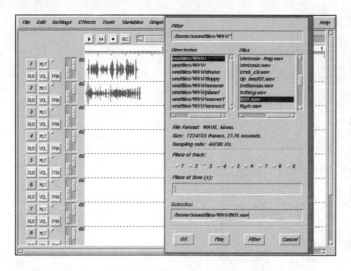

Figure 8-17: The Add Soundfile box in Mix

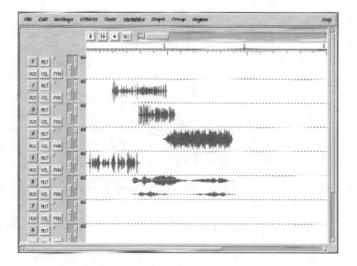

Figure 8-18: Mix after selecting sounds

new track called new_piece; the option to monitor the input signal ("monitor audio input") is selected—an important option if you want to hear what you're recording while listening to what you've already recorded.

After you close the **Record File** window and make sure that your software mixer has selected the proper input and levels, simply press the **Record** button to start recording and the **Stop** button to halt it.

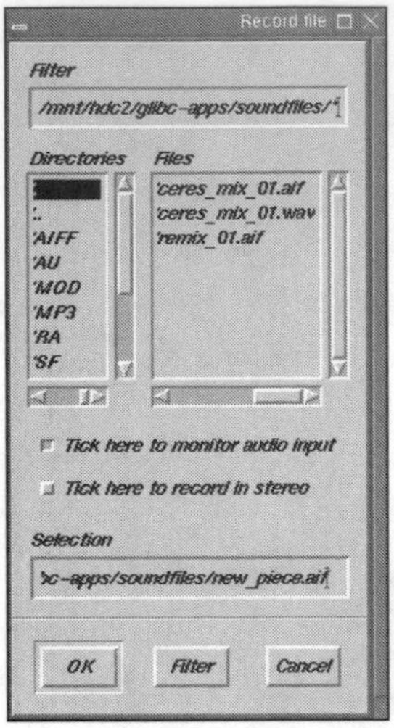

Figure 8-19: Recording directly with Mix

Editing

Once you've recorded your track(s), you can splice and dice them by manipulating each track's graphic representation. The graphic displays can be positioned anywhere in the mix by clicking the right mouse button over your selection and dragging it to where you want it placed—even across tracks.

If you want to edit a track further, left-clicking on the graphic representation of the sound you want to edit will open the dialog box shown in Figure 8-20.

This dialog presents a number of useful functions, including Mute, Play, Delete, and Duplicate. It also lets you:

- Call your external soundfile editor and refresh the graphic display after editing

- Disable any further positioning of the soundfile by ticking the lock option

- Edit start and stop times

- Reset the track designation

- Set the number of times for a file to play repeatedly with the looping function

The grayscale screenshot in Figure 8-20 can't show it, but the segments that have been copied and inserted are in blue; the original material is in red (the default color for soundfiles).

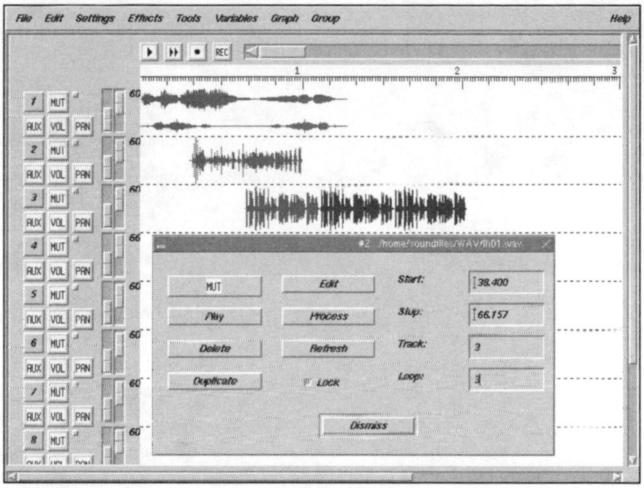

Figure 8-20: Track editing in Mix

The Mix Menus

Once you have your soundfiles the way you want and placed into tracks, you can start mixing them, a task for which Mix provides a variety of useful tools.

File

The File menu manages basic soundfile loading and also loads and saves mixture specification files (or just "mix files"), which are ASCII text indicating the soundfiles used and the state of the mix at the time of the save, including start times, effects curves, track parameters, etc. You can then edit a mix file in any common text editor (such as vi or emacs) to refine the mix outside the program itself. Here is the edited mix file for Figure 8-18:

```
samplerate 44100
   channels 2
buffersize   0.50
linearvol 0
monitor 0
recstereo 0
bpmscale 0
bpm 120
bpbar 4
quant 1
autoquant 0
showlinear 0
shownumbers 0
showgrid 0
```

```
smallfont 0
showallgraphs 0
autoscroll 0
fastdraw 0

plugin Chorus 0.000000 0.000000
plugin Compress 0.000000
plugin Echo 0.000000 0.000000
plugin Filter 0.000000 0.000000 0.000000
plugin Harmonizer 0.000000
plugin Reverb 0.000000
plugin Ring 0.000000

    sound /home/soundfiles/warp_keep_02.wav          0.000  5         1
    sound /home/soundfiles/WAV/chrismix.wav         18.300  2         1
    sound /home/soundfiles/WAV/lh01.wav     38.400  3         1
    sound /home/soundfiles/WAV/bb01.wav.resampled.aif          57.000  4         1
    sound /home/soundfiles/WAV/am004.wav    34.200  6         1

volume 1 60
quadpos 1 1
  ...

volumegraph 1
0.00 60
1920.00 60
end
  ...

pangraph 1
0.00 30
1920.00 30
end
  ...

auxgraph 1
0.00 0
1920.00 0
end
  ...
```

If you have some programming skill, it is a straightforward hack to write an algorithmic mixing program, particularly using a language strong in text manipulation (such as Perl or LISP) which would produce a mix file that can be loaded and edited further in Mix itself. If you're not a programmer, all you need to know is that a mix file saves all the specifications of a mix in a standard text document.

The File menu also provides the rather important option to write the mix to disk as a stereo soundfile. Use this option when you're satisfied with a mix and want to save it as a finished piece.

The Refresh option redisplays the screen to remove any X artifacts.

Edit

The Edit menu offers only a few basic operations: The familiar cut/copy/paste actions are provided, along with Insert and Undo functions. This selection of edit functions might seem embarrassingly meager, but remember that, by left-clicking on a sound graphic, you can call your preferred soundfile editor to perform more detailed and extensive edits.

Settings

We have already looked at the Record File dialog available from the Settings menu in Figure 8-19. Figure 8-21 shows the dialog windows for the Audio, Time, and Display settings.

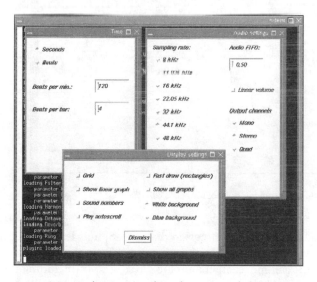

Figure 8-21: Audio, Time, and Display settings dialog boxes

The Time dialog lets the user select whether the time will be displayed as seconds or beats. When represented as beats, a tempo and beats per bar can be indicated. These settings are especially important when using the Time Machine in the Tools menu.

The Internet Slaves option on the Settings Menu is not yet working under Linux. Check the Mix Web site for updates on Mix's capabilities.

Effects

Mix's effects include chorus, compression, echo, filter, harmonizer, octave divider, reverb, and ring modulation. Although the list sounds extensive, Figure 8-22 shows that parameter control is not exactly fine (though efforts are being made to improve Mix's effects).

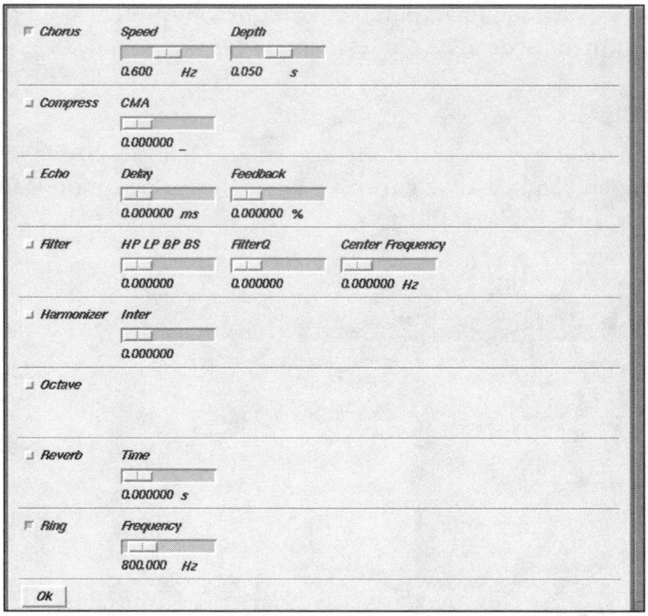

Figure 8-22: Parameter control for Mix's effects

You can adjust the effects in realtime. Simply leave the Effects window open, start playback, and adjust the effects from the panel. Note that, to adjust effects in realtime, each channel in "Aux" graph (including the Master track at the bottom of the track display) must be turned on and dragged to maximum level.

NOTE *Guenter Geiger has created a programming interface for Mix that allows effects devices to be used as loadable software modules (plug-ins). Because Linux Mix is an open-source GPL'd project, Guenter's API is free for use by any Linux audio software developer.*

Tools

The Tools menu calls the Time Machine and Sounds Overview internal helpers and also links Mix to the external helpers specified in the Mix resource file (the Mix.ad file, which **make install** will place as "Mix" in your **/usr/X11R6/lib/X11/app-defaults** directory). Figure 8-23 displays the Time Machine and Sounds Overview dialogs and Figure 8-24 shows the AIFF sound-file player Aifplay, the soundfile editor Snd, and the file format converter Xsox all being used under Mix.

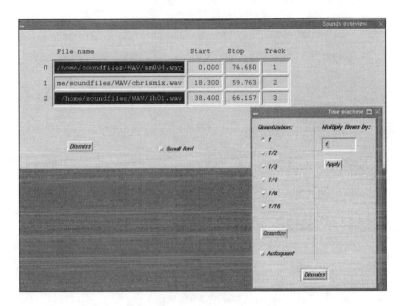

Figure 8-23: The Time Machine and Sounds Overview dialogs

The Time Machine is a powerful tool that works in coordination with the Time options in the Settings menu. It lets you quantize (place on a preferred beat) soundfile start times from whole note to sixteenth-note precision, auto-quantize, and expand or contract the entire mix time by the "Multiply times by" value.

The Sounds Overview box details the names of all the files included in the mix, their start and stop times, and their track assignments. All of this information can be edited, with the exception of the file names and paths. To add a file to the list of grouped files (the highlighted files in the Sounds Overview window), hold the SHIFT key while left-clicking on a file name in the Overview box. Other options in the Tools menu will eventually include the following functions, but they are not yet fully operable. The Write to PostScript function will write a PostScript graphic file depicting the layout of the mix, but at the time of this

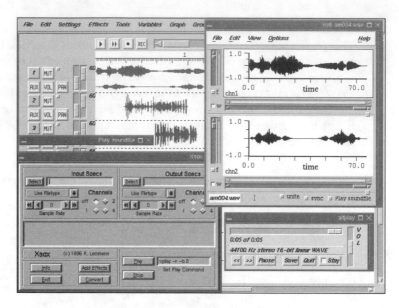

Figure 8-24: Aifplay, Snd, and Xsox under Mix

writing it is not working correctly. The 3D Viewer option calls another external helper, in this case "ivview" from the Apprentice for Linux package, to display a three-dimensional view of the mix in the SGI Inventor format. As of this writing, the 3D Viewer does display an image, but it is not accurate.

Variables

The Variables menu enables drop-in values for effects and other parameters to be placed anywhere within a mix. For instance, a dramatic increase in reverb time can be achieved simply by placing the appropriate variable value wherever needed.

Figure 8-25 shows a track with four variables already inserted along the waveform; the parameter values window is opened for a fourth variable object (the Variables are numbered from 0). In this instance, a reverb effect is applied at 72% strength at 14.18 seconds into the track.

In the Variables Overview window (shown in Figure 8-26) you can delete or duplicate the variable object, redefine its insertion point and track number, and edit its parameter value.

Graph

The Graph menu lets you delete volume, aux, and pan nodes (the small squares for adjusting graph levels) from existing graphs. It also provides a list of nodes for a selected graph, as seen in Figure 8-27 on page 174 (the Pan control nodes for Track 3). Nodes can be deleted by erasing them from the list, or by simply clicking on the node and pressing the DELETE key.

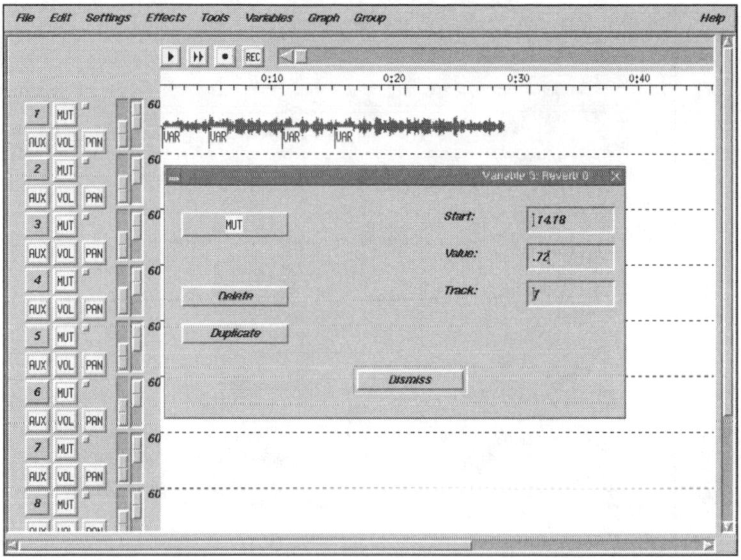

Figure 8-25: Using variables to modify a track

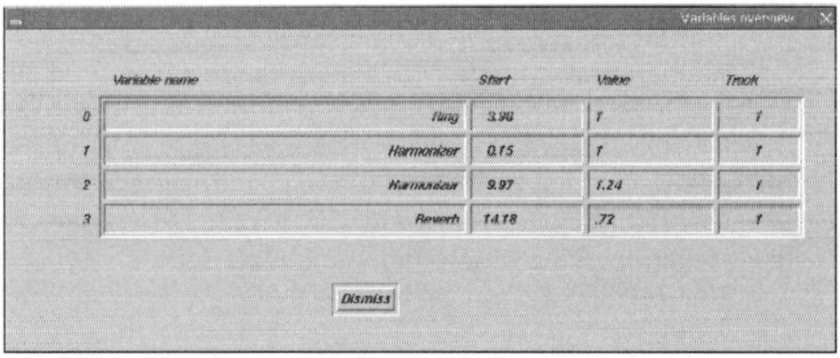

Figure 8-26: The Variables Overview window

Group

Grouping lets you drag an entire mix as one file (by choosing **Group All**), retaining the relative start and end times of each file in the mix. You can make a group using selected sounds from a mix or add sounds to an already existing group at any time simply by holding the SHIFT key and clicking the left mouse button on the desired sounds' graphic representations. The **Group** menu also lets you delete or duplicate grouped sounds and then mute the affected tracks. If necessary, you can ungroup grouped sounds from this menu too.

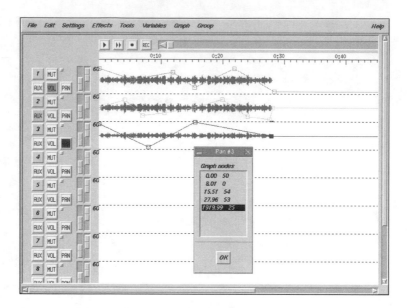

Figure 8-27: The Graph menu can display a list of nodes

Final Words on Mix

In true Linux fashion, Mix has been worked on by several developers, and I expect the "committee method" will continue to work for Linux Mix. Perhaps by now Mix already has such amenities as Region edits and improved effects processing. But don't let its few drawbacks discourage you from using Mix: It is usable right now, and is an excellent tool for composers, arrangers, and researchers working with sound and Linux.

9

SOFTWARE SOUND SYNTHESIS

Some of the finest Linux audio and music applications come
under the rubric of software sound synthesis (SWSS), a method
for the manipulation of sound using a programming language
(sometimes called a "waveform compiler") and a computer. Audio
synthesis and processing languages let you create, edit, analyze, and
resynthesize sounds by providing language elements, or opcodes, for working
with digital audio (such as Csound's signal generating and processing opcodes).
Examples of SWSS include computer music stalwarts such as Csound, Cmix, and
Common LISP Music, as well as newer developments like Craig Stuart Sapp's
Sig++ and the SAOL project led by Eric Scheirer. Graphic interfaces include
sound design and composition environments such as Cecilia (from Jean Piche
and Alexandre Burton), the Atelier Planck group's HPKComposer, and Michael
Gogins' Silence. All of these programs are profiled in this chapter, making it
easily the largest chapter in the book. (Realtime software synthesizers such as
aRts, Quasimodo, and RTSynth constitute their own class of Linux sound and
music software, so I have dedicated a separate chapter to them: See Chapter 10.)

Warning: Brainwaves Required!

SWSS is an advanced topic in digital audio. If you are not a programmer, much
of what follows may seem incomprehensible. Learning a software synthesis

language can seem quite daunting if you have no previous programming experience, but the languages presented here are not especially difficult to learn. Both Csound and Cmix enjoy the assistance of graphic user interfaces, and the background contained here in their respective profiles may help you reach a deeper understanding of the engines behind their GUIs. If you want to dive into Csound without going through the material presented in its profile, jump to the sections on Cecilia or HPKComposer. Those programs are designed especially for musicians with no previous knowledge of any synthesis programming language.

Csound

Author: Barry Vercoe
Version profiled: 3.57, official and unofficial versions
Web site: http://mitpress.mit.edu/e-books/csound/frontpage.html; (also see http://web.tiscalinet.it/mupuxeddu for unofficial versions)
FTP site: ftp://ftp.maths.bath.ac.uk/pub/dream (official); ftp://mustec.bgsu.edu/pub/linux (unofficial)
Maintained: Yes
Availability: Free, open-source
License: Copyright held by the Massachusetts Institute of Technology (MIT)
Capsule summary: Most popular SWSS language, with the greatest range of opcodes (operations and instructions) and widest variety of support software

Csound is an exceptionally powerful general purpose digital audio specification language. It can be used to design new computer-based instruments, or it can analyze existing sounds and resynthesize them based on the analysis data. Csound can be used as a music composition environment, an audio research tool, or a realtime MIDI-controllable synthesizer. Csound is one of the oldest SWSS languages and has the largest selection of modules for generating and processing sound.

History

Csound evolved out of MIT Professor Barry Vercoe's original 1973 MUSIC11 program when, in 1986, it was ported from PDP-11 assembler to UNIX C. MUSIC11 itself was derived from the pioneering MusicV program, written in 1966 by Max Mathews, perhaps the most revered founder of computer music technology. One of MusicV's major innovations was the implementation of the unit generator, a "black box" concept that allowed great extensibility (the ability to add to and expand a program or language) to the language. Since its inception, Csound has continuously evolved, quickly accommodating new synthesis methods, composition utilities, and digital signal processing (DSP) algorithms.

Getting It, Building It

Two Distinct Csound Packages

Csound is available for Linux in at least two distinct packages. John Fitch maintains the primary repository for Csound's source code at Bath in England and provides a Linux package built from those sources. Nicola Bernardini, from the Linux Csound Development group, maintains a version of Csound that was also built from the canonical sources at AIMI (Associazione di Informatica Musicale Italiana). The AIMI version, which is available in various popular Linux distribution formats (such as Red Hat's RPM and Debian's DEB), is completely compatible with existing orc/sco files and includes all opcodes found in the Bath sources.

Here is a summary of features available only in the AIMI version:

- Enhanced makefile system, with autoconf and configure support for site-specific build

- Support for Jaroslav Kysela's ALSA sound drivers

- Support for 64-bit Alpha systems

- Enhanced OSS/Linux realtime audio support

- Shared library (libcsound.so) for greatly reduced memory footprint

- Robin Whittle's random number generator

- A high-priority scheduler for improving realtime I/O on slower or heavily loaded systems

Two Distinct Build Procedures

The AIMI and Bath versions differ somewhat in the way in which Csound is compiled, or built, from its source code.

The Bath package includes a top-level makefile, which you edit for such items as audio and X support. After editing the makefile, run the **make** command to build the binary. After the binary is built, you can place it anywhere available to the system's PATH environment variable (/usr/local/bin is a good choice). You will also need to place the csound.txt file (the source for all text messages produced by Csound) in /usr/local/lib.

The development group version (also known as the "unofficial" version) utilizes the configure utility and a greatly expanded set of makefiles and make procedures. This version is built by running **./configure** with any necessary flags (for instance, with or without X, realtime audio, ALSA), then **make depend**, **make**, and finally (as root) **make install**. A typical installation will place the shared library, the binary, and the include files in the /usr/local/ hierarchy.

Whichever version you choose, once the binary is in the system PATH, Csound is ready for operation.

NOTE *The Csound examples presented in this chapter have been compiled under various releases of the development version but, because that version tries to stay in step with the canonical version, you should have no problem compiling the examples under either version.*

Creating a Soundfile in Csound

Csound requires two source files (text files created in any text editor or word processor). The first, called an orc (orchestra) file, designs a Csound instrument, which might be anything from an FM oscillator (foscil) to a sample playback engine (loscil or soundin). You write your orc and sco files as common text files in an editor such as vi or emacs. You can define your instrument's parameters solely within the orc file, or you can specify that it receives them from the second source file, the sco file. Along with instrument parameters, a sco (short for score) file also specifies event start times, duration, and any required stored-function tables (that is, pre-calculated functions such as waveforms and envelope curves).

Defining an Instrument

We begin by defining an instrument (a simple oscillator) by creating it in a text editor and saving it as **my.orc**. The semicolon is the comment delineator in Csound, and the comments need not be entered into your score; however, commenting your code is always good programming practice.

```
        sr=22050                ; sets sampling rate
        kr=441                  ; sets control rate for k-rate components (as opposed to a-
                                  rate or audio signals)
        ksmps=50                ; sr/kr, number of samples per control period
        nchnls=1                ; monaural output
        instr1
kamp  =        10000            ; raw amplitude
kfreq =        440              ; the musical pitch 'A' at 440 cps
ifn   =        1                ; stored function table 1
asig  oscil    kamp, kfreq, ifn ; an audio signal is created by an oscillator playing a
                                  stored sinewave at kamp and kfreq
      out      asig             ; the audio signal is sent out
      endin                     ; end instrument
```

Each line of a Csound instrument follows the same general design: output – generator or modifier – parameter list. The line

```
asig    oscil    kamp, kfreq, ifn
```

from the my.orc file is a perfect example: asig is a symbol for an audio signal that we wish to create by use of the oscil (simple oscillator) generator, which is defined by the amplitude, frequency, and waveform indicated by the kamp, kfreq, and ifn values.

Defining the Score

Following is an example of a score file, which we'll call my.sco. When your orc and sco files are compiled with the **csound** command, the score will be played by the instrument defined in the my.orc file above.

```
f1 0 8192 10 1   ; function table #1 (supplied by user), a stored sine wave
i1 0 3           ; instrument 1 plays for 3 seconds, start-time at 0
e                ; end score
```

The function table designation is constructed in this manner:

F1 Indicates that it is the first numbered table (ifn in my.orc).

0 Tells the Csound compiler that it is ready for use at time point 0 (that is, right away).

8192 The number of points in the table—and therefore the resolution of the stored function (higher numbers mean smoother functions).

10 The GEN function used to fill the table, in this case GEN10, a function for storing waveforms made up of summed sine waves.

1 Indicates that the first partial (a frequency component) is the only one present and it is at full strength (measured from 0 to 1).

Compiling the orc and sco Files

As already mentioned, the finished orc and sco files are compiled with the **csound** command. The command line

```
csound -o my.wav -W my.orc my.sco
```

compiles my.orc and my.sco to a WAV format soundfile called my.wav. The -o flag names the output file or device, and the -W flag defines the output as a WAV format file.

If run in an X session, Csound will pop up a small window with a graphic display of the function tables in the sco file. Click anywhere within that window to allow compilation to begin, and a series of messages will appear in the starting xterm.

And that's all there is to it. You can edit the new soundfile with MiXViews, DAP, Snd, or any other Linux soundfile editor (see Chapter 4).

The Csound csd Unified File Format

Csound also supports the csd file format. A csd file unifies the orc and sco files into one file along with the desired command options. Open your favorite text editor and create a new file named `my.csd`. Enter the following text:

```
<CsoundSynthesizer>

<CsOptions>
-o my.wav -Wdm6
</CsOptions>

<CsInstruments>
instr 1
kamp    =       10000
kfreq   =       440
ifn     =       1
asig    oscil   kamp, kfreq, ifn
        out     asig
        endin
</CsInstruments>

<CsScore>
f1 0 8192 10 1
i1 0 3
e
</CsScore>

</CsoundSynthesizer>
```

A `csd` file begins and ends with the CsoundSynthesizer tag pair and contains the CsOptions, CsInstruments, and CsScore tag pairs. Instruments and scores are composed exactly as they are in standard orc and sco files (the file above uses the orc and sco files defined in the previous section), and the command options are the same as if entered on the command-line.

Save your new `my.csd` file. Compile it with **csound my.csd** and that's all there is to it. Now play the results. . . .

Playback

You can play the resulting soundfile with any WAV player. If you wish to send the sound output directly to the soundcard DAC, use the following command line:

```
csound -o devaudio -W -dm6 my.orc my.sco
```

where -o devaudio sends output to audio device in realtime, -W creates WAV format (uses /dev/dsp for audio device), and -dm6 turns down messaging for better realtime response.

Simultaneous Input and Output

With a full-duplex soundcard, you can have simultaneous audio input and output, allowing realtime signal processing. If you're using the ALSA driver, the command line looks like this:

```
csound -i ADC -o DAC inout.orc inout.sco
```

where -i ADC is input to soundcard analog-to-digital converters and -o DAC is the output to soundcard digital-to-analog converters.

If you're using the OSS/Linux driver, a command line for simultaneous audio input and output looks like this:

```
csound -i devaudio -o /dev/dspW inout.orc inout.sco
```

> **NOTE** *Fred Floberg's high-priority scheduler, available only in the "unofficial" version of Linux Csound, is invoked with either −sched or −sked. Both commands place Csound's realtime output first in the timing queue, which will help keep playback free of interference from the system as it performs its own tasks, such as checking disk integrity or polling for network connectivity.*

Shortening the Command Line

To make the command line shorter, you can group the various commands and use wildcards (asterisks) for file extensions. Thus,

```
csound -Wdm6 -o devaudio myfoo.*
```

is functionally the same as

```
csound -o devaudio -W -d -m6 myfoo.orc myfoo.sco
```

> **NOTE** *In the above example, a wildcard ending will work only if there are no other filenames beginning with "myfoo" in the working directory, including files such as myfoo.sco.bak or myfoo.wav. Also, options that require parameters cannot be grouped (or must be the last member of a group, such as m6 in the example above).*

Realtime MIDI Input

Now, assuming you have a MIDI interface properly installed (see Chapter 2), you can play your first instrument (my.orc) by adding a dummy table to the score file (the dummy table keeps the instrument active yet does not supply it with any parameters), as follows:

```
f1 0 8192 10 1
f0 10000    ; dummy table, keeps the instrument active for 10000 secs
e
```

and compiling your orc/sco files with

```
csound -o devaudio -W -dm6 -M/dev/midi my.orc my.sco
```

where -M/dev/midi tells Csound to look for its note information from the MIDI input device instead of a Csound score.

Another way of triggering my.orc is to use a MIDI file. The orc/sco can be used as in the last example, but the command line changes to

```
csound -o devaudio -W -dm6 -F my.mid my.orc my.sco
```

where -F my.mid tells Csound to expect input from the MIDI file my.mid.

To make your sounds more interesting, you can map MIDI values into the orc file and arbitrarily utilize that data. In the following example the value for inum is derived from the incoming MIDI note number (using the notnum opcode). That value is then used to determine which of two function tables will be assigned to the ifn parameter for the oscil opcode (the determination is made in the lines beginning with if inum).

```
    instr 1
inum notnum              ; note number
kfreq     cpsmidib       ; MIDI to frequency
iamp ampmidi   inum*100  ; MIDI to amplitude (scaled within range)
if inum > 60 goto fun1   ; if the inum value is greater than 60 go to the
                         ; line labeled "fun1:" and proceed from there
if inum < 61 goto fun2   ; as above, but go to "fun2:" if inum is less than 61
fun1:
    ifn    =       1
    goto      contin
fun2:
    ifn    =       2
    goto      contin
asig oscil   iamp,kfreq,ifn
    out       asig endin
```

Our score file is the same as before, but we have added another function table:

```
f1 0 8192 10 1                         ; sine wave
f2 0 8192 10 1 .9 .8 .7 .6 .5 .4 .3 .2 .1  ; ramp wave
f0 10000
e
```

These files can be compiled for control by either a MIDI input device or a MIDI file. They demonstrate that simple Csound components can be easily built into elaborate sounds and control structures: I have here used the simplest instrument, but already it is quickly evolving into greater complexity.

Realtime MIDI Output

Now let's have Csound create a realtime MIDI output stream. The next example, using Gabriel Maldonado's MIDI output opcodes, demonstrates a more complex control system than what we've seen so far.

The moscil Opcode

The moscil (MIDI oscillator) opcode—by controlling MIDI channel, note-number, velocity, duration, and time between notes—can be used to create an "indeterminacy" aspect in composition, producing notes and other MIDI messages using Csound's randomization routines. In the following instrument, knum and kvel control the output of MIDI notes and their velocities over p3 (note-stream duration as specified in the score). The kran random output is used for kdur (actual duration) and kpause (pause between notes).

```
;;; MIDI OUT opcodes
;;; Name: mussle.orc
        instr 1
kchan   =          0
knum    linseg     40,p3/7,60,p3/7,46,p3/7,54,p3/7,24,p3/7,58,p3/7,48,p3/7,80
kvel    linseg     20,p3/2,39,p3/2,33
kran    pcauchy 23 ; calls a particular randomizing function known as a Cauchy distribution
kdur    =          int(kran)+.46
kpause  =          frac(kran)
        moscil     kchan, knum, kvel, kdur, kpause
        endin
```

knum and kvel are the results (and are control or k-rate signals), linseg is an opcode that creates an envelope (a modifying function), and P3 is the event duration passed to the orc from the sco file. P3/7 indicates that each segment of the envelope is equal in length to the event duration divided by seven. The numbers between each p3/7 are MIDI note numbers.

So in the above example, the knum statement creates an envelope function whose segments provide a linear movement between the indicated MIDI note numbers at the rate of p3/7.

Controlling Change Messages

The next two instruments control MIDI Program Change messages (see Chapter 6 for more details about MIDI) sent to my external synthesizer and my MIDI-controlled mixer.

```
      instr 11
kchan = 0
kprog = 2.
kmin  = 1.
kmax  = 128.
      koutpc kchan, kprog, kmin, kmax
      endin

      instr 100
kchan = 8
kprog = 6.
kmin  = 1.
kmax  = 128.
      koutpc kchan, kprog, kmin, kmax
      endin
```

Here is the sco file for this instrument:

```
;;; MIDI OUT opcodes
;;; mussle.sco

t 0 60          ; tempo indicator
i1 1.0 1.0      ; the different p3 durations will stretch out
                ; the play of the notes indicated by knum
i1 2.0 7.0
i1 9.0 18.0 i1 18.0 17.0
i11 0.0 1 i100 0 1
e
```

The command line for compiling these files is

```
csound -Q0 -n -dm6 mussle.orc mussle.sco
```

where -Q0 selects the first MIDI device and -n suppresses write to disk (for performance enhancement).

Given a fast enough CPU and hard disk, you can combine the various realtime I/O options. I have tested simultaneous realtime audio with MIDI output opcodes: It works, but with a noticeable performance slowdown on a Pentium 166.

Csound Helpers

Csound is especially rich in helper applications, some of which are included in the canonical source tree. The source package includes Cscore (a C library for the creation and manipulation of Csound scores), sndinfo, which displays information about a selected soundfile, and a collection of powerful analysis utilities for providing data files to the Csound resynthesis opcodes.

Csound has many other powerful and useful tools in addition to those that come with the source package. Analysis data editors, composition environments, score processing utilities, and drum machines are all freely available. Cecilia, HPKComposer, and Silence are three large-scale Csound helpers; Midi2CS and hYdraJ are two excellent examples of smaller sized assistants. We'll discuss the latter programs first.

Midi2CS

Author: Ruediger Borrman
Version profiled: 0.95/2
Web site: http://www.snafu.de/~rubo/songlab/midi2cs
FTP site: n/a
Maintained: Yes
Availability: Free, binary-only
License: Copyright held by author
Capsule summary: Handy utility to convert your favorite MIDI files to Csound scores

Ruediger Borrman's Midi2CS converts standard MIDI files to WAV files using Csound as its rendering engine. Midi2CS can use either user-selected samples (in AIFF or WAV format) or user-defined Csound instruments. With this feature, Midi2CS can orchestrate MIDIfiles in ways commercially available MIDI sequencers cannot. Midi2CS comes with a unique looping feature that makes it ideal for creating techno and other dance-music mixes; however, the program can be used to create almost any type of music. If you're interested, take a look at Ruediger's excellent Midi2CS tutorial on his Web site (see above).

Midi2CS is available for Linux in binary form only, so setting up the program is easy. Make a new Midi2CS directory in /home or /usr/local and download the latest Midi2CS package from the Web site listed above into the new directory. Midi2CS is packaged as a gzipped binary, so just run **gunzip midi2cs.gz** to unpack the program. You may need to set the permission on the file by running **chmod a+x midi2cs** before you can use it. With the correct permission, Midi2CS is now ready to rock.

Rendering a MIDI file to a WAV is a three-step procedure. Run **midi2cs** without parameters to create a project file template named midi2cs.pro. You edit this project file to let Midi2CS know what MIDI file to process, what names to give to the output orc and sco files, and what soundfiles or Csound instruments will be used to render the MIDI file. Run **midi2cs** (without parameters) again to create your Csound orc/sco files. Figure 9-1 shows the results of this second step:

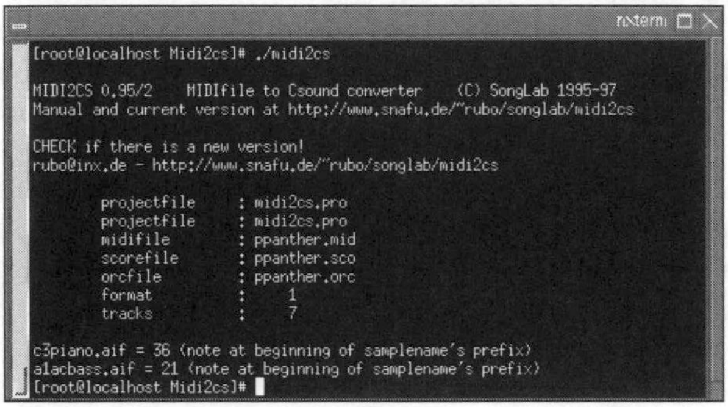

Figure 9-1: Midi2CS in the second stage

For the final step run Csound to compile your new orc and sco into a WAV format soundfile:

```
csound -W -o ppanther.wav ppanther.orc ppanther.sco
```

That example would compile the ppanther (Pink Panther) orc and sco files listed in Figure 9-1. You can automate the final step by writing a script file (call it **cs.scr**) containing this one line:

```
csound -W -o $1.wav $1.orc $1.sco
```

Make the script executable with **chmod +x cs.scr**. Using the script file, you can now run the command

```
./cs.scr my_project_name
```

and automate the rendering process. Thus, the Pink Panther example could be compiled with **./cs.scr ppanther**.

Midi2CS is an excellent tool for converting MIDI files to soundfiles, combining the strengths of both the MIDI file format and the Csound synthesis engine. It is usable from the console or X, and it is highly recommended software.

hYdraJ

Author: Malte Steiner
Version profiled: 1.20
Web site: http://members.aol.com/additiv/
FTP site: n/a
Maintained: Yes
Availability: Freeware
License: Copyright held by author
Capsule summary: Simple, useful graphic editor for Csound's *hetro* analysis data files

The hetro utility, one of Csound's analysis tools, supplies heterodyne filtering, a process that calculates the individual frequency and amplitude components of a sound and renders them to a data file (see the entries for "hetro" and "adsyn" in the Csound manuals available from David Boothe's Web site at http:// www.lakewoodsound.com/csound/). Typically, the Csound adsyn opcode is used to resynthesize the analysis data back into a soundfile. hYdraJ is a tool for editing hetro data files.

Malte Steiner first developed hYdra as a command-line utility, and hYdraJ is the Java version of hYdra. hYdraJ provides graphic editors for harmonic strength and amplitude/frequency envelopes. Editing analysis files is an intuitive process with hYdraJ's GUI.

I recommend running hYdraJ under the Blackdown group's JDK 1.1.7 or 1.1.8. These packages are versions of Java for Linux and are available at www.blackdown.org. Versions of JDK 1.2 work with hYdraJ but disable the Spektrumfilter display.

To install hYdraJ, download the package from Malte's Web site into your /home directory and unpack it with **tar xzvf hydraj-latest.tar.gz**. To start the program, enter your new hYdraJ directory, and run **java hydra**. When the main window appears, select **File • Open** to load the hetro analysis data into hYdraJ. Figure 9-2 shows hYdraJ opened to the main display of the analysis data's frequency components and the Spektrumfilter opened behind it.

Select **Process • Open Editor** from the menu bar of the main display. The editor simultaneously displays the frequency and amplitude components of an analysis channel. In Figure 9-3 the flat line in the middle represents the channel frequency curve, while the more active line (shown toggled for editing) represents the channel amplitude curve.

Save your edited data from the main display's File menu. Data can be saved in the Csound analysis file `.ads` format or exported as a Csound orc file.

With hYdraJ's GUI you can graphically edit a hetro analysis file with full control over the strength of each analyzed frequency and the envelope contours for both frequency and amplitude. That's what it sets out to do, and that's all there is to it. It's an excellent Csound utility.

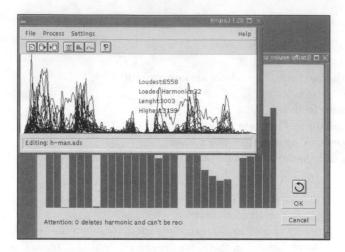

Figure 9-2: hYdraJ's main display

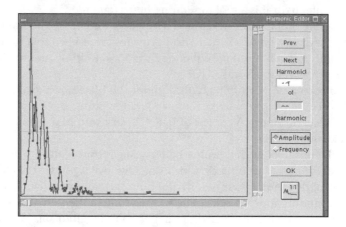

Figure 9-3: hYdraJ's editor

Cecilia

Authors: Jean Piche and Alexandre Burton
Version profiled: 2.0.2
Web site: http://www.musique.umontreal.ca/electro/CEC/index.html
FTP site: n/a
Maintained: Yes
Availability: Free, binary only
License: Held by the authors
Capsule summary: Complete music composition/production environment and front-end for Csound

Cecilia is a user-friendly and complete front-end for Csound. It provides a graphic interface for every aspect of Csound, including orc/sco composition, the analysis utilities, documentation, and the command-line options. The interface includes a user-programmable grapher for drawing control curves with the mouse. The system also contains its own scoring language, called Cybil. Cecilia is highly interactive, capable of realtime performance, and a complete environment for computer music composition and sound design. Although the program utilizes Csound as its rendering engine, no knowledge of Csound is needed to use Cecilia. It's a comprehensive, powerful tool that I highly recommend.

Getting It, Building It

Retrieve the latest Cecilia package from the Web site listed above. Unpack it in your /home directory with **tar xzvf cecilia-latest.tar.gz**. Move into the new Cecilia directory and run the installation script. As root, enter **./install.sh** at the command prompt and the installation will proceed automatically. When it's finished, type **cecilia** in an xterm window to start the program.

Setting It Up

When Cecilia opens, you will see its attractive splash screen with a loading status display at the bottom of the window. When the program components have loaded, the splash screen will disappear, leaving Cecilia's main window open. This window contains various global settings, including output choice (direct to soundcard or write to disk), output file name, Csound orc file header values (sample rate, control rate, number of samples per control pass, number of channels, Csound GEN function table size), and compilation controls. The menus at the top provide file management, the full range of Csound command-line options, access to the Csound analysis utilities, and a manager for Cecilia's windows.

To begin your acquaintance with Cecilia, open **File • Preferences** and edit the information in the **Preferences** window. Figure 9-4 shows the default main window and my preferences.

Be sure to indicate the correct path to the Csound binary. If you have set the Csound environment variables SSDIR (location for soundfile input), SFDIR (location for soundfile output), and SADIR (location for analysis files) you can pass those settings to Cecilia by pressing the **sync to env** button (at the far right of Figure 9-4). You can also choose a new color scheme and assign shortcut keys for the playback controls. When you are satisfied with your selections, press **OK**. You are now ready to open a Cecilia module.

The Cecilia Module

In Cecilia, a "module" includes the general settings in the main window, the components of the grapher window (if a GUI is used by the module), and a text editor for creating instruments and score specifications.

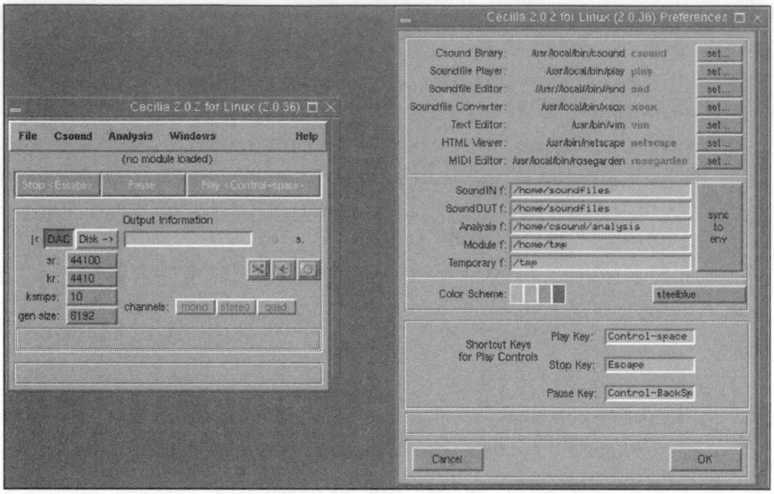

Figure 9-4: Cecilia's main window (left) and Preferences window (right)

Open the CybilExample module from **File • New • Cybil**. In the main window, select **Windows • Show Editor** from the menu. Your screen should now look like Figure 9-5.

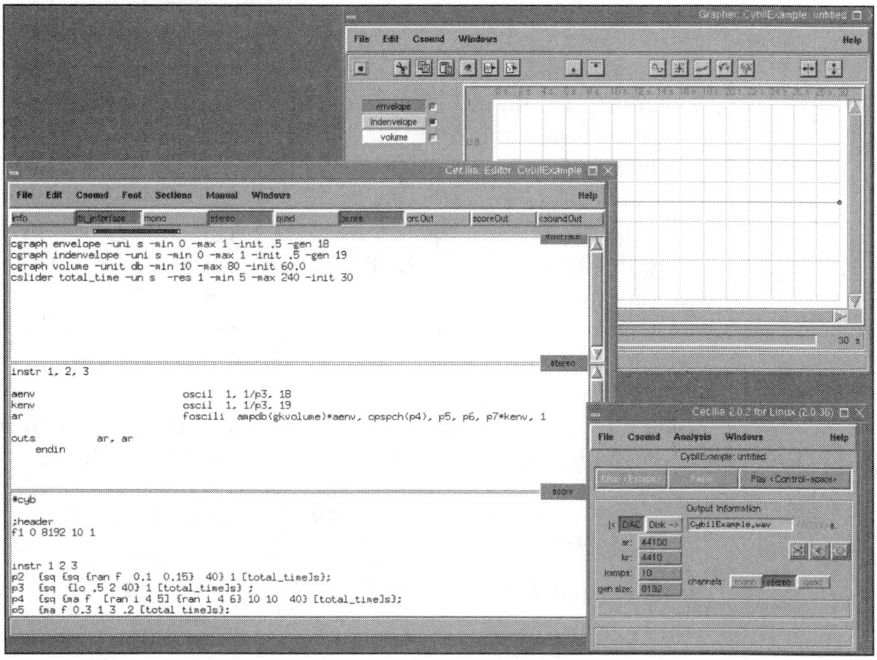

Figure 9-5: Front to back: The main window, text editor, and grapher window in Cecilia

Select **File • Save Module As**, rename and save CybilExample as
`my_first.cec`, then select **File • Reinit Module**. You are now ready to edit your
first Cecilia module.

The Grapher

Let's explore the grapher first. Figure 9-6 provides a better look at the
grapher in the `my_first` example.

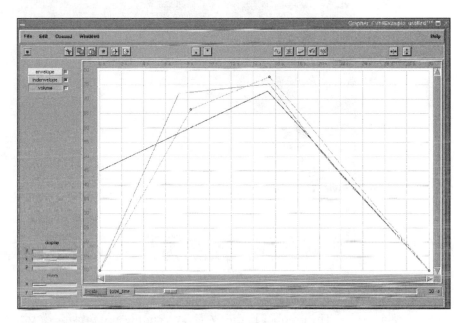

Figure 9-6: Cecilia's grapher

I've added simple line-segment graphs for the three graph-controlled
functions (envelope, indenvelope, volume). Unfortunately, the grayscale
screenshots can't show off Cecilia's use of color coding: Each envelope curve
is a different color, which helps when the grapher is filled with curves. The
entire program makes good use of color schemes and coding.

To edit or create a line-segment control envelope, select a function by
clicking on its label (at the left side of the graph window). Its line will be highlighted in the grapher, and you can now add points to it by left-clicking the
mouse pointer anywhere within the graph display. Points can be dragged
around the graph, and you can delete points with a middle-button click (or a
simultaneous right/left click on a two-button mouse).

To move an entire curve, bring the pointer over the curve you want to
move. When the line turns white, click and hold the left mouse button and
drag the curve to a new location.

You can also switch between line-segment curves and spline curves. A line-segment curve simply interpolates a straight line between points, but a spline curve is smooth and rounded between its points. Figure 9-7 shows another view of the my_first example's function graphs, now with two of the functions controlled by spline curves and the other controlled by a line-segment curve.

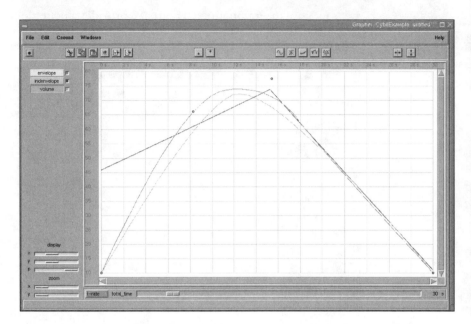

Figure 9-7: Controlled curves in Cecilia's grapher

The grapher in the my_first example also provides a total_time slider. Adjusting this slider will determine the length of the output file. The other sliders (to the left side of the graph display) control the grid intensity and the zoom view into or out of the grid.

The intensity and zoom sliders are default parts of the Cecilia grapher. Other default parts of the grapher include the menu bar and the toolbar directly beneath it.

The File, Csound, Windows, and Help menus are the same as those on the main window. The toolbar contains a variety of useful tools for creating, editing, and randomizing graph curves. The leftmost button removes the toolbar from the grapher, displaying the tools in their own window. In Figure 9-7 the tools are, from left to right, the "scissors group," which includes buttons for cut/copy/paste operations, along with a reset function (the eraser) and two buttons for file save and load (Cecilia can save and load graphs); a pair of buttons to nudge the display up or down slightly; the "sine wave" group, which includes functions for generating and randomizing waveforms; and two buttons to expand and contract the display vertically and horizontally.

Let's look at what a randomization function can do in the grapher.

The Randomization Function

Go to **File** and select **Reinit Module**. The grapher will now contain only three straight lines. Open the drunk walk dialog by right-clicking on the middle icon in the sine wave group, then enter some values for the points and walk parameters. A drunk walk steps through a random course between the start and end points, stopping at a user-specified number of points in between, and deviating from the straight path by a user-specifed degree. The grapher and the drunk walk dialog should look like the display in Figure 9-8.

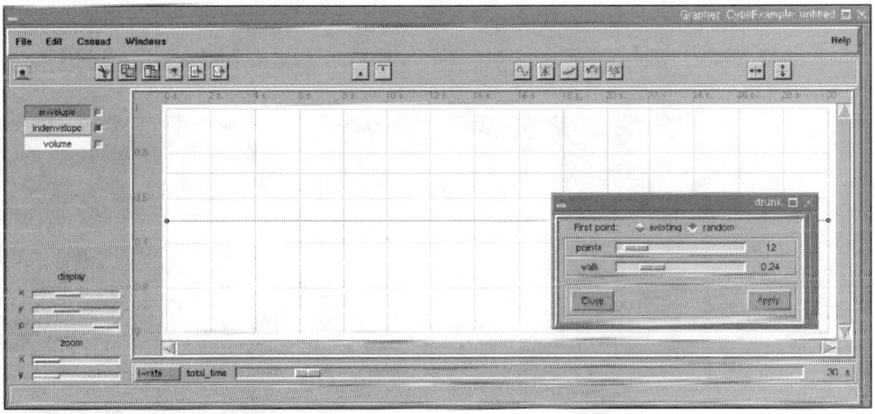

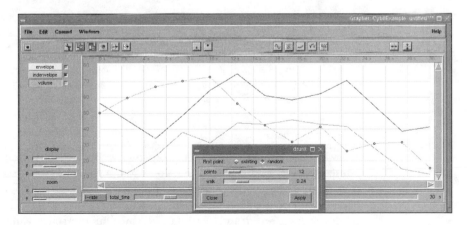

Figure 9-8: Cecilia's grapher with the drunk walk dialog

Now select in turn the envelope, indenvelope, and volume functions, and apply the drunk walk to each one. Your grapher will now look something like the screen in Figure 9-9.

Figure 9-9: Cecilia's grapher with drunk walk applied

You can now edit the breakpoints directly, change the line-segment curves to splines, or use the eraser tool (in the "scissors group") to reinitialize each curve and start over.

When you are content with the appearance of your control curves in the grapher, click on **Open Csound Window** in the Csound menu, then press the **Play** button in the main window (or use CTRL-**spacebar** if you want to stay in the grapher). An xterm window will appear, running Csound and compiling the my_first example. When the compile is finished, type CTRL-**C** in the Csound window to close it. You can now edit and audition your new soundfile by going to Cecilia's main window and clicking on either the scissors or speaker icon. Figure 9-10 displays the my_first example with the Csound window and the soundfile editor (Kwave in this picture) opened.

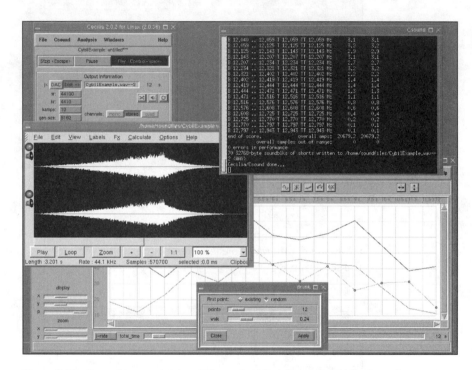

Figure 9-10: Csound (upper right) and Kwave (middle left) opened in Cecilia with main window, grapher, and drunk walk dialog

Cecilia's Editor

Now let's look into the Cecilia editor window. By default, the editor window is closed when a module is opened. You can open the editor window by choosing either **Editor** or **Show Editor** from the **Window** menu. Panels are available for editing the text that creates the instruments, the score (with separate panels for mono, stereo, and quad output), and the interface components. Figure 9-11 displays the my_first.cec editor.

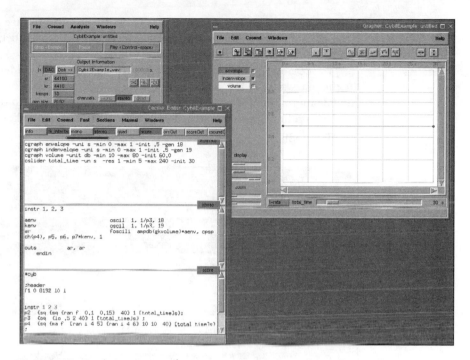

Figure 9-11: Cecilia's editor window

The Cecilia editor is the Csound programming heart of the application. By closely studying the editor for the original my_first.cec module, you can see how the interface components are related to the elements of both the instrument and the score. This design is very powerful: The grapher can control the amplitude, pitch, and waveform curves (instrument-level factors) at the same time that it controls the tempo, event duration, total duration of the piece, and density of events (performance-level factors).

The editor is divided into three panels: one each for the interface, the instrument, and the score. Panels are opened and closed by pressing their buttons, which appear just below the menu bar.

The Interface Panel

Compare the elements of the interface panel (the top panel in the window labeled Cecilia Editor CybilExample in Figure 9-11) with what you see in the grapher in the same figure. The last line in the panel reads cslider total_time -un s -res 1 -min 5 -max 240 -init 30, and the grapher does show a slider labeled total_time, sitting at a value of 30 seconds (-un s sets the unit of movement to seconds). Move the slider to the right until it stops at 240, its maximum value. Note that when the slider moves, it increments or decrements by units of 1. Bring the slider to the left until it stops at its minimum value of 5. Every part of the cslider definition is clearly seen in the graphic slider. The cgraph interface components work in the same way: Each line in the interface panel applies to an element seen in the graph window, providing the type, label, range, initial setting, and other aspects of the graphic interface component.

To see how the interface definitions work, change the cslider init value to **10**, the max value to **100**, and the min value to **0**. Choose **Save Module** from the **File** menu, then **Reinit Module** (these steps are required to update the display to reflect your changes). The grapher will then look like the display shown in Figure 9-12.

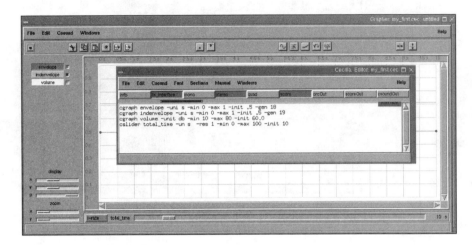

Figure 9-12: The grapher after modifying various sliders

As you see, the slider now defaults to the 10-second position. Move it to the right end-point, and the display will read **100 s**. The minimal position will read **0 s**. Again, you must run through the sequence **File • Save Module** and **File • Reinit Module** before the grapher updates with your changes.

The Instrument Panel

The next panel (in the center of the lower left window in Figure 9-11) is where you design your instruments. Separate panels are available for mono, stereo, and quad output, and any or all may be used. The output selector in the main window will determine the output channels; however, if no panel exists for an output type, it will be grayed out. Our my_first example has only a stereo instrument panel, so a good exercise will be to add a mono panel to it.

To Add A Panel

Click on the mono panel selector under the menu bar, and a new empty panel will appear in the editor. For the my_first example, simply copy and paste the stereo panel contents into the new panel. Select the text in the stereo panel by left-clicking and dragging the mouse over the text. Choose **Copy** from the **Edit** menu (or use the ALT-C keyboard accelerator) to copy the selected text. Click inside the mono panel to activate it, then select **Edit • Paste** or use ALT-V to paste the copied text into the mono panel.

This instrument was designed for stereo output, so you need to change **outs** (Csound stereo output designator) in the original stereo instrument (as seen in Figure 9-11) to **out**. Delete one of the two **ar** definitions (again seen in Figure 9-11) on the same line, then save and reinitialize the module. Figure 9-13 shows the editor and main window after adding the mono output panel. Mono output has been selected:

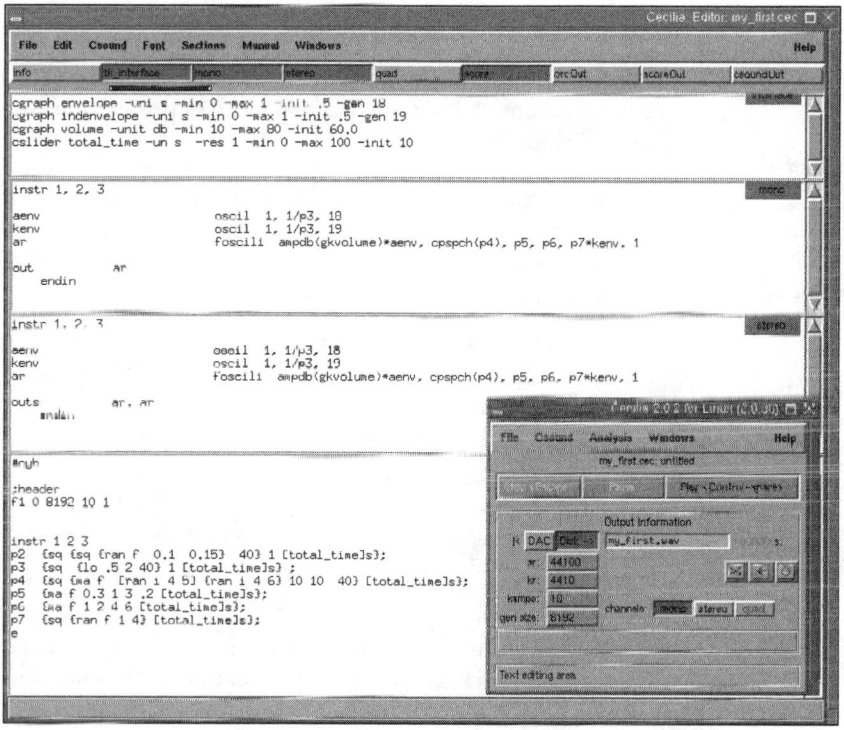

Figure 9-13: Cecilia's editor and main window with added mono panel

To force mono-only output, delete the contents of the stereo panel, then click on the **stereo** button under the menu bar to remove that panel from the editor. After another save/reinit cycle, both the quad and stereo selectors will be grayed out in the main window.

Now let's look deeper into the mono instrument panel of Figure 9-13. The instrument in my_first is based on the Csound foscili opcode, an FM synthesis generator. The amplitude is controlled by the cgraph volume interface element, indicated in the instrument as the gkvolume variable.

The aenv and kenv oscillators directly above it produce amplitude and frequency envelopes. For each of those oscillators the last parameter is a function table number. That number corresponds to the GEN table number assigned to the cgraph envelope and cgraph indenvelope interface elements.

Note that the instrument block delimiter instr 1, 2, 3 will create three instances of the foscili instrument.

Our module connects its interface elements and their data to the instrument by graphs assigned to GEN function tables and by variables corresponding to the interface component type. Now let's see what kind of interconnections exist with the Cecilia score.

Four Scores

Cecilia recognizes four types of scores. Ordinary Csound score (sco) files are of course accepted, but Cecilia also processes three other interesting score types: #minimum, tcl, and cyb.

- A score created with the #minimum keyword contains a single event for instrument 1 (i1). The event lasts for the length of the longest active soundfile or for the duration indicated by the total_time slider. A #minimum score is especially useful for interactive work.

- If a score starts with #tcl, it will be interpreted as a Tcl (tool command language) procedure or program. A score will be compiled and then passed on to Csound. Tcl is a scripting language usually associated with Tk, a set of graphics widgets (GUI components). It is a popular modern programming language with support for arrays and complex control structures. It is also the language in which Cecilia is written. It is beyond the purpose of this book to teach you how to use Tcl/Tk, but interested readers should look into the book *Practical Programming in Tcl and Tk*, by Brent B. Welch[1].

- A #cyb score indicates that what follows is written in the Cybil scoring language. Cybil is a language for the creation of Csound note lists (as in Csound sco files). The language is easy to learn and use, yet quite powerful.

Let's look at the score in the modified my_first.cec module in Figure 9-13. A Csound score event strictly defines only the first three parameter fields (p-fields). The instrument number is p1, p2 is the event start time, and p3 is the event duration. Although p4 and p5 are often used for amplitude and frequency, all p-fields beyond p3 are arbitrarily assigned to components of the instrument.

1 Upper Saddle River: Prentice Hall PTR, 2nd ed., 1997. ISBN 0136168302.

P-Fields and Tendency Masks

Cybil creates data for p-fields. According to the excellent documentation, the general syntax for a statement in Cybil is

```
{algorithm duration} [ operator {function} ]
```

In your score, p2 is defined as

```
p2 {sq {sq {ran f  0.1  0.15} 40} 1 [total_time]s};
```

The Cybil algorithm sq creates a sequence of events and loops them. Sequences can be nested. Taking this nest apart, we find that p2 is generated by a sequence of 40 floating-point random numbers in a range between 0.1 and 0.15, followed by a value of 1, then looped for the time set by the GUI total_time slider. The process is repeated for each of the three instruments. Similar operations are carried out for all p-fields.

For instance, the foscili opcode has the following syntax:

```
ar foscili xamp,kcps,kcar,kmod,kndx,ifn[,phs]
```

In your mono instrument, the opcode is employed with these values and variables:

```
ar foscili ampdb(gkvolume)*aenv, cpspch(p4), p5, p6, p7*kenv, 1
```

The opcode receives its amplitude data from the volume graph (gkvolume), converts it from decibels to linear amplitude data (where 60 db equals 1,000, 66 db equals 2,000, 72 db equals 4,000, and so forth), and modulates it with the aenv oscillator. The note pitch is determined by the output of the Cybil score for p-field 4, then converted to cycles per second (Hz). With the exception of the final parameter (the function table number), the remaining parameters are generated by Cybil formulas in the score.

The function table number is indicated in the score in exactly the same way as in a standard Csound score. Anything between #cyb and the first instr is considered a Csound score statement, including function tables and tempo sequences.

P5 is the carrier frequency in the FM synthesis. The following line in the score calculates each occurrence of p5:

```
p5 {ma f 0.3 1 3 .2 [total_time]s};
```

The ma algorithm generates a tendency mask, a range created by the two lines generated by values 1 and 3 (minimum line), and values 2 and 4 (maximum line). In the my_first example, the lines cross: One line of floating-point numbers extends from 0.3 to 3, whereas the other goes from 1 to 0.2. P5 is gen-

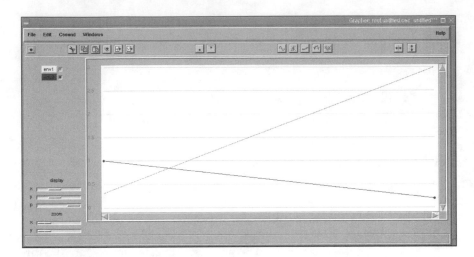

Figure 9-14: A tendency mask in Cecilia's grapher

erated as a random number from the space between the two lines. Figure 9-14 shows the example tendency mask as drawn in the Cecilia graph window.

You can check the output of the tendency mask (and all the other parameter generators) by investigating the contents of the scoreOut panel (shown in Figure 9-15). Make your graphs in the grapher, then compile the module by pressing **Play** in the main window. If the scoreOut panel is open in the editor, you will see the score events stream by as Csound compiles the instrument and score. The scoreOut panel displays events in ordinary Csound score syntax, so you can easily check a parameter's realized value against its proposed ranges in the Cybil score.

The orcOut panel (also shown in Figure 9-15) displays the contents of the orc file passed to the Csound compiler, and the csoundOut panel shows the command line used. An info panel contains any pertinent information you want to enter. Figure 9-15 shows our my_first example with all of these panels active.

Summary

Congratulations! If you came this far you are ready to forge ahead, and Cecilia can take you much farther. I have shown you only a little of what Cecilia can do. The interface invites experimentation, the example modules provide plenty of starting points for learning the deeper aspects of the program, and the documentation is thorough and clearly written. Cecilia is definitely "Most Recommended" software for signal processing, sound design, or Csound composition. I've used the program extensively, yet I'm far from exhausting its possibilities. In my opinion, Cecilia is simply splendid.

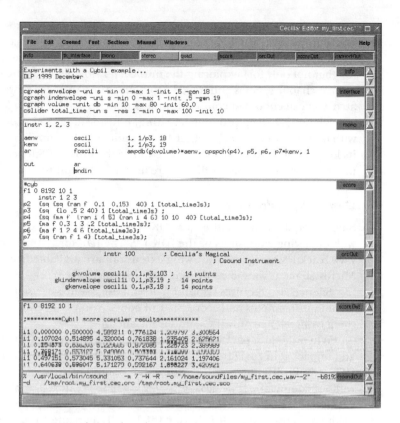

Figure 9-15: The Cecilia editor with active panels for info, interface, mono instrument, score, orcOut, scoreOut, and csoundOut

Silence

Author: Michael Gogins
Version profiled: 4.1.1
Web site: http://www.pipeline.com/~gogins/
FTP site: n/a
Maintained: Yes
Availability: Free for non-profit use, open-source
License: GPL
Capsule summary: Rich environment for exploring music composition using algorithms and mathematics. Renders audio via Csound; can also output standard MIDI file

On the Silence Web page, Michael Gogins describes his program as

> ... *an extensible system for making music on computers by means of software alone. It is an instrument for music that could not be performed, composed, or even imagined without computers. It is specifically designed to support algorithmic composition using software synthesis.*

Silence creates Csound scores from numeric systems (such as Lindenmayer fractal formulae), MIDI files, and graphics files in the GIF format. Silence is not a realtime synthesizer, nor does it provide any interactive controls. It is designed for (but not only for) exploring the musical possibilities of exotic mathematics such as chaotic systems and fractal geometry. After a Silence score has been created, you can choose to compile it with Csound or render it as a MIDI file.

Silence is a deep program, creating, transforming, and processing sound with tools not found in any other Linux audio or MIDI application. However, its logical interface makes it easy to explore the world of Silence, and its documentation clearly explains the nature and use of its unusual tools.

Getting It, Building It

Silence requires Java—either the JDK (Java Development Kit) 1.1.7 or higher with the Swing extensions or the JDK 1.2. The JDK for Linux is available from www.blackdown.org and the Swing extensions are available from Sun Microsystems at www.javasoft.com. Both packages are free.

Silence also requires Csound. You can use Silence by itself to create Csound instruments and scores, but of course you will be able to compile them from Silence only if Csound is installed.

When the Java packages are installed, retrieve Silence from its Web site and unpack it in /usr/local/ or your /home directory. Silence is packaged as a DOS-style PKZIP file, but fortunately the ubiquitous gzip will uncompress it without complaint. Type **gunzip Silence.zip** to create a new Silence directory. Change to that directory and edit the **Silence.cfg** file to designate your external helper applications for viewing the HTML help and for playing and editing soundfiles. Here is how my **Silence.cfg** file appears:

```
silenceHelpPath = /home/Silence/Silence.htm
   csoundHelpPath = /home//CsManual/TITLE.html
   instrumentLibraryPath = /home/Silence/instr
   instrumentPath = Instruments.
   unitPath = Units.
   nodePath = /home/Silence/Nodes
   play wav = xplay
   edit wav = snd
   play aif = xplay
   edit aif = snd
   play mid = playmidi -e
   edit mid = jazz-pp
   open html = xterm -e lynx
   open htm = xterm -e lynx
   csound = csound
```

Note that the nodePath does not include a trailing period.

You will also need to download the AXCsound package from the Silence site. All you need from that package is the JCsound directory. Unzip the AXCsound package wherever you like, copy the JCsound directory to the Silence tree, then configure the JCsoundManager.cfg in the **Silence • JCsound • JCsound** directory. Here is my JCsoundManager configuration file:

```
soundfilePlayer = xplay
    helpCommand = xterm -e lynx /home/Silence/AXCsound.htm
    externalCsound = true
```

With these steps completed, you can now launch and use Silence.

Using Silence

From the Silence top directory, start the program with the following command (substituting the correct paths for your installation) in an xterm window:

```
java -classpath .:/home/Silence/calc:/home/Silence/JCsound:/home -mx72m -ms64m
Silence.Framework.MMLManager
```

The -mx and -ml options specify the optimal starting memory for Java and Silence (72 megabytes and 64 megabytes in this example). You may need to adjust those amounts to accommodate the size of your system's memory.

When Silence starts, it opens to the Music Modeling window shown in Figure 9-16.

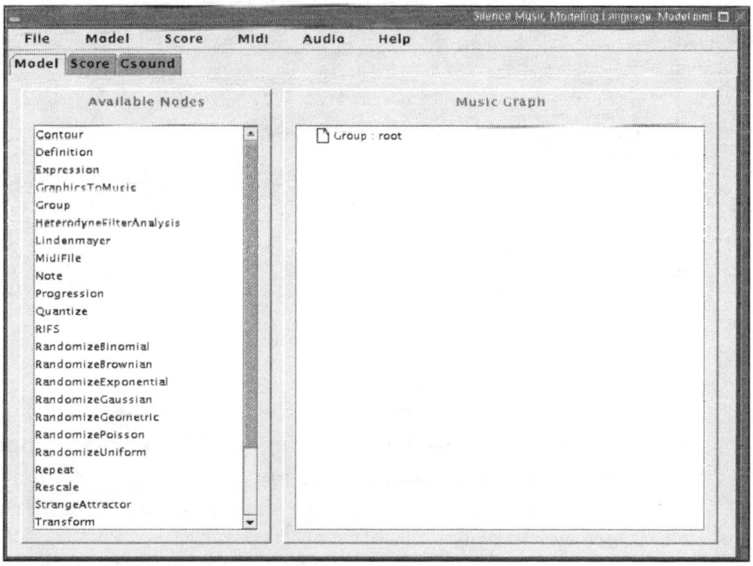

Figure 9-16: Silence's Music Modeling window

You create a Silence composition by selecting **Nodes** and arranging them along the hierarchical tree of the Music Graph. When you are satisfied with your structure, select **Score • Generate Score** from the menu bar, and Silence will switch to the Score window—where it will display your new creation as a piano-roll style graph.

Silence loads and saves a variety of file types. An entire Silence creation is saved as a Music Modeling Language file with the .mml extension. Silence scores can also be saved as Csound sco files, as MIDI files, and as scores within the Csound csd unified file format.

Render a MIDI File to a Silence Score

For our first experiment with Silence, we'll render a MIDI file to a Silence score. Select the **MidiFile** node from the list of **Available Nodes** and press the **Insert** key to add the node to the Music Graph. Right-click on the **MidiFile** node in the **Music Graph**, choose a MIDI file to render, and rename the node. Figure 9-17 illustrates the process.

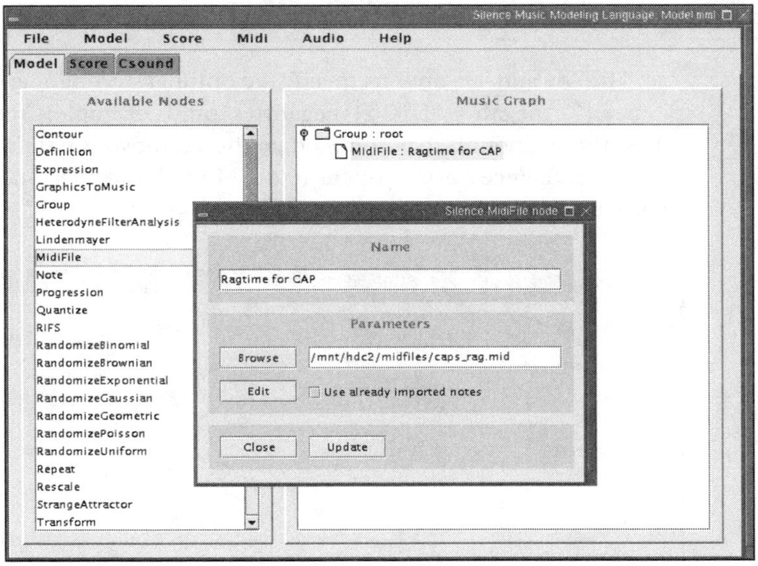

Figure 9-17: Rendering a MIDI file in Silence

Select **Score • Generate Score** from the top menu, and the display will automatically switch to the Score window while Silence computes the new score. When the score has been computed, you will see a new display in the Score window. Figure 9-18 shows the "ragtime" example MIDI file rendered to a Silence score display.

You can now select **Score • Edit Score** to edit the events in your new score. Events can be inserted and deleted singly or in blocks, and individual

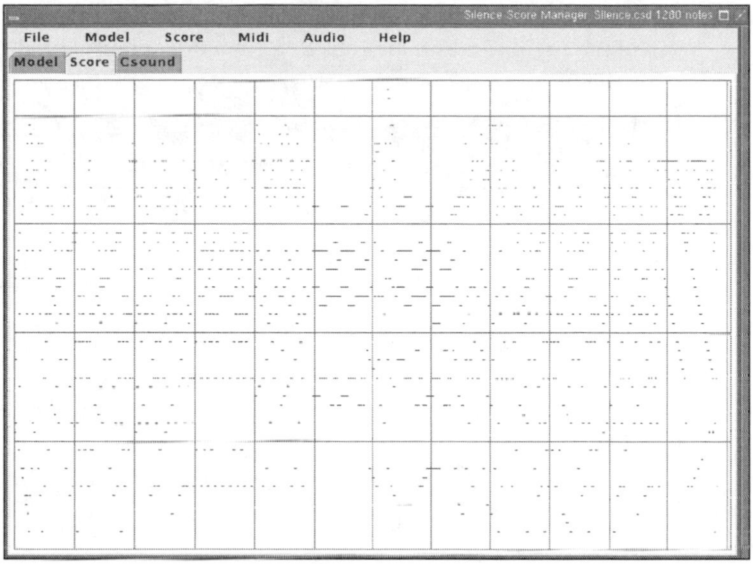

Figure 9-18: The MIDI file rendered to a Silence score

events can be edited in fine detail. Instrument number, start time, duration, MIDI note number, even the event's spatial coordinates (the x, y, and z plane values) can be changed freely; you can also change the nature of the event's MIDI status. Figure 9-19 shows the Note Editor opened for our example. The Status for each event shown is 144, which is the MIDI note-on message in decimal, but you can redefine it as any type of MIDI message in the Note Editor.

When you finish your edits, click on the **Close** button to save your changes.

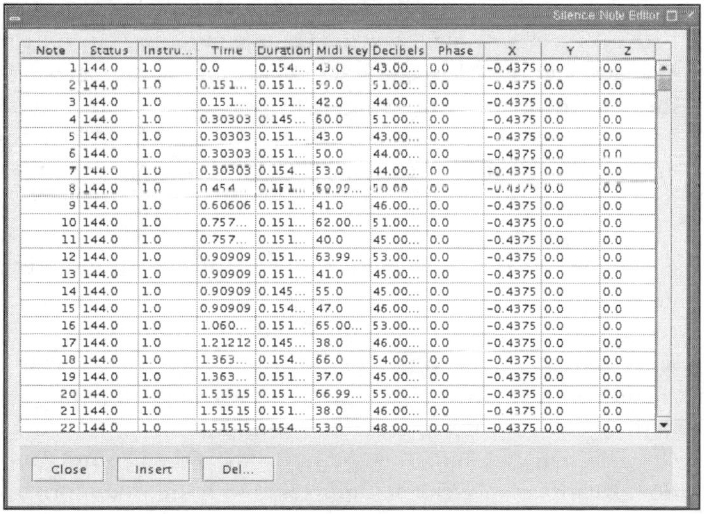

Note	Status	Instru...	Time	Duration	Midi key	Decibels	Phase	X	Y	Z
1	144.0	1.0	0.0	0.154...	43.0	43.00...	0.0	-0.4375	0.0	0.0
2	144.0	1.0	0.151...	0.151...	59.0	51.00...	0.0	-0.4375	0.0	0.0
3	144.0	1.0	0.151...	0.151...	42.0	44.00	0.0	-0.4375	0.0	0.0
4	144.0	1.0	0.30303	0.145...	60.0	51.00...	0.0	-0.4375	0.0	0.0
5	144.0	1.0	0.30303	0.151...	43.0	43.00...	0.0	-0.4375	0.0	0.0
6	144.0	1.0	0.30303	0.151...	50.0	44.00...	0.0	-0.4375	0.0	0.0
7	144.0	1.0	0.30303	0.154...	53.0	44.00...	0.0	-0.4375	0.0	0.0
8	144.0	1.0	0.454	0.151...	60.99...	50.00	0.0	-0.4375	0.0	0.0
9	144.0	1.0	0.60606	0.151...	41.0	46.00...	0.0	-0.4375	0.0	0.0
10	144.0	1.0	0.757...	0.151...	62.00...	51.00...	0.0	-0.4375	0.0	0.0
11	144.0	1.0	0.757...	0.151...	40.0	45.00...	0.0	-0.4375	0.0	0.0
12	144.0	1.0	0.90909	0.151...	63.99...	53.00...	0.0	-0.4375	0.0	0.0
13	144.0	1.0	0.90909	0.151...	41.0	45.00...	0.0	-0.4375	0.0	0.0
14	144.0	1.0	0.90909	0.145...	55.0	45.00...	0.0	-0.4375	0.0	0.0
15	144.0	1.0	0.90909	0.154...	47.0	46.00...	0.0	-0.4375	0.0	0.0
16	144.0	1.0	1.060...	0.151...	65.00...	53.00...	0.0	-0.4375	0.0	0.0
17	144.0	1.0	1.21212	0.145...	38.0	46.00...	0.0	-0.4375	0.0	0.0
18	144.0	1.0	1.363...	0.154...	66.0	54.00...	0.0	-0.4375	0.0	0.0
19	144.0	1.0	1.363...	0.151...	37.0	45.00...	0.0	-0.4375	0.0	0.0
20	144.0	1.0	1.51515	0.151...	66.99...	55.00...	0.0	-0.4375	0.0	0.0
21	144.0	1.0	1.51515	0.151...	38.0	46.00...	0.0	-0.4375	0.0	0.0
22	144.0	1.0	1.51515	0.154...	53.0	48.00...	0.0	-0.4375	0.0	0.0

Close   Insert   Del...

Figure 9-19: Silence's Note Editor

When you're satisfied with the details of your score, click on the **Csound** tab of the main window. Figure 9-20 shows the default panel that will appear.

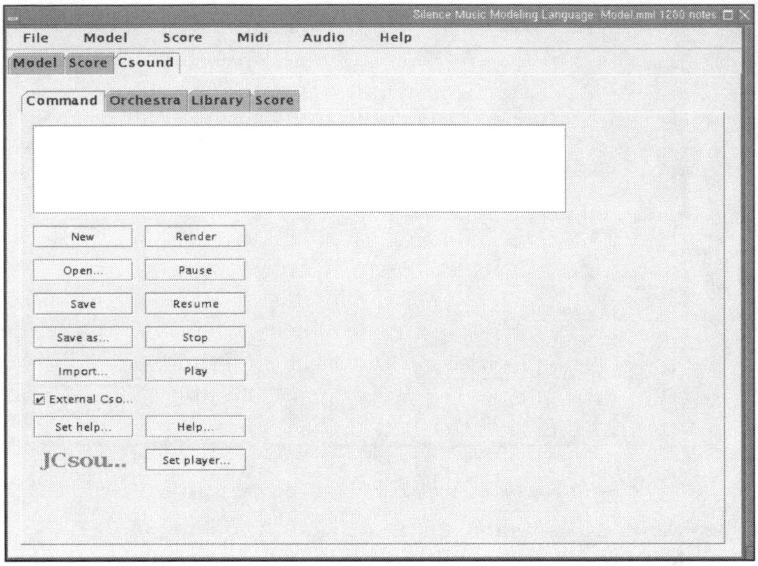

Figure 9-20: Csound in Silence

Click on the **Csound • Score** tab, and you should see your new score represented in Csound sco format. The text in this panel (and the other panels of the Csound tab) can be directly edited. You can freely add function tables, tempo designators, section markers, comments, and any other element of the Csound scoring syntax. Press the **Update** button at any time to save your changes. Figure 9-21 is a look at our ragtime example score as a Csound sco file, with the addition of a single function table (the f1 statement).

Now click on the **Csound • Orchestra** tab. The default window will be empty, and you can write a Csound orc file directly into the edit area. Figure 9-22 is a look at the Orchestra window containing a Csound orc file.

With your Csound orc and sco files defined, click the **Csound • Command** tab. Again, the default condition is an empty panel, and it is here that you will enter your Csound command string. The default orc/sco filenames are temp.orc and temp.sco. Press the **Render** button to begin compiling your orc and sco files and, when the compile is finished, press **Play** to listen to the new soundfile. In Figure 9-23, you can see the compilation options defined for rendering your orc and sco files into a soundfile.

The window containing the sine wave is the Csound function table window. Its appearance can be suppressed with the -d option, but it's a good idea to keep your Csound messaging at the default level (graphics on, all messages echoed to the root window), because Silence doesn't ring a bell or otherwise

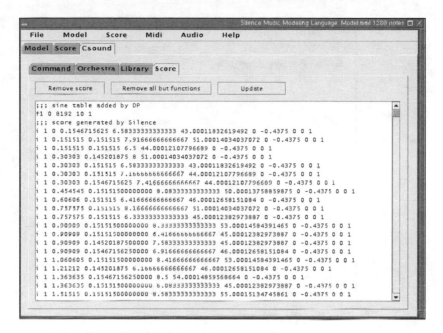

Figure 9-21: The example score as a sco file

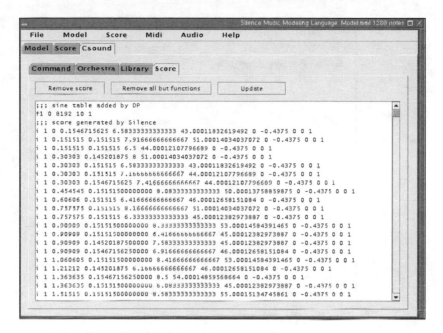

Figure 9-22: The Orchestra window

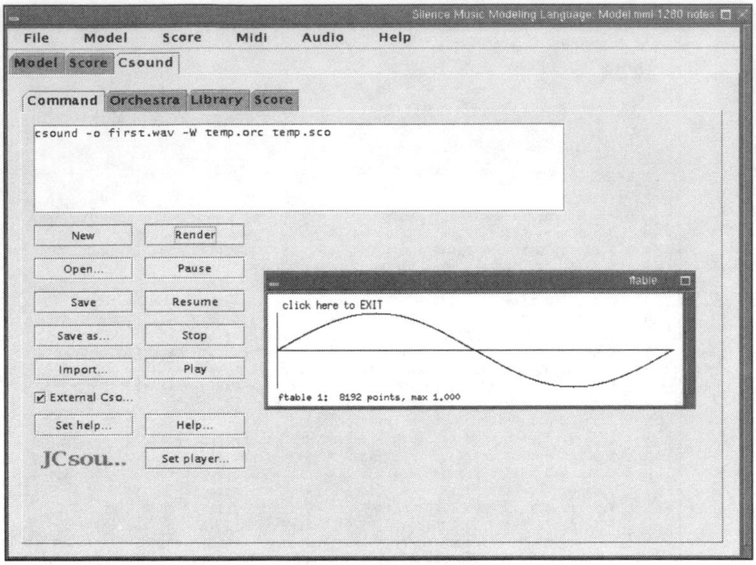

Figure 9-23: Compilation options

notify you when the compiling is done. Return to the **Music Modeling** window and save your session work as `midifile.mml`.

If you've come this far, you now have a good starting point for exploring the deeper aspects of Silence. The next example demonstrates a more complex use of the program.

Triptych: An Advanced Example

The Silence package includes some example mml files, one of which is titled `Triptych.mml`. "Triptych" (TRIP-titch) is a term from classical art meaning a painting or picture made of three panels (commonly medieval altarpieces), and this piece (by Michael Gogins) displays a very clear three-part structure.

Load `Triptych.mml` from **File • Open** in the **Music Modeling** window. When the file is loaded, you should see only a locked Group icon on the Music Graph. Left-click on the lock lever, then unlock each consecutive locked icon until all icons are unlocked. You should see the display (I have renamed the nodes for this example) shown in Figure 9-24.

The large-scale structure is **Group • Progression • Contour**. Each Contour opens to the deep structure **Contour • Rescale • Strange Attractor**. Let's investigate each type of node on the tree, starting with the Strange Attractor node.

The documentation for the Strange Attractor tells us that the node " . . . generates notes by searching for a chaotic dynamical system defined by a polynomial equation or partial differential equation using Julien C." Readers with knowledge of chaos mathematics will know more precisely what that description means, but for now we need only know that the node is a data or signal generator. Figure 9-25 shows the node opened for editing.

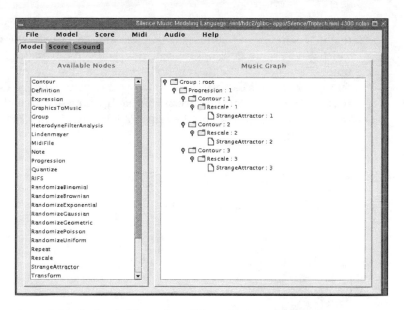

Figure 9-24: The loaded Tryptych.mml file and unlocked icons

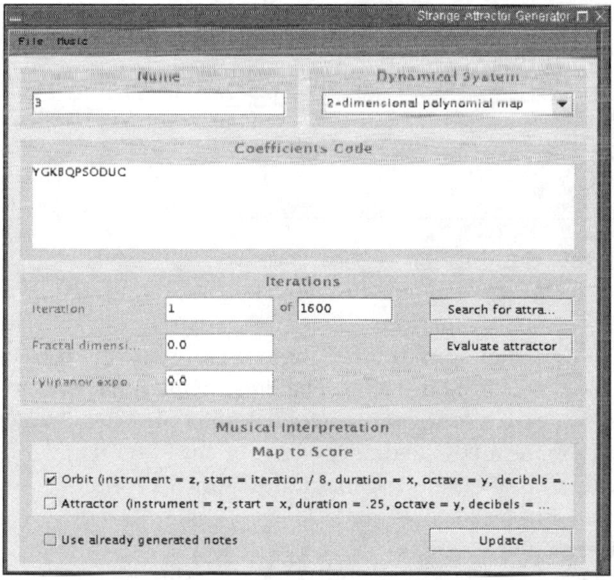

Figure 9-25: A node opened for editing in the Strange Attractor

Moving up the hierarchy, the documentation for the Rescale node tells us that it " . . . defines a bounding hypercube of note space in the score, into which will be refitted, by appropriate translating and rescaling, all the child notes of this node." The Rescale node is the first filter through which the Strange Attractor's data will pass. Among other parameters, it establishes the start and end times for its processing, what instruments are included, the range of note durations, and the range of loudness. Figure 9-26 shows the Rescale edit window.

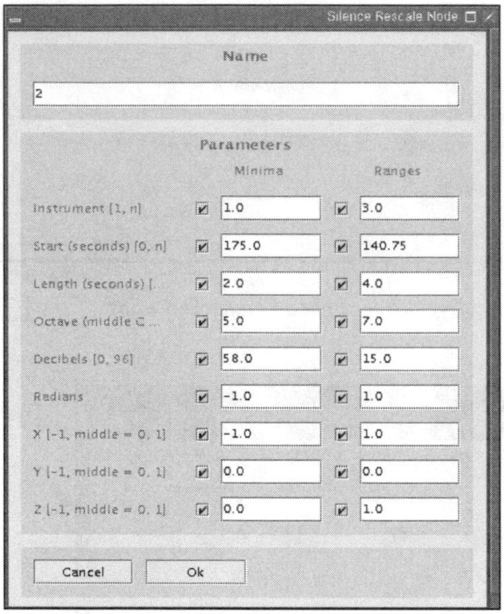

Figure 9-26: The Rescale edit window

The next step upward brings us to the Contour node. As its name implies, this node is a shaping function. The documentation states that it " . . . contains the definition of a series of exponential functions from breakpoint to breakpoint in the form [[delta-time level exponent]. . .]." Think of the Contour node as a kind of envelope generator. Figure 9-27 shows the details of the Contour edit window.

Note that by scaling to 1.0, you can easily create complex segmented shapes with Contour, because your segments have only to add up to 1. In Figure 9-27, the breakpoints occur at delta times 0.0, 0.6, and 0.4, adding up to 1.0.

Before continuing, note that Silence processes the nodes along the Music Graph from the deepest level upward. In Triptych, that means that the output of Contour 3 will be created first, then Contour 2, and Contour 1 last.

Going up one step farther, we come to the Progression node. According to the documentation, Progression " . . . defines a temporal sequence of pitch-class

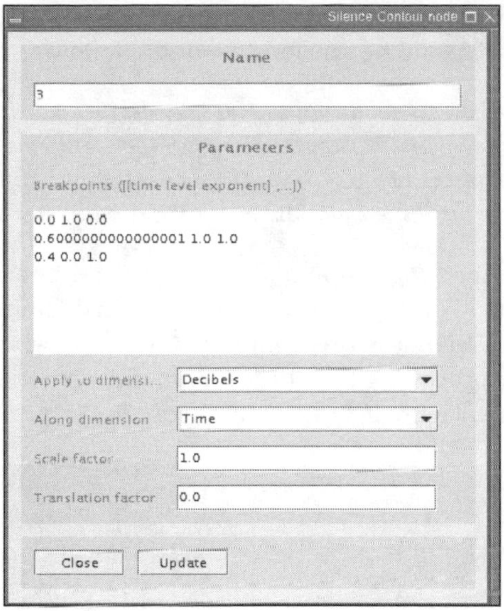

Figure 9-27: The Contour edit window

sets to which the child notes of the progression will be conformed." The format for a Progression entry is [time transposition pitch-class set]. The pitch set is represented as selections from a master 12-note set, written as 0123456789ab. If the base pitch-class (0) is C, that notation represents a chromatic scale beginning on C, and the set 02367b would represent C D Eb F# G B; the set 02478a represents C D E G Ab Bb, and so forth. Figure 9-28 shows Progression in edit mode.

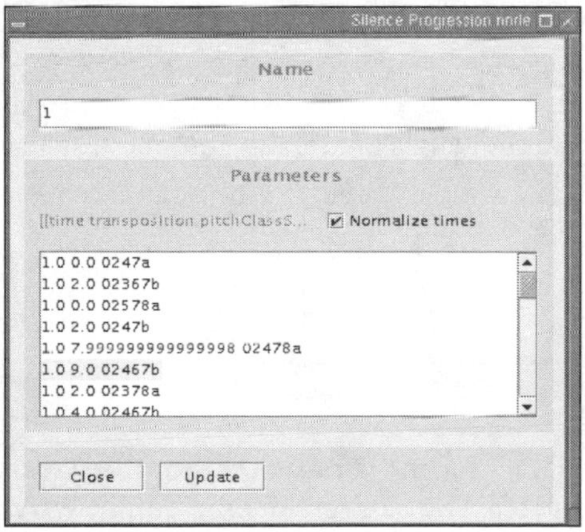

Figure 9-28: Progression in edit mode

I asked the author for some clarification regarding how the Progression node works in Triptych, and he graciously sent the following description:

Time is usually relative: total duration 100 seconds, time a is 1, time b is 3, then a lasts 25 and b lasts 75 seconds. The pitch-class set IS the scale: [the] C major scale is 0 transposition 024579b, D major is 2 transposition 024579b. Or the pitch-class set is just a chord: Bb major 9th is a transposition 0247b.

In other words, the Progression node is a filter of scales and harmonies for the Contour data to pass through. It is also the final filter in the Group tree. Select **Score • Generate Score** from the MML window's menu. When Silence has finished processing the Music Graph, the Score will be drawn in the Score tab window. Figure 9-29 shows the score for Triptych.

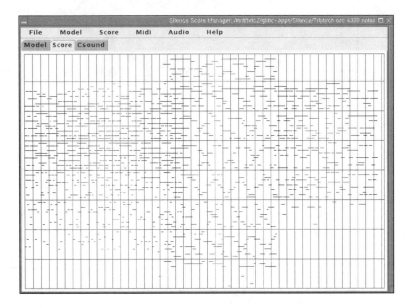

Figure 9-29: The Triptych score

Proceed to the **Csound** tab. The default command string is

```
csound -RWmo7 ./Triptych.wav ./temp.orc ./temp.sco
```

Change it to this:

```
csound -o Triptych.wav -W temp.orc temp.sco
```

The default filenames for the Csound orc/sco files created within Silence are `temp.orc` and `temp.sco`. You can rename the output WAV file to anything you like; in fact, you can rewrite the command string to include any Csound options you prefer.

Your Silence display should now look something like Figure 9-30.

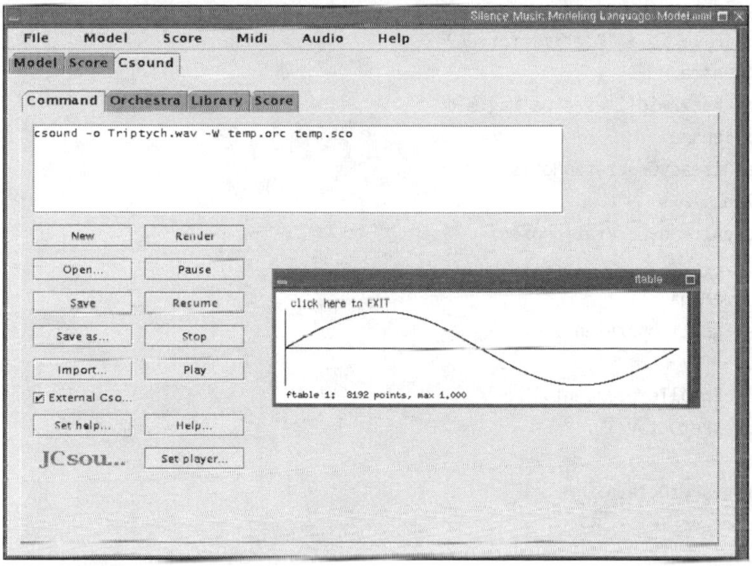

Figure 9-30: Silence Score view of Triptych

Press the **Render** button. If you used the command string given above, you should see the Csound function table window pop up. When the compiling is finished, a "Click here to exit" message will appear in that window. Click it, and your new `Triptych.wav` soundfile is ready to play and edit.

NOTE *The copyright for Triptych is held by Michael Gogins. Public performance of Triptych is forbidden without the author's permission.*

The MML File Format

Before leaving Silence, let's take a very brief look at the MML file format. Using any text editor (such as vi or emacs), open your **midifile.mml** file. You will see a type of programming language known as a mark-up language, similar to the HTML and XML mark-up languages well known to Web page programmers. The MML file format is directly editable within your text editor, allowing you to change the file without opening Silence itself. Here's a look at the inside of `midifile.mml`, opened with the vi text editor (note that some material has been deleted for clarity):

```
<MMLManager id = "root">
<Group id = "root">
<Children>
<MidiFile id = "Ragtime for CAP">
<filename>
/mnt/hdc2/midfiles/caps_rag.mid
</filename>
<useAlreadyGeneratedNotes>
false
</useAlreadyGeneratedNotes>

<ScoreManager>
<useEqualTemperament>
true
</useEqualTemperament>
<tonesPerOctave>
12.0
</tonesPerOctave>
<autoRescale>
false
</autoRescale>
<Rescale>
<scaleActualMinima>
[144.0 1.0 0.0 1.0 8.0 72.0 0.0 0.0 0.0 0.0 1.0]
</scaleActualMinima>
<scaleActualRanges>
[144.0 1.0 0.0 1.0 8.0 72.0 0.0 0.0 0.0 0.0 1.0]
</scaleActualRanges>
<scaleTargetMinima>
[144.0 1.0 0.0 0.5 6.0 60.0 -1.0 -0.5 -0.5 -0.5 1.0]
</scaleTargetMinima>
<scaleTargetRanges>
[144.0 4.0 240.0 2.0 6.0 20.0 2.0 1.0 1.0 1.0 1.0]
</scaleTargetRanges>
<rescaleMinima>
[true true true true true true true true true true true]
</rescaleMinima>
<rescaleRanges>
[true true true true true true true true true true true]
</rescaleRanges>
<Children>
<Note>
<v>
```

```
[144.0 1.0 0.0 0.1546715625 6.583333333333334 43.00011832619492 0.0 -0.4375 0.0 0.0 1.0]
</v>
</Note>
.................[material cut out here]
</Children>
</Rescale>
</ScoreManager>

<CsoundSynthesizer>     <CsOptions>
csound -o ragtime.wav -W temp.orc temp.sco
</CsOptions>
<CsInstruments>
sr=44100
kr=441
ksmps=100
nchnls=1      instr 1
kamp = ampdb(p5)
kfreq = cpspch(p4)
ifn = 1
asig   oscil   kamp,kfreq,1fn
kenv   linseg  0,p3/2,1,p3/2,0
       out     asig
       endin

</CsInstruments>
<CsScore>
i 1 0 0.1546715625 6.58333333333333 43.00011832619492 0 -0.4375 0 0 1
.................[material cut out here]
</CsScore>

</CsoundSynthesizer>
</MMLManager>
```

In this example you can see that the format is divided into three major sections: the MMLManager, the ScoreManager, and the CsoundSynthesizer (which is similar to the Csound csd unified file format). The file format simply provides a text interface to everything you've done in the Music Graph, including the contents of the MIDI file (I have deleted some lengthy chains of notes from the ScoreManager and the CsScore subheading in the CsoundSynthesizer section). Using a text editor's cut/copy/paste routines and other amenities to edit an MML file is a humble but powerful method for making changes in your work. Changes made to an MML file will be enabled when you reopen it in Silence.

Summary

This profile is a mere glance at the power of Silence. The program is very deep, but the interface invites participation and experimentation and the documentation is thorough. Perhaps Silence's immediate appeal will be limited to readers with good backgrounds in mathematics and algebra; however, it is also designed for experimentation even by the most mathematically naive user (such as myself). Michael Gogins is committed to developing and maintaining Silence, and I can think of no better recommendation than to quote once more from his Web page: "If you have ever composed by writing a program, or by doing mathematics, or wanted to, then Silence is for you."

HPKComposer

Authors: Didiel Debril and Jean-Pierre Lemoine
Version profiled: 2.0
Web site: http://hplank.inetpc.com/
FTP site: n/a
Maintained: Yes
Availability: Free, binary-only
License: Held by the authors
Capsule summary: Beautiful graphic interface to Csound and Cmask. Supports audio, MIDI, and VRML output

The HPKComposer Web page describes the application as ". . . a 3D Art composition tool for Csound"—an accurate characterization. HPKComposer presents Csound as a virtual synthesizer, concealing the orchestra language behind a well-designed graphic user interface. A graphic interface is also used to display the tendency masks created by the algorithmic generators.

Getting It, Building It

Download the latest HPKComposer zipfile from the Web site listed above. Create a directory named HPKC, move the zipped file into it, and unpack it with **gunzip hpkc-latest.zip**. Because the program is distributed only as a binary, no building instructions are necessary.

HPKComposer requires Java, either the JDK (Java Development Kit) 1.1.6 (or higher) with the Swing extensions or the JDK 1.2, which does not require the Swing software. You can download the JDK from the Blackdown Group's Web site at www.blackdown.org, and the Swing extensions are available from Sun Microsystems at www.javasoft.com. Follow the instructions included in the package to install the software: It is beyond the scope of this book to detail the installation of Java, but it isn't difficult to do, and you must have a recommended JDK installed before you can use HPKComposer.

HPKComposer is packaged with Windows-specific start-up batch files that you can use as guides for writing your own Linux-specific scripts. I have two versions of Java installed on my machine, and I have two separate scripts for starting HPKComposer. Here is my script for starting it with the JDK 1.1.7 and Swing:

```
java -classpath .:/usr/local/java/lib/classes.zip:/home/swing/swing-
1.1/swingall.jar:hpkc.jar hpkc.commonview.CSoundApplication
```

My JDK 1.1.7 installation is my default Java. To start HPKComposer with the JDK 1.2, I use this script:

```
/home/jdk1.2/bin/java -classpath .:/home/hpkc/hpkc.jar hpkc.commonview.CSoundApplication
```

NOTE *On my system (described in Chapter 2), HPKComposer's performance is significantly better when using the JDK 1.1.7. However, development work proceeds on the JDK 1.2 and it may therefore be more usable by the time this book has been published. HPKComposer was relatively sluggish with the JDK 1.2, but that may be due to my slow processor (a Pentium 166).*

Copy the appropriate script as **go.hpkc**, then run **chmod +x go.hpkc** to give it executable permission (you may need root privileges to do so). As presented here, these start-up scripts must be run from the HPKComposer home directory.

Once you have written the start-up scripts, you're ready to work with HPKComposer.

HPKComposer Setup

Run your preferred starting script. When HPKComposer opens, you will see the screen shown in Figure 9-31.

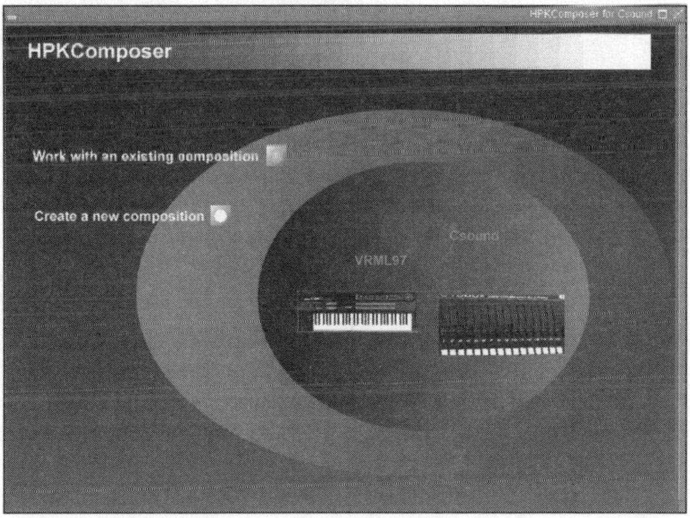

Figure 9-31: HPKComposer

Click on the **Create a new composition** button. A Files dialog box will appear. Type **my_new.hpk** in the entry box, click the **Open** button, and in a few moments you will see the Composition Structure screen (also called the Synoptic view in the program documentation) shown in Figure 9-32.

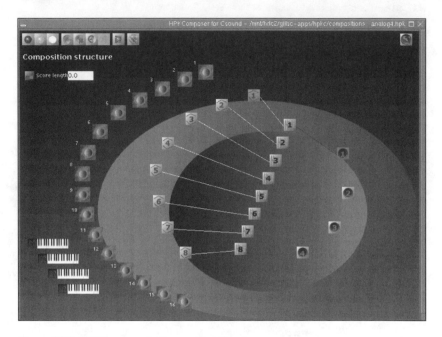

Figure 9-32: HPKComposer's Composition Structure screen

By default, tooltips are active: Move the mouse pointer over an icon and let it rest there, and a small box will appear with a short definition of the icon's function. Move the pointer around the Synoptic view to see the tooltips for the various buttons and icons.

The row of buttons at the upper left corner of the screen provides file management functions, soundfile generation and play, preferences and external helper settings, and modules database management. The button in the top right corner calls the HPKComposer VRML scene editor.

Four sets of numbered edit buttons fill the greater part of the Composition Structure display. From left to right, you see a curving set of sixteen buttons for editing the VRML graphic objects (more about that later), a set of eight buttons for editing the Structure (the Csound score), another eight buttons for editing your instrument (Csound orc file), and a group of four buttons for editing the global effects (such as reverb and echo).

In the bottom left corner, four keyboard icons represent the MIDI connections to the VRML display. The MIDI-to-VRML connection is currently unavailable in the Linux version of HPKComposer, so these keyboards may be ignored. The remaining icon, near the upper left corner, is a toggle for setting a duration that overrides any other setting for the score length.

Before going farther into HPKComposer, press the **Edit Settings** button
and declare your preferred external soundfile player and your Csound executable. Figure 9-33 shows my settings in the Output tab.

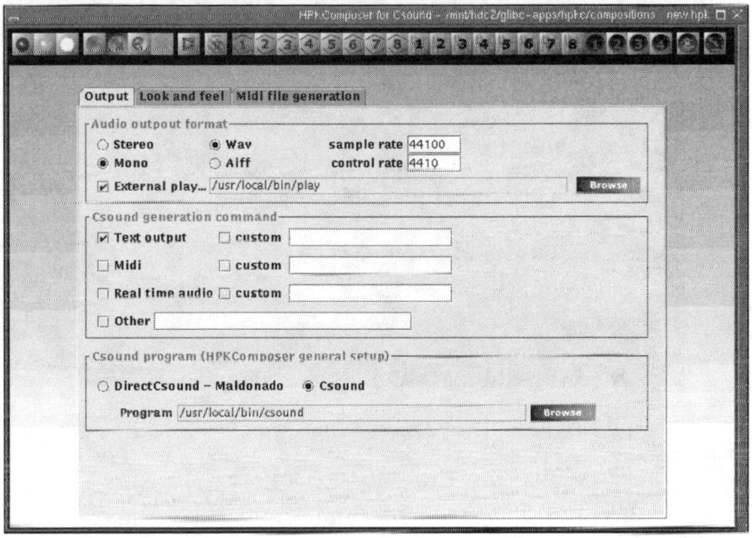

Figure 9-33: Output settings

The Look and feel tab lets you make changes in the interface appearance.
The MIDI File Generation tab provides toggles for MIDI file creation and program change MIDI message transmission. As of this writing, JavaSound is not
yet implemented in Linux Java, so you must indicate an external player in
your **Output** settings. The other controls available on this tab include instrument selection and a MIDI controller assignment table. MIDI channel and an
initial Program Change message can also be set here.

Using HPKComposer

Because our focus is on HPKComposer as a GUI for Csound, we will begin our
explorations by building an instrument (orc file), creating a score (sco file),
compiling the orc and sco files into a WAV file, and playing the output soundfile.

Building an Instrument

Building a simple instrument is easy. From the **Synoptic** view, click on the
Edit Instrument button. The edit screen will open to the HPKSynthe default
display, a GUI for a software synthesizer based on predefined Csound instruments. The HPKComposer window should now look like the screenshot in
Figure 9-34.

Figure 9-34: The HPKSynthe default display

To open the Csound instrument editor itself, click on the drop-down menu at the top right corner (labeled HPKSynthe) and select **Csound Orc**. When the Instrument display opens, click the **instr** button in the row of buttons labeled instr/functions/parameters/global/output. Type in the instrument seen in Figure 9-35 (you can leave out the comments after the semicolons).

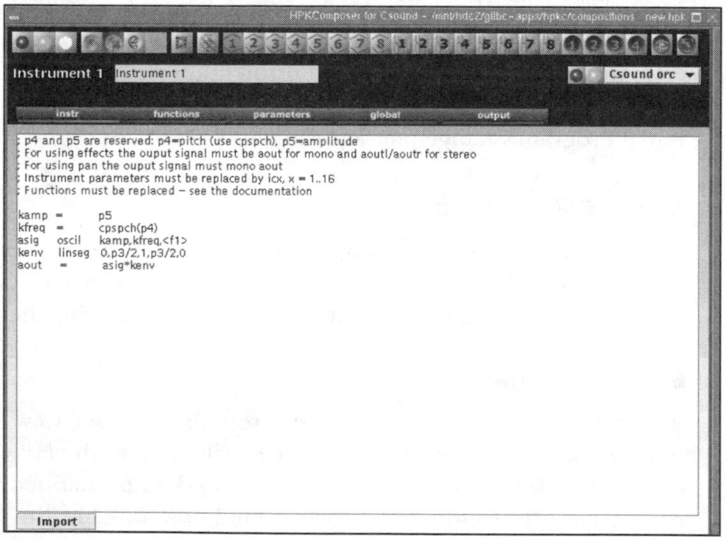

Figure 9-35: HPKComposer's Csound instrument editor

As you can see, there are some significant differences from the standard Csound orc file syntax. The parameters p4 and p5 are reserved for frequency and amplitude respectively, function table numbers must be entered in a special format, no instr 1 heading is required, endin is not required, and the output must be labeled aout (for monaural output) or aoutl/aoutr (for stereo). Other restrictions apply to the notation for panning and effects processing. You can import an existing Csound orc file, but you must make the required alterations before it will work in HPKComposer.

To add a function table, click the **Functions** button. Enter the table number and definition, then press **Add** to add it to the set of recognized functions. This process should produce the screen shown in Figure 9-36.

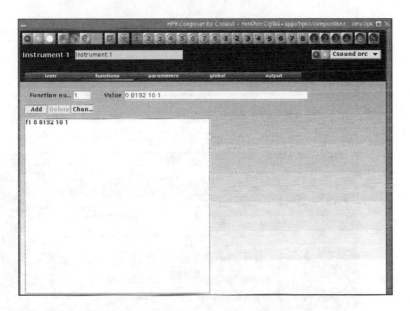

Figure 9-36: HPKComposer's function table editor

For our example, we will skip the instrument's parameters and global sections. Click on the **output** button and set the display to the configuration shown in Figure 9-37.

This configuration sets the output as a mono signal without panning. Click on the first button in the **Dry/Effects** panel to apply a global effect to the output, then click one of the **Edit Effects** buttons at the top of the window (the ones labeled 1 through 4 only). The display will change to the screen shown in Figure 9-38. Note that the globals and parameters labels in Fig. 9-38 apply only to the **Effects Edit** window.

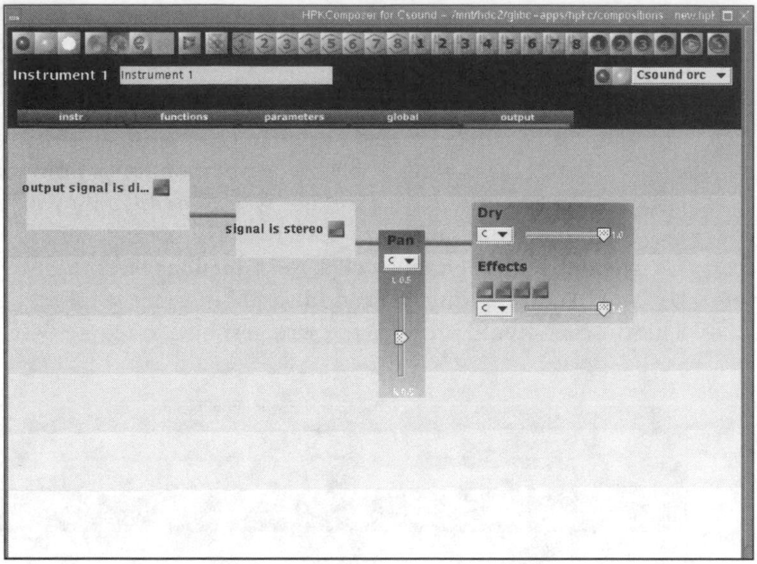

Figure 9-37: Output definition display

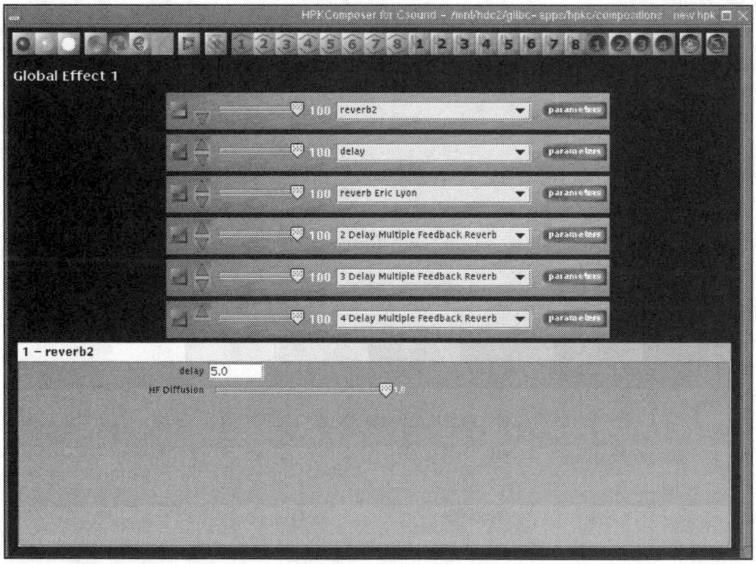

Figure 9-38: The Edit Effects screen

Press the **on/off** button in the **reverb2** panel to activate the connection to your instrument. Click on the **Synoptic** view button (the second button from the top right corner) to see the new connection in your Composition Structure (shown in Figure 9-39).

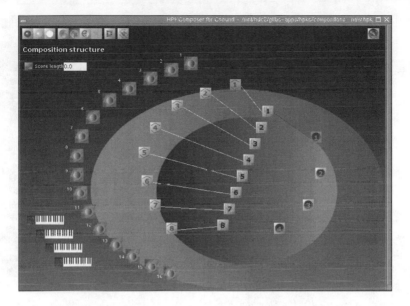

Figure 9-39: Synoptic view

NOTE *The grayscale images in this book may not clearly show various connections and highlighting, but HPKComposer makes good use of color throughout the program.*

Your instrument is now complete and ready for processing by HPKComposer. Now you need to create a score for your instrument to play.

Creating the Score

You may have noticed that all of the edit buttons seen in the Synoptic view are now placed at the top of the display. Press one of the **Edit Structure** buttons (at the right of the 16 VRML buttons) to begin defining your score.

HPKComposer has integrated Andre Bartetzki's CMask algorithmic generators into its design, along with extensions created by the HPKComposer team. CMask is a set of algorithms that create tendency masks. By using a tendency mask, the user can control or constrain a set of random numbers, forcing the selection of a number into the area described by the mask. Various masking algorithms are available, including probability constraints, fractal distribution, and random pattern generation. Many of those algorithms have a further set of adjustable parameters. For example, the List algorithm includes a subset of methods for choosing values from the list, such as cycle or random.

Figure 9-40 shows the Structure 1 screen with the Range algorithm employed.

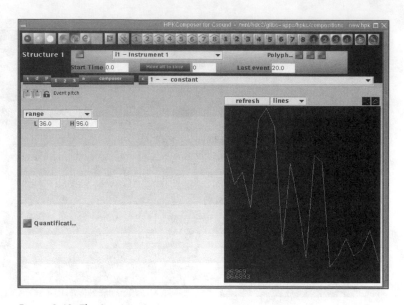

Figure 9-40: The Structure 1 screen

Let's take a closer look at this screen. The parameter shown is Event Pitch, and the algorithm is set to produce pitches between 36 and 96 (MIDI note numbering). Pressing the **Refresh** button will graph the output of the masked random distribution (which can be represented as points or lines). Press **Refresh** again to create and view a new distribution.

Mask graphs can be created for event density, duration, pitch, amplitude, polyphony, and MIDI controller. Tendency masks are a very powerful way to create compositional order out of random output from the CMask generators.

Up to eight Structures can be used to define your score, each with its own algorithmic generation parameters, using any one of the eight Instruments. When you are satisfied with your Structure, Instrument, and Effects settings, you are ready to generate the Csound orc/sco files.

Press the **Generate Files & Sound** button (in the top row of buttons, the fifth from the left). If you checked the Text Output box in your Output settings, you should see a screen like the one in Figure 9-41.

Compile and Play Your Composition

Unless specified otherwise in your Output settings, the Csound compiler will open the function table display. When the compile is completed, click on the table display and that box will disappear. All that remains is for you to press the **Play Generated Soundfile** button (immediately to the right of the Generate Files & Sound button) to hear your new HPKComposer composition.

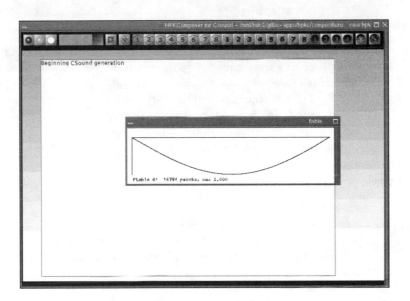

Figure 9-41: Csound generation

HPKComposer and VRML

VRML stands for Virtual Reality Modeling Language. According to the comp.lang.vrml newsgroup FAQ (Frequently Asked Questions) sheet, it is " . . . a scene description language that describes the geometry and behavior of a 3D scene or 'world'." HPKComposer can generate worlds in the VRML .wrl file format; unfortunately, it is beyond the scope of this profile to describe the VRML aspects of HPKComposer in more detail. Interested readers should access the FreeWRL Web page at www.crc.ca/FreeWRL for more information regarding a free VRML97 viewer for Linux.

Summary

Like the other large applications reviewed in this book, HPKComposer offers a multitude of sophisticated features, and it is impossible to fully describe them all here. If you made it through our tutorial example, you can start to dig more deeply into the program's features on your own. Much fascination awaits you: The GUI synthesizer, the MIDI connections, and VRML scene creation are some of the areas left for you to explore. If you have the programming skills, you can extend HPKComposer's capabilities by writing new Java classes and adding them to the modules database. The program is consistently maintained, with very good documentation and examples for study, and the authors are quick to respond to suggestions and criticisms. I have used HPKComposer since its first appearance: In my humble opinion, it is definitely a "Most Recommended" Linux sound and music application.

Other Helpers

Ceres, a soundfile editor (see Chapter 4), is a powerful Csound helper. After directly editing the frequency components of a sound, Ceres can render its output as a Csound score.

For links to other Csound support software, the interested reader should look on the Linux Soundapps page, in the section listing Csound helpers (www.bright.net/~dlphilp/linuxsound/cshelp.html). The latest edition of the Linux Soundapps page is included on the CD with this book.

Cmix Classic

Author: Paul Lansky
Version profiled: cmix-linux-3-31-97.tar.gz
Web site: http://silvertone.princeton.edu/winham/PSK
FTP site: ftp://ftp.princeton.edu/pub/music/cmix.linux.src.tar.gz
Maintained: No
Availability: Free, open-source
License: Copyright held by author
Capsule summary: Non-realtime sound synthesis language with very C-like syntax

Cmix is another venerable software sound synthesis language. Originally designed to create and manipulate soundfiles, Cmix, like Csound, developed far beyond its designers' original intentions.

The canonical Cmix package is available from the principal Web site at Princeton University (see above). Building and installing Cmix is straightforward (simply unpack the Cmix source package with **tar xzvf cmix-latest. tar.gz** and run **make**), though it's possible you'll have to search for a few arcane headers and libraries. Once the system is installed, it's ready for use.

Cmix isn't a language so much as a library of C functions optimized for sound processing. The Cmix score (the control data file) is directed to a command parser called MINC (Minc Is Not C), where the appropriate functions are called as needed, receive their parameter values, and are finally linked with soundfile objects to create Cmix performances and write them to disk.

Getting into Cmix

Cmix's command parser presents itself in a very C-like manner and includes familiar control flow structures such as the for loop and if/else conditional statements. A typical Cmix score looks like this:

```
/*my_first.sco*/
/* Cmix example score */
/* note the use of C-style commenting */
/*
    * fminst -- simple fm instrument
    * p0 = start time
```

```
 *  p1 = duration
 *  p2 = pitch of carrier (Hz or oct.pc)
 *  p3 = pitch of modulator (Hz or oct.pc)
 *  p4 = FM index (low)
 *  p5 = FM index (high)
 *  p6 = amp
 *  p7 = stereo spread (0-1) <optional>
 *  function slot 1 is oscillator waveform, slot 2 is the amp envelope,
 *  slot 3 is index guide
 */
output("foo.snd") /* the output soundfile MUST exist beforehand ! */
makegen(1, 10, 1024, 1)  /* the oscillator waveform, a simple sine */
makegen(2, 7, 1024,  0, 512, 1, 512, 0) /* the amplitude envelope */
makegen(3, 24, 1000, 0,1, 2,0) /* index guide envelope; note arbitrary table length ! */
nfms = 1 /* a counter */
/* repeat the following code body 15 times */
    /* incrementing the start time by .5 seconds on each loop */
    for (start = 0; start < 15; start = start + 0.5) {
    /* begin at pitch class middle C */
    /* play the enclosed FM instrument code block twice */
    /* raising the pitch a whole step on each loop */
    freq = 8.00
for (n = 0; n < nfms; n = n + 1) {
        fminst(start, 1.5, freq, 179, 0, 10, 1000)
    freq = freq + 0.02 }
    nfms = nfms + 1
    }
```

Before Cmix can process this score, you must first create an empty sound-file. This invocation of the sfcreate utility

```
sfcreate -r 44100 -c 1 -i foo.snd
```

creates an integer monaural soundfile in NeXT/IRCAM SND format with a sampling rate of 44.1 kHz. This command makes foo.snd a container for what-ever the input score wishes to pour into it.

A comments block in the score indicates the parameters and permissible ranges available to the called function, in this case the fminst.

You can run my_first.sco (created in Cecilia earlier in this chapter) on the instrument fminst with the command

```
fminst < my_first.sco
```

After some messages fly by, you should now have a soundfile named foo.snd, which is playable by any player that supports the NeXT/IRCAM file format (the Cmix package includes such a player).

If you want the soundfile to play immediately upon compilation, you need only to add this line to the end of the score (after the closing parenthesis):

```
system("play foo.snd")
```

Cmix was not originally intended to be a realtime or interactive computer music language. However, as computers have become more powerful, some very interesting realtime and interactive features have been added to the package. One result of these additions is RTcmix.

RTcmix

Authors: Brad Garton and Dave Topper
Version profiled: 2.0
Web site: http://www.music.columbia.edu/cmix/
FTP site: ftp://presto.music.virginia.edu/pub/rtcmix/
Maintained: Yes
Availability: Free, open-source
License: Copyright held by Paul Lansky
Capsule summary: Excellent update of Cmix with new unit generators and support for realtime audio input/output

In 1995, Brad Garton and Dave Topper began work on a new version of Cmix for the "Indy," a computer manufactured by SGI and designed for superb multimedia performance. It was soon apparent that a number of Cmix instruments could run in realtime. The Cmix synthesis engine was then connected directly to the Indy's digital-to-analog converters, and RTcmix was born.

RTcmix has since been ported to Linux and has maintained good cross-platform compatibility with the versions for SGI computers. It now reads data over TCP sockets, which has liberated the synthesis engine from the interface/parser. MIDI I/O is available. RTcmix instrument parameters can be controlled in realtime via software interfaces (such as the Looching example presented later in this section) or MIDI controllers (such as keyboards or fader boxes).

NOTE *RTcmix is distributed by Columbia University and is significantly different from the Princeton (Cmix) package. The RTcmix documentation pages should clarify compatibility problems that may arise when using scores written for classic Cmix.*

GUIs for RTcmix

Brad Garton has prepared a package of interfaces for RTcmix, including GUIs for X/Motif, OpenGL, and Java. Console interfaces are included for MIDI control and hooking into the LISP programming language. As of June 1999, these interfaces were not yet optimized for Linux, but they are easily converted with a little hacking. Dave Topper's GTK interfaces also offer possibilities for realtime interactive instrument design.

Looching is an RTcmix program that creates relaxing ambient sounds in styles selected by the user. The two columns of radio buttons list the available styles and the scale degrees for the chords of the music. Figure 9-42 shows RTcmix running Looching in its X/Motif interface:

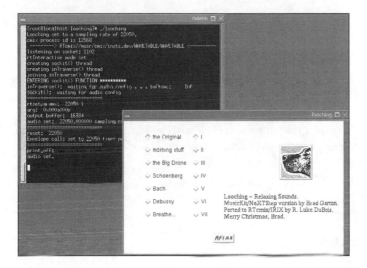

Figure 9-42: RTcmix with realtime interface

Once started, the music will play continuously. The user can change styles and degrees at any time.

MIDI I/O is also being developed for RTcmix. RTcmix 2.0 includes a group of interactive instruments that sense and react to MIDI input.

Realtime Audio Output

RTcmix is a new world for Cmix users. It has excellent realtime audio, a range of new interactive interfaces, and supports full-duplex I/O (permitting some interesting realtime signal processing).

Realtime audio output is achieved by calling one of the instruments especially coded for realtime performance. Here is our Cmix example, but now programmed for realtime audio:

```
/* my_first_rt.sco */
rtsetparams(44100,1) /* set sampling rate and channels for audio output */
makegen(1, 10, 1024, 1)
makegen(2, 7, 1024, 0, 512, 1, 512, 0)
makegen(3, 24, 1000, 0,1, 2,0)
nfms = 1
    for (start = 0; start < 15; start = start + 0.5) {
```

```
        freq = 8.00
                for (n = 0; n < nfms; n = n + 1) {
            FMINST(start, 1.5, freq, 179, 0, 10, 1000)    /* call realtime version of FM
instrument */
                    freq = freq +  0.02 }
      nfms = nfms + 1
      }
```

The command FMINST < my_first_rt.sco runs the score.

Another new feature of RTcmix is the automatic creation of a generalized CMIX instrument. In classic Cmix, the user must create her own generalized instrument, i.e., a Cmix "meta-instrument" containing all other instruments. RTcmix automatically creates such an instrument, neatly named CMIX. To use the meta-instrument, a new line is added to our example score:

```
  /* my_first_rt.sco */
    load("FMINST")   /* calls and loads libFMINST.so */
    rtsetparams(44100,1)
    makegen(1, 10, 1024, 1)
    makegen(2, 7, 1024, 0,  512, 1, 512, 0)
    makegen(3, 24, 1000, 0,1, 2,0)
    nfms = 1
for (start = 0; start < 15; start = start + 0.5) {
    freq = 8.00
            for (n = 0; n < nfms; n = n + 1) {
        FMINST(start, 1.5, freq, 179, 0, 10, 1000)
freq = freq + 0.02 }
    nfms = nfms + 1
    }
```

CMIX < my_first_rt.sco runs the score and should output a scale run played by an FM instrument in realtime.

Using RTcmix over a TCP/IP Network

We can extend our score's complexity by establishing a condition for its activation over a TCP/IP network. This is a very exciting development in RTcmix, so we'll look at it in some detail.

The following score illustrates the basic operation of RTcmix over a TCP/IP connection:

```
  /* strumscale -- very simple RTcmix socket interface to generate a scale
   * uses the STRUM instrument * * BGG
   */
```

```
#include <stdio.h>
/* include RTcmix realtime socket header file */
#include "/musr/cmix/interface/lib/RTsockfuncs.h"
int theSock;
main() {
    int i; int RTpid; float start,pitch;
/* define realtime process ID as iSTRUM, received via an open socket */
/* iSTRUM is the STRUM instrument
    specially enhanced for interactive
    realtime work
 */
    RTpid = RTopensocket(0, "iSTRUM");
sleep(3);
  /* define the socket as localhost (or whatever server) */
    theSock = RTsock("localhost", 0);
  /* send parameters to iSTRUM in realtime over TCP/IP */
    RTsendsock("rtsetparams", theSock, 2, 44100.0, 1.0);
sleep(1);
    for (i = 0; i <= 12; i++) {
            start = (float)i * 0.2;
pitch = 8.00 + ((float)i/100.0);
            RTsendsock("START", theSock, 7, start, 0.3, pitch, 0.3, 0.2, 10000.0, 1.0);
    }
    sleep(4);
    RTkillsocket(theSock, RTpid);
  }
```

Unlike the previous examples, this code must be compiled by a C compiler. The makefile that builds it looks like this:

```
CFLAGS = -O
RTOBJS = /musr/cmix/interface/lib/RTsockfuncs.o  /musr/cmix/interface/lib/randfuncs.o
all: strumscale
  strumscale: strumscale.c
    gcc ${CFLAGS} -o strumscale strumscale.c $(RTOBJS) -lm
```

The application is then run as `./strumscale` at the command line. If all is well, you should see something like the following message display:

```
cmix process id is 3871
    ---------> RTcmix/iSTRUM <----------
    listening on socket: 1102
    rtInteractive mode set
```

```
creating sockit() thread
creating inTraverse() thread
joining inTraverse() thread
ENTERING sockit() FUNCTION **********
inTraverse():  waiting for audio_config . . .
buftime:
Inf sockit():
waiting for audio config
============================
rtsetparams:  44100 1
arg: 0x000a000e
output buffer: 16384
audio set:  44100.000000 sampling  rate, 1 channels
audio set.
========<rt-queueing>=======
START:  0.000000 0.300000 8.000000   0.300000 0.200000 10000.000000 1.000000
========<rt-queueing>=======
START:  0.200000 0.300000 8.010000 0.300000 0.200000 10000.000000 1.000000
========<rt-queueing>=======
START:  0.400000 0.300000 8.020000 0.300000 0.200000 10000.000000 1.000000
========<rt-queueing>=======
START:  0.600000 0.300000 8.030000   0.300000 0.200000 10000.000000 1.000000
========<rt-queueing>=======
START:  0.800000 0.300000 8.040000 0.300000 0.200000 10000.000000 1.000000
========<rt-queueing>=======
START:  1.000000 0.300000 8.050000 0.300000 0.200000 10000.000000 1.000000
========<rt-queueing>=======
START:  1.200000 0.300000 8.060000 0.300000 0.200000 10000.000000 1.000000
========<rt-queueing>=======
START:  1.400000 0.300000 8.070000 0.300000 0.200000 10000.000000 1.000000
========<rt-queueing>=======
START:  1.600000 0.300000 8.080000 0.300000 0.200000 10000.000000 1.000000
========<rt-queueing>=======
START:  1.800000 0.300000 8.090000 0.300000 0.200000 10000.000000 1.000000
========<rt-queueing>=======
START:  2.000000 0.300000 8.100000 0.300000 0.200000 10000.000000 1.000000
========<rt-queueing>=======
START:  2.200000  0.300000 8.110000 0.300000 0.200000 10000.000000 1.000000
========<rt-queueing>=======
START:  2.400000 0.300000 8.120000 0.300000 0.200000 10000.000000 1.000000
```

. . . and you should hear a medium-tempo scale played with a guitar-like sound.

A much more complex example, Brad Garton's Looching with an X/Motif interface (seen in Figure 9-42), is included on the CD-ROM that comes with this book. The Looching example illustrates the possibilities of a realtime interactive performance interface for RTcmix.

Realtime Effects Processing in RTcmix

This final example demonstrates a delay effects processor applied to a realtime audio stream read from the soundcard's microphone input:

```
/* rt_delay.sco */
load("DELAY")  /* load libDELAY.so */
rtsetparams(44100, 1, 64, 1)  /* set realtime parameters: sampling rate, channels, buffer
size, ? */
rtinput("AUDIO")  /* tell the scheduler where the input comes from */
makegen(1, 24, 1000, 0,0, 0.5,1, 3.5,1, 7,0)  /* apply amplitude envelope to output */
DELAY(0, 0, 7, 0.7,.14, 0.7, 3.5)  /* apply delay effect to input signal */
```

This score is run with this command sequence:

```
CMIX < rt delay.sco
```

The realtime response is quite good even on a P166. Faster machines should permit more complex processing.

The Future of RTcmix

Although the Cmix community is small compared to the Csound user base, it is an active group dedicated to improving the power and presentation of the language. Dave Topper has generously donated his time and energy to maintaining the Linux version of RTcmix, and he hopes to improve it continuously. With the availability of graphic user interfaces for it, I expect Cmix's popularity to grow.

Other Languages

With its UNIX lineage, Linux inherited a rich tradition of academic music and sound software. Csound and Cmix are only two of the many software sound synthesis languages available for Linux; others include Common LISP Music, SAOL, Nyquist, and Music4C. Many of these languages expand upon the MusicN series of computer music technologies, but new approaches have come into use, such as the composition of audio processing classes for direct use with the C++ programming language.

Sig++

Author: Craig Stuart Sapp
Version profiled: 1.0.0
Web site: http://hummer.stanford.edu/sig/
FTP site: n/a
Maintained: Yes
Availability: Free, open source
License: Copyright held by author
Capsule summary: Sound synthesis and processing language similar to C++

Craig Stuart Sapp describes his Sig++ as ". . . a set of C++ classes for use in creating sound synthesis/filtering programs—primarily for the uninterpreted elegant environment of a Unix command line."

Like Cmix, Sig++ is really a library of audio signal processing functions that can be linked into regular C and C++ code. To programmers already conversant with those languages, using Sig++ is a simple matter of learning its functions. To novices with sounding souls and a desire to learn more about C/C++ programming, Sig++'s C++ classes and predefined functions provide an elegant solution.

A Sig++ Example: The White Noise Generator

Following is the example code for a white noise generator, written in C++:

```
//
// Programmer:     Craig Stuart Sapp <craig@ccrma.stanford.edu>
// Creation Date: Wed Apr 30 14:17:37 GMT-0800 1997
// Last Modified: Mon Jan 19 04:21:15 GMT-0800 1998
// Filename:       ../sig/code/Generator/WhiteNoise/WhiteNoise.cpp
// Syntax:        C++
// $Smake:        cc -Wall -g -c %b.cpp -I../../../include && rm -f %b.o
//
#include "WhiteNoise.h"
#include <iostream.h>
#include <stdlib.h>
#include <limits.h>
#include <time.h>
/////////////////////////////
//
// WhiteNoise::WhiteNoise
// default values: aMaxAmplitude = 1.0, randomSeed = 0
//
WhiteNoise::WhiteNoise(sampleType aMaxAmplitude, int randomSeed) {
   setName("WhiteNoise"); setAmplitude(aMaxAmplitude); seed(randomSeed);
   outputValue = 0; brandname = GENERATOR; action();
}
```

```
/////////////////////////////
//
// WhiteNoise::~WhiteNoise
//
WhiteNoise::~WhiteNoise() { }
/////////////////////////////
//
// WhiteNoise::action
//
void WhiteNoise::action(void) {
   outputValue = amplitude * ((float)rand()/RAND_MAX*2.0 - 1.0);
}
/////////////////////////////
//
// WhiteNoise::getAmplitude
//
sampleType WhiteNoise::getAmplitude(void) {
   return amplitude;
}
/////////////////////////////
//
// WhiteNoise::output
//
sampleType WhiteNoise::output(int channel) {
   return outputValue;
}
/////////////////////////////
//
// WhiteNoise::printState
//
void WhiteNoise::printState(void) {
   cerr << "WhiteNoise amplitude = " << amplitude << endl;
}
/////////////////////////////
//
// WhiteNoise::seed
//      defaultvalue: aSeed = 0
//
void WhiteNoise::seed(int aSeed) {
   if (aSeed == 0) {
      srand(time(NULL));
   } else {
      srand(aSeed);
   }
}
/////////////////////////////
```

```
//
// WhiteNoise::setAmplitude
//
void WhiteNoise::setAmplitude(sampleType anAmplitude) {
    amplitude = anAmplitude;
}
```

This code is compiled at the command line with

```
g++ -DLINUX -O3 -o whitenoise whitenoise.cpp -lpthread -L/usr/local/lib -lsig && strip
whitenoise
```

Running whitenoise results in this help display:

Figure 9-43: Sig++ help display

In Figure 9-43, you can also see the refurbished command line at the bottom of the display, ready to add an amplitude envelope to my new three-second-long noisy WAV file.

The entire Sig++ package includes the C++ source code for libsig.a and for the packaged examples. Documentation and a manual are available from the Sig++ Web site (see above), and a tutorial is in the making.

SAOL and sfront

Authors: Eric Scheirer (SAOL) and John Lazzaro (sfront)
Version profiled: 1.0 (SAOL), 0.44 (sfront)
Web site: http://sound.media.mit.edu/~eds/mpeg4 (SAOL)
         http://www.cs.berkeley.edu/~lazzaro/sa/index.html (sfront)
FTP site: n/a
Maintained: Yes
Availability: Free, open-source
License: GPL
Capsule summary: Very promising modern sound synthesis environment based on MPEG-4 specifications

SAOL is the Structured Audio Orchestra Language. It is designed to work with the emerging MPEG-4 audio specification (see the SAOL Web site for detailed information regarding MPEG-4). In the author's own words, it provides " . . . a powerful, flexible language for describing music synthesis, and integrating synthetic sound with 'natural' (recorded) sound in an MPEG-4 bitstream. MPEG-4 integrates the two common methods of describing audio on the WWW today: streaming low-bitrate coding (like RealAudio) and structured audio description (like MIDI files). However, the quality and flexibility of the MPEG-4 tools is greater than other audio tools available today."

Currently, the primary tools for SAOL users are the compiler (saolc) and the encoder (saolenc). saolc will compile an MPEG-4 bitstream or an SAOL orchestra file into an AIFF audio file, an SAOL score, or a Standard MIDI file. The saolc compiler is presently "reference" software: It proves the viability of the concept of a music description and synthesis language based on the MPEG-4 specification. saolenc will encode audio files into an MPEG-4 bitstream (see Chapter 7 for more information regarding MPEG and bitstreams).

sfront translates SAOL programs into C code. Its tools make the use of SAOL easier for first-time users. It performs the same duties as saolc, but it is capable of much faster compile times, and it is packaged with a comprehensive set of tutorial examples and documentation.

The remainder of this profile will focus on the sfront tools, because they provide better and more explicit support for Linux.

How to Make sfront

After retrieving the sfront source package, unpack it with **tar xzvf sfront-latest.tar.gz** and change into the newly created sfront directory. Move into the src directory and edit the Makefile to indicate where you want sfront installed. Type **make**, and after a few minutes you should have a brand-new copy of the sfront binary. **make install** (run as root) will place the program in your selected installation directory, and you can now run the various examples.

What It Does

The best way to see what sfront will do is to run one of the examples included in the sfront/examples directory. For our example, we will use sfront as an audio rendering tool. We'll take an SAOL-compliant source file (such as my_foo.mp4 or my_foo.saol) and convert it to a C program. The resulting C code will then be compiled into a soundfile by using a native C compiler (typically gcc on most Linux systems).

In the sfront/examples/speedt directory, we find this simple SAOL instrument:

```
// speedt.saol
// Tests speedt opcode and templates
// Written by John Lazzaro
```

```
//
//
// Both samples from analogue2@aol.com's collection
// of Moog Rogue samples.
//
  global {
  srate 44100;
krate 100;
outchannels 1;
table noise(sample,-1,"noise.wav");
table bass(sample,-1,"bass.wav");
  }
  //
// Noise played at three sizes
//
  template <noise, twicenoise, halfnoise> ()
map {factor, size} with { <1, 381952>, <2, 2*381952+1>, <0.5, 190976> }
  {
  imports exports table noise;
table newnoise (empty,size);
speedt(noise,newnoise,factor);
output(0.4*doscil(newnoise));
  }


//
// Bass played at three sizes
//
  template <bass, twicebass, halfbass> ()
map {factor, size} with { <1, 110848>, <2, 2*110848+1>, <0.5, 55424> }

  {
      imports exports table bass;
  table newbass (empty,size);
  speedt(bass,newbass,factor);
  output(0.4*doscil(newbass));
      }
```

In this example you can see some similarity to Csound code, particularly in the header statement and in its use of pre-filled function tables. However, the differences are striking. The SAOL language supports modern programming models, including support for templates, arrays, conditional tests, and more.

Running **sfront -o sa.c -orc speedt.saol** will create sa.c (the default name for the C code produced by sfront). sa.c can then be compiled into the sa binary by running **gcc -g -O3 sa.c -lm -o sa**. Running **./sa** will create a WAV soundfile with the default name output.wav.

sfront's author has included a Makefile with each example to automate the process, so it is necessary only to type make in any of the example directories to create the output.wav file.

After creating output.wav, you can play and edit it with any WAV-compatible Linux audio software.

Where It's Going

SAOL continues to evolve under the watchful supervision of Eric Scheirer, and its importance will grow as audio software programmers and hardware manufacturers adopt the MPEG-4 specification.

Computer musicians are increasingly attracted to SAOL's orchestra language and its support for modern programming techniques, and tools such as sfront increase SAOL's efficiency even more. I have only recently begun to work with SAOL and sfront, but I do not hesitate to recommend them to anyone who wants to take a look at and work with the next generation of synthesis software for Linux.

Recommendations

All of the systems profiled and reviewed here have their unique values. Csound is certainly richest in opcodes, and its user base is very large. It also has the most helper applications. I recommend it to anyone wanting to learn more about synthesis methodologies and digital signal processing. If you are interested in using more modern language styles, then I would steer you to Cmix and RTcmix. RTcmix also has the best realtime response of the systems I've used, though Csound's isn't far behind. C++ programmers will find lots to like in Sig++. And SAOL and sfront are indicators of the "cutting edge" of SWSS languages.

10

REALTIME SOFTWARE
SYNTHESIZERS

A realtime software synthesizer provides an interface (not nec
essarily but usually a GUI) designed for control of a set of
instantly responsive synthesis parameters. Some realtime synthesizers (such as Quasimodo and RTSynth) are designed to emulate
the control interface to a hardware synthesizer, while others (such
as aRts and jMax) present a more abstract interface in the form of iconic patching structures.

The realtime software synthesis applications presented in this chapter are
different than the Csound GUIs (discussed in Chapter 9), in that the following
synthesizers provide their own synthesis engines—i.e., they are not front-ends
for Csound or any other software synthesis language. Realtime software synthesizers are optimized for response time and immediate access to synthesis
parameters. They are indeed serious tools, but they are also just plain fun to
play with. MIDI input (from a keyboard or hardware sequencer) is usually
assumed for the performance interface. The synthesizer is designed to respond
to a variety of MIDI messages and to treat the computer as a synthesizer module capable of any digital audio synthesis technique. Some, such as aRts, are
evolving into complete production environments, with sequencers and the
capacity to save performances as files. Others, like RTSynth, are purely control
interfaces for realtime synthesis engines.

Table 10-1 is a quick profile of the realtime software synthesizers presented in this chapter.

Table 10-1: Overview of realtime software synthesizers

Program	Synthesis	MIDI control	Extensible?	Command-line	GUI toolkit
aRts	Various	Yes	Yes	Yes	Qt
RTSynth	Physical modeling	Yes	No	No	FLTK
Quasimodo	Various	Yes	Yes	Yes	Gtk
jMax	Various	Yes	Yes	No	Java
Aube	Additive synthesis	No	Yes	No	Gtk

NOTE *Each program profiled here was tested on a rather low-end machine (a Pentium 166), yet response was excellent in every test.*

aRts

Authors: Stefan Westerfeld and Harald Lapp
Version profiled: 0.3.4
Web site: http://linux.twc.de/arts/
FTP site: n/a
Maintained: Yes
Availability: Free, open-source
License: GPL
Capsule summary: Blends analog synthesis emulation with sequencing and external MIDI control, provides a client/server architecture for working with concurrent aRts-compatible processes

aRts (Analog Realtime Synthesizer) was inspired by the modular patching synthesizers popular in the 1970s. Those machines presented the player with racks and banks of hardware modules, each performing a unique function, and each capable of "patching" (plugging a cable) into any other. A patching synthesizer has an entirely open interface, which means that any output can be routed to any input. aRts works in a similar manner; the only difference is that the physical boxes of yesteryear are now replaced by software modules.

Getting It, Building It

aRts is available on this book's CD and from the Web site listed above. After downloading it, unpack the tarball with `tar xzvf arts-latest.tar.gz`. Enter your new aRts directory and read the current installation instructions in the README and INSTALL files.

Before compiling aRts, you need to install the KDE (www.kde.org) development libraries and headers, along with the Qt (www.troll.no) GUI libraries and headers. KDE and Qt are found in most modern Linux distributions, and you can download the latest packages for free from their Web sites.

You will also need to download and install a package called MICO (www.mico.org). MICO ("Mico Is Corba") is an implementation of CORBA, the Common Object Request Brokering Architecture. MICO provides services for separately running aRts programs and processes, such as interprocess communication (which sets up and manages communications channels), message passing (which exchanges data and instructions), and TCP/IP network connectivity. The MICO package contains instructions for building and installing MICO.

NOTE *Be sure to configure MICO with the* `--disable-mini-stl` *option. aRts will not build otherwise.*

When the required packages are successfully installed, run **./configure --help** to view aRts' configuration options, then run **./configure**. The configuration process will notify you if any needed parts are missing. If all the pieces are in place, type **make** and (as root, of course) **make install** to build and install aRts.

Using aRts

Because aRts employs a client/server architecture, you start the artsserver (the synthesizer server) as a background process by entering **artsserver &** in an xterm window (Figure 10-1). Then type in **artsbuilder** to call the client that presents the aRts GUI (Figure 10-2). From this point you select, set, and patch various modules into a sound-creating instrument. When your instrument is complete, its structure is sent to the server, and the server sends the output to the sound system.

In the following examples, you will first patch together modules for waveform, frequency, and amplitude to create a synthesized sound. Then you will add modules for controlling that sound with a note sequencer and MIDI control.

Figure 10-1: Starting the artsserver in an xterm window

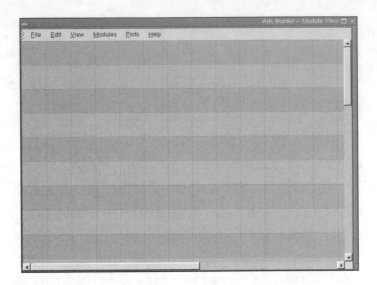

Figure 10-2: The default aRts GUI

Creating a New Structure

Now, you select some modules to patch together into a new structure. Here's the process:

1. Go to **Modules • Synthesis • SoundIO • Synth_PLAY** and the mouse pointer will change to a cross-hairs in the grid. Left-click anywhere within the grid to drop the **Synth_PLAY** module (a basic sound output module with two input ports and a channel definition).

2. Double-click the **cha** (channels) port and set the constant value to **2** (for two-channel output). Figure 10-3 shows the process thus far.

3. Choose **File • Save** to name and save your new structure—we'll assume the name my_01.arts.

Sending an Audio Signal and Synthesizing the Sound

Now you need something to send an audio signal to the output module.

1. Choose **Synth_WAVE_SIN** (a sine wave generator) from **Modules • Synthesis • WaveForms** and drop it above your **Synth_PLAY** module as shown in Figure 10-4.

2. Connect the ports of the output module to the generator: Single-click on the **outv** port, then single-click on the left port of the output module. Then single-click on the **outv** port again and single-click on the right port of the output module.

3. Your display should look like Figure 10-4.

Figure 10-3: The cha port

Figure 10-4: Connecting an audio signal to a module

4. The Synth_WAVE_SIN pos (position) port receives the output of a frequency module. Drop a **Synth_FREQUENCY** module (from **Modules • Synthesis • Oscillation&Modulation**) above the sine generator (as shown in Figure 10-5) and connect their pos ports.

5. Double-click the **freq** (frequency) port of the **Synth_FREQUENCY** module and enter a constant value of **440**. The display should now look like Figure 10-5.

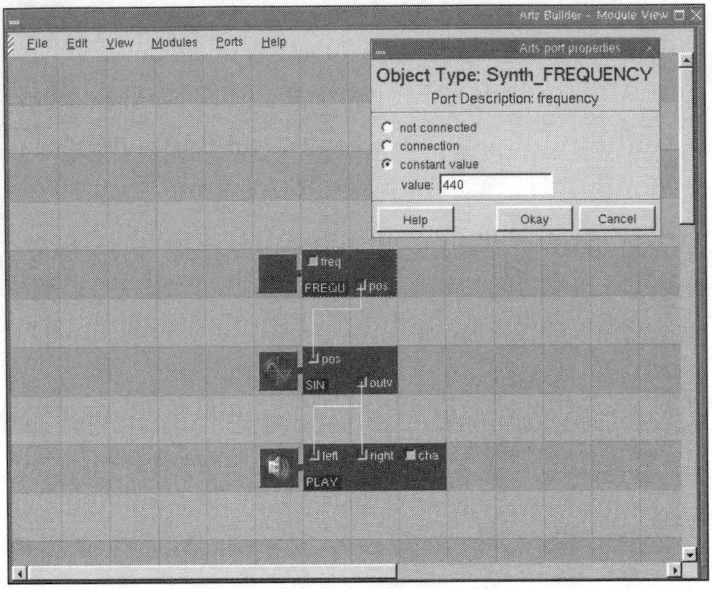

Figure 10-5: Adding a frequency module

6. You are now ready to synthesize the sound. Select **Execute Structure** from the **File** menu. The grid display will be replaced by the status box shown in Figure 10-6, and you should immediately hear your newly synthesized sound.

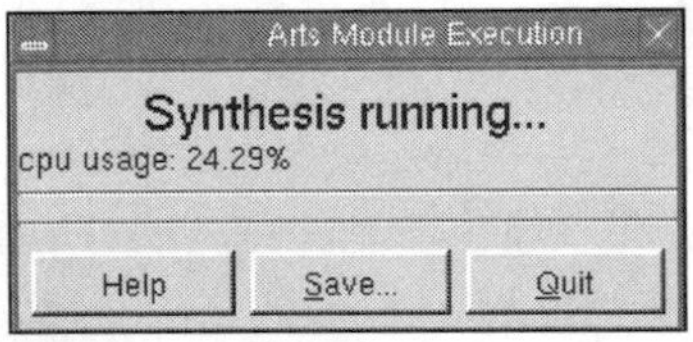

Figure 10-6: Execution status box

If you don't hear anything, double check your connections in aRts (the port connections), your mixer settings for the PCM and master volume channels, and all external connections and settings. If all is well, you will hear a sine wave with a frequency of 440 Hz playing through your speakers. Press **Quit** to stop the sound and return to your structure.

Making a More Complex Structure

To make a more interesting structure, you could add a sequencer with these steps:

1. Open a **Synth_SEQUENCE** module from **Modules • Synthesis • Midi+Sequencing** and place it above the **Synth_FREQUENCY** module.

2. Connect their **freq** ports, then set the sequence speed by double-clicking the **spe** (speed) port and entering some value into the constant entry field. The documentation suggests starting with a value of 0.13; 0.26 will slow it by half, 0.065 will run the sequence twice as fast.

3. Double-click the **seq** (sequence) port and enter your sequence as a constant. Use the format "pitch-class/octave," with a semicolon as a separator. Note duration is determined by the clock-tick divided by the number of notes you specify within the sequence. In Figure 10-7, the first note is a C in the fourth octave (following the layout of octaves on a piano keyboard), followed by a B in the third octave, a D in the fourth, and a G in the third. Thus, these four notes will be played between successive clock-ticks (with the clock-tick **spe** value set to 0.13).

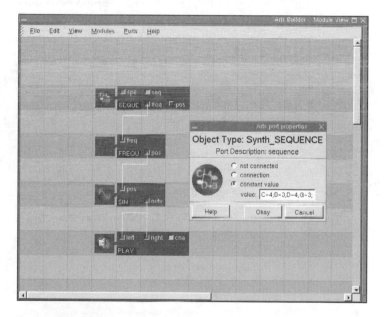

Figure 10-7: Adding a sequencer

> **NOTE** *aRts may crash if you don't give the* Synth_SEQUENCE *module a note sequence and a speed.*

4. Select **Execute Structure** from the **File** menu to hear the sequencer play your simple sine wave. Press **Quit** to stop the sound and automatically return to the structure display.

Using PSCALE

The following steps show you how to use the Synth_PSCALE module to add a simple amplitude envelope to each note in your sequence, scaling the volume from 0 (silence) to 1 (peak) and back to 0:

1. Open a Synth_PSCALE module from **Modules • Synthesis • Envelopes**, drop it near the sine module, and disconnect the sine module's **outv** (out value) port (double-click on that port and choose "not connected").

2. Connect the Synth_WAVE_SIN **outv** to the Synth_PSCALE **inv** (in value) port, the Synth_PSCALE **outv** to both the left and right input ports on the Synth_PLAY module, and the sequencer **pos** to the Synth_PSCALE **pos** as shown in Figure 10-8.

3. Double-click on the Synth_PSCALE **top** box and set it to a constant value of **0.10**. The **top** value indicates that 10 percent of the note duration will elapse before the amplitude reaches 1 (its peak) starting from silence, at which time it immediately begins to decay back toward the 0 (silence). Your display should now appear like Figure 10-8.

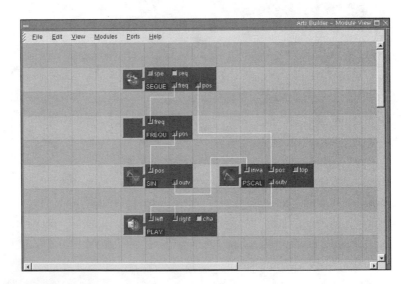

Figure 10-8: Adding a PSCALE envelope

4. Select **File • Execute Structure** to play the sequence. You should clearly hear the effect of the amplitude envelope scaling; if you don't, check all your onscreen connections to and from the Synth_PSCALE module. It is easy to miss a step or enter a bad value as the connections become more numerous and complex. Press **Quit** to stop the sequence and return to the grid display.

5. Save your work.

Setting Up for MIDI

Now you can set up the structure to respond to incoming MIDI events:

1. Replace the Synth_PLAY module with Synth_BUS_UPLINK (from the **Modules • Synthesis Busses** menu).

2. Delete the Synth_SEQUENCER module, replace it with an Interface_MIDI_NOTE module (from **Modules • Synthesis • Midi+Sequencing**), and connect the **MIDI_NOTE** and **Synth_FREQUENCY** freq ports.

Now you need a way to specify how long your signal will be played, because there is no way to predict how long a player will hold a note on a MIDI keyboard (or other MIDI input device). The MIDI note module therefore includes a port named pressed, indicating either 1 (pressed) or 0 (released). The Synth_PSCALE envelope will not work with keyboard MIDI note input (because the envelope must know how long the note will be played), so Synth_PSCALE must be replaced by the Synth_ENVELOPE_ADSR module, which controls stages of the envelope (attack, decay, sustain, release).

Here's how you do it:

1. Connect the MIDI note **pres** (key pressed) port to the ADSR envelope **acti** (activate envelope) port, then connect the sine wave **outv** and the ADSR **inv** ports.

2. In the ADSR module, set **atta** (the envelope attack time) to **0.1**, **dec** (decay time) to **0.2**, **sust** (sustain level) to **0.7**, and **rele** (release time) to **0.1**. These values (suggested by the aRts documentation) will create a perceptible modulation in the amplitude of the output signal.

3. Connect the ADSR **outv** to the **Synth_BUS_UPLINK** left and right ports.

4. Drop a Synth_STRUCT_KILL module beneath the ADSR envelope and connect the **read** and **don** (done) ports. The kill module shuts off the sound when the MIDI key is released. By this time your structure should appear like Figure 10-9.

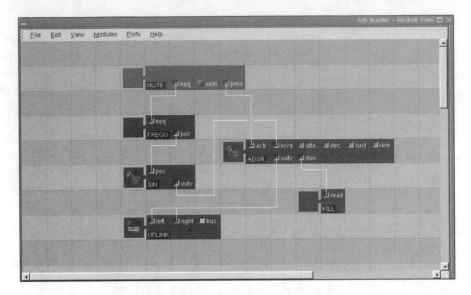

Figure 10-9: Setting up aRts for MIDI input

5. Now choose **File • Publish Structure!** to register my_01.arts (or whatever you named it) with the artsserver database. Your structure is now available on demand to other structures.

Linking to Other Structures

Now we'll create another structure for MIDI control of the one we just saved. Follow these simple steps:

1. Open another xterm and then another artsbuilder.

2. Build a structure connecting a Synth_PLAY and a Synth_BUS_DOWNLINK module to receive data from the MIDI bus. Assign the name **audio** to the downlink **bus** port, then name the client (the clie port) **my_01.arts**; my_01.arts will interpret your MIDI input.

3. Place a Synth_MIDI_ROUTER module over the downlink. Set the **cha** (router channel) port to **0** and the **max** (maximum voices) to **4**. If you're using a relatively slow computer (under 200 MHz), you may need to lower the maximum voice limit. Set the bus name to **audio** and leave the **x**, **y**, **parent**, and **count** ports at their defaults.

4. Run **File • Execute Structure** for this structure and leave it active.

5. Open another xterm window and type in **midisend**.

If your MIDI system is correctly configured, you can now play the aRts synthesizer from your MIDI keyboard. Figure 10-10 shows the entire system described so far.

Figure 10-10: A system set up to receive MIDI input

You now know how to select and arrange modules, connect and define ports, build and run a structure for synthesis and sequencing, and control your structure from an external MIDI keyboard. However, this profile has only introduced you to aRts: The program provides modules for interface and synthesis components, pre-defined instruments and mixer elements, and didactic examples and templates. I leave the further exploration of aRts as your next exercise.

Advanced aRts

The aRts MIDI server creates and manages a MIDI connectivity channel called the midibus. Any midibus-aware clients can be connected to one another for communication over the bus line. Chapter 6 presented a detailed example of a midibus connection in the profile of the Brahms MIDI sequencer.

Summary

The design spirit of modular synthesizers encourages arbitrary connections between the hardware modules that define the synthesis parameters. aRts carries this philosophy into the free arrangement and connection of software modules but, unlike the hardware synths, aRts can call virtually any number of modules desired. Despite the rather daunting set of modules, once you understand the program's basic operations, even a novice can immediately begin building complex structures. The documentation is excellent, the mail-list is responsive, and the authors are dedicated to continuing aRts' development. Whether you want to explore a software replication of a modular synth or just play in an iconic synthesis environment, aRts is definitely worth your attention. Very highly recommended.

RTSynth

Author: Stefan Nitschke
Version profiled: 1.6.2b
Web site: http://www.vtourist.com/rtsynth/
FTP site: n/a
Maintained: Yes
Availability: Free, binary-only
License: Held by the author
Capsule summary: **Excellent visual interface to physical modeling synthesizer, supports external control via MIDI keyboard or concurrently running MIDI sequencer**

RTSynth consists of two synthesis engines, one for polyphonic string sounds (including plucked strings) and one for monophonic flute (or other end-blown instrument) sounds. The effects panel offers realtime control over parameters for distortion, filtering, resonators, chorus, reverb, and delay. With its internal processing done in 32-bit floating point numbers, RTSynth produces very high-quality synthesized sounds and effects.

RTSynth uses the synthesis methodology known as physical modeling. Unlike most other synthesis methods, physical modeling doesn't combine or filter or modulate waveforms to create its sound: Instead it presents controls over the physical properties of an instrument, such as string or tube length, as well as controls for aspects of its playing technique, such as bow pressure or plucking point.

Physical modeling can be rather confusing to sound designers familiar with the older synthesis strategies, because getting a good sound with physical modeling requires some knowledge of an instrument's physical and performance properties. RTSynth provides a simple, effective interface for experimenting with those properties.

Getting It, Building It

Retrieve the RTSynth package from this book's CD or from the RTSynth Web site and unpack it with `tar xzvf rtsynth-latest.tar.gz`. To install the program, simply copy or soft-link the binary anywhere you prefer. `/usr/local/bin` is a good choice. However, you should first set the ownership permission for the program. For best performance, set RTSynth to root user identity with `chown root RTSynth; chmod +s RTSynth` (you may need to become the root user to make this change). Now the program will use the realtime scheduler for best run-time behavior. When you finish your session with RTSynth, it resets the root priority to normal user status.

You should have at least a Pentium 90 to run RTSynth. Of course, a faster machine will improve response time and increase the total polyphony.

Using RTSynth

MIDI control of RTSynth is quite flexible. The program will read MIDI input from a pipe from stdin (the command line), a named pipe (FIFO), or a device such as /dev/midi. MIDI messages currently recognized by RTSynth include Note-On, Note-Off, All Notes/Sounds Off, Velocity, Hold Pedal, Volume (controller #7), Pitch, and Pan. The default output device is /dev/dsp, but the default I/O devices can be replaced by specifying the required alternatives at the command line.

If you start RTSynth with **RTSynth** in an xterm window, the program appears in normal operation mode, reading events from /dev/midi00 and routing the synthesis output to /dev/dsp. Figure 10-11 shows the program opened with the default tiles (the icons are called tiles) for the string synthesizer, flute synthesizer, and the effects.

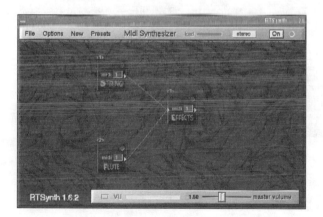

Figure 10-11: RTSynth and its default tiles

The tiles are connected by left-clicking an output tab (shown as a white arrow) and dragging a connector line to an input tab. The synthesis tiles have only output tabs, whereas the Effects tile has both input and output tabs. Right-click anywhere on the **Effects** tile, and a menu will pop up. Select **Open**, and the panel shown in Figure 10-12 will appear.

Close the **Effects** panel, then double-click on the **String** and **Flute** tiles to view their parameter displays. Figures 10-13 and 10-14 show the string and flute synthesizer panels respectively.

Every control in each panel is interactive and adjustable in realtime.

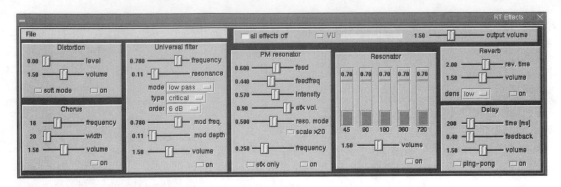

Figure 10-12: The Effects panel

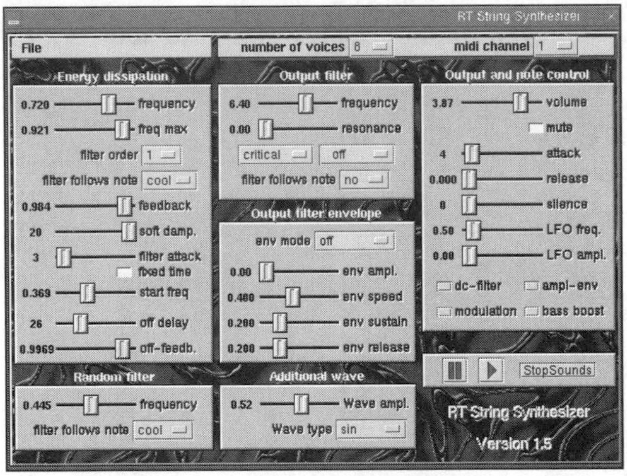

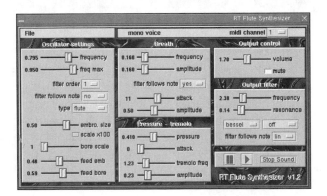

Figure 10-13: The string synthesizer panel

Figure 10-14: The flute synthesizer panel

The string and flute tiles each have a MIDI channel selector (left-click to increase, right-click to decrease) and an on/off toggle (the button in the upper right corner). Turn on each tile, then press the **On** button at the upper right corner in the menu bar. Play some notes on your MIDI keyboard. If every piece is in place, you will hear a plucked string instrument combined with a clarinet-like sound, with no effects. Open the **Effects** panel again and turn on the **Reverb** and **Chorus** modules. In the **Reverb** pane, click on the **dens** key and set the reverb density factor to **hi 1** to deepen the sound of the reverberation. Leave the **Chorus** module at its default settings. The panel should look like Figure 10-15.

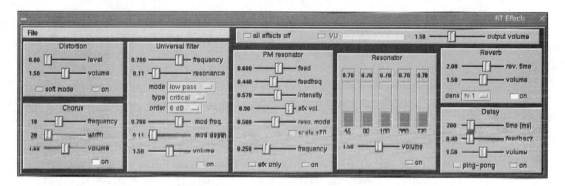

Figure 10-15: Setting the chorus and reverb effects

Now when you play your keyboard, your notes should have a noticeable reverberation. Change the reverb density to low if the effect is too strong. Remember, each tile's panel is interactive and you can open as many tiles and panels as you wish. Their parameters update in realtime; you don't have to close a panel for your adjustments to take effect.

These steps have taken you through the basic use of the program. This profile does not intend to teach the technique of physical modeling synthesis; the interested reader should consult the relevant material in Curtis Roads' *Computer Music Tutorial*.[1] However, like all of the applications profiled in this chapter, RTSynth invites exploration and experimentation. No previous knowledge is required to tweak the parameters of a preset or to create a multi-channel multi-instrument patch.

1 Roads, Curtis. *A Computer Music Tutorial.* Cambridge, MA: The MIT Press, 1996. ISBN 0-252-18158-4.

Advanced Use

You can also invoke RTSynth with the following command strings:

```
RTSynth -o /dev/dspW
```

which routes output to the /dev/dspW device. The line

```
RTSynth </dev/midi01
```

accepts the MIDI stream from /dev/midi01 and sends it to RTSynth.

Pipes

A standard UNIX pipe connects the output of one process to the input of another. A normal pipe uses the | operator to allow several processes to be grouped together on the command line and literally pipes data from one process into another. This command sequence:

```
ps -a | sort -d | more
```

takes the output from the ps -a command (lists all running processes) and sends it to the sort -d command for sorting (in dictionary order), then sends the sorted list to the more command for displaying one screen full of information at a time.

A named pipe (FIFO, for "first in, first out") is a special UNIX file type: It exists as a name in your file system, but it behaves as a standard pipe. Using a named pipe enables RTSynth to respond to input from concurrent processes (such as a MIDI sequencer or software MIDI keyboard).

Let's use a named pipe to control RTSynth with Simon Kågedal's Clavier (available for free from www.sdf.se/~simon/clavier.html), a software keyboard controller with a Gtk graphic interface. Run this series of commands in an xterm window:

```
mkfifo /tmp/midiFIFO
RTSynth </tmp/midiFIFO &
clavier -o /tmp/midiFIFO
```

This feature is especially valuable if you don't own an external MIDI keyboard: You can just use Clavier to play the sounds you design with RTSynth (Figure 10-16).

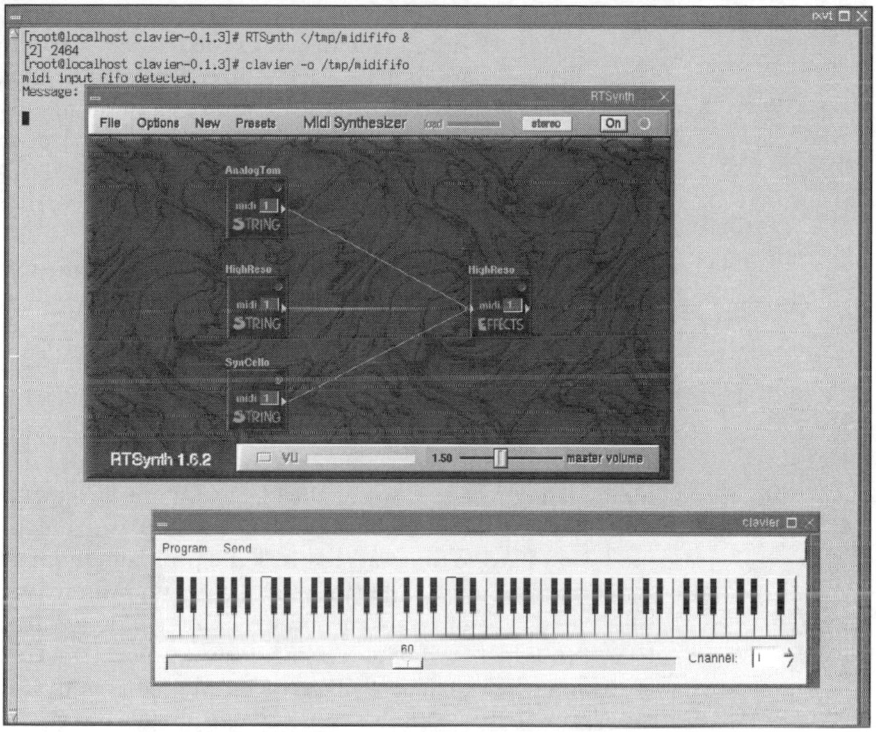

Figure 10-16: Clavier with RTSynth

Effects

You can save and reload your patch files to build your own libraries of sounds and effects. The RTSynth distribution package includes presets for guitar, cello, piano, organ, bass, clarinet, and flute sounds. Those presets are excellent tutorial examples, especially when supplemented by the brief but informative documentation.

Quasimodo

Author: Paul Barton-Davis
Version profiled: 1.0.0
Web site: http://quasimodo.org
FTP site: ftp://ftp.quasimodo.org/pub
Maintained: Yes
Availability: Free, open-source
License: GPL
Capsule summary: Multi-faceted synthesis/composition/signal processing program, with Csound compatibility and excellent performance GUI

Quasimodo is an environment for generating and processing audio and MIDI data. Its powerful synthesis engine allows you to use a MIDI input device (e.g., a synthesizer keyboard or a MIDI fader box) to control realtime audio output or simply run a standard Csound score to write a soundfile to disk. It has two interfaces: Its Gtk interface looks like a modular synthesizer combined with a rack of signal processors, complete with patch cords, sockets, knobs, and switches; and its user interface is for playing audio and MIDI compositions. (We'll demonstrate the Gtk interface below.)

Quasimodo is arguably the most flexible Linux realtime software synthesizer. You can alter or extend its behavior at many different levels (e.g., redefine the interface, add plug-in functions, change graphics), its internal engine is extremely efficient, and it has a significantly greater number of functional modules than any other Linux realtime synth. Furthermore, Quasimodo's code features an advanced object-oriented design, multithreading, formal grammars, high-precision timing, and a highly portable GUI toolkit. It runs on advanced and stable operating systems based on the POSIX OS specification, such as Linux.

Keep in mind, though, that Quasimodo is still very much under development. It isn't hard to find ways to break the program, there are numerous cryptic error messages, and many modules are underdeveloped and/or poorly implemented. The program currently requires you to use the Csound language to write new modules, which may be a problem if you don't already know Csound (see Chapter 9 for more information about Csound).

But despite these drawbacks, the system already has enormous potential. If you want the full power of a Linux realtime software synthesizer and the ability to control almost every aspect of its behavior, then Quasimodo is for you.

Getting It, Building It

The full Quasimodo environment is a large and complex piece of software that relies on many external libraries. Building Quasimodo from source code requires at least the Gtk development packages (available for free from www.gtk.org), the X11 libraries and header files (standard packages in almost all Linux distributions), and the libsigc package (available for free from www.ece.ucdavis.edu/~kenelson/libsigc++/). Requirements for building Quasimodo may change, so you should check with the Quasimodo Web site for updates on required packages.

Quasimodo is designed to utilize both processors in a dual CPU system, but it can be configured for a single-CPU machine. The base processor should be nothing less than the floating-point equivalent of a Pentium II-200.

When you have assembled and installed the various necessary external parts, download the latest Quasimodo packages from the Web site listed above. Read the Compiling Quasimodo Web page at www.quasimodo.org/compiling.html for a description of the current compile and installation procedures. It's best to build Quasimodo from source code, but prebuilt binaries may also be available in RPM format (see the Compiling Quasimodo page on the Quasimodo Web site for details on installing Quasimodo from the RPM packages). Remember to read the configuration instructions at the Quasimodo Web site and edit your configuration files to define your soundcards, MIDI interfaces, and data file paths.

Using Quasimodo

In the following examples, we'll invoke Quasimodo in its Gtk form. This GUI is easy to understand, presenting the various Quasimodo modules in an attractive virtual "rack-mounted synth" display.

Playing Quasimodo

The following steps will set up Quasimodo as a simple through-connection between the recording source of your soundcard and the soundcard output:

1. Open an xterm window and type **Gtk-quasimodo** at the command prompt. A large window (called a cabinet) will open with a menu bar along the top.

2. Select the **Modules** item, and a second window will open showing a list of available modules.

3. Select the **Input** marker, click on the **StereoInput** module, and a panel with two patch sockets will appear in the cabinet.

4. Select **Output** from the modules list, open the **StereoOutput** module, and a second panel will appear in the cabinet.

5. Move the mouse cursor over one of the **Input** sockets, press the left button, and drag the connection to one of the **Output** sockets. Release the button when you get there. Do the same for the other pair of **Input/Output** sockets. Figure 10-17 illustrates these connections.

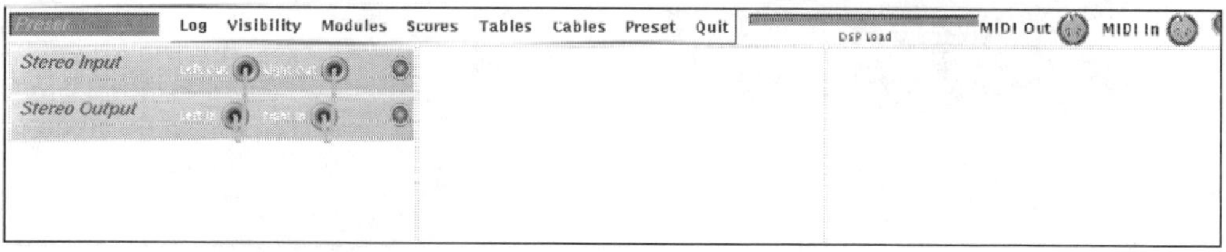

Figure 10-17: A simple Quasimodo structure

To make this connection actually produce sound, use your mixer application to select a recording source for the soundcard and set the volume for PCM playback to a reasonable level.

Quasimodo as a Delay Line

Now let's turn Quasimodo into a delay line to add a realtime echo to an input signal. Here's the process:

1. Go to the modules list, select the **Audio/FX** marker, then select the **Delay** item below it. A new panel will appear in the cabinet.

2. Select the **Audio/Mixers** marker, then the **SliderMixer**. A four-channel mixer with sliders will open.

3. Use the mouse to connect one of the **StereoInput** sockets to the **Input** socket on the **Delay** module.

4. Connect the **Output** socket of the **Delay** module to one of the **SliderMixer** inputs.

5. Go to the **StereoOutput** module and click the middle mouse button (or the left and right buttons simultaneously on a two-button mouse) on the **Input** sockets to disconnect the patchcords.

6. Connect these sockets to the **Output** of the SliderMixer.

7. Finally, use the mouse to connect the **StereoInput** module to two more inputs on the **SliderMixer**.

Your cabinet should now look like Figure 10-18.

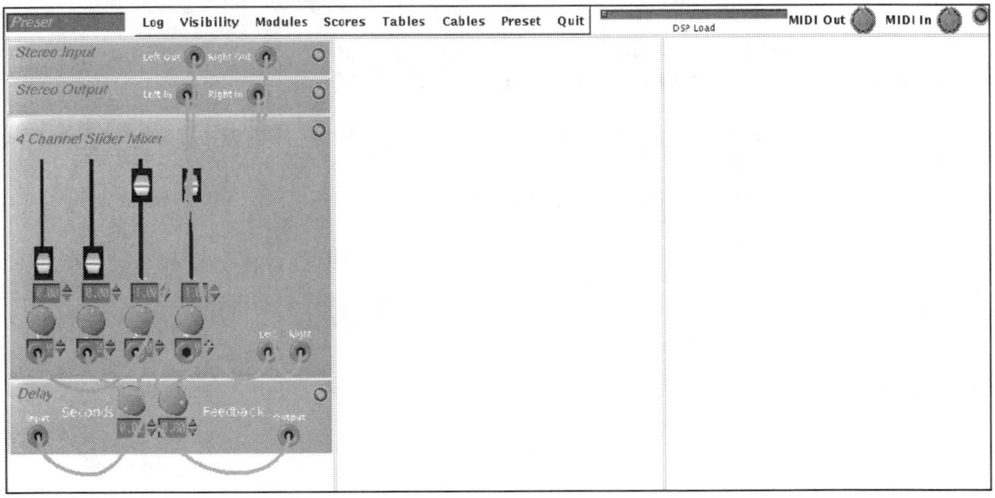

Figure 10-18: A Quasimodo delay line

Note that, in order to start a new connection to a socket already patched to another module, you must first disconnect the patchcords connected to the socket or click on a part of the socket that is not covered by the existing patchcord.

At this point, you should immediately hear any sound coming into the soundcard's recording source. Go to the **Delay** knob on the **Delay** module, press the left mouse button, and rotate the knob to change the delay. The effect should be clearly audible. If you can hear the audio input but not the delay, step through the instructions again and double-check all your connections.

You now have a realtime delay processor running on your Linux box, but unlike other applications that can do this, yours has been built entirely from modular components. To see how the modules make their magic, press the middle mouse button on the big red button of the **Delay** module and select **Show Definition**. A window will pop up showing you how the **Delay** module was written. You can do the same for any module loaded into Quasimodo.

The Future of Quasimodo

Paul Barton-Davis is dedicated to extending and perfecting the program. Plans for future versions include support for other languages for module design and a set of modules emulating the Nord Lead and CreamWare Pulsar hardware synthesizers.

NOTE *The author would like to thank Paul Barton-Davis for his extensive contribution to this profile.*

jMax

Authors: Maurizio de Cecco, Francois Dechelles, Enzo Maggi, Norbert Schnell
Version profiled: 2.4.9c
Web site: http://www.ircam.fr/equipes/temps-reel/jmax/
FTP site: ftp://ftp.ircam.fr/pub/IRCAM/equipes/temps-reel/jmax/releases/
Maintained: Yes
Availability: Free, open-source
License: GPL
Capsule summary: Powerful sophisticated iconic patching language for real-time synthesis and digital signal processing, includes MIDI I/O support.

Its Internet home page describes jMax as "a graphical programming environment for interactive realtime audio applications"—translated, this means you create your sounds by positioning icons on a blank drawing board, specifying their characteristics, and "wiring" them together. jMax is a Java implementation of Max, a music and sound programming environment designed by Miller Puckette at IRCAM (Institut de Recherche et Coordination Acoustique/Musique), a prestigious facility for research in music and acoustics.

jMax blends its language and interface, presenting components that themselves represent large families of services and functions. Unlike the other software synthesizers reviewed in this chapter, jMax includes an interactive MIDI composition and performance environment. MIDI input/output provides an interactive control interface for your digital audio devices and your MIDI equipment.

Getting It, Building it

jMax requires the Java Development Kit (JDK), version 1.1.6 or higher, which is available for Linux from the Blackdown Organization (www.blackdown.org). jMax also needs the Java Swing classes library, available online from Sun Microsystems at http://java.sun.com:80/products/jfc/index.html. The JDK and Swing are free downloads, and you must have them both successfully installed on your machine in order to build and run jMax. As of this writing, jMax is incompatible with the JDK 1.2, and the developers are working to remedy that situation.

You will also need to install Michael Pruett's audiofile library and headers, available from www.gnome.org. Be sure you have installed version 0.1.9 or higher: Earlier versions will crash jMax if it attempts to read or write an AIFF soundfile.

Once you have the required support files, retrieve the jMax package from this book's CD or from the FTP site listed above and unpack it with **tar xzvf jmax-latest.tar.gz**. Read the installation instructions in your newly created jmax directory, then begin the build process. For Intel CPUs you can do **make i386-linux** or **make i686-linux**. Build options are also available for other processors (see the jMax installation files for details). jMax is an X application, so building it will require the standard X libraries and header files. When the build is complete, become the root user and run **make install i386-linux**. Now you can start using jMax.

NOTE *If you have the Kaffe Java compiler installed on your system, it may interfere with the compilation process. You may need to disable or uninstall Kaffe if you have problems compiling the Java parts of jMax.*

Configuring jMax

The **.jmaxrc** resource file must be configured correctly and placed in your **/home** directory. This file designates your audio and MIDI input and output hardware and the default sample rate for jMax's audio I/O. Note that at present jMax supports only external MIDI synthesizers; soundcard synths are not supported. Here is my **.jmaxrc** file, set up for a SoundBlaster PCI128:

```
set jmaxHostType linuxpc
set jmaxSplashScreen "show"
set jmaxFastFileBox "true"

when start {
# set up PCI128 audio          # a comment
   jmaxSetSampleRate 22050      # These lines should be defined
   jmaxSetAudioBuffer 1024      # for your own system
   openDefaultAudioOut stereoOut  # Be sure that your soundcard
```

```
    openDefaultAudioIn stereoIn        # actually includes the features
# set up PCI128 MIDI                    # indicated.
    openDefaultMidi midi                #
}
```

Depending on your machine's CPU and hard-disk speeds, some trial and error may be necessary to adjust the audio buffer setting (jmaxSetAudioBuffer) if you have problems with the continuity of your sound. The jMax Console window will inform you of any problems caused by a faulty .jmaxrc file.

Using jMax

jMax provides various sound and MIDI functions represented as graphic icons that you connect to create what jMax calls a *patch*. Patches can be designed for synthesis, signal processing, sending and receiving MIDI, and interactive performance controls.

jMax is a very deep application, but space allows for only a few simple examples. However, jMax is well documented and includes several example patches (many patches written originally for the Max application will also run under jMax). For information more specific to Max, I recommend the chapters on the Max language in *A Computer Music Tutorial.*[9]

Before building your own jMax patch, try loading an example patch to test your jMax installation. Open an xterm window and go to the jMax home directory (usually /usr/lib/jmax/). Enter the bin subdirectory and launch the program by typing ./jmax at the command prompt.

Check the status reports in the open jMax Console window. If everything looks good, select **File • Open** and then open the **/usr/local/max/tests** directory. Double-click on the **testone.jmax** file to load the patch.

Figure 10-19 shows the jMax console (lower left corner), the files window (upper right corner), and the opened testone.jmax patch (lower right corner).

The **testone.jmax** patch is divided into three sections. The Sine section tests the audio synthesis, whereas the MIDI in and MIDI out sections test the MIDI I/O. As you can see, jMax patches can be self-describing with visible comments and instructions, making it easy to document your patch building.

In the Sine area, left-click on the **Start** box and move the **Frequency** slider (at the far left) upward. If your audio system agrees with the jMax configuration, you should hear a sine wave steadily rising in pitch. The sound's volume can be similarly raised or lowered. Click on the **Stop** box to halt the wave play, then left-click on the empty square beneath the **Random notes out** label in the MIDI out section. If the MIDI output is correctly configured, you will hear a random stream of single notes played on your external MIDI synthesizer. Click the square again to stop the MIDI output. You can also test MIDI output by successively clicking on the **Note on** and **Note off** boxes. Click on the **Start**

2 Ibid.

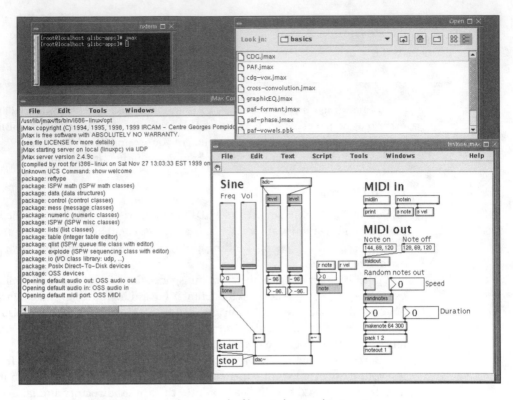

Figure 10-19: The jMax start window, console, files window, and testone.jmax

box again, but this time first bring the **Sine Freq** slider down to 0, leaving the **Volume** slider at the halfway point. Play some notes on your MIDI keyboard: If your MIDI input configuration is correct, you should hear the sine wave played with its frequencies determined by the MIDI input. You can also try all three sections simultaneously if your machine is fast enough (I can do so on my Pentium 166). When you are satisfied that jMax is correctly configured, close the `testone.jmax` file.

jMax Modules

Select **New** from the **File** menu, and a new Patcher will open. The Patcher is where you build and edit jMax patches by connecting various generative and processing modules. Figure 10-20 shows the different types of icons used to represent those modules.

The box icons accept data entry in the form of numbers or character strings, and an icon's function is determined both by its type and its definition. For instance, an Object box may be defined as an oscillator (`osc1~`), a soundfile reader (`readsf~`), or an envelope generator (`line~`). Help for every jMax function definition is available from the Help menu. Opening the **Signal Objects** help file yields the display shown in Figure 10-21.

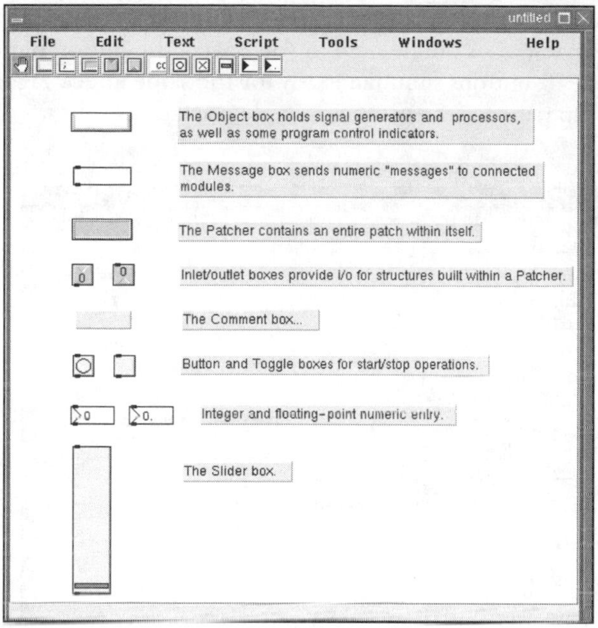

The first screenshot shows a "untitled" window with menu bar: File, Edit, Text, Script, Tools, Windows, Help, and a toolbar. The content area lists:

The Object box holds signal generators and processors, as well as some program control indicators.

The Message box sends numeric "messages" to connected modules.

The Patcher contains an entire patch within itself.

Inlet/outlet boxes provide i/o for structures built within a Patcher.

The Comment box...

Button and Toggle boxes for start/stop operations.

Integer and floating-point numeric entry.

The Slider box.

Figure 10-20: JMax icons

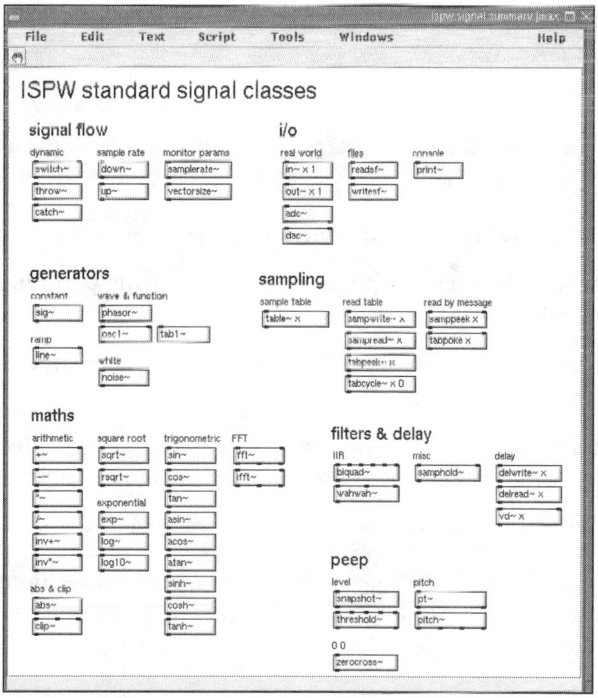

The second screenshot window titled "ispw signal summary.jmax" with menu bar: File, Edit, Text, Script, Tools, Windows, Help.

ISPW standard signal classes

signal flow

dynamic
switch~
throw~
catch~

sample rate
down~
up~

monitor params
samplerate~
vectorsize~

i/o

real world
in~ × 1
out~ × 1
adc~
dac~

files
readsf~
writesf~

console
print~

generators

constant
sig~

ramp
line~

wave & function
phasor~
osc1~   tab1~

white
noise~

sampling

sample table
table~ × x

read table
sampwrite~ × x
sampread~ × x
tabpeek~ x
tabcycle~ × 0

read by message
samppeek x
tabpoke x

maths

arithmetic
+~
-~
*~
/~
inv+~
inv*~

square root
sqrt~
rsqrt~

exponential
exp~
log~
log10~

trigonometric
sin~
cos~
tan~
asin~
acos~
atan~
sinh~
cosh~
tanh~

FFT
fft~
ifft~

abs & clip
abs~
clip~

filters & delay

IIR
biquad~
wahwah~

misc
samphold~

delay
delwrite~ × x
delread~ × x
vd~ × x

peep

level
snapshot~
threshold~

pitch
pt~
pitch~

0 0
zerocross~

Figure 10-21: Signal Objects help

If you have a three-button mouse, center-click on an icon to see an exploded view of its online help. If you have a two-button mouse, click the right and left buttons simultaneously for the same effect. Figure 10-22 is a look at the Help page for the osc1~ wavetable oscillator.

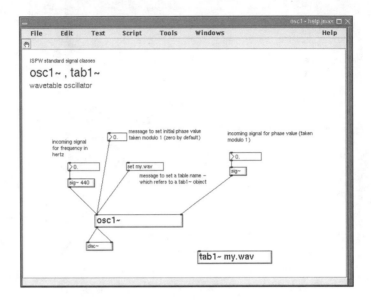

Figure 10-22: Detailed help page for osc1~

In this figure, the boxes attached to osc1~ provide various parameter values to the oscillator. Here's the breakdown:

- The sig~ 440 box provides the waveform frequency.

- A message box sets the phase value (the starting point in a cyclic waveform's duty cycle).

- The set box names a soundfile for use by the oscillator (provided by the tab1~ box).

- The sig~ box at top right provides an incoming signal for the waveform phase value (instead of using the static value in the message box).

- The dac~ box receives the numbers from osc1~ for conversion to sound.

Message boxes with values of 0 initialize their connections. Also, note that it is not necessary to use all of these parameters at once. At its simplest, osc1~ requires only a frequency value.

Building a jMax Patch

Now that you know the available tools and how to find out what they do, you are ready to build your first jMax patch.

1. If any jMax patches are open, close them. Select **File • New** from the **Console** window, and a new Patcher window will open, ready for editing.

2. Left-click on an **Object** icon and move the cursor into the canvas (the blank area underneath the icon menu). A cross-hair cursor will appear, and another mouse click will drop the icon at the location of the cross-hair cursor.

3. Click on the newly dropped box again, type **osc1~** into it, then click anywhere outside the icon to accept this definition.

4. Bring another **Object** box into the canvas, drop it, and define it by typing **dac~** into it. After defining the boxes, small black tabs will appear on both of the Objects: These are the input/output ports for the defined function: Tabs on top are input points, tabs on the bottom are the output points.

5. Move the cursor over one of the tabs, and the tab will immediately become active. To create a connecting wire, hold the left mouse button down while over the i/o tab at the bottom of the osc1~ box and drag the "wire" to the left input tab of the dac~ box.

6. Repeat the connection for the right dac~ input.

7. Bring another **Object** box into the area, type **sig~ 440** into it, and connect it to the top left input of the osc1~ box. This action sends a frequency of 440 cps to the oscillator waveform.

8. Bring two **Message** boxes into the area. Enter **start** into one and **stop** into the other and connect their outputs to the top left input to the dac~ box. Your display should now look like Figure 10-23.

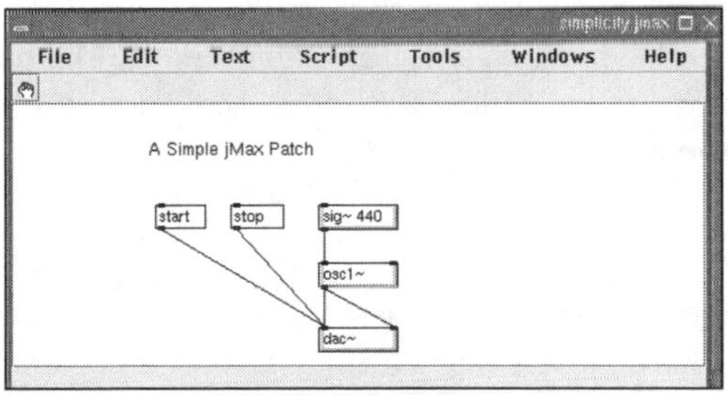

Figure 10-23: a jMax patch

9. Click on the open-hand icon (at the left end of menu bar), and it will turn into a closed hand, indicating that the patch is ready for performance. The icon menu bar will also disappear. Click on the **start** box and you will hear a steady sine wave at 440 Hz. Click the **stop** box and the sound will halt.

10. Congratulations, you've built and run your first jMax patch!

Editing a jMax Patch

Editing a patch is easy. Cut/copy/paste operations are available, and groups of icons can be selected for block edits. Holding the SHIFT key while selecting icons will place them into a group, as will drawing a box around a group of icons. Groups can be moved around the canvas, and the Patcher window will scroll sideways and up or down automatically to accommodate icons and groups as you reposition them. The selected icons can then be moved, deleted, and duplicated wherever you like.

jMax Performs: A Complex Example

jMax patches can become quite complex. The jMax package includes some very interesting examples, and many patches written for the original Max program will work with jMax too. Figure 10-24 illustrates a more complicated jMax patch (included with the jMax package) that creates a complex synthesized sound that is continuously modulated by a variety of means, including random data generators, interactive presets, and user-controlled sliders. It also provides a volume slider for a MIDI-controllable mixer.

To set it all in motion, first click on the **Toggle** for the **randnotes** boxes (the square labeled "toggle randomizations" at left center), then click the **start** box (at lower left). A random sequence of notes will trigger the synthesis patch (the various osc1~ boxes); if you move the slider or click on any of the tempo presets, you can change the tempo of the output. If you have a MIDI-controlled mixer, you can edit the ctlout **Object** box to control its parameters (it sends continuous controller data to MIDI devices) and remotely manipulate the device from jMax by moving the slider attached to ctlout. If you want to explore more complex patches, a useful set of Max tutorial patches is available from http://www.ircam.fr/equipes/temps-reel/fts/doc/tutorials/SignalObjectTutorials.

Summary

Simply put, jMax is terrific. I consider it one of the best reasons for getting into the world of Linux music and sound. jMax is exceptionally well designed and is easy to learn and use. By drawing upon the legacy of the Max iconic programming language, jMax provides the user with excellent documentation and examples to speed the learning process, and the program is certainly rich enough in features to keep you occupied for a long time. The developers have

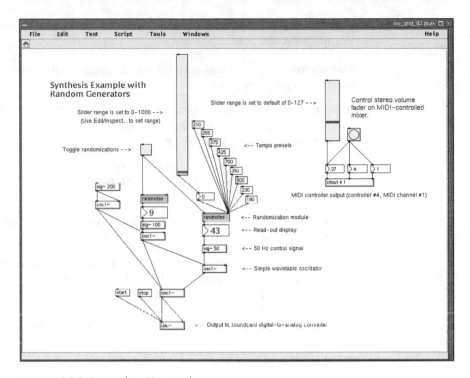

Figure 10-24: A complex jMax patch

established a very active mail-list, and they are quickly responsive to users' questions, comments, and criticisms. With open source code and licensing under the GPL, jMax has great appeal to the Linux audio development community, and I look forward to watching it expand and evolve. Lovely software, most highly recommended.

Aube

Author: Conrad Parker
Version profiled: 0.21.1
Web site: http://www.cse.unsw.edu.au/~conradp/aube/
FTP site: ftp://ftp.cse.unsw.edu.au/pub/users/conradp/aube/
Maintained: Yes
Availability: Free, open-source
License: GPL
Capsule summary: All-in-one realtime additive synthesizer, sample playback engine, and drum machine

Its Web page refers to Aube (it's pronounced "oh-bay") as "the beast within your system," and the program certainly lives up to the promise of untamed power in that description. In one easy-to-use environment, you will find this shopping list of features:

Instruments   A virtual keyboard (Simon Kågedal's clavier again), a drum machine, a loop sequencer.

Applications   A rudimentary tracker (that will generate random sequences); a module for sequencing samples (with arbitrary control input); Syre, an additive synthesizer; a sample recorder.

More toys   A white noise generator, a resonant low pass filter, effects modules for delay (echo), normal panning (left-right placement in a stereo field), and a four-way panner for a "false quadraphonic" sound.

Support   Available for OSS/Free and OSS/Linux drivers (coming soon: support for ALSA and EsounD).

Aube is exceptionally easy to build, install, and use. Its Gtk graphic interface is a pleasure to navigate, and the entire program is great fun as well as serious software for making music in Linux. You may be especially interested in Aube if you're a dance beat composer (Aube has excellent pattern sequencing aids) or if you're interested in learning more about additive synthesis.

Getting It, Building It

Aube requires the Gtk development libraries and header files, available for free from www.gtk.org. It also requires Michael Pruett's libaudiofile, available for free from www.gnome.org. These packages must be installed before you can build Aube. Check the Aube Web site for an up-to-date list of any other required packages.

After retrieving the package from this book's CD or from the Aube Web site, unpack it in your /home directory or /usr/local, or wherever you prefer to unwrap your new Linux packages. Enter **tar xzvf aube-latest.tar.gz** to create a new Aube directory and then run **./configure —help** to see what configuration options are available. Run ./**configure,** then **make**. Become the root user, run **make install**, and you will have the beast at your command.

Using Aube

Aube is a collection of modules—controllers, generators, sequencers, filters, effects, mixers, and input/output ports—each of which performs some specific function in the system. Making sound in Aube consists of creating a sound generator, connecting it to a controller or sequencer, adding effects or filtering, and mixing audio channels to send to the output stage. This profile focuses on Aube as a realtime software synthesizer, so let's set up an Aube system using the Syre additive synthesis module for our sound generation engine.

Setting Up a System

Type **aube** in an xterm window. A single module will appear containing the BPM (beats per minute) tempo slider, and a menu bar with File and Modules menus (shown in the upper left corner of Figure 10-25). Your first arrangement of Aube modules will be designed to drive an additive synthesizer by a note-sequencer, adding some delay to the sound and mixing the synthesis and delay outputs to the final audio output stage. Select the following modules from the BPM window's Modules menu and set their inputs according to Table 10-2.

Table 10-2: Aube module input settings

Module	Input
Atonal Loop	(None)
Syre	Atonal Loop
Delay	Syre
Mixer	Syre/Delay
Output	Mixer

The resulting Aube audio chain, Sequencer • Synthesizer • Effects Unit • Mixer Output, is shown in Figure 10-25. Bear in mind that this chain is only one possible arrangement. Each module that receives input can select from any of the output sources (Syre, the delay line, and the mixer in this example), and the mixer expands to accommodate more generators as needed.

Activate this structure by clicking the **On** button in the top left corner of each module, saving the **Line Out** module for last. Before turning on the line-out, bring the mixer's master volume down to the half-way point or lower to avoid any sudden spike in the audio output. (An audio spike can potentially damage your speakers.)

Because the settings are self-explanatory for the mixer, the delay line, and the output module, we'll take a closer look at just the modules for the sequencer and the synth.

The Sequencer

The Atonal Loop module (Figure 10-26) is a simple looping pattern sequencer. Its basic loop is a sequence of four beats, each divided into four parts (that is, 16 sixteenth notes in 4/4 time). The slider determines the pitch, and the button beneath each slider toggles the accented and unaccented beat. A beat is silent if the slider is at the 0 position.

The Synthesizer

Additive synthesis is the technique of adding different sine waves together to create a sound. But because additive synthesis requires at least 24 sine waves to

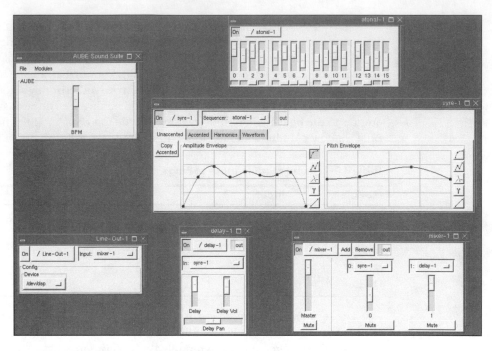

Figure 10-25: The system outlined in Table 10-2

Figure 10-26: The Atonal Loop module

create a complex, interesting sound, the required control over the separate envelopes and phase points becomes more a curse than a blessing. Various methods have been devised to ease this odd problem of having *too much* control over sound generation in additive synthesis, and Aube's Syre synthesizer provides a couple of handy tools for designing an additive synth sound.

Harmonics

The sliders in the Harmonics window adjust the intensity for each of 32 harmonics. You can manually adjust each slider yourself, or you can use Syre's handy randomization button, then clear only the odd-numbered harmonics. You can also clear all the slider settings to a "flat" distribution and start over. Figure 10-27 shows the result of a Clear • Randomize • Clear-Odd sequence.

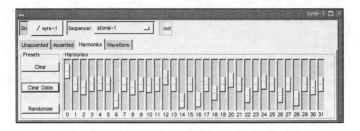

Figure 10-27: The Harmonics window

Graphic Envelope Editors

Using the graphic envelope editors is straightforward: Click anywhere in the graph to add a node to the envelope shape. Bring the cross-hair pointer over a node to pull it into a new position. The drawing toolkit provides line-segment and spline (smooth) curves, a freehand drawing pencil, a ramped line, and a gamma curve creation tool. The ability to copy between the accented and unaccented envelopes is another nice touch to the editor.

Figure 10-28 shows the Accented envelope editor with its settings copied from the Unaccented tab shown in Figure 10-25.

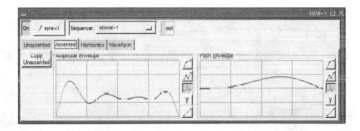

Figure 10-28: The Accented envelope editor

Waveforms

Classical additive synthesis assumes only the sine wave for its waveform source, but Syre provides sine, square, and sawtooth waveforms as well as white noise. Click the **Waveform** tab for the display in Figure 10-29.

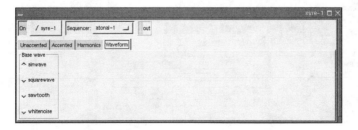

Figure 10-29: The Waveform tab

Experiment with the Example

Make some settings in the loop sequencer and adjust some sliders in the synth. Double-check that all other **On** buttons are depressed, then turn on the **Line Output** module. Assuming your audio connections are correct and you have raised the levels for the master volume and PCM channels in your soundcard mixer, you should immediately hear a looping sequence playing with the sound created by your additive synthesizer.

Now play around with the settings in any and all of the modules, turning them on and off at will. Audio output can be halted either by pressing the **Mute** button beneath the **Master** slider in the mixer or by turning off the **Line-out** module. Aube will update parameter changes in realtime. However, some edits will cause sequence output to stagger, at least on my Pentium 166. A faster machine may eliminate that undesirable effect.

Select **Save Workspace** in the **File** menu to save your work.

Going Farther with Aube

Aube is much more than a realtime additive synthesizer. Figure 10-30 shows Aube set up as a drum machine, triggering a user-defined sample set. See if you can figure the connections between the modules in the display.

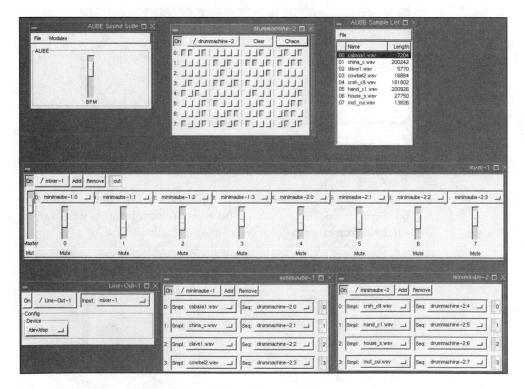

Figure 10-30: Aube set up as a drum machine

I leave the rest of Aube for you to discover.

Closing Remarks

Aube is still in development, so you should check the Web site for news about the latest versions. The documentation was almost nonexistent (a single manual page) when I tested version 0.21.1, but the program is so easy to use that I never missed it. The author is responsive to email inquiries and requests for help, and he continues to develop the beast in my Linux system. I look forward to our next confrontation.

11

MUSIC NOTATION PROGRAMS

Music notation programs, which allow you to print high-quality scores on any PostScript-capable printer, come in two major types: programs that transcribe an input file or performance into standard notation, and music formatting programs based on a music specification language. This chapter covers three Linux music notation applications: Common Music Notation (one of the oldest and most sophisticated packages for the preparation of musical scores), Rosegarden, and Mup.

Of the three programs profiled, Common Music Notation is my first choice for complex scoring, Rosegarden is best for quick MIDI-to-notation conversion, and Mup is well-suited for preparing scores for small- to medium-size musical groups. I consider these particular programs to be the best Linux music notation software available, based on the criteria of ease of installation, ease of use, and range of notation symbols.

Common Music Notation

Author: Bill Schottstaedt
Version profiled: Common Music Notation 17-Aug-99
Web site: http://ccrma-www.stanford.edu/CCRMA/Software/cmn/
cmn-manual/cmn.html
FTP site: ftp://ccrma-ftp.stanford.edu/pub/LISP/
Maintained: Yes
Availability: Free, open-source
License: Held by the author
Capsule summary: Exceptionally flexible symbol palette, perfect for notating
arbitrarily complex scores

Common Music Notation (CMN) is a powerful system for creating and editing complex musical scores. It is a LISP-based language, easy to learn and use, and has a full complement of music symbols and other scoring amenities (such as score sizing and text underlay). You can view CMN-created encapsulated Post-Script (eps) files with the standard Linux PostScript viewers (e.g., Ghostview and Ghostscript) or the program's own handy viewer (xcmnw), which can be called from within a CMN specification file. You can print files with any Post-Script-compatible printer.

Common Music Notation is one of the most powerful notation programs I've ever worked with, even though it lacks a mouse-entry graphic interface. The language itself is really quite straightforward and easy to learn, as are its viewing and printing capabilities. If you need a notation program capable of handling almost any scoring requirement, Common Music Notation might be just what you're looking for.

Getting It, Building It

To use CMN, you must have a working version of the LISP language installed. Most Linux distributions include some version of LISP as an installable development package. Almost all versions of LISP should work fine with Common Music Notation, but I highly recommend Allegro Common Lisp, available for free from Franz, Inc. at www.franz.com.

When you have LISP installed, download the latest version of Common Music Notation from the Stanford FTP site listed above. Place it in `/usr/local` or your `/home` directory, unpack the software with `tar xzvf cmn.tar.gz`, enter your newly created `cmn` directory, and invoke your LISP interpreter. When the LISP prompt appears, type in `(load "cmn-all.lisp")` and grab a cup of coffee while LISP builds the Common Music Notation "fast-load" (`fasl`) files. This will take a while, but subsequent loads will take place very quickly. After all the files have loaded, type `(in-package :cmn)` at the LISP prompt, and the entire wealth of Common Music Notation will now be accessible.

xcmnw

By default, Common Music Notation sends its output to an eps file named `aaa.eps`. Like everything else in CMN, this default output designation can be changed. However, CMN's in-line viewer, xcmnw, lets you instantly preview your score without a PostScript viewer, so there is no need to change the default output designation.

You can build xcmnw with the following command:

```
gcc xcmnw.c -o xcmnw -L/usr/X11R6/lib -lXm -lXp -lXt -lXext -lX11 -lm
```

Note that xcmnw requires either the Motif graphics libraries or the free LessTif (www.lesstif.org) libraries (I built xcmnw with LessTif with no problems). The other required X libraries are standard with nearly all Linux distributions. Also note that CMN does not require xcmnw, which is provided only as an amenity for quick previewing.

Using Common Music Notation

In an xterm (or at the console if you won't use the xcmnw program), call the Common Music Notation image with **(load "cmn-all.lisp")** and load the package with **(in-package :cmn)** to get to the Common Music Notation prompt. The LISP interpreter is now set up to process Common Music Notation directives. Entering this line at the interpreter prompt:

```
(cmn staff treble c4 q)
```

instructs Common Music Notation to create a single staff with a treble clef and a quarter note at middle C. CMN uses common practice notation—if you are unfamiliar with this subject, you should check out George Heussenstamm's *Norton Manual of Music Notation*[1] or Gerd Castan's online material at http://www.s-line.de/homepages/gerd_castan/compmus/musicnotation_e.html.

To view the resulting `aaa.eps` output file created by the code above, use your PostScript viewer or add an output designator to view it with xcmnw. Typing this line at the prompt:

```
(cmn (output-type :x) staff treble c4 q)
```

will open the xcmnw window with the display shown in Figure 11-1.

---

1 Heussenstamm, George. *The Norton Manual of Music Notation.* New York W. W. Norton, 1987. ISBN 0393955265.

Figure 11-1: Middle C in xcmnw

Now add a few more notes by entering this line into the interpreter:

```
(cmn (output-type :x) staff treble c4 q d4 e e4 e f4 h)
```

You should then see the xcmnw window display the screen shown in Figure 11-2.

Figure 11-2: A slightly more complex CMN example

Save your file by entering **(cmn-store)** at the interpreter prompt. It will be saved as hi.cmn by default, but if you want to rename it during the save, enter this command at the prompt:

```
(cmn-store *cmn-score* "my_new.cmn")
```

You can then load your file later with this command:

```
(load "my_new.cmn")
```

Congratulations, you have already mastered the basics of Common Music Notation! It really is that simple to use.

Advanced Use

Now let's move on to a more complex example. The following is a slightly altered version of an example from the excellent Common Music Notation documentation:

```
(cmn (output-type :x) (size 40)
  (system brace
    (staff treble (meter 6 8)
      (c4 e. tenuto) (d4 s) (ef4 e sf)
      (c4 e) (d4 s) (en4 s) (fs4 e (fingering 3)))
    (staff treble (meter 3 4)
      (c5 e. marcato) (d5 s bartok-pizzicato) (ef5 e)
      (c5 e staccato tenuto) (d5 s down-bow) (en5 s) (fs5 e)))
  (system bracket
    (staff bar bass (meter 6 16)
      (c4 e. wedge) (d4 s staccato) (ef4 e left-hand-pizzicato)
      (c4 e tenuto accent rfz) (d4 s mordent) (en4 s pp) (fs4 e fermata))))
```

This example illustrates one of the program's greatest strengths, its conformance to standard music notation terminology. This "common practice notation"—including such terms as brace, staff, meter, tenuto, marcato, and so on—makes it very easy for musicians to understand the meaning of a CMN score specification file.

Figure 11-3 shows the above example in the xcmnw window.

Figure 11-3: An even more complex CMN example

You can type longer files such as the above example directly into the interpreter, but this method quickly becomes unmanageable. One way to put a large code listing into the interpreter is to open an xterm window, invoke your favorite text editor (vi, of course), edit the CMN specification files there, then copy and paste from the xterm into the LISP interpreter. Of course, you can also simply save the code as a `.cmn` file in vi and load it in CMN as described in the previous section.

As you can see, Common Music Notation provides a wealth of performance technique indicators as well as a full range of note types, rests, and other musical symbols. Another of CMN's great strengths is the freedom to arrange symbols in virtually any fashion, lending Common Music Notation the power to create very complex scores, as seen in author Bill Schottstaedt's example from the CMN documentation, rendered in the Ghostview PostScript file viewer (Figure 11-4).

The following code listing creates the contents of the treble clef in the upper system (the grand staff at the top) of Figure 11-4:

```
;;; -*- syntax: common-lisp; package: cmn; base: 10; mode: lisp -*-
;;; This example shows uses of invisible notes (a note with (scale 0 0))
;;; to attach slurs to, and the dy message to an explicit beam.
(cmn (size 40)
 (automatic-ties nil)
 (automatic-rests nil)
 (system brace
   (setf stf1 (staff treble
   (a3 (rq 1/16) (scale 0 0) (setf slur1 (begin-slur (dy0 -.5))))
   (cs4 (rq 1/16) (onset 1/16) (setf ib1 (beam- (dy .25))) (setf sl1 (tie-)))
   (e4 (rq 1/16) (-beam- ib1) (setf sl2 (tie-)))
   (b4 (rq 1/16) (-beam- ib1) (setf sl3 (tie- (tie-curvature .33))))
   (as4 (rq 1/16) (-beam- ib1) (setf sl4 (tie-)))
   (ds5 (rq 1/16) (-beam- ib1) (setf sl5 (tie- (tie-direction :down))))
   (g5 (rq 1/16) (-beam- ib1) (setf sl6 (tie- (tie-direction :down))))
   (as5 (rq 1/16) (-beam- ib1) (setf sl7 (tie-)))
   (d6 (onset .5) (scale 0 0) (end-slur slur1))
       (chord (notes (c4 (-tie sl1))
                     (e4 (-tie sl2))
                     (a4 (-tie sl3))
                     (b4 (-tie sl4))
                     (d5 (-tie sl5))
                     (g5 (-tie sl6))
                     (a5 (-tie sl7)))
       h (onset .5) stem-down (diminuendo (onset-offset .25) (duration 1.25)))
     (cs4 e (onset (+ 2.5 .25)) stem-down begin-beam)
     (cn4 s (onset (+ 2.5 .75)) stem-down end-beam (begin-tie (tie-direction :down)))
     (c4 q (pp (dy -.75)) stem-down end-tie)))
```

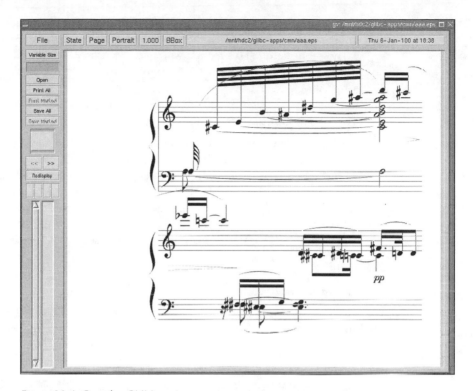

Figure 11-4: Complex CMN scoring

Closing Remarks

Figure 11-4 clearly demonstrates the power and flexibility of Common Music Notation, yet we've barely scratched the surface: Among other features, CMN lets you underlay text, colorize symbols, and add new graphics. There is also an interface for Common Music Notation and the Common LISP Music synthesis language that lets you play your scores via the synthesis methods in Common LISP Music. If you run into trouble, Bill Schottstaedt continues to develop Common Music Notation and is quick to help with any difficulties.

Rosegarden

Authors: Chris Cannam, Andy Green, Richard Bown
Version profiled: 2.1
Web site: http://www.bath.ac.uk/~masjpf/rose.html
FTP site: n/a
Maintained: Yes
Availability: Free, open-source
License: GPL
Capsule summary: Integrated MIDI sequencer/notation program with graphic notation editor

Rosegarden wears many hats: It is a full-featured MIDI sequencer, a Csound score-creation utility, and a tool for the creation and editing of music scores in standard notation. This section will focus on its application as a notation editor, but we shall see how this feature integrates with the other aspects of the program.

Getting It, Building It

Retrieve the latest version from the Rosegarden Web site and download it to your /home directory or to /usr/local/. Unpack it with **tar xzvf rosegarden-latest.tar.gz**, switch into the new Rosegarden directory, and follow the instructions in the README for building the program. Rosegarden is easily compiled, requiring only a C compiler and the standard X libraries and headers. Running **./configure** and **make** will build the program, and **./do-install** will complete the installation. Typing **rosegarden** in an xterm window will launch the program.

Using Rosegarden

Because our focus is on Rosegarden's notation capability, we'll head straight for its notation editing screens. When you start Rosegarden, you will see a small box with buttons for selecting the sequencer and the notator. Click on the

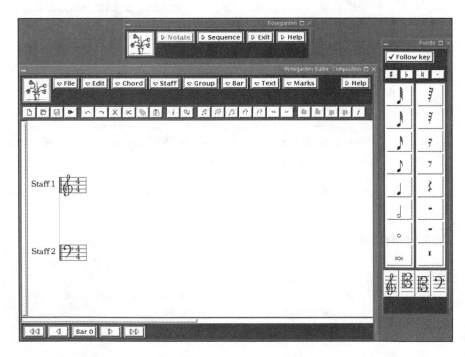

Figure 11-5: A bass and treble staff in a Rosegarden score

Notate button, and the notation editor will open with a blank canvas for entering notes and other musical symbols from the Palette box (which stretches down the right side of the screen). Select **File • New**, enter a staff count of 2 (i.e., treble and bass), and the notator display will look like Figure 11-5.

Creating a Score

Creating a score is simplicity itself: You enter notes into the staves by left-clicking on the desired symbol in the **Palette**, then left-clicking again in the notator canvas, dropping the note (or other symbol) into the appropriate staff. Figure 11-6 shows a few measures of music entered into our two-staff canvas.

As you can see, Rosegarden's flexibility allows for lyrics, legato indicators, accidentals, and fermata markers to be added to your scores.

Editing Your Score

Left-click and drag the mouse to prepare an area for a block-area edit. Area editing includes the basic cut/copy/paste routines, as well as the insertion and deletion of ligatures, tuplets, and lyrics. In addition to these usual operations, Rosegarden's area editing can transpose, invert, and reverse the selected block. This capability adds a nice touch for composers, particularly given that you can audition your notated work at any time merely by pressing the Sequence button.

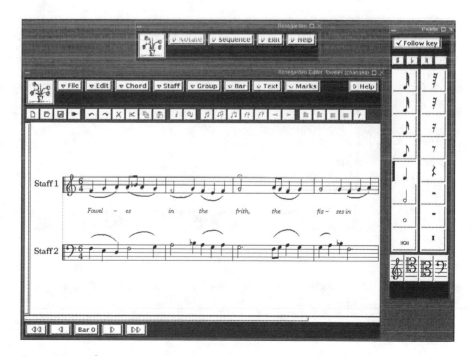

Figure 11-6: A few measures in a Rosegarden score

Saving and Printing Your Score

You can save your work as a Rosegarden or MIDI file. Rosegarden files do not require any particular extension, but I usually save them as `.rg` files.

In order to print your Rosegarden score, you must first convert it to a MusicTeX, OpusTeX, or PMX file. Most Linux distributions include a LaTeX package that will perform the necessary conversions to render these formats into printable files. For more information regarding MusicTeX and its relatives (MusiXTeX, OpusTeX, MuTeX, and PMX) see the MusiXTeX Web page at http://www.gmd.de/Misc/Music/Welcome.html.

Importing MIDI Files

Rosegarden can also import and export standard MIDI files. Select **File •
Import MIDI** to bring a MIDI file into the notator. After a few moments, you should see your MIDI music represented in standard notation. Figure 11-7 shows a notation screen after loading a MIDI file into Rosegarden.

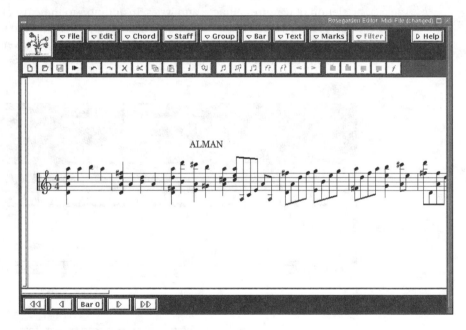

Figure 11-7: A MIDI file imported into Rosegarden

As is typical with programs that transcribe MIDI performances, some manual editing will probably be required before your score is clearly readable.

Closing Remarks

Though this brief profile has focused only on Rosegarden's notation facility, don't forget that it's also a fine MIDI sequencer with recording, playback, and editing capabilities. These two features, along with its Csound scoring option, make Rosegarden a very powerful program. You can write your music using standard notation, render and play it as a MIDI file, convert it to a Csound score, and print out your work all within Rosegarden. No other Linux music application provides all of these features in one bundle. This brief profile has shown the flexibility and power of its notator, and I leave you to the happy experience of discovering everything else that Rosegarden can do. Enjoy!

Mup

Authors: John Krallmann and Bill Krauss
Version profiled: 3.5
Web site: http://www.arkkra.com
FTP site: ftp://ftp.arkkra.com
Maintained: Yes
Availability: Commercial (US$29), open-source shareware
License: Held by authors
Capsule summary: Great easy-to-use package for small to medium scores

Mup ("music publisher") is essentially a specification language for music notation that takes a formatted text file and creates a PostScript file for printing. It can also produce a standard MIDI file for rendering your music to sound.

Here is just a partial list of the complex scoring demands Mup can handle:

- Automatic transposition of music and chord marks per staff

- Up to 32 staffs, including one-line, five-line, and tablature staffs

- One or two voices per staff, up to 70 simultaneous notes per voice

- Double whole to 256th notes, with any number of dots

- Lyrics can be placed above, below, or between staffs; unlimited number of verses, with control of font and size

- Optional rehearsal marks and/or automatic measure numbering

- 8th note and shorter notes can have either flags or beams; beams can be cross-staff

- Staffs can be grouped with braces or brackets

As the following examples will attest, Mup delivers all this and more.

Getting It, Building It

Mup is available in source code or as a pre-compiled binary. If you've downloaded the binary, you can place it anywhere in your system PATH (/usr/local/bin is always a good choice) and run the program by entering **mup** in an xterm window.

Building Mup from Source Code

If you want to build Mup, you must obtain the source package and place it in your /home or /usr/local directory. Unpack the compressed file with **tar xzvf mup-latest.tar.gz** and follow the build instructions in the README file. Compiling Mup is easy; just switch to your new mup directory and run this command:

```
gcc -o mup *.c -lm
```

After building the program, you must create an empty file called .mup and place it in either your root directory or in the Mup directory itself. You can now run Mup, but you may want to compile the Mup display program first.

mupdisp

Most Linux distributions include PostScript file viewers, such as Ghostview or Ghostscript, that will work perfectly well with the PostScript files created by Mup. However, you can preview your Mup files before rendering them into the PostScript format by using the mupdisp program. It is not necessary to build and use mupdisp, but it is a handy tool. You build mupdisp by switching to the mupdisp directory and issuing the following command:

```
gcc -o mupdisp *.c -lvga -L/usr/X11R6/lib -lX11 -lm
```

This will build the mupdisp program. Place it in the same directory as your mup binary. You can now view Mup files in console mode or in X by simply running **mupdisp my_file.mup**.

Mup Documentation

Mup's documentation is available as a separate package. Simply download and unpack it into your existing Mup directory. The docs are in PostScript and HTML formats, and brief man (manual) pages are also provided. The PostScript and HTML pages can be installed wherever you like, but the man pages should be placed in /usr/man/man1 or /usr/local/man/man1. You can then invoke the Mup and mupdisp manual pages in an xterm or at the console with **man mup** and **man mupdisp**. The man pages are useful for a quick overview of Mup's usage, but the full documentation is in the PostScript and HTML pages.

Using Mup

For our introduction to Mup, we'll create a simple two-bar phrase to demonstrate the language and its syntax.

Open your text editor (vi is my choice) and create a new file called **my_first.mup**. Copy the following lines into this new file and then save the file.

```
header
     title (18) "My First Mup"                     // centered title, 18-point font
     title (14) "Learning how it's done..."        // subtitle
     title "Y2K" "David L. Phillips"               // composer information, change as you like

footer
     title "\(copyright) Copyright 2000 Musique_DLP" // copyright notice, change as you like

score
     time = 4/4                                    // time signature
     key = 0#                                       // key signature
     staffs = 2                                     // number of staffs
     clef = treble                                  // clef
     beamstyle = 2,2                                // beaming style

     staff 2                                        // indicates that the following spec
                                                    // applies only to staff 2
     clef = bass                                    // set clef for staff 2

music

     1: mr;                                         // rest for measure 1, staff 1
     2: 2c; 2e;                                     // notes in staff 2
     bar                                            // bar is finished

     1: 4e; 4d; 2e;                                 // notes for staff 1
     2: 8g; 8a; 4h; 2c+;                            // notes for staff 2
     endbar                                         // double-bar for ending
```

As you can see, a Mup input file is organized into various sections (header, footer, score, music) that describe some aspect of the score's layout and music. Although our first example is quite simple, Mup can render very complex scoring indications, as we shall see in a moment.

Preview your new creation by running **mupdisp my_first.mup**. The display should look like Figure 11-8.

NOTE *The watermark will appear on-screen and in print until you have registered Mup.*

Now convert my_first.mup to PostScript format with the following command:

```
mup -f my_first.ps my_first.mup
```

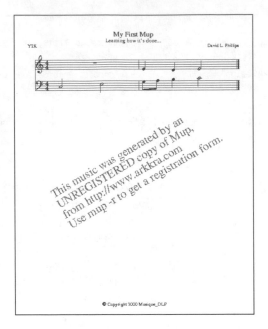

Figure 11-8: A Mup score in mupdisp

To view your new PostScript file with Ghostscript, simply run **gs my_first. ps**. Your music is now ready for printing on any PostScript-compatible printer.

Advanced Use

Our example only scratches the surface of Mup's capabilities. Your /home/mpu/ doc directory includes an example named sample.mup. Run **mup -f sample.ps sample.mup** to produce a PostScript file, seen in Ghostscript in Figure 11-9.

The following code fragment creates the first two measures for the foghorn and drum parts in Figure 11-9:

```
staff 3
    label = "foghorn\nin G\(smflat)"
    clef = baritone
    transpose = down dim 5

    // set different default octave
    defoct = 4

staff 4
    // make staff 4 a 1-line staff
    stafflines = 1

// define a macro to allow saying "DRUM" instead of "4:" for the 4th staff
```

Figure 11-9: The first page of the sample.mup score

```
define DRUM 4:  @

// a grace note and an accent on staff 3
   3: [grace; slash 1]c; [with >] 2.d;4.r;

// measure rest for staff 4
   DRUM mr;

// include a note with a double flat
   3: 2.e&&;4.r;

// you can specify a pitch for a 1-line staff, even though all notes will be
// placed on the line. The pitch will be used for MIDI output, if you use
// the -m option to Mup to get a MIDI file instead of printed output.
   DRUM 4.f&;2.r;

   // double bar
   dblbar
```

To render the `sample.mup` Mup file to a Type 1 Standard MIDI file, use the following command:

```
mup -m sample.mid sample.mup
```

You can then play it with playmidi, TiMidity, or any other Linux MIDI player or sequencer.

Closing Remarks

Mup allows a degree of output customization not commonly encountered in notation programs dependent on graphic interfaces. For instance, a textual music specification language lets you pre-process and filter the specification data with other programs, something that is impossible to do with graphic interface programs. The language itself is very easy to learn, and with a little practice you can enter even complex scoring indications quickly and accurately. Mup is powerful and flexible, and every detail of the score layout can be adjusted to suit your own needs. Using the mupdisp program to preview Mup's output enables you to edit, view, and print your music in a very fast working cycle. Arkkra Enterprises has consistently maintained Mup since 1997, and it is in use at many prestigious schools and other organizations. At a cost of only $29 (US), Mup is a great bargain. Consider it another "Most Highly Recommended" music application for Linux.

12

NETWORK AUDIO SOFTWARE

Network audio software provides audio services to a network of computers, such as an office or school LAN (large area network), a group of connected computers in your own home, or the Internet. Typical services include music broadcasting, network telephony, and the distribution of audio support throughout a network.

In this chapter we'll look at a player for the popular Real Audio format (RealPlayer G2), a streaming MP3 server (Icecast), an Internet telephone connection (Speak Freely), and a client/server network audio I/O service provider (NAS).

RealPlayer G2

Authors: Real.com
Version profiled: 7.0 alpha
Web site: http://proforma.real.com/real/player/linuxplayer.html
FTP site: n/a
Maintained: Yes
Availability: Binary-only
License: Commercial, held by Real.com
Capsule summary: The one and *only* Real Audio/Real Movie player for Linux

RealPlayer G2 is a variable bandwidth audio/video player for files in the RA (Real Audio) and RM (Real Movie) formats. The RA soundfile format was the first popular Internet streaming audio protocol. Thanks to Real.com's foresight in providing inexpensive encoders and players, today thousands of Web sites offer sound and video clips in the RA/RM formats.

Getting It, Building It

Download the latest binary from http://proforma.real.com/real/player/ linuxplayer.html. Be sure you read the installation instructions on that Web page: The Linux version is offered as alpha-stage software, and installation requirements are updated on the Web page. RealPlayer G2 is currently distributed in the standard `.tar.gz` format and as an RPM package.

If you download the RPM package, create an empty holding directory (something like `/usr/local/RealPlayer` is good), download the package into it, and unpack the software with `rpm -iv RealPlayer-latest.rpm`. Unpacking the RPM file automatically installs everything.

If you download the `.tar.gz` package, create an empty holding directory (such as `/usr/local/RealPlayer`), download the package to that directory, and unpack it with `tar xzvf RealPlayer-latest.tar.gz`. From the RealPlayer directory run `./install.sh` to place the program files in their correct locations.

Using RealPlayer

Before using RealPlayer G2 for the first time, go to **View • Preferences** and set the Performance and Connection values for your system. RealPlayer's playback quality depends upon the speed of your network connection: With a 14.4 modem, the sound will approximate that of an AM radio, at 28.8 kbps the sound is closer to an FM radio transmission, and higher-speed connections yield correspondingly higher-quality audio. Video playback is more severely affected: Connections under 56 kbps will suffer from frame loss and poor audio/video synchronization; higher-speed connections will greatly improve performance.

After setting the Preferences, you can use RealPlayer G2 from an xterm simply by entering **realplay** at the command prompt. However, because you'll probably want to access RA files in real time over the Internet, you must configure your browser to use RealPlayer when you click a link to a Real Audio soundfile. I have my Netscape Preferences configured in this manner:

```
Description: Real Audio
MIME Type:   audio/x-pn-realaudio
Suffixes:    ra,ram
Application: /usr/bin/realplay %s
```

With the above settings, I can click on a RealAudio link and listen to the sound as it streams to my player. In Figure 12-1 RealPlayer is playing a Real-Audio-encoded Csound composition by Michael Coble, available at http://www.panix.com/~coble/Coble/music/.

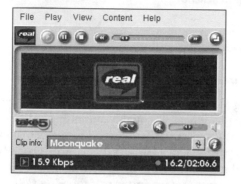

Figure 12-1: RealPlayer G2 playing a RealAudio file

Figure 12-2 shows RealPlayer G2 playing a music video found on Real.com's music page at http://realguide.real.com.

Figure 12-2: Playing a music video with RealPlayer G2

There's really not much more to say about RealPlayer G2. It is a straightforward application, easy to install and use. Real.com maintains excellent listings for RA sites on the Internet, so you should have no trouble finding hours of streaming media for your network audio pleasure.

Icecast

Authors: Jack Moffitt, Barath Raghavan, many others
Version profiled: 1.3.0
Web site: http://www.icecast.org
FTP site: n/a
Maintained: Yes
Availability: Free, open-source
License: GPL
Capsule summary: Streaming MP3 and live audio for network broadcasting

Icecast is a streaming MP3 server that lets anyone with a sufficiently fast network connection broadcast near-CD quality audio (e.g., MP3s—see Chapter 7 for more information) live over the Internet. Starting Icecast invokes the server (icecast), starts the encoder (shout) that converts your MP3s into streaming audio, and streams them to the server. Icecast is incredibly cool (excuse the pun) and easy to set up and use. If there's a radio disc jockey inside you, Icecast is your chance to become an instant broadcast celebrity over the Internet or your local area network. Icecast is wonderful Linux audio software that definitely deserves a Most Highly Recommended status.

Getting It, Building It

Get Icecast from www.icecast.org or this book's CD-ROM, place it into an empty directory, and unpack it with **tar xzvf icecast-latest.tar.gz**. Enter your newly created Icecast directory, read the installation instructions, and then run **./configure --help** to see what configuration options are available. Icecast requires no special libraries and should compile without problems on any Linux system. Run **./configure** and **make icecast** to build Icecast. You will also want to build the shout encoder and liveice (live Icecast) binaries with **make shout** and **make liveice** in their respective subdirectories.

Using Icecast

Setting up your network broadcasting station is simple with Icecast. Edit the icecast.conf file (in the Icecast home directory) to reflect such items as your host location, server name, aliases, and so forth. This file is rather lengthy, but it is also very well documented. Study it carefully to make sure your settings are right.

Testing Your Configuration

After you've edited the configuration file, start the Icecast server by entering **./icecast** at the command prompt. To test your broadcast system on your home machine, open another xterm, enter the Icecast shout subdirectory, then run the following command sequence:

```
shout localhost -P itsme -p /home/soundfiles/MP3/playlist -l -g various -n "Your Icecast Show"
```

With this command, shout uses the Linux network loopback device (local-host) to connect to localhost with the password **itsme** (set in icecast.conf), stream the files listed in the /home/soundfiles/MP3/playlist file, loop the playlist, identify the genre of music as various, and name the broadcast My Ice-cast Show. You can now listen to the Icecast stream by running **mpg123 http://localhost.localdomain:8000** or **xmms http://localhost.localdomain:8000**. Figure 12-3 displays the Icecast session described above with XMMS as the client.

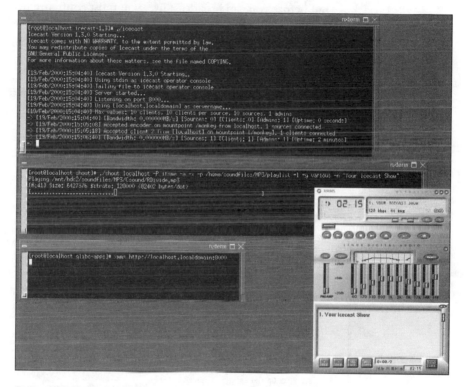

Figure 12-3: Icecast run in XMMS

Broadcasting to the World

To broadcast your pre-composed playlist over a TCP/IP connection and out to the world, append this line to your shout command sequence:

```
-u http://your.IP.address.here:port
```

If you have a static IP address, you can permanently add it into the icecast.conf file. If your address is dynamically assigned (as occurs with most dial-up connections), you must explicitly declare it (as in the above line) whenever you start the shout program. A static IP address makes it easy for listeners to tune in at any time; if you have a dynamic address, you must announce it via a Web page or IRC channel each time you broadcast. Don't forget the port address (it's usually 8000)—users need it to connect to the icecast server.

Live Broadcasting with Icecast

You can also broadcast interactive Icecast sessions using the liveice program.

But before you can broadcast live, you must configure liveice for your system by editing the liveice.cfg file (in the liveice subdirectory). You can edit that file using any text editor or with the handy Tcl/Tk utility seen in Figure 12-4.

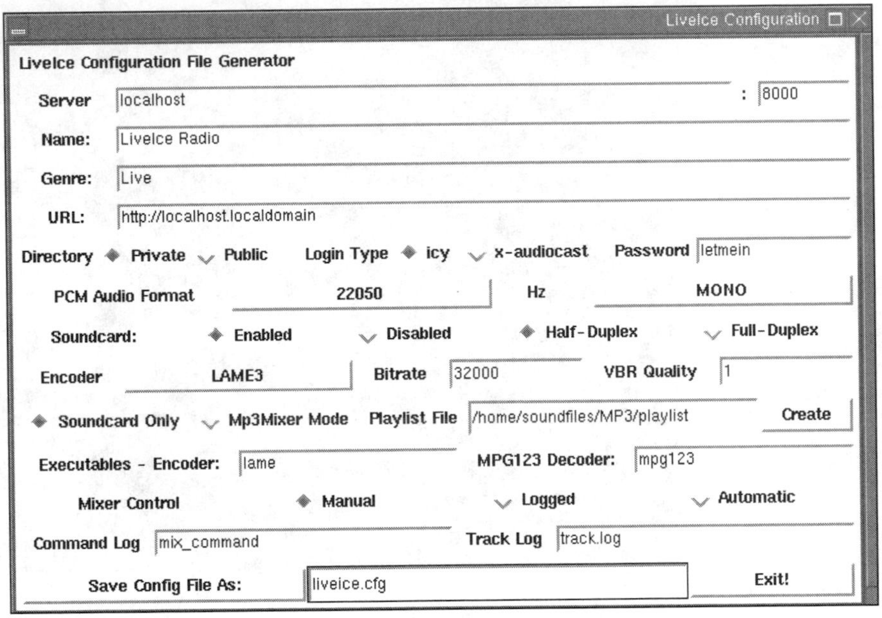

Figure 12-4: Liveice configuration utility

To broadcast live, start the icecast server as described in the previous section. Then enter the liveice subdirectory and run **./liveice**. Figure 12-5 shows a liveice broadcast over the network loopback device. You can see the icecast server running in the lower right window, with the liveice interface running in the upper left window. XMMS has been launched with the loopback address (see middle left window), and a software mixer (smix) has been opened to control output and input volume.

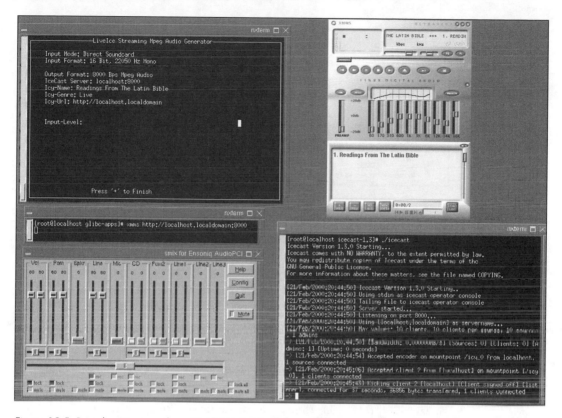

Figure 12-5: Broadcasting over the network loopback device with liveice

To broadcast live over a TCP/IP network, simply change the URL entry in the liveice.cfg file to your IP address (as you did with shout).

You can now make realtime modifications to your broadcast via the liveice interface and its various control commands (described in the liveice documentation) or with the Tcl/Tk front-end (Figure 12-6).

Performance Considerations

Bandwidth and connection speed determine the quality of your network broadcast audio. Although the MP3 format is remarkable for its compression ratios, it is still a rather dense data format for streaming audio and requires a fast CPU (I recommend at least a 266 MHz Pentium or equivalent) and a fast network connection for the smoothest transmission and reception. An ISDN, cable modem, or DSL/ASDL connection is a must for high-quality broadcasting.

Your icecast station's bitrate can be adjusted downward to accommodate lower-powered machines and connections, but be aware that audio quality will be compromised, most noticeably if you are sending music streams. Spoken-word broadcasts can use the lower rates with much less noticeable degradation.

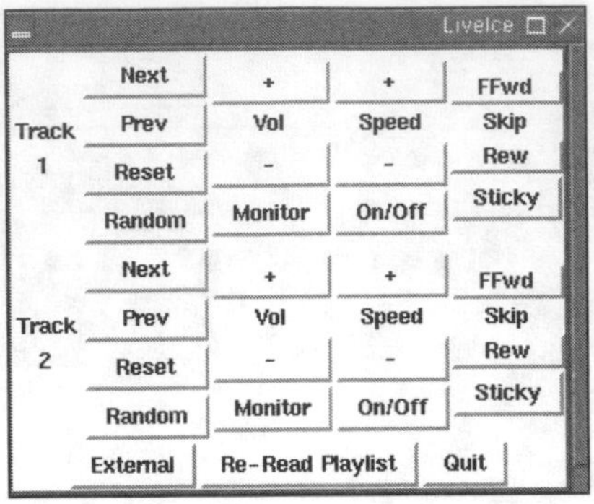

Figure 12-6: The liveice Tcl/Tk frontend

Speak Freely

Author: John Walker
Version profiled: 7.1
Web site: http://www.fourmilab.ch/speakfree/unix/index.html
FTP site: n/a
Maintained: Yes
Availability: Free, open-source
License: public domain
Capsule summary: Turns a soundcard and microphone into a network telephone

Speak Freely turns your Linux box into a network telephone and does so
extremely well. If you and your friends have Speak Freely installed on your
local machines, you can call each other over your network connection. The
difference between making a telephone call and using a computer network is
that the computer network call uses a soundcard for audio services (sound
input/output), the network connection for the carrier line, and Speak Freely
for the software agent that makes it all work together. Whether your needs are
corporate-wide or just buddy-to-buddy, Speak Freely is your "must-have" Linux
network telephony solution.

Getting It, Building It

Get the sources from this book's CD-ROM or the Speak Freely Web site at
www.fourmilab.ch/speakfree/unix/index.html, place the package in your
/home or /usr/local/ directory, and unpack it with **tar xzvf speak_freely-
latest.tar.gz**. Enter the new **Speak Freely** directory and study the README
and INSTALL files before attempting the build. Compiling Speak Freely is
easy (it requires only common libraries found in every mainstream Linux distribution), but be sure to read the Makefile and edit it to accommodate your
specific hardware. Run **make** and (as root) **make install** and you are all set to
make that first call.

Using Speak Freely

Speak Freely is a software suite that includes the following command-line applications:

sfecho	Echoes transmission back to host; a debugging tool
sflaunch	Opens audio device, starts mic and speaker applications (sfmike and sfspeaker)
sflwl	Look Who's Listening client; lists users connected to LWL server
sflwld	The LWL server daemon
sfmike	Sound transmission utility
sfreflect	Conference call reflector
sfspeaker	Sound reception utility
sfvod	Voice-on-demand server

Speak Freely's excellent man pages provide complete descriptions and explanations for these programs and their command options. For our look at Speak Freely, we will limit ourselves to initiating, controlling, and terminating a telephony connection over a TCP/IP network with sflaunch.

Starting sflaunch and Testing Speak Freely

Start sflaunch from the command prompt in an xterm or at the Linux console. You should see the following appear:

```
[dlphilp@localhost]$ sflaunch localhost.localdomain:2074
Space bar switches talk/pause, Esc or "q" to quit, "." for chat text
Pause:
```

At this point, simply press the **Spacebar** to initiate a talk connection over your network loopback device on port 2074 (the default). Test your connection by pressing the space bar and saying a few words into your microphone. After a slight delay, your voice will come back through your speakers. If Speak Freely seems to be doing everything it should but you hear nothing, make sure your soundcard mixer levels are up far enough and that the mic input is selected for Record.

Connecting to a Network IP

To connect to a network IP address, issue the following command:

```
[dlphilp@localhost]$ sflaunch 209.143.49.133:2074
```

The above command uses an IP address in its "dotted quad" form (four decimal numbers separated by dots), but you can just as easily use a domain name instead, as in this example:

```
[dlphilp@localhost]$ sflaunch brutus.myown.net:2074
```

Of course, your intended receiver must also have Speak Freely installed and set to your network address and port in order to hear and respond to your transmission.

In addition to voice, you can send chat text and even music over a Speak Freely connection (see the sflaunch manual page for more details). However, Speak Freely is most commonly used as machine-to-machine network telephony software. As with the other programs reviewed in this chapter, your available connection speed and bandwidth will determine the quality of your network audio. If your network connection is a dial-up Internet service provider (ISP), you might want to explore the various compression schemes in Speak Freely to minimize latency and fragmentation of your sound.

sflwd and sflwl

The sflwd and sflwl programs deserve special mention. sflwld is a daemon (a server that runs as a background process) that will automatically add your name and IP address to a database on an LWL-compliant machine (LWL is the Look Who's Listening software that builds the database of registered users). Using the sflwl client, you can see who is available for a Speak Freely connection, and your address will also be available for others to call.

Speak Freely and X

The console tools work fine with Speak Freely, but if you prefer a fancy GUI you can choose between a Tcl/Tk interface (Shawn Pearce's xspeakfree, available from http://www.spearce.org/projects/xspeakfree/) and one for Java (Neil Clayton's JSF, available from http://www.germane-software.com/SpeakFreely/jsf/index.html). Figures 12-7 and 12-8 show the xspeakfree and JSF front-ends at work.

The GUIs introduce no new features, but they do make using Speak Freely a little more transparent. Note that you must have Speak Freely installed to use the GUIs, because they are simply front-ends for the console commands.

Need More Information?

Speak Freely has been in development since 1995, is stable and feature-rich, and is still maintained. The original program documentation is excellent, and Sean Russell's page at www.germane-software.com/SpeakFreely/ is dedicated to disseminating information about running Speak Freely specifically under Linux.

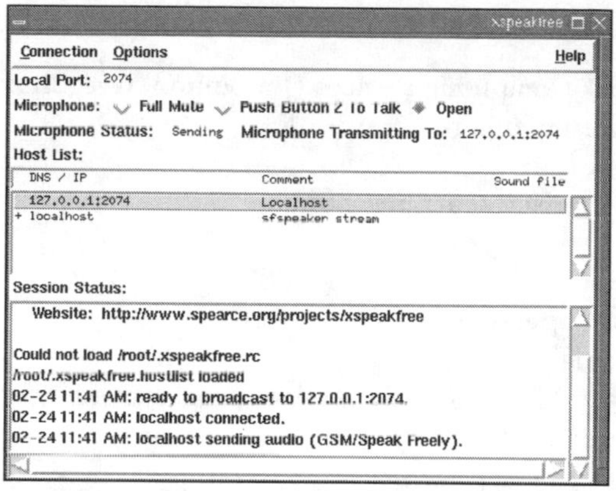

Figure 12-7: xspeakfree

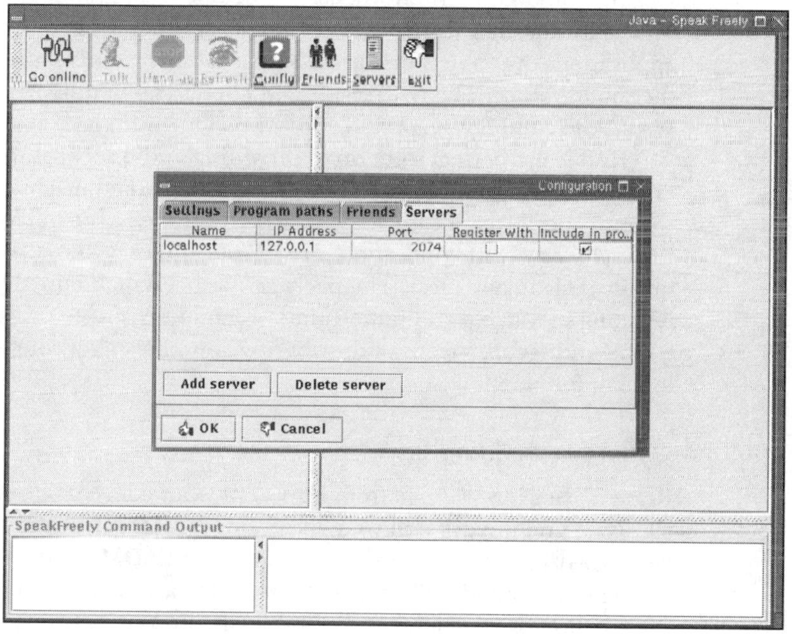

Figure 12-8: Java Speak Freely

NAS

Authors: Network Computing Devices (Jim Fulton, Greg Renda, Dave Lemke), Jon Trulson, others
Version profiled: 1.3e
Web site: http://radscan.com/nas.html
FTP site: n/a
Maintained: Yes
Availability: Free, open-source
License: Held by authors
Capsule summary: Network audio services provider with client/server software architecture

Network Audio System (NAS) lets you play, record, and manipulate audio data over a network. The system provides an audio server (nasd), more than a dozen client applications and utilities, and extensive documentation in man (manual) and PostScript formats. The server makes low-level connections with sound hardware, provides audio I/O services to small "lightweight" client applications over a network, and allows multiple clients simultaneous access to the sound device. The NAS server and clients can handle AU/SND, VOC, WAV, AIFF, and 8SVX soundfile formats.

NAS is the perfect solution to providing audio services to LANs (local area networks), diskless workstations, and networked machines without soundcards. Its performance is excellent: The nasd server is completely transparent, the included client applications are simple and easy to use, and the sound quality is clean and clear. The package has been maintained since 1995, resulting in a stable and powerful network audio service provider. If you need a solid and secure means of distributing sound over your network, you're looking for NAS.

Getting It, Building It

Retrieve the NAS package from http://radscan.com/nas.html or this book's CD-ROM and unpack it in your /home or /usr/local/ directory. Enter the new **nas-latest** directory and carefully study the README and BUILDNOTES files.

The NAS build utilizes a template called an Imakefile that sets rules for the creation of a top-level Makefile specific to your machine architecture (NAS will build on Sun, SGI, HP, and Intel-based machines). Run **xmkmf** in the NAS top directory to create the top Makefile, then run the following command line to build NAS:

```
make WORLDOPTS="-k CDEBUGFLAGS='-O2 -D__USE_BSD_SIGNAL'" World
```

Run **make install** and **make install.man** to install the NAS server, clients, and manual pages.

Before starting your new NAS server, go to **/etc/nas/** and copy the example **nasd.conf.eg** file to **nasd.conf**. You may need to do **chmod +w nasd.conf** to edit the file (its default condition is read-only). Change the following sections to reflect the capabilities of your soundcard:

```
inputsection
    device          "/dev/dsp"      # SB PCI128 is full-duplex
    maxrate  48000                  # maximum sample rate for the card
    minrate  5000                   # minimum sample rate
    maxfrags 3                      # low latency
    minfrags 2                      # the default
    fragsize 256                    # low latency
    wordsize 16                     # i/o is 16-bit on the PCI128
    numchans 2                      # and stereo
end

outputsection
    device          "/dev/dsp"
    maxrate  48000
    minrate  5000
    maxfrags 3
    minfrags 2
    fragsize 256
    wordsize 16
    numchans 2
end
```

When the nasd server starts, it will use these values for the system recording and playback defaults.

Using NAS

Start NAS from the xterm or console prompt with the **nasd &** command (the & puts the process in the background). While the server is running, any of the NAS clients can access its services as long as they know the server's network address. Now type **audemo** to launch the record/play demonstration client (Figure 12-9). The interface is self-explanatory.

Select **Record** and the window in Figure 12-10 will appear. Again, the record interface is self-explanatory. Press the **Record** button to start your recording, then press **Dismiss** to stop and close the window. The audemo files panel will update automatically. Simply double-click on your new soundfile to listen to it. Note that the info panel will also update with information about your file, as shown in Figure 12-11.

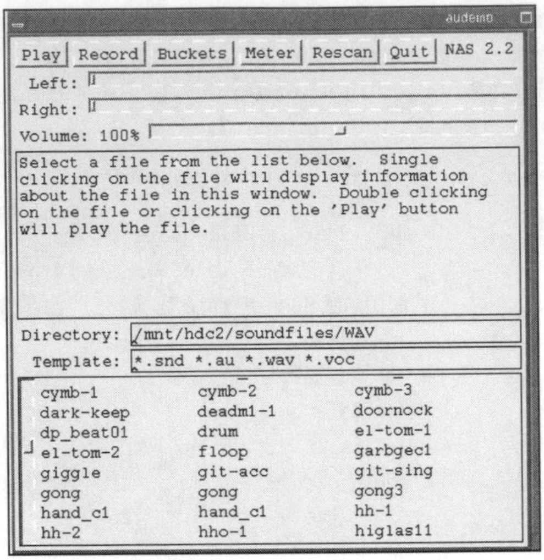

Figure 12-9: audemo in NAS

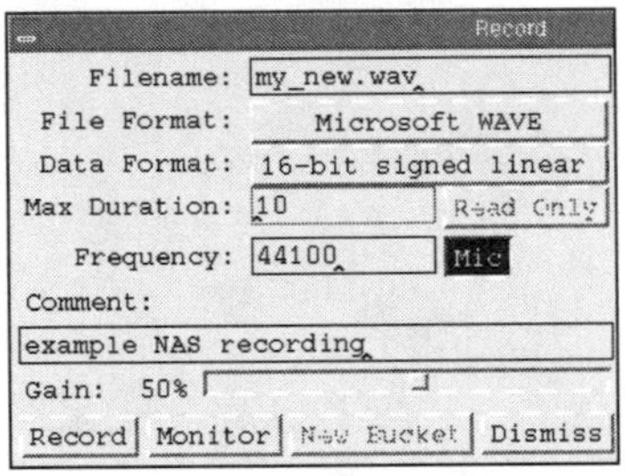

Figure 12-10: Recording in audemo

Now let's try another NAS client. Quit the audemo program and start the auedit application, a rudimentary but efficient soundfile editor. Figure 12-12 shows auedit loaded with our new recording.

auedit lets you perform simple cut/copy/paste edits and add a few amplitude effects. You can also record and play back from auedit.

More NAS

Other NAS clients include a network telephone connection (auphone), a server monitor and control tool (auctl), a soundfile format converter (auconvert), as well as players (auplay, autool, audemo) and recorders (aurecord, auedit, audemo). Some are command-line applications; others will run only under X. Like auedit and audemo, they are all simple and small.

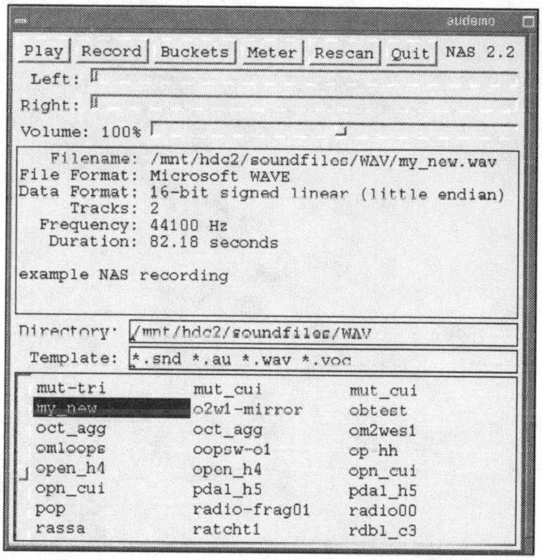

Figure 12-11: An updated audemo info panel

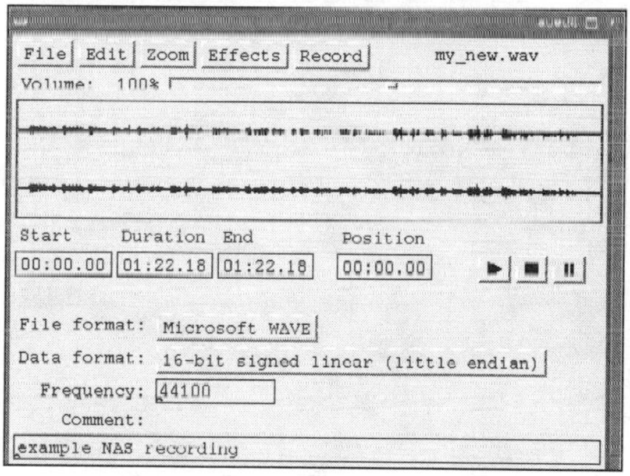

Figure 12-12: auedit

XMMS (www.xmms.org), mpg123 (www.mpg123.org), and Keith Packard's MIDI/AudioPlayer (www.ctrl-alt-del.com/keithp/linux/midiplay.html) also support NAS, extending its capabilities to the MP3 and MIDI file types.

13

LINUX AND THE DIGITAL DJ

If you're a rap or hip-hop musician, Linux offers you, free of charge, a variety of solid programs that have everything needed to cut your own deep grooves and backing beats. With digital re-creations of tools like samplers, scratch turntables, and ancient beat-boxes such as the Roland TB303, TR808, and TR909 drum machines, Linux enables and empowers the latest variety of Linux music-makers: the digital DJ.

In this chapter I'll cover a DJ mixer (Oolaboola), a software "scratcher" (terminatorX), a drum machine/groove composer (Green Box), and an integrated bass synth/sample player (Freebirth). I consider these selections to be the best of their kind for Linux: They are certainly powerful enough for the professional DJ, but they are also designed to be immediately rewarding for the novice.

Oolaboola

Author: Eric S. Tiedemann
Version profiled: 0.2.0
Web site: http://www.hyperreal.org/~est/oolaboola
FTP site: n/a
Maintained: Yes
Availability: Free, open-source
License: GPL
Capsule summary: DJ mixer suitable for live performance or studio recording work

Oolaboola, an "open-source cyber-shamanic noise-maker," is a system for mixing sound files in real time that also lets you alter the speed and volume during playback. In other words, it is a software mixer ideally suited for the Linux digital DJ.

Getting It, Building It

Copy the `oolaboola-latest.tar.gz` from this book's CD-ROM or download the latest version from Oolaboola's Web site. In an empty directory, unpack it with **tar xzvf oolaboola-latest.tar.gz** and read the instructions for compiling and setting up the program. Oolaboola uses the Python language library and header files, so you will need to install Python before building Oolaboola. Python is packaged with most Linux distributions, and the latest version is available from www.python.org. You will also need a version of the GIMP Toolkit (GTK) higher than 1.2.1. GTK is also bundled with most Linux distributions, but you can retrieve the latest version from www.gtk.org. Finally, you will need the Python/GTK bindings from ftp://ftp.gtk.org/pub/gtk/python/.

When all the other pieces are in place, move to the `oolaboola-latest` directory. Run **./configure —help** to see the available options for the configuration process. Then run **./configure** followed by **make**; **make install** (you must become the root user for the installation). Type **oolaboola** in any open xterm window to start the program. You should hear Eric Tiedemann singing the Oolaboola theme once through. If you don't hear Eric, double-check all your connections and settings and make sure that you have installed the latest versions of Python, GTK, and the PyGTK software.

Playing Oolaboola

Figure 13-1 shows Oolaboola's self-explanatory interface as it appears on startup.

Each player panel has its own file selector and sliders for volume, sample playback rate, and position within the selected soundfile. Soundfile length is displayed along with the amount of the file played and the amount remaining. You can control Oolaboola with the mouse, from the keyboard, and with a MIDI input device such as a synthesizer or MIDI fader box. The program comes alive when all of these controls are utilized together during realtime playback.

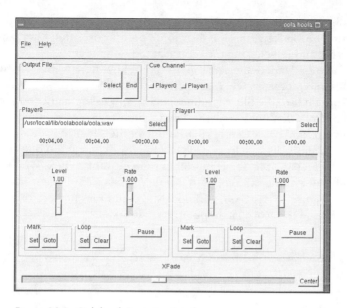

Figure 13-1: Oolaboola's startup interface

Play may be paused and restarted at will either by moving the cursor to the **Pause** control and pressing ENTER, by clicking on the button with the mouse pointer, or, if the Linux MIDI device /dev/midi is available, by pressing **middle C** and the **D** above it on a MIDI keyboard (respectively starting and stopping play). The Oolaboola manual page describes each of the program's control interfaces (mouse, keyboard, MIDI input) in detail. Type `man oola-boola` in an xterm window for a list of controls.

You can move one second forward or backward in the soundfile with the right and left arrow keys. CTRL-ARROW increases the position increment to 10 seconds, ALT-ARROW reduces the increment to 1/10 of a second, CTRL-ALT-ARROW reduces it to 1/100 of a second. The Home and End keys move the position pointer to the beginning and end of the soundfile, and a cue channel toggle controls which player's output is sent to the cue channel (a channel waiting to be cued for its entry into the mix).

To get a feel for operating the program, play with the various controls on the `oola.wav` file loaded at startup. The GUI is intuitive and easy to navigate, so you should soon master the basics of Oolaboola.

Using Oolaboola

Before you record anything, familiarize yourself with the program by working with two soundfiles at the same time (without selecting a file for recording). First load soundfiles into each of the player panels. Each file will autoplay once through. Press **Loop Set** (shown in Figure 13-1) to start playing a file again and **Loop Clear** to stop loop playback. You can manually start both soundfiles simultaneously by positioning the cursor over one panel's Loop Set (use the TAB key), placing the mouse pointer over the other, and pressing ENTER and left-clicking the mouse at the same time.

Press **Mark Set** to set a "go-to" point anywhere within the file (you can do this in realtime, so feel free to click on Mark Set anytime). When you press the **Goto** button, the file will immediately jump to the mark you specified and play from that point. Use the **XFade** slider to cross-fade the volumes of your players, and press **Center** to instantly set the slider to its midpoint. Now let's make a mix. First, select or name a file for digital audio output (see Chapter 1) by pressing the **Select** button in the **Output File** box. When you start your mix, everything will record to this file.

Figure 13-2 shows Oolaboola with soundfiles loaded for each player and prepared to record its output to test.raw.

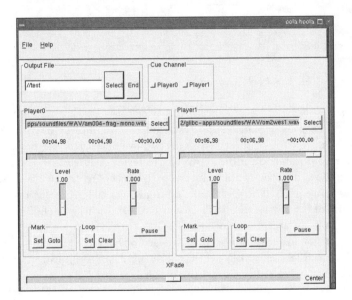

Figure 13-2: Two soundfiles loaded in Oolaboola

You will be recording from the time you start one of the player panels with Loop Set until you press the **Output File End** button. If you like, you can later change the file format with the SoX utility (profiled in Chapter 3) or the MiXViews soundfile editor (reviewed in Chapter 4).

C-oola-ing Down

Oolaboola's uncluttered, easy-to-learn interface lets even a novice make interesting mixes almost immediately. No special knowledge is required, and with a little practice you'll be mixing like a pro. Oolaboola is an excellent partner with terminatorX and Green Box (reviewed below): After saving a mix from

Oolaboola, you can combine it in terminatorX with a drum loop created in Green Box. New features are added regularly, and the author is dedicated to continually improving the program. If I had a major criticism of Oolaboola, it would be that it's hard to stop playing with it once you've started. There's a little Linux DJ in us all: Let Oolaboola bring yours out to center stage.

terminatorX

Author: Alexander Koenig
Version profiled: 3.51
Web site: http://www.stud.fht-esslingen.de/~alkoit00/tX
            http://termx.cjb.net
FTP site: n/a
Maintained: Yes
Availability: Free, open-source
License: GPL
Capsule summary: Virtual turntables for the Linux "scratcher," with excellent intuitive GUI

Alexander Koenig named terminatorX after the DJ for the famous rap group Public Enemy. The author describes his software as ". . . a realtime audio synthesizer that allows you to 'scratch' on digitally sampled audio data . . . just like you might have heard hip-hop DJs scratch on vinyl records. . . ." With one soundfile for a background loop and another for the scratch loop, scratching and stuttering are just a few mouse clicks away.

Getting It, Building It

terminatorX requires the GTK libraries and header files found in most Linux distributions. If your GTK installation is out of date or if you do not have it installed at all, you can retrieve the latest package from www.gtk.org.

After downloading the latest version of terminatorX from the its Web site, put the package in your /home or /usr/local/ directory and unpack it with `tar xzvf terminatorx-latest.tar.gz`. Move into the new `terminatorx-latest` directory and read the installation instructions. The build process is a straightforward `./configure`, `make`, and (as root user) `make install`. Type `terminatorX` in an xterm window, and the program will open to the display in Figure 13-3. terminatorX is now ready to use.

Using terminatorX

Session Options

The program's default opening condition is a single turntable window. But before we add another turntable and set up loops for beats and scratching, let's first take a look at the session options. Figure 13-4 shows the Options panel and its available parameters.

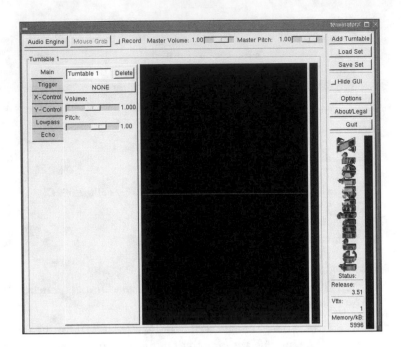

Figure 13-3: terminatorX's opening display

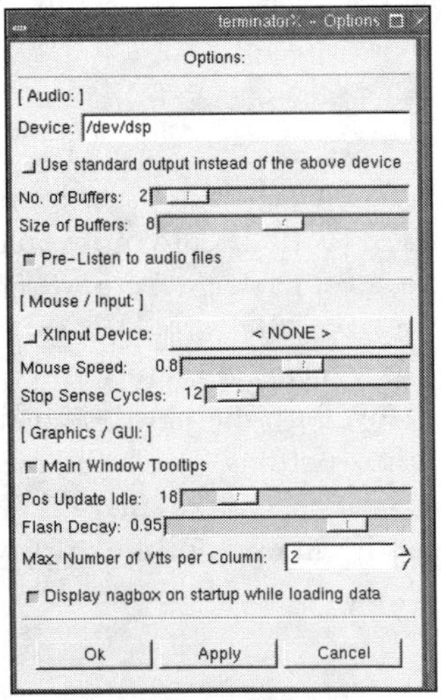

Figure 13-4: terminatorX options

The choices are mostly self-explanatory, and the defaults will usually be acceptable. Tooltips open over any non-obvious function or option (such as the XInput Device radio button), and the program's README file explains each option in detail. Close the panel when you are satisfied with your Options choices.

Creating a Scratch File and Adding Turntables

Click on the **Record Radio** button at the top of the display, and a dialog box will ask you to name your new scratch soundfile—this is the file that will save your scratches. Now click on the **Add Turntable** button to choose the tracks you want to mix and scratch. Select a soundfile in WAV, AU, or MP3 format for each turntable by clicking on the **Main** tab and pressing the selector button that says **NONE** on it. When your soundfiles are loaded, click on the **Audio Engine** button, and the files will play together, looping smoothly through their individual file lengths. You can click on the **Main** tab (visible in Figure 13-5) in each **Turntable** panel to name your turntable and set its volume and pitch, even while the soundfile is playing.

Scratching and Recording

After you've added some turntables and selected soundfiles for them, your screen will resemble Figure 13-5. Click on the **Mouse Grab** button to start scratching.

NOTE   *You can always exit the Mouse Grab mode by pressing the ESCAPE key.*

Scratching is a simple procedure: Click and hold the left button in the scratch loop window to allow forward and backward (or upward and downward) scratching over the waveform. To prepare for scratching (and other effects) in Mouse Grab mode, click on the **Y-Control** and **X-Control** tabs to set the mouse's vertical and horizontal movement to control scratching, volume, low-pass filtering, echo, or nothing at all. If you select the filter or echo effects, click on their edit tabs (as seen in Figure 13-5) to enable them and to set their parameters.

At this point you may want to save your terminatorX session setup. Click on **Save Set** and enter a filename (a .tX extension will be added by the program). You can click on **Load Set** at any time to reload an entire session configuration. Now begin recording by clicking on **Audio Engine** (to stop recording, click on **Audio Engine** again). If you have four turntables, your screen should look something like Figure 13-5.

Use the function keys (**F1** through **F4**) to select the active turntable window. While the Audio Engine is running, click on the **Mouse Grab** button. This locks the mouse pointer on the Mouse Grab button and outlines the active scratch turntable waveform window in red. Now, any motions you make with the mouse will affect the active turntable, depending on how you set the X and Y controls. For instance, if you selected scratching for the X axis for

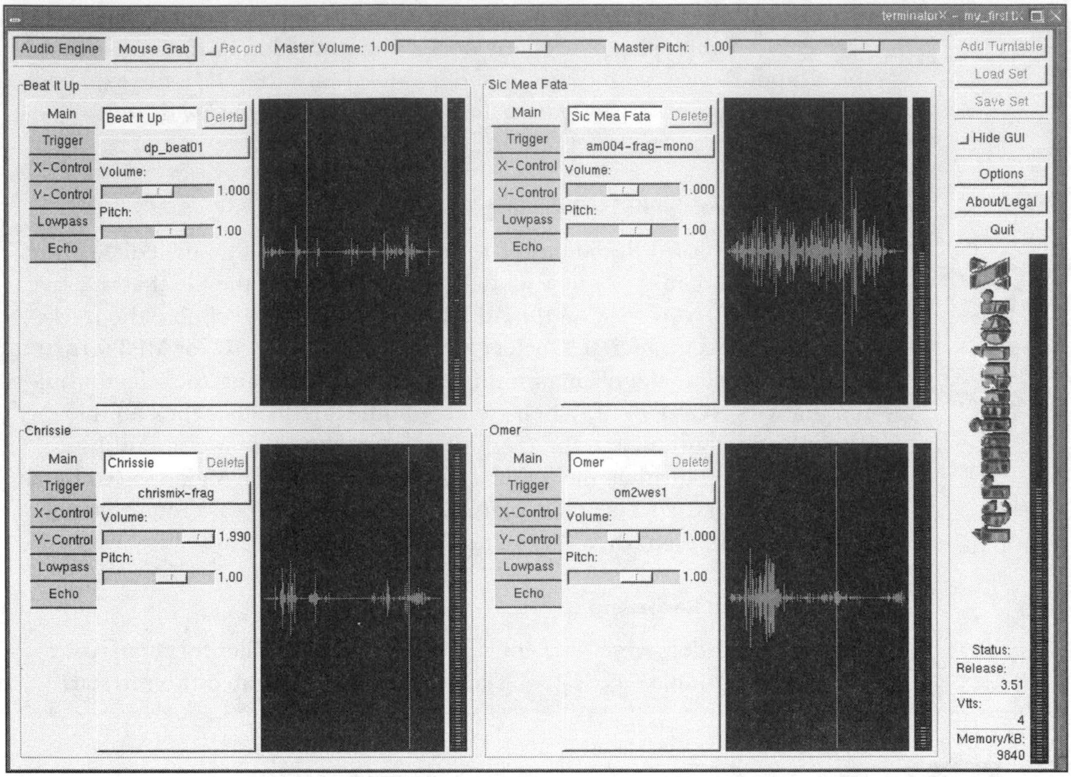

Figure 13-5: terminatorX with four turntables

Turntable 1, moving the mouse back and forth horizontally will scratch that soundfile, visibly controlling the movement of the selected turntable's cursor line. If the Y control is set for low-pass filtering, then moving the mouse vertically will control the brightness of the soundfile. Obviously, this combination of effects in terminatorX produces some very interesting sounds.

Keyboard Controls

When you want to leave Mouse Grab mode, just hit the ESC key. Because the mouse pointer is unavailable in Mouse Grab mode, you must learn the keyboard controls for full use of the program. Here is the list of keyboard and mouse controls currently available:

Keyboard:

TAB	Select next turntable
F1 to F12	Select turntable 1 to 12
RETURN	Triggers the turntable
Backspace	Stops the turntable

S	Toggles "Sync Client"
Spacebar	Maps turntable speed to mouse speed (scratching)
ALT	Mute on/off
CTRL	Mute on/off (inverted)
F	("Fast") Warp mode while scratching
W	Same as above but mutes audio while warping

Mouse:

Left button	Same as Spacebar
Right button	Select next turntable
Middle button	Mute on/off

With a little experimenting with these controls you can quickly master the various terminatorX operations and start to cut your own cool grooves. If you need beat patterns, a starter package of ten is available from the terminatorX Web site. However, you don't necessarily have to use beat pattern soundfiles in terminatorX: The program will happily process any sort of soundfile you desire.

Terminating Remarks

There's really not much more to say about terminatorX: It's easy to operate, it works, it's fun, and it can be a powerful and useful music-making tool. It's stable enough for both live performance and recording situations. terminatorX runs well even on my Pentium 166. I set up multiple turntables, and the program produced smooth audio output.

Even if you've never even seen a real turntable, you will find terminatorX to be an excellent substitute and a great way to learn about hip-hop–style scratching. Trust me: terminatorX is definitely dope Linux software.

Green Box

Author: Daniel Venkitachalam
Version profiled: 0.03
Web site: http://www.ecel.uwa.edu.au/~dvenkita/greenbox.htm
FTP site: n/a
Maintained: No
Availability: Free, open-source
License: GPL
Capsule summary: Straightforward, easy-to-use beat-box with some unique features

Daniel Venkitachalam's Green Box is a fine example of the virtual drum machine. It is a software incarnation of beat-boxes such as the Roland TR-808 and TR-909, the Alesis SR-16, and other popular drum modules. It is also inspired by the many software drum machines currently available for other platforms, particularly Rebirth and Drum Station for Windows.

The Green Box feature list is impressive: It has an attractive Qt with color-coded interface, imports 16-bit 44.1 kHz monaural WAV-format soundfiles for sound sources, saves patterns and loops in WAV format, and functions as an excellent partner to programs such as Oolaboola and terminatorX. It also offers:

- Internal resolution at 128 pulses per bar (32 ppq)

- Sixteen channels (instruments), each with its own volume and velocity (dynamics) controls

- Independent tempo that can be set anywhere from 30 to 400 bpm for every channel

- A mixer section that maintains overall balance of instrument sounds

- A master tempo control that can adjust all the channel tempos at once

- A "reversed 16th note" effect that plays the sound backward on the selected beats

- A clipping light to indicate soundcard buffer overflow

- A tracking display of current bar position following the selected channel's tempo

A lot to learn, perhaps—but read on, and the way will become clear. . . .

Getting It, Building It

Green Box requires the Qt libraries and header files. If you have the KDE desktop installed, you should have these files already placed in your system PATH. The latest Qt packages are always available for free from www.troll.no. You must also have Michael Pruett's libaudiofile installed; it can be downloaded from http://www.68k.org/~michael/audiofile.

Setting up Green Box is easy: Download the latest package and unpack it with **tar xzvf greenbox-latest.tar.gz** in your /home or /usr/local directory. A binary is included with the package: Run **ldd greenbox** to determine whether you have the required libraries to run it. If ldd shows no unresolved dependencies, you can simply use the included binary. If you need to build your own binary, follow the compiling instructions, edit the Makefile as necessary, then run **make** and (as root) **make install** to complete the build procedure.

Learning the Layout

Type **./greenbox** in the Green Box directory. The program must be launched from its home directory so it can find the images in the gfx subdirectory. In a moment you will see the display shown in Figure 13-6.

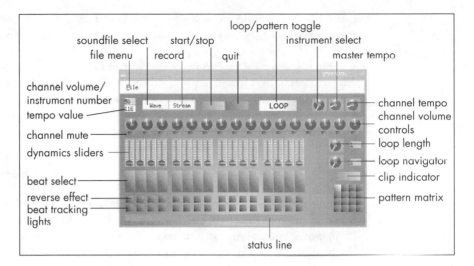

Figure 13-6: Green Box's opening display

Unfortunately the grayscale image cannot communicate the way color defines the various parts of Green Box. However, Green Box's layout is easy to understand.

The File menu lets you open and save the machine state (i.e., the session configuration and patterns) or quit the program. The two small numerical displays in the upper left corner are a general status display (on the top) for any changed value, such as when you increase a knob's value, and the overall tempo display (on the bottom). The Wave and Stream buttons open dialogs for selecting soundfiles and an output file name for streaming your loops and patterns to disk. To the right of those buttons are two colored tabs: The left (green) one toggles the start/stop play status, the right (red) one closes the program. The Loop/Pattern button toggles between the looping and pattern play modes. To the right of the Loop/Pattern button is a set of three knobs: The left (aqua) knob is the channel selector, the center (red) knob is the Master Tempo control, and the right (red) knob is the Channel Tempo control. Right-click on a knob to increase its value, left-click to decrease.

NOTE *The Channel Tempo is an experimental feature that permits multiple simultaneous tempos, but it may not always sync the audio streams correctly. Performance is best on CPUs faster than 266 MHz.*

The next row of sixteen knobs is the mixer section. The small tab underneath each knob toggles the channel mute; the knob itself controls the channel volume (right-click to increase, left-click to decrease).

The vertical sliders below the mixer section control the dynamics of the pattern of beats. We'll return to this section when we set up our first loop. The blue strips directly beneath the sliders are the beat select switches. Underneath the beat selectors you see two rows of red squares. The top row toggles the reversed sound effect for that particular beat, and the bottom row sets the active beats of the loop.

Finally, the two large knobs at the far right control the length of the loop (the top knob) and locate any pattern within the loop (the bottom knob). The green strip underneath these knobs indicates clipping (distortion from a too-loud signal). Below that is a pattern matrix for selecting new pattern spaces.

If you are a little confused by now, hang on! In a moment we'll create a loop and pattern to clarify the use of all these knobs, sliders, and tabs.

Using the Green Box

Composing loops and patterns with Green Box will feel very familiar to anyone who has had experience with typical drum machines and their software emulations. You assign instruments to channels, start loop play, then click on the beat line to add an event to any particular beat. You then switch to the next channel, repeat the process for that instrument, and so on until the pattern is acceptable. Select a new pattern from the grid of the thirty-two available pattern forms (empty by default) and start the process again, editing your rhythm patterns in real time.

Loading Sounds

First you need to load some sounds into Green Box. Click on the **Wave** button to open the file selector box and select an appropriate mono WAV-format file (a bass drum will be good for our first example). The current channel (instrument) is now set to your selected sound.

Entering a Rhythm

Now enter a rhythm. The blue strips beneath the sliders represent 16th notes. When you click on a slider, a light appears on the blue strip and the slider above it moves to the halfway point. Click on the 1st, 5th, 9th and 13th blue strips to enter a sequence of bass drum beats on the first, second, third, and fourth beats of a measure in 4/4 time. In short, use the blue buttons to enter the rhythm and the sliders to alter dynamics of a channel.

Figure 13-7 shows Green Box programmed for our bass drum beat.

Note that the top numerical display in the upper left corner shows a 0 because the sixteen instruments in Green Box are numbered 0 through 15. Also note that the status line across the bottom of the display shows the currently edited instrument channel.

Playing and Adjusting Your Rhythm

Press the green play strip next to the Stream button. You should now hear your bass drum beating a regular series of quarter notes in 4/4. While the beat pattern plays, accent the first beat of the pattern by moving the first slider

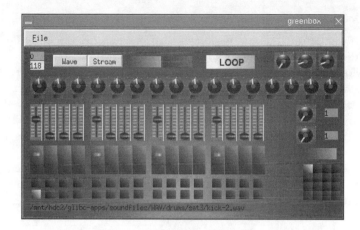

Figure 13-7: A bass drum beat in Green Box

upward. Now the first beat sounds louder than the others. Continue adjusting the rhythm and dynamics until you have a pattern you like.

Adding Another Channel

Of course, one instrument on one channel is not enough to make an interesting beat pattern. A typical drum pattern uses snare, bass, and hi-hat sounds. Move to another channel by adjusting the aqua Channel Selector knob in the top right corner or clicking on the appropriate mixer knobs with your middle mouse button. You can now open new WAV files for the sounds you want to include.

Figure 13-8 shows the pattern programmed for our hi-hat.

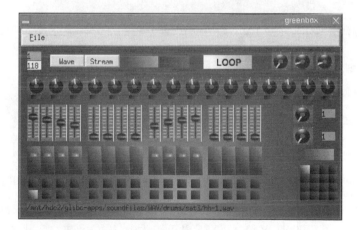

Figure 13-8: Green Box programmed for a hi-hat

Making Complex Loops

If you want to make loops longer than one bar, use the **Loop Length** knob at the right (the top aqua knob) to set the loop anywhere from 1 to 50 bars long. For our example, we'll make a four-bar loop. Set the **Loop Length** to 4, press **Play** (the green button next to Stream), and the current pattern will repeat itself four times. To introduce a new rhythm into the loop, use the lower aqua knob to select where to insert the rhythm. For our example, adjust the **Locator** knob to 2 and then choose a new (blank) pattern from the pattern matrix in the bottom right-hand corner.

Now enter a different rhythm for this part of the loop sequence. You can lock any particular pattern to play by toggling the **Pattern/Loop** button so you don't move on to the next part of the loop when the pattern ends. Edit the other two bars in your loop by selecting a previous rhythm or creating a new one.

Figure 13-9 illustrates an edit of instrument channel 2 (the snare drum), in bar 4 (pattern 2) of a four-bar loop.

Use the **Locator** knob to move to the beginning of the loop, then toggle the **Pattern/Loop** button to **Loop** mode and press **Play** to hear the entire loop. Press the **Stream** button to save your loop as a WAV file, and open **File • Save State**. . . to save your session configuration and rhythm patterns.

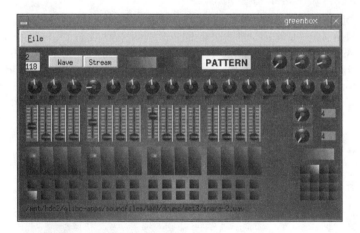

Figure 13-9: Editing instrument channel 2

Closing the Box

Green Box sequences patterns to create elaborate rhythm loops, making it an excellent companion to Oolaboola and terminatorX. Its design is deliberately based on the rhythmically strict beat-box, presenting only a single rhythm grid in 4/4 time. However, once you master the interface, Green Box opens itself to some uses quite beyond the beat-box model. Any WAV sound source can be utilized, and independent channel tempo control is included as an experimental feature. Green Box is a very useful tool, especially when combined with the other digital DJ tools presented in this chapter. Get it, learn it, have fun with Green Box.

Freebirth

Author: Topher Lafata, Jake Donham; graphics by Steve de Brun
Version profiled: 0.3.1
Web site: http://www.bitmechanic.com/projects/freebirth/
FTP site: n/a
Maintained: Yes
Availability: Free, open-source
License: GPL
Capsule summary: "All in one" sample-player/bass-synth/beat-box software designed for live performance

Essentially for performance, Freebirth is a software sample player, bass synthesizer, and step-sequencer. It has no soundfile saving functions, nor does it provide a way to recall your session settings, but its interface is exceptionally easy to navigate and play. Its bass synthesizer is modeled somewhat after the Roland TB303, and its step-sequencer is based on the Roland TR606 drum machine. Thus Freebirth is ideal as a "bass and drums" accompaniment for soloists—the 303 and the 606 were originally intended to be used together for that purpose.

Although the authors indicate their debt to the Roland TB303 and TR606, they state clearly that they have not tried to emulate those devices, and they note that Freebirth improves on them in many ways. Freebirth has three oscillators (sawtooth, square, and sine waves), each with separate tuning control, phase offset, and filter and volume envelopes; two effects busses for reverb and delay; and a step-sequencer that can trigger five arbitrary samples in RAW format. Freebirth's sample set makes up a very basic drum kit, but users can replace those samples with their own.

Getting It, Building It: Freebirth Day

Before building Freebirth, you must install the GTK, GDK, and GLIB libraries and header files. These are included with any Linux distribution carrying the GNOME desktop, but you can always find the latest packages at www.gtk.org.

Retrieve the latest Freebirth package from its Web site. Unpack it with **tar xzvf freebirth-latest.tar.gz** in your /home or /usr/local directory. Read the installation instructions, edit the Makefile as necessary, and run **make**. When the build is complete, type **./freebirth** to start the program. The binary must be run from the Freebirth home directory in order to access the samples and image bitmaps.

Using Freebirth

When the program opens, you will see the trio of windows shown in Figure 13-10.

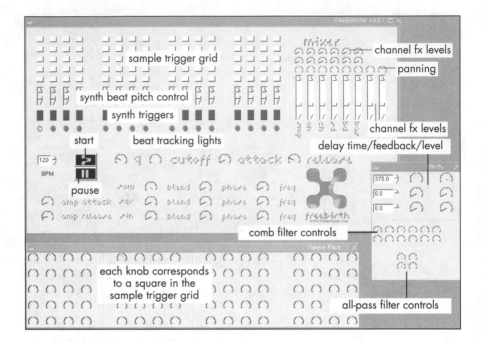

Figure 13-10: Freebirth's opening three windows

The top left panel of the largest window, consisting of four identical modules, is the step-sequencer—where you will compose your rhythm patterns and bass lines. Each module is composed of four identical vertical strips, and each strip contains (from top to bottom) five rhythm grid toggles for the five sampled sounds, a slider for the pitch of the bass synth, a toggle for the synth hit point, and a beat tracking light.

The top right section of this window is the mixer section, which provides sliders and knobs to control the relative channel volumes and panning positions as well as the effects line send and return values. Six sliders are labeled smp (sampled sound), oh (open hi-hat), ch (closed hi-hat), sn (snare), bd (bass drum), and bas (bass synth). The remaining two unlabeled sliders control the master volumes for the effects.

The virtual knobs in the lower half of the main window control the bass synthesizer. The synthesizer's global parameters include filter Q (resonance), cutoff frequency, and envelope attack and release times. The three oscillators have controls for their blend, phase, and frequencies, and the synth's output amplitude envelope has controls for its attack and release times. The synth panel also contains the Start/Stop and tempo controls.

The Sample Pitch window—immediately below the main window, across the bottom of the display—lets the user tune the sampled sounds. This is a very cool control, permitting some outrageous effects with realtime pitch-shifting. Used subtly, it helps create a more realistic dynamic space (a slight detuning adds realism to drum sounds, for instance). The Effects window—the smallest window, at the right of the display—controls the integrated delay (the top half) and reverb (the bottom half). The delay module is a set of three delay lines with parameters for delay time in milliseconds, feedback of the delay tapped, and the amount of the tap that will be sent to the module output. The reverb module displays six pairs of controls for delay time and feedback amount for each of the comb filters (which make the reverb) and two pairs of controls for phase and feedback values for the allpass filters. As in the Sample Pitch window, realtime control of the effects can produce some fascinating sonorities. Figure 13-11 shows Freebirth with settings for rhythm patterns, bass synthesis, sample pitch, and effects.

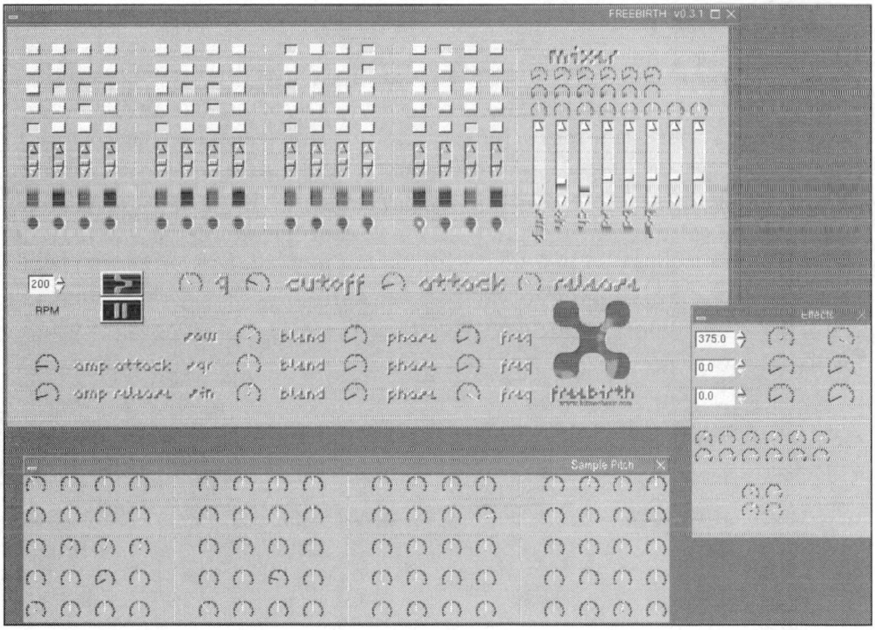

Figure 13-11: Freebirth with various settings

All of Freebirth's parameters are controllable in real time, and even if you know nothing about programming a synthesizer or a drum machine, you'll be able to quickly generate some great sounds and patterns. There's not much more to say about using Freebirth: The rest is all interactive.

Saving Sessions

One way to get around Freebirth's lack of a Save State function is to make a screenshot of a session setting. Although not the most elegant of solutions, this snapshot of your settings will at least give you a model to work from if you try to recreate the session later.

Freely Speaking

Freebirth is easy to use, incredibly fun, and sounds great. At the time of this writing, the program is strictly a performance-oriented virtual machine. The developers are considering ways to implement a digital audio save function, but even in its current state it has some very cool features. Freebirth will appeal especially to composers who want to create dance rhythm tracks for bass and drums, but its flexibilities should interest any Linux musician. Definitely recommended.

Togetherness . . .

You can integrate the software profiled in this chapter into a powerful toolkit. For example, you can use Green Box to create beat loops for use behind scratch tracks created in terminatorX, or save your recordings from terminatorX for use in the Oolaboola mixer. If you have external recording facilities (such as a tape or hard-disk recorder) you can save Freebirth performances and record them back into your computer for use as material for Oolaboola and terminatorX. And those of us fortunate enough to have two computers running Linux can play Freebirth on one machine while a friend plays Oolaboola on the other—a def jam, indeed.

14

LINUX GAMES

Computer games are the best indicators of how well a computer can present fast action in high-resolution graphics, seamless animations, scrolling text (often in unusual fonts), and of course high-quality sound in MIDI, MOD, and other digital audio formats. Until recently, games for Linux meant the various Pacman clones, Tetris variants, and chessboards available from the famous MetaLab (formerly sunsite) software repository (http://metalab.unc.edu). Many of those games are fun to play, but they are no match for the range and complexity of the commercial games familiar to Mac and Windows users.

However, in the late 1990s the maturity of Linux attracted the attention of serious game developers. id Software (www.idsoftware.com), creators of the enormously popular Doom, announced the commercial release of Quake III: Arena for Linux. The era of commercially available shrink-wrapped Linux games had arrived. Loki Entertainment (www.lokigames.com) has partnered with a variety of companies (including id Software) to bring the latest games to Linux, and at last Linux users can play the hottest new games on the hottest new operating system.

And things will only get better. Game development in the free software community benefits from the continuing expansion of game software development kits (SDK)—such as ClanLib (www.clanlib.org) and the SDL (Simple DirectMedia Layer) project (www.devolution.com/~slouken/projects/SDL/)

—that provide support for graphics and sound routines, freeing the game designer to concentrate on design.

Sound support in Linux games is relatively uncomplicated. If your sound system is set up properly and you can play WAV, MOD, and MIDI files, then you should have few if any problems getting great sound from your Linux gaming experience. Some games (such as Doom) may require a separate sound server, but most will provide transparent support for sound with no special software requirements.

The games presented in this chapter have been chosen for their availability, playability, and support for sound. Linux gaming is a rapidly developing activity—as I write this chapter in mid-2000, I can safely say that the fun is just beginning.

Quake

Authors: id Software (John Carmack, John Romero, Adrian Carmack, Zoid, others)
Version profiled: 1.0
Web sites: http://www.linuxquake.com
FTP site: ftp://ftp.idsoftware.com/idstuff
Maintained: Yes
Availability: Free, open-source
License: GPL
Capsule summary: Extremely fast 1st-person shooter with much violence and gore (rated PG)

Unless you've lived under a rock for the last decade, it's hard not to have heard about id Software's Doom and its even more intense successor, Quake. These games are fast, wild, and even frightening journeys through nightmarish scenarios populated by hellish monsters and mindless zombies, all of which you must avoid or destroy (before they destroy you) to reach the next level of the game. When it was first released, Doom set a new standard for action games, and Quake has advanced the standard even farther.

In 1999, id Software announced that the Quake source code would be opened and licensed under the GPL. Linux game developers considered this a major coup that made it easier to find and fix remaining bugs and add new features to a commercial-grade game. In addition, developers could sharpen their coding and design skills by studying the sources for a commercially successful large-scale game.

Getting It, Building—or Downloading—It

Generally speaking, if a package is available in source code, I usually prefer building it myself. However in the case of Quake, I advise downloading the pre-built binaries. The Quake source code is designed to compile under the Microsoft Visual C++ compiler and masm, the Microsoft assembler (to compile the parts written in assembly language). Although it is possible to use the native Linux assembler (named "as") and the GNU C/C++ compilers (gcc and g++), building Quake is definitely a task for the experienced Linux programmer. If you absolutely must build the game yourself, the q1source.txt file on the id Software ftp site (see above) contains the instructions for compiling it. For the purpose of this chapter, I will assume you are using one of the pre-built versions.

Free binaries for Quake are available for X11 and SVGA, but you will also need the data files from the Windows shareware version. Again, the LinuxQuake HOWTO will direct you to various sites for acquiring the binaries. Create a new directory for these files in your /home or /usr/local/ directory, then unpack the binaries with **tar xzvf quake-package.tar.gz**.

Next you need some levels to play. The id Software ftp site offers a free single-episode version of Quake. Download the quake106.zip file to your /home or /usr/local directory, create a new directory named **Quake**, then move the zipfile into it. Enter the Quake directory and unzip the archive with **gunzip quake106.zip**. A file named resource.1 will be created: This file is an lha archive and requires the lha file compression utility to unpack it. (If lha is not already on your system, you can find it at ftp://sunsite.unc.edu/pub/linux/utils/compress/lha-1.00.tar.z). Run lha e resource.1: A number of files and directories will be created, including the /id1 directory containing the data files for the various Quake levels.

NOTE *If you already have Quake installed in Windows, you can simply copy the* id1 *directory (and its files) to your Linux Quake directory. Alternately, you can copy the* resource.1 *archive file from the Quake CD-ROM and unpack it as described above.*

To start the game in X, open an xterm window, enter your Quake home directory and type **quake**. To start Quake from the console, enter **squake** at the command prompt.

Before You Begin

Quake starts up with a high-speed demonstration run through the first level. Hit your ESC key at any time to start the game, but before jumping into the fray you should set your preferences in the **Options** menu as shown in Figure 14-1.

The game includes a built-in CD player, so you can choose (from the **Options** menu) to listen to the music from the original distribution discs or any other audio CD in your collection. You can also set your competency rating, the graphics brightness, the mouse sensitivity, and the sound effects volume. With your preferred settings you can now chop, blast, frag (blow up an opponent with a fragmentation bomb), and race your way through the demonic world of Quake.

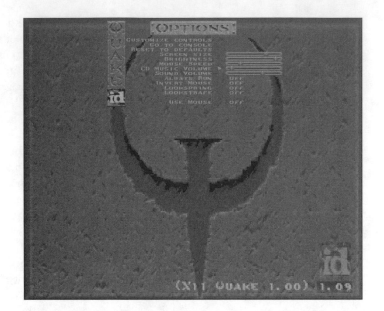

Figure 14-1: The Quake Options menu

Playing Quake

This is Quake: Monsters want to kill you before you can reach the gate to the next level, so your primary activity is to stay alive as you move through each scenario picking up life extenders such as health packs, protective armor, and new weapons and ammunition. You can save your game at any time, making it easy for you to learn the tricks without having to start over from the beginning each time you get slaughtered by some mindless zombie.

Beyond that, you're on your own.

Quake's graphics and sound are designed to invoke dread and caution. At all times a grim sky is moving overhead, while lurid lighting effects flicker and pulsate around you. Even when you can't see them, you hear the sounds of creatures just around the corner, warning you to stay locked and loaded for the next fast-action firefight. The sound effects were created by Trent Reznor (of Nine Inch Nails fame) and are employed to great effect throughout the game: a low moaning wind whenever you enter an area open to the sky, the distinctive growl of each type of creature, and appropriately loud weaponry. More ethereal sounds are heard when Quake "secrets," such as magic runes and hidden passages, are discovered.

Figure 14-2 shows a typical Quake scene.

Quakin' All Over

The free version of Quake is very easy to set up and play, and the commercial versions provide extended features such as network play, more levels, and of

Figure 14-2: Quake carnage

course commercial support. id Software has also developed Quake 2 and Quake 3: Arena for players who just can't get enough of those zombies, and developer John Carmack is particularly devoted to providing the highest quality gaming experience to Linux players. Many gamers consider Quake the greatest first-person shooter game ever written, but you don't have to take anyone else's word for it. Download it, play it, and see for yourself why I consider it a "Must Have" game for Linux. Frag on!

Roll 'Em Up

Authors: Lost Boys Media Lab (Taco Kampstra, others)
Version profiled: n/a
Web site: http://medialab.lostboys.nl
FTP site: ftp://usa.lostboys.nl/pub/medialab/rollemup/Linux/Rollemup.tar.gz
Maintained: No
Availability: Binary-only demo
License: Held by authors
Capsule summary: Software pinball at its finest, fastest, and loudest

I love pinball games. When I was much (much!) younger I played in bar bands, and playing pinball was a routine activity during rehearsal breaks and between sets. When I went looking for a good pinball simulator for Linux, I had no idea anything like Roll 'Em Up existed. The game motto says it all: "multi-ball, multi-player, multi-platform, multi-media, multi-cool."

Getting It, Building It

Download the binary package from the ftp site listed above. The size of the package is about 20 MB, so if you have a slow connection to the Internet you should be aware that the download will take quite a while. Once the package is downloaded, open it in your /home or /usr/local/ directory with **tar xzvf Rollemup.tar.gz**. A new Rollemup directory will be created, containing the binary, a README file, and a sample `Rollemup.ini` file.

Because the game is binary-only, you must have specific libraries installed for it to run at all. Here is a list of the necessary libraries:

```
libX11.so.6
libXext.so.6
libpthread.so.0
libstdc++.so.2.8
libm.so.6
libc.so.6
/lib/ld-linux.so.2
```

Run **ldd Rollemup** to see if your system meets these dependencies. Mainstream Linux distributions will include them as a matter of course, but if they are not present on your system, you can find them all at the MetaLab site (http://metalab.unc.edu).

Figure 14-3: Roll 'Em Up's splash screen

Playing Roll 'Em Up

Come on, it's a pinball game! About all you need to know is that the z and /
keys operate the flippers, the ENTER key launches the ball, and the Spacebar
"shakes" the machine. The ESC key will bring up a list of top scores along with
a drop-down menu for toggling the sound support and quitting the game.

Figures 14-3 through 14-5 display Roll 'Em Up's splash screen, Help
menu, and game table, respectively.

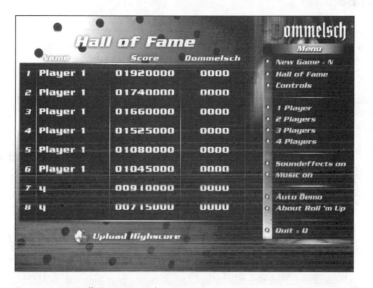

Figure 14-4: Roll 'Em Up's Help menu

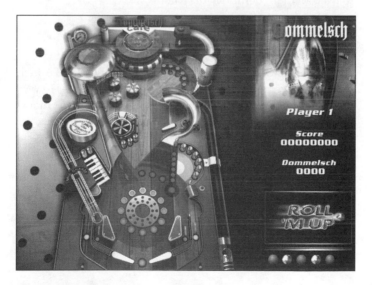

Figure 14-5: Roll 'Em Up's game table

Rolling It Up

Roll 'Em Up is an impressive game. It runs quickly and smoothly even on my P166, a very slow machine by contemporary standards. With its beautiful graphics, excellent ballistics and soundtrack, Roll 'Em Up is an easy winner of Most Recommended Linux Game status.

Myth2: Soulblighter

Authors: Bungie Software
Version profiled: 1.3d (demo)
Web site: http://www.lokigames.com/
FTP site: ftp://ftp.linuxgames.com/loki/demos/myth2/
Maintained: Yes
Availability: Binary-only
License: Commercial
Price: $49.95 US
Capsule summary: Fantasy adventure at its best, with superb graphics, animation, and sound

Myth2: Soulblighter is a fantasy action/strategy game in which you are "[i]n command of a ragtag army of berserkers, dwarves, soldiers and sorcerers," and must save "the folk of Madrigal and the West from the evil might of Soulblighter and his minions."

Fantasy action/strategy games typically involve long-range planning, troop maintenance and deployment, battle tactics and strategies, and knowing the ways of magic and sorcery. If that sounds like the kind of game you'd like to play, Myth2 is definitely for you.

Getting It, Building It

The version profiled here is the demo available from the Loki Software site (www.lokigames.com). The download is a hefty 66 MB, which should be no problem on fast ADSL or cable modem connections. However, if your Internet connection is slow or disconnects after a certain number of hours, you will want to download and use the wget (ftp://prep.ai.mit.edu/pub/gnu/) program to retrieve the file. The following command will repeatedly download the game until it has been entirely transferred:

```
wget -o logfile -c "ftp://ftp.linuxgames.com/loki/demos/myth2/myth2-demo.run"
```

Simply enter ./myth2-demo.run to create the myth2_demo directory and install the game. Move into the new directory, read the README file, then run ./setup.sh to determine your system architecture for the game. Now type ./myth2 (while still in the myth2_demo directory) to start playing.

Playing Myth2

The demo begins with a short movie depicting scenes from the story, accompanied by an excellent soundtrack. When the movie ends, you will be greeted by the ominous screen shown in Figure 14-6.

Select **Preferences** to set the various options seen in Figure 14-7.

Figure 14-6: Greetings from Myth2

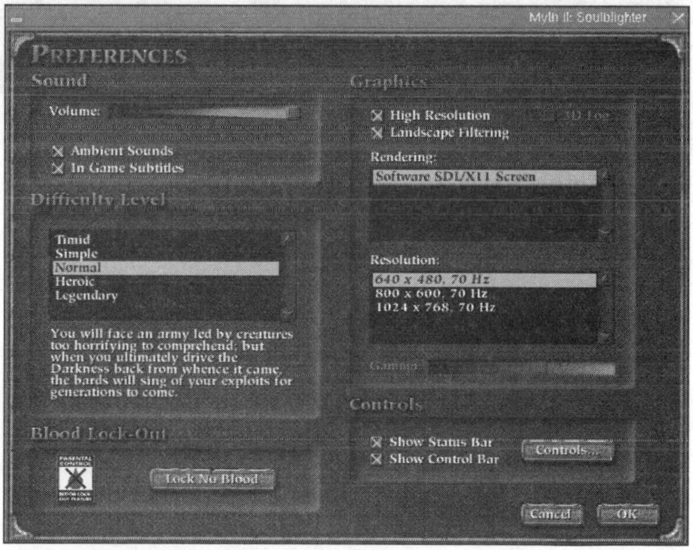

Figure 14-7: Setting your preferences in Myth2

Click on **OK** when you have set your preferences, then select **Tutorial** to learn how to control your combatants. Knights, archers, dwarves, and sorcerers are the sorts of characters you will equip and guide into battle to save the good folk of Madrigal from the evil Soulblighter, and each of them has a special skill. A voice-over describes camera control, single-character and group movements, and the finer points of swordplay, archery, satchel bombs, and fireballs.

The tutorial beautifully demonstrates the game's audio support: Characters respond vocally to your orders (knights are soldierly, dwarves are grumpy), weaponry is appropriately noisy, and your training is accompanied by the ambient sounds of a quasi-medieval countryside, complete with creaking windmills and clucking chickens. Figure 14-8 shows a typical scene from the tutorial.

Figure 14-8: Myth2 tutorial: Your knights prepare to chop up pumpkin-headed scarecrows

Quit the tutorial and select **New Game** from the **Main** menu. An animated story line (shown in Figure 14-9) will scroll past, accompanied by another voice-over describing the situation you and your army will face.

After the introduction, the screen will display your mission objectives as shown in Figure 14-10.

You must now march onward and vanquish (or be vanquished by) the minions of Soulblighter.

Closing the Myth

I have given you only a glimpse of Myth2: Soulblighter, but I hope you will be inspired to enter its world on your own. It is truly a splendid game, far richer

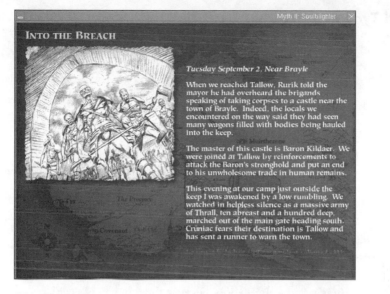

Figure 14-9: The Myth2 story line

Figure 14-10: Your mission objectives

than I can indicate in this profile. If you're lucky and skilled, you'll have a chance to defeat the "army led by creatures too horrifying to comprehend." If you succeed, "the bards will sing of your exploits for generations to come. . . . "

Railroad Tycoon II

Authors: PopTop Software
Version profiled: 1.54 (demo)
Web site: http://www.lokigames.com
FTP site: ftp://ftp.linuxgames.com/loki/demos/rt2
Maintained: Yes
Availability: Binary-only
License: Commercial
Price: $49.95 US
**Capsule summary: Sophisticated simulation game with excellent graphics
and sound**

Railroad Tycoon II (RT2) is another commercially available game from Loki
Games. In this game, you set out to build a railroad empire and become an
industry baron. Beginning with an initial capital outlay, you start your own
railway company and spend your money wisely (or not) to lay track, build stations, and maintain and expand your company interests. This type of game is
often called a simulation, because the game play simulates real-world developments and necessities. RT2 requires great skill in managing and deploying
resources, but with practice you too can become a virtual railroad tycoon.

Getting It, Building It

As with Myth2, this review is based on the free demo version of RT2 available
from the Loki Games Web site. The package weighs in at about 50 MB, so if
you have trouble retrieving it, please read the Myth2 profile for instructions
on using the `wget` utility.

Unpack the package with **`tar xzvf rt2-demo.tar.gz`**, enter the new **RT2**
directory, and study the README file for the most recent news about the
game. Because the game is available in binary form only, simply type in **`./rt2`**
(while still in the RT2 directory) to start it. The Loki splash screen will appear,
followed by the startup menu shown in Figure 14-11.

Working on the Railroad

If you've played other "sim" games, RT2 will feel quite familiar, but if you're new
to the genre you should work through the tutorial. Select **Load Scenario** from
the startup menu and click on the **Tutorial**. This scenario presents an 1870s English landscape in which you will connect the various towns and villages, gradually
expanding the reach of your new railroad. Because building the railroad
depletes your cash, you must also deliver and manage services to generate rev-
enue in order to keep expanding. The basic procedure is to lay track, add
stations, buy trains, and then provide transportation and other services to
increase your total wealth. Figure 14-12 shows a look at the tutorial scenario.

The tutorial will walk you through the various aspects of game play, such
as founding your company and building your railways. The game itself is very

Figure 14-11: The RT2 startup menu

Figure 14-12: RT2 tutorial

easy to play, but your success as a railroad tycoon depends on the intelligent use of your resources and your ability to weather such vagaries as bandits, train wrecks, and stock market reversals.

Once you've mastered the tutorial, it's time to build your empire. Return to the **Main** menu and select **New Scenario**, choose a new map and difficulty level, then click on **OK** to start playing. Figure 14-13 shows the New Scenario setup window.

Figure 14-13: Selecting a New Scenario in Railroad Tycoon II

Figure 14-14: Chicago, from the Heartland USA scenario

Figure 14-14 shows the map for the Chicago area in the "Heartland USA" scenario.

As you can see, the graphics are superb, even when zoomed in to high detail. Audio support is likewise excellent, with a full complement of the sounds and noises of the trains and with ambient sounds appropriate to your current location. It is a credit to the designers that, although the sound is constant, it is never annoying and always seems well integrated with the activity on-screen.

Getting off This Train

RT2 is easy to learn but quite challenging. Like Myth2, it lives up to Loki's goal of providing a top-quality gaming experience for Linux gamers, with first-rate graphics and sound and a highly intelligent game plan. If amassing a fortune by building your own railroad appeals to you, or if you just like the sight and sounds of trains, then you need to play RT2. Another "Most Recommended" game from Loki.

Clanbomber

Authors: Andreas Hundt, Denis Oliver Kropp
Version profiled: 1.00
Web site: http://www.clanbomber.de
FTP site: n/a
Maintained: Yes
Availability: Free, open-source
License: GPL
Capsule summary: Easy, noisy game play, and great fun for all ages

Clanbomber is modeled on the popular Bomberman game. The main activity in Clanbomber consists of moving around the game area and planting very loud explosives to rid yourself of your opponents (who, of course, are trying to do the same thing to you). You can play against computer-controlled players, but the authors recommend playing with as many as eight friends for the most fun.

Getting It, Building It

Clanbomber requires the zLib, ClanLib, and Hermes libraries for its graphics and sound support, and they are all available from the Clanbomber Web site. With those libraries installed, download the latest version of Clanbomber from www.clanbomber.de. Put the package in your /home or /usr/local/ directory and unpack it with **tar xzvf clanbomber-latest.tar.gz**. Enter the new Clanbomber directory and run **./configure**, followed by **make** and (as root) **make install**. Now let's play Clanbomber!

Playing Clanbomber

Enter **clanbomber** at the command prompt in an xterm window or at the console. You will be asked what video display type should be used. Enter the appropriate type; after a brief splash screen, you will see the display shown in Figure 14-15.

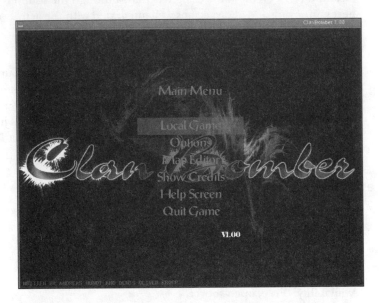

Figure 14-15: The Clanbomber Main menu

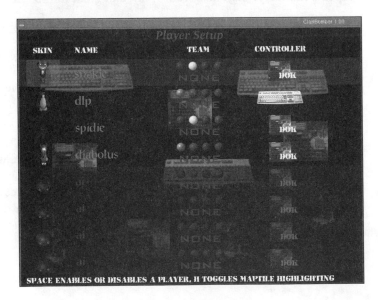

Figure 14-16: Player Setup in Clanbomber

Figure 14-17: Beginning Clanbomber

Open the **Options** menu to toggle the music track and various other settings. Press the ESC key to return to the **Main** menu, then select **Local Game**. When that menu opens, select **Player Setup** to choose your players and set up teams. Figure 14-16 shows the **Player Setup** window.

When you've completed the player setup, return to the **Local Game** menu. Set the round time and the number of points needed to win, select a terrain map, and start the game. The screen shown in Figure 14-17 will appear.

From here on out, planting bombs and avoiding the bombs planted by your opponents are your primary activities. As squares on the board are blown up, various new powers are revealed (such as hurling bombs and getting two-for-one explosions). Acquiring those powers can help you collect points, but your time is always running out in Clanbomber. Eventually a big rubber ball will enter the playing field. It will bounce around and punch empty spaces at random, leaving you with less and less room to move. Finally, your score is assessed and you proceed to the next level.

Bombing Out

My description hardly does justice to the game and the fun of playing it. With the incessant motion of your opponents, the bombs exploding constantly, and the continuous music soundtrack, Clanbomber's excitement level is quite high. Game play is fast, and the graphics and sound are very good. Clanbomber is easy to build, easy to play, and easy to enjoy. In short, it's a blast. . . . <groan>

15

OPERATING SYSTEM EMULATORS

 This chapter covers Linux operating system emulation programs for MS-DOS (DOSemu), the Apple Macintosh OS (ARDI Executor), and Windows (WINE). Because many of these emulators are designed for users who wish to play their old favorite games on their new favorite operating system, developers have paid particular attention to audio support.

The Linux Sound & Music Applications page at http://www.bright.net/ ~dlphilp/linuxsound contains a list of the emulation systems currently available for Linux that support audio and/or MIDI.

Sound Check

Before downloading any of this software, remember to check the application's most current documentation for sound system status reports. If you intend to run a particular sound or MIDI application, your chance of success will depend on the emulator's support for the necessary file formats, audio sampling rates, and MIDI drivers.

DOSemu

Authors: Matthias Lautner, Robert Sanders, James MacLean, Hans Lermen, many others
Version profiled: 0.98.6
Web site: http://www.dosemu.org
FTP site: n/a
Maintained: Yes
Availability: Free, open-source
License: Held by the DOSemu Development Team, some parts under the GPL
Capsule summary: Complete, stable MS-DOS emulation. Runs nearly all DOS-specific software, including many audio and MIDI applications

DOSemu is an MS-DOS emulator for Linux.

Among its capabilities, DOSemu can trap and emulate a DOS program's system calls, including calls to basic Sound Blaster (or compatible) audio and MIDI services. PCM audio, the UART MIDI interface, and some of the sound-card mixer functions (master volume, PCM audio level, CD level) are currently supported.

Getting It, Building It

To use DOSemu you need a working copy of MS-DOS on your hard disk. If you have a dual-boot machine with Windows and Linux installed, you should have no trouble setting up DOSemu. If DOS is not installed, you can try using FreeDOS, a free clone of MS-DOS available from www.freedos.org.

DOSemu is available as an installable package in most Linux distributions. If you do not have such a distribution, simply retrieve the DOSemu package from this book's CD-ROM or the Web site listed above, unpack it into an empty directory with **tar xzvf dosemu-latest.tgz**, and follow the build and installation instructions.

Know Your Configuration!

The configuration instructions are especially important: DOSemu depends upon a file named `dosemu.conf` that is typically placed in your `/etc` directory. Here is a look at the relevant portion of that file configured for my system:

```
$_sound = (on)            # sound support on/off
$_sb_base = (0x220)
$_sb_irq = (5)
$_sb_dma = (1)
$_sb_dsp = "/dev/dsp"
$_sb_mixer = "/dev/mixer"
$_mpu_base = "0x330"
```

As you can see, you need to know the base address of your soundcard, the numbers for the IRQ and DMA ports DOSemu will use, the MIDI port's base address, and the names for the Linux audio and mixer devices. The port numbers and base addresses are normally found in your soundcard's documentation. If you don't have that information, it is unlikely that you have a working Linux sound system anyway, and you may need to contact the card manufacturer for the needed specifications.

While in dosemu.conf, you should probably also set the aptly named hogthreshold to **0**. This ensures that the CPU will devote all its processing to DOSemu, which is necessary to avoid gaps and stuttering during playback.

Other important settings in dosemu.conf include designations for your mouse and your video support. Detailed instructions for customizing this file are included in the DOSemu package. Because each system will present unique hardware settings, it is not possible to cover the entire DOSemu setup, but if you follow the documentation you should have few or no problems with the configuration. DOSemu has been in development since 1992 and is an exceptionally stable and well-documented program.

DOSemu runs in both console mode and X:

To launch in console mode: Simply enter **dos** at the console prompt to call up the ancient MS-DOS prompt. Note that if you have Windows 95 or later installed, you may have to select the Command-prompt only mode from the startup menu presented during the Windows boot process.

To launch in X: Type **xdos** in an xterm window, and a separate window will open for your DOS session.

Whichever mode you choose, when you've reached the DOS prompt you are ready to start testing your DOS MIDI software under Linux.

Using DOSemu with DOS MIDI Programs

Your success with DOSemu will depend on a variety of factors. The most important is whether a native DOS MIDI or audio driver will work with the emulator. Many early DOS sequencers and other MIDI applications simply accessed the MIDI interface in what is known as UART or dumb mode (so called because it does not recognize or generate advanced features such as timing synchronization or multiport hardware). You can probably get such programs working in DOSemu without any special setup. For example, I got both the RAVEL and MusicBox programs working with relatively little effort, because they both use the interface in UART mode.

I have been able to run most of my favorite DOS MIDI software on DOSemu. Here is the list of the programs I could run at the time of this book's printing:

Application	Description	Version	Author/Manufacturer
Sequencer Plus Gold	MIDI sequencer	4.09	Voyetra Technologies (http://www.voyetra.com)
Sideman D/TX	Synthesizer editor	—	Voyetra Technologies (http://www.voyetra.com)
M/pc	Algorithmic music maker	1.10b	Voyetra Technologies (http://www.voyetra.com)
Drummer	Drum machine composer	2.0	Cool Shoes Software (unavailable)
RAVEL	MIDI programming environment	3.0	Jim Binkley (ftp://ftp.cs.pdx.edu/pub/music/ravel/)
MusicBox	MIDI programming environment	—	John Dunn (http://algoart.com)

The directions for audio support given in the DOSemu package are simple enough: A link is established with /dev/midi or /dev/sequencer, and all native DOS calls to the MIDI hardware are intercepted by DOSemu and rerouted to the appropriate Linux MIDI device. However, Voyetra's software will not transmit or receive MIDI data unless a Voyetra MIDI interface (VAPI) driver is present, which presents a problem: Only one of the VAPI drivers will work (vapimpu.com), and then only at certain version levels (1.26 and 1.33). In order to use either of those drivers, you must add the IRQ number. Here's the command I use in DOSemu to load the VAPIMPU driver:

```
vapimpu /IRQ:7
```

The specific version level of the driver is quite important: I tried using version 1.51, but even with the IRQ flag it would not load.

Software Support

My experience with running the Voyetra MIDI programs underscores the importance of having all the support software at hand, such as Voyetra's drivers or the Cool Shoes graphics files. Consider it a basic rule that whatever was required to run the application natively in MS-DOS will also be required to run it under DOSemu.

Some Cool DOS Music Programs to Try with DOSemu

Sequencer Plus Gold and M/pc

Sequencer Plus Gold (shown in Figure 15-1) is my favorite MS-DOS MIDI sequencer, and I'm quite pleased with its performance in DOSemu. I have also been able to use Voyetra's M/pc (version 1.10b), which is a port of M 2.0 (by

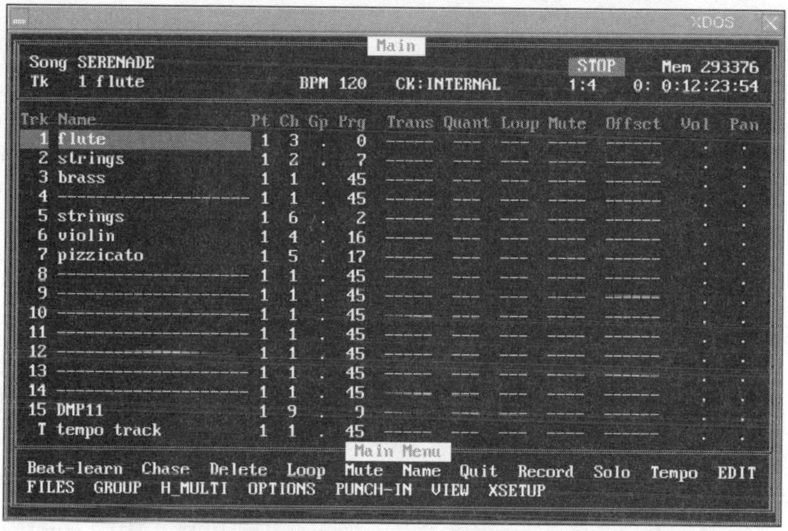

Figure 15-1: The main screen in Sequencer Plus Gold under DOSemu

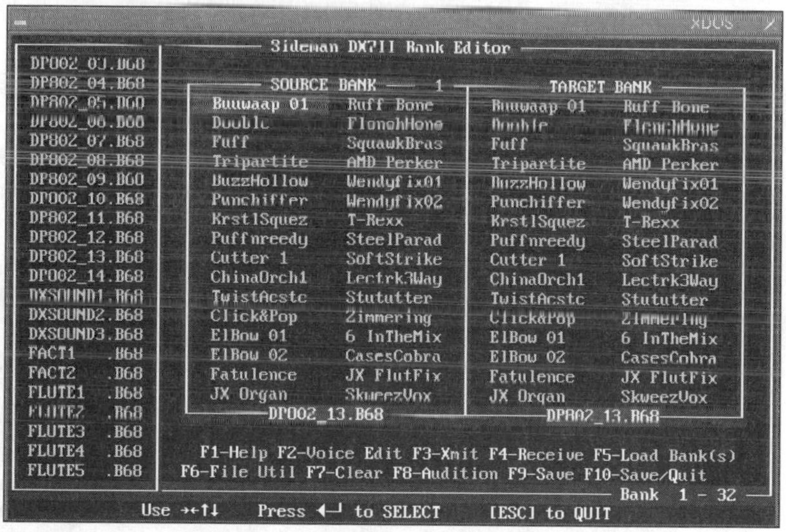

Figure 15-2: Sideman D/TX DX7 editor in DOSemu

Joel Chadabe and David Zicarelli) for the Macintosh. M is a fascinating MIDI composition environment with an excellent interactive GUI. Interestingly, M/pc utilizes a run-time version of Windows 2.0, which DOSemu handles with no problems. And thanks to DOSemu, I can still use Voyetra's Sideman D/TX editor with my Yamaha TX802 synthesizer—it's shown in Figure 15-2.

Drummer

Cool Shoes Software's wonderful Drummer 2.0 is an excellent MS-DOS MIDI program "loosely modeled on a drum machine" that lets you arrange beat patterns into your own score. Its performance is quite stable under DOSemu. I have been unable to find a music software distributor still carrying Drummer, but if you are fortunate enough to own a copy you should definitely try it out under DOSemu.

RAVEL

Jim Binkley's RAVEL is a C-like MIDI programming environment especially well suited to exploring algorithmic composition. No special drivers or other software is required for RAVEL to run under Linux: It ran perfectly the first time I tried it under DOSemu.

MusicBox

MusicBox (Figure 15-3) is a unique algorithmic MIDI composition environment from John Dunn. It utilizes a cryptic ASCII interface, yet is an amazingly powerful program: Various modules are linked together to process and output any type of MIDI events, including system-exclusive messages. I've used MusicBox to create a sequencer, a virtual drum machine, and an editor for a Kawai K4 synthesizer. A mouse must be loaded for the program to run but, as with RAVEL, no VAPI or other proprietary driver needs to be installed. The MIDI setup recommended in the DOSemu documentation is sufficient for using MusicBox under Linux. Readers interested in trying MusicBox can download it at ftp://mustec.bgsu.edu/pub/linux/mbox.tar.gz.

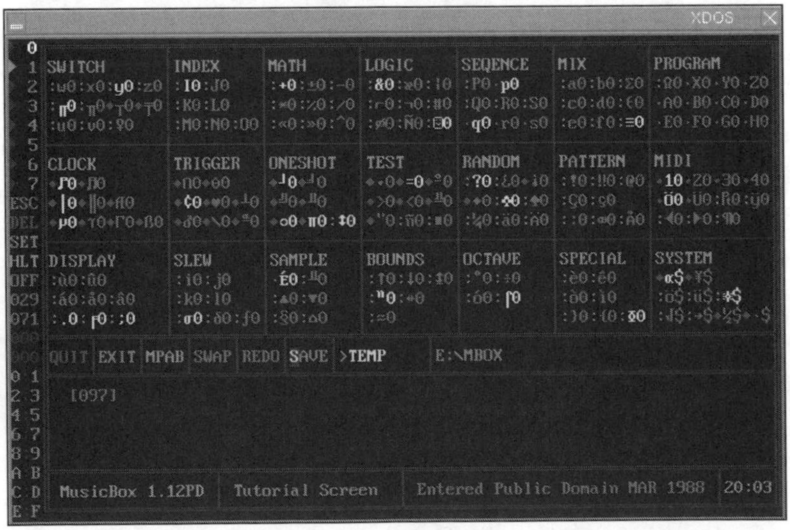

Figure 15-3: MusicBox running under DOSemu

Music Printer Plus, Convert, and pcmusic

Other significant successes with music and sound software under DOSemu include Music Printer Plus, an excellent DOS-based music notation program (see http://www.musicwareinc.com/mppfaq.htm for more information) and Jesus Villena's Convert (http://www.th-zwickau.de/%7emaz/convert.html), a soundfile conversion utility that supports a wide variety of formats. Professor F. Richard Moore's pcmusic, a DOS port of his venerable cmusic software synthesis language, runs very well under DOSemu. It is available from ftp://wendy.ucsd.edu/pub/pcmusic. And as might be expected, Csound for DOS also runs well.

Summary Remarks

Your success or failure at running a DOS music or sound program depends on its ability to support the basic Sound Blaster configuration. Programs that let you select the MIDI or audio devices will fare better than programs requiring special hardware or vendor-specific drivers. If you lack certain pieces of support software, you can try writing to the manufacturer (if they're still in business), but it will be the rare company that still supports their ancient MS-DOS MIDI software. You may have to scour the Internet, asking for help on various relevant newsgroups (such as comp.os.msdos.apps and comp.os.msdos.misc), but with some persistence you may be able to revive some good and useful DOS MIDI software.

ARDI Executor

Author: Cliff Matthews
Version profiled: 2.1pre6 demo
Web site: http://www.ardi.com
FTP site: n/a
Maintained: Yes
Availability: Commercial
License: Held by ARDI Inc.
Price: US$75 (regular), US$35 (student)

ARDI Executor is designed to let you run Macintosh applications on a PC. The compatibility page (http://www.ardi.com/compat/search.phtml) lists hundreds of Macintosh programs that will run under Executor, including many sound and music applications. Executor has been in continuous development since 1986, and the ARDI company regards Linux as its primary target platform. Its years of development have resulted in a remarkably powerful and stable emulator.

Setting Up Executor

After retrieving the software from this book's CD-ROM or the ARDI Web site, simply unpack it in an empty directory and follow the installation instructions. Executor is available in binary form only, so there is no build procedure, and you can place the software wherever you like. If you download the RPM (Red Hat Package Manager) bundle, you can automate the entire setup by typing `rpm -iv executor-glibc-demo-2.1pr6-1.i386.rpm`. Repeat this procedure for any other packages included with the distribution: Separate RPMs are included for the X and SVGA versions of Executor.

Running Executor

Typing `executor-demo` in an xterm window calls the Executor splash screen and then the license agreement. After clicking the **Accept** button, you're ready to use Executor.

But before you get excited at the prospect of running Opcode's Studio Vision or Mark Of The Unicorn's synthesizer editors, I must warn you that Executor does not support MIDI. In general, Executor's sound support is primitive at this time. However, you can still create audio files to play with your regular Linux soundfile players, and some truly excellent Macintosh audio software is available for free over the Internet. Try the repository at ftp://notam.uio.no/pub/mac/audio_old/ for a large collection of free Mac music software.

Executor In Action

. . . with SoundHack

Tom Erbe's SoundHack is an impressive utility for performing a variety of interesting operations on soundfiles. Binaural filtering (placing the sound in space relative to the listener), convolution (a method for reverberating a signal), spectral dynamics processing (compressing and expanding a signal's frequency levels), and phase vocoding (analyzing a signal's amplitude and frequency content) are all available in SoundHack. The documentation will tell you all you need to know about using SoundHack. Meanwhile, Figure 15-4 shows the program running under Executor in Linux.

. . . with Spliner

Spliner provides a graphic interface for drawing smooth curves (known as cubic-spline curves) for use in Csound function tables. Points can be subsequently added or removed from the graph, and the table values are calculated and displayed at the bottom of the graph window. The brief documentation explains the program's use and history. Figure 15-5 shows off Spliner doing what it does best.

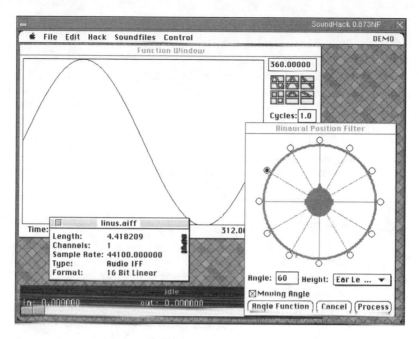

Figure 15-4: SoundHack under Executor

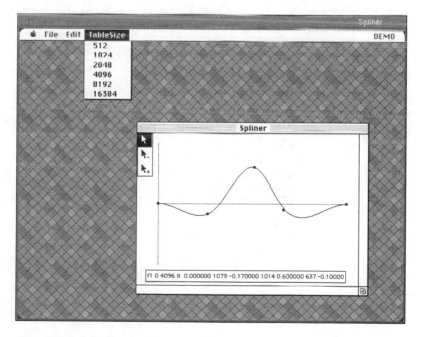

Figure 15-5: Spliner under Executor

. . . with Out Of Phase

For my last example I've chosen Out Of Phase, an ". . . almost real time wavetable and algorithm based synthesis language." The interface includes built-in editors for waveforms, standard music notation symbols, and text (for writing synthesis and composition algorithms). Out Of Phase is too complex to explain further here, but Figure 15-6 should give you some notion of the program at work.

SoundHack, Spliner, and Out Of Phase are all available from the NoTAM ftp site mentioned above. Look for the packages SH0873.hqx, spliner.cpt.hqx, and out-of-phase-13.hqx. Executor comes with the handy StuffIt! Expander software to unpack this software.

Summary

Executor runs a wide variety of Macintosh programs, and its years of development have clearly paid off in an outstanding program. Cliff Matthews has indicated that audio support is important to Executor's evolution, and we can expect improved audio functions in upcoming releases. Executor is stable and very usable: If you want to run some of your favorite Mac applications, or if you'd like to learn about Macintosh software without buying a Mac, ARDI Executor is definitely the way to go.

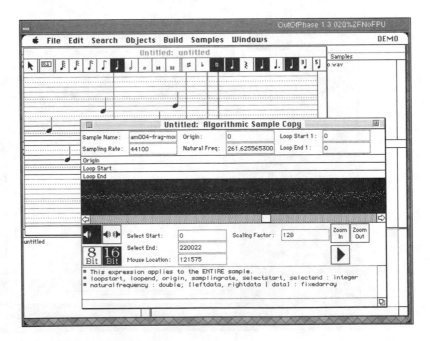

Figure 15-6: Out Of Phase under Executor

WINE

Authors: Too many to list (see the AUTHORS file in the WINE package)
Version profiled: wine-000112
Web site: http://www.winehq.com
FTP site: n/a
Maintained: Yes
Availability: Open-source, free
License: BSD-style

WINE is an acronym for either "WINdows Emulator" or "Wine Is Not an Emulator." Curiously, both interpretations are correct. WINE itself is indeed a Windows environment emulator, enabling some Windows programs to run under Linux as though they were native Linux applications. The WINE project is also focused on the libwine library, a code base designed to make easier ports of software from Windows to Linux and other UNIX environments.

Support for sound and MIDI in WINE includes the basic Sound Blaster functions (similar to those supported by DOSemu) and other audio extensions, such as Microsoft's DirectX. However, providing such support in an emulated Windows environment has proven much more difficult than it has been for DOSemu. You probably won't be able to run Cakewalk or Cool Edit Pro, but WINE can run a variety of lighter-weight sound and music applications. Check the WINE Web site for links to lists that enumerate users' successes and failures in running specific applications under WINE, including a number of music and sound applications.

WINE is still considered an alpha-stage project. It is not uncommon for an application to work under one WINE release, only to be broken by the next release. The WINE documentation gives detailed instructions for submitting useful bug reports, so if you find that your favorite Windows program isn't working anymore under WINE, you can help the project by submitting a report, usually to the comp.os.emulators.windows newsgroup. That forum is also an excellent source of information about successes and failures with specific Windows applications under WINE. You may find that someone else on the newsgroup has already supplied just what you need to know in order to get your favorite Windows program up and running in your favorite operating system (Linux, of course).

Getting It, Building It

Before you can do anything with WINE, you need to have Windows installed and working. You will also need to mount the drive (while still in Linux) containing the installation in order to make your Windows programs available to the emulator. Here's how I do it on my system:

```
mount /dev/hda1 /mnt/dosc
```

And, of course, if you want to run any music or sound applications under WINE you will need a working Linux audio system (see Chapter 2).

Download the latest binary or source package from the WINE Web site, or copy the version included on this book's CD-ROM. Red Hat Linux users will be happy to learn that RPMs of the most recent releases are available at various sites listed on the WINE Web pages. Building WINE isn't terribly difficult, but the RPM packages simplify the installation process for users who just want to test the waters before jumping in.

Keep in mind that WINE's development pace is quite rapid, with new versions released nearly every week (the version number is the date of release, so the version profiled here was released on January 12, 2000). System requirements and building procedures may change from version to version, so if you decide to build WINE be sure to follow the installation instructions included with the source package.

Using WINE

Using WINE is easy. The documentation suggests trying to run the Windows Solitaire card game as a test case, because it exemplifies the basic usage. After the emulator has been installed, type the following in an xterm window:

```
wine /mnt/dosc/windows/sol.exe
```

Replace the /mnt/dosc pathname with the drive where your Windows installation is located (the Solitaire program is normally found under the /windows directory). When the familiar card game appears, you'll be ready to try running some Windows music and sound applications.

More WINE, Please . . .

Sound support under WINE is transparent—that is, no special setup is required. However, it is safe to say that more complex programs, such as Cakewalk or other MIDI programs, are unlikely to work. The WINE Web site lists hundreds of applications that have been rated on how well they run under the emulator, but very few audio programs receive the highest rating (0 indicates failure, 5 indicates a complete success). Two that have received the highest marks are Rasmus Ekman's GranuLab (available from http://hem.passagen.se/rasmuse/Granny.htm) and David Billen's SimSynth (available at http://ellisdee.onestop.net).

GranuLab

GranuLab takes a WAV-format soundfile as input and performs a synthesis technique known as granulation on it.[1] The program is meant to run in real time, and performances can be saved to disk.

---

1 For more information on granular synthesis, see the relevant material in Curtis Roads' *A Computer Music Tutorial*. Cambridge, Mass.: MIT Press, 1996. ISBN 0-252-18158-4.

No special DLLs are required, and it is a testament to the author's coding style that GranuLab runs smoothly under WINE.

Launch the program under WINE with **wine /dosc/granny/granulab.exe** (substituting the directory paths correct for your system). Figure 15-7 shows GranuLab's controls.

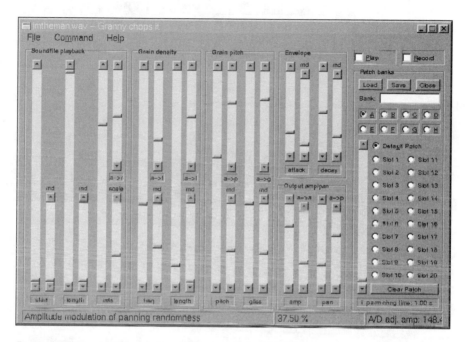

Figure 15-7: Rasmus Ekman's GranuLab running under WINE

Basic operation of GranuLab is simple: Load a soundfile, check the **Play** box, then move the sliders to control various parameters of the granulation of your soundfile. The soundfile will loop continuously until you stop play, and you will hear your parameter changes immediately. For more details concerning GranuLab's operation, see the program's excellent documentation.

SimSynth

SimSynth is a software synthesizer with realtime parameter controls that attempts to emulate the classic analog synthesizers of yesteryear. Like those ancient electronic instruments, SimSynth presents a control interface consisting of knobs and switches for the realtime adjustment of a sound's parameters. A mouse-controlled keyboard is provided, and an external MIDI keyboard can also control the synthesizer.

Figure 15-8 shows SimSynth in action. The setup in this figure creates an FM (frequency modulation) bass sound. The SimSynth package includes a

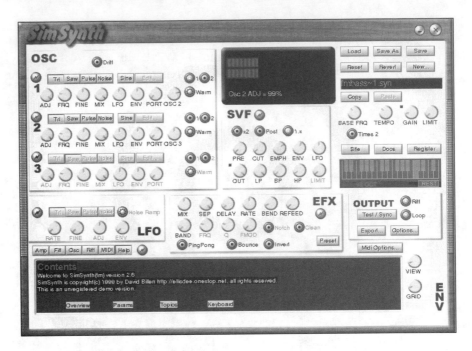

Figure 15-8: SimSynth running under WINE

variety of synthesizer emulations, each of which can be controlled in real time,
tweaked to your liking, and saved as a new patch.

See the SimSynth documentation for more information.

Closing Comments

Thanks to similar projects carried out under other flavors of UNIX, Linux has
inherited a rich tradition of operating system emulation software. However,
Linux's popularity has inspired programmers to new and innovative efforts at
accommodating other systems and their software under Linux.

Ideally, we would see native Linux applications replacing their Windows,
Macintosh, and OS/2 counterparts. But until that happy time, the emulators
profiled and mentioned in this chapter are the only solution. Let's hope they
will work well enough to let you run the one or few applications that still have
no Linux equivalents.

AFTERWORD

Taking Leave

I have had the great pleasure of watching and helping the growth of Linux music and sound software, and I'll certainly continue to encourage and follow its development. An amazing amount of outstanding software has appeared in a few years, and our journey is just beginning. Like Linux itself, the ride might be a little bumpy, but that's to be expected on the road less traveled.

Join Up!

If you've come this far, I invite you to journey onward. The development of high-quality Linux audio and MIDI software depends upon your involvement, regardless of whether you are a seasoned C programmer or a Linux newbie. If you can contribute code, then join in an existing project or pick up an orphaned application. Join the Linux Audio Development group (at http://www.linuxdj.com/audio/lad). If you can't contribute code, then be a tester or contribute ideas. Sign on to one of the Linux audio mail lists found at http://www.bright.net/~dlphilp/linuxsound/mlists.html. Help with documentation is always welcome. Compose a Web page for your favorite Linux sound program. Put your original music online with a notice that it's "Made In Linux."

I hope you have enjoyed this tour of the world of Linux MIDI and sound software. Perhaps you've discovered programs unique to Linux (such as jMax or Quasimodo), or just reacquainted yourself with familiar applications like MP3 players and MOD trackers. However you have used this book, I hope it has led you to some interesting and useful music and sound software.

Above all, I hope you've had fun with the programs I've profiled here. And remember: The fun is just beginning. . . .

GLOSSARY

ADC (analog-to-digital converter)   A device that processes an electrical stream into a series of numbers.

additive synthesis   A synthesis method that creates complex sounds by adding frequency components, usually in the form of sine waves.

ADSR (attack, decay, sustain, release)   Defines the shape of a sound's envelope in four stages.

AIFF (audio interchange file format)   A soundfile format from Apple Computer.

algorithm   A procedure for solving a problem or accomplishing a task wherein each step of the procedure is strictly defined.

amplitude   In digital audio, the value of a signal's largest sample. Directly proportional to the perceived intensity and loudness of a sound.

arpeggiation   Breaking a chord into a series of pitches.

attack   The first part of an ADSR envelope, also called the rise-time segment.

AU   A soundfile format from Sun Microsystems.

bit   A binary digit, either 0 or 1. The smallest unit of information understood by a computer.

bitrate   The rate (in kilobits per second) at which a soundfile is converted to an MP3 soundfile. Files encoded at 128 kbps approach CD-quality audio fidelity. Higher bitrates ensure better sound, but require more storage space.

bit resolution   The number of bits used to define a single sound sample (usually 8, 16, or 32 bits). In digital audio, a sampled sound's dynamic range depends on its bit resolution. Low-resolution sound (8-bit) is adequate for non-musical applications, whereas higher resolutions (16-bit and 32-bit) are preferred for music and other sonically critical applications.

bitstream   The flow of the bits of an MP3 soundfile.

CD audio   Digital audio sampled at 44.1 kHz in 16-bit resolution.

channel   In audio terminology, a specified path for signal input/output in either hardware or software.

cue channel   A mixer channel that waits for a signal before it opens its sound output.

DAC (digital-to-analog converter)   A device that converts a series of numbers to an electrical stream.

decay   The second segment of an ADSR amplitude envelope, reaching from the end-point of the attack to the start of the sustain stage.

decibel   A unit of measurement for the relative amplitudes of a sound (abbreviated dB).

delay line   An algorithm that delays the output of an incoming signal (e.g., an echo effect).

DMA (direct memory access)   A method of transferring data directly in and out of a computer's memory, bypassing the control of the CPU.

DSP (digital signal processing)   Creating or editing signals in the digital domain. Typical DSP applications include radar and telecommunications devices (such as modems), as well as audio and image processing software.

dynamic range   The full range of amplitudes that can be represented by an audio system.

effect bus   The part of a mixer that routes a signal to and from an effects processor.

envelope   The shape of a sound's amplitude variation.

fader   A software or hardware slider that controls an input or output level.

FFT analysis (fast Fourier transform analysis)   A technique used to determine the relative amplitudes of a signal's frequencies to determine the shape of a wave.

filter   A device or algorithm that lets some frequencies through and rejects others, modifying the frequency content of a signal.

frequency   How often a periodic waveform repeats itself over a unit of time (usually one second).

full duplex   The ability of a soundcard to simultaneously record and play back sound.

gain   The ratio of an audio device's output amplitude to the input amplitude.

Hertz   A measurement unit for frequency equal to one cycle per second (abbreviated Hz).

iconic synthesis environment   Software synthesis by means of patching icons together in a graphic interface.

interrupt   A signal from a device that demands the immediate attention of the CPU.

I/O   Input/output.

IRQ (interrupt request)   A signal from a program to the computer, asking it to attend to a particular device (such as a modem or soundcard) via the device's interrupt number.

LISP (list processing)   A computer programming language especially well suited for artificial intelligence and the exploration of algorithms for the creation of music.

loop   To play a portion of or an entire recording repeatedly.

LPC (linear predictive coding)   A method of analyzing and encoding a digital signal. LPC resynthesis works by calculating (i.e., predicting) its output samples using data from samples already calculated.

Markov chain   A randomization process that calculates higher-order probabilities from first-order probabilities.

MIDI (musical instrument digital interface)   A specification for hardware and software protocols that allows digital musical instruments (such as synthesizers and drum machines) from different manufacturers to communicate with each other.

mixer A device for blending multiple sound inputs into a balanced output signal.

MOD (music module) A soundfile format commonly used by digital audio tracking software. *See* tracking.

MP3 (MPEG audio specification, layer 3) An audio data compression format designed by the Motion Pictures Engineering Group (MPEG).

MPEG (Motion Pictures Engineering Group) An organization formed to design and implement standards used in commercial and industrial audio and video applications.

music specification language A programming language that represents musical notation symbols and functions.

note-off A MIDI message indicating the end of a note.

note-on A MIDI message indicating the start of a note.

opcode (operation code) A programming language directive that tells the computer to perform a specific task. In the Csound language, an opcode may be a signal generator or modifier, a mathematics function (including the =, +, −, *, and / signs), or some other process that acts upon incoming data.

oscillator A software or hardware device that generates a waveform.

parameter A numerical characteristic of an algorithm that controls some characteristic of the sound created by the algorithm.

patching Connecting modules by real or virtual cables.

PCM (pulse code modulation) A standard digital sound encoding technique; the sampling process whereby electrical impulses are converted into numbers.

periodic wave An audio signal consisting of a repeating waveform at a specific frequency. Pitched sounds, such as those made by musical instruments, are periodic waves.

phase The starting point of a waveform, represented in the radian degrees of a unit circle.

pitch The subjective response to the frequency of an audio signal. Pitch is perceived as higher or lower as the signal frequency rises or falls.

pitch-shifting Raising or lowering the pitch of a signal.

polyphony A musical term indicating the simultaneous motion of multiple voices or melodies. Also used to indicate a synthesizer's simultaneous sound capability.

probability   The likelihood of an event occurring.

program change   A MIDI message that tells a device to change to a particular stored sound.

pulse code modulation   *See* PCM.

quantize   The technique of converting a continuous analog signal into discrete bits. In MIDI terminology, the process of rounding an event's duration and/or start time to a user-defined value.

realtime synthesis   The process of synthesizing sound samples faster than the sampling rate and sending the sound directly to a DAC instead of saving it to disk.

release   The final stage of an ADSR envelope. Typically this stage starts from the last point of the sustain stage and descends to an amplitude level of zero.

resolution   The degree of detail (usually referred to in terms of bits) possible in digital computer output—either audio or visual.

sampling rate   The frequency in Hertz at which a sound is sampled, e.g., 22050 Hz or 44100 Hz (cycles per second).

scratching   Manually operating a record turntable forward or backward to produce a distinctive rasping sound.

SND   A soundfile format used extensively on NeXT computers.

software mixer   *See* soundcard mixer.

software synthesis   A method of creating sound using programs for digital computers and processors.

soundcard mixer   A software application for managing levels, mute and solo status, input gain, and other aspects of a soundcard's capabilities.

sound synthesis   A general term for methods of creating sound using electronic devices (such as analog and digital synthesizers).

spectral dynamics processing   A process that changes the strength of a signal's frequency content.

spectrum   The amplitude and phase of a sound's frequency components.

spline curve   A smooth curve with no discontinuities.

sustain   The third stage of an ADSR amplitude envelope, representing the "steady state" portion of the sound.

synthesis   The process of converting electronic signals into acoustic sound.

track   A specific hardware or software channel for recording and playing audio or MIDI data. Different components—bass, drums, voices—may occupy different tracks.

tracking   A method of arranging sound samples in tracks and then looping and sequencing the tracks.

transport controls   The start/stop/pause and rewind/fast-forward controls of a recording or playback device.

unit generator   An algorithm that generates, modifies, or combines sounds.

VU meter   A software or hardware device that indicates input or output levels.

WAV   A popular soundfile format from Microsoft.

wavetable synthesis   A type of synthesis that uses stored, precalculated functions to produce a waveform.

ABOUT THE LINUX MUSIC
& SOUND CD-ROM

The CD-ROM that accompanies this book contains as many of the profiled applications as legally possible.

Almost all of the software here can be considered "in development," but that certainly does not mean it is broken or useless. As shown in the book, even packages in the developmental stages can be quite sophisticated. However, given the variety of Linux distributions and the occasional differences between file systems, some applications may not compile and/or run on your system without some determined hacking. If you have persistent problems building, installing, or using a package, write to the author or maintainer of the software in question. Describe your problems clearly and keep in mind the fact that most of this software is available for free.

Linux software is a quickly moving target. For the most up-to-date versions, I encourage the reader to visit the Web sites listed in the Linux Music and Sound Applications Pages for all of the software packages profiled in this book and included on the disk.

The disk is organized exactly like the book: Software in Chapter 2 of the book will be found in the Chapter_2 directory on the CD, software in Chapter 3 in the Chapter_3 directory, and so forth. The /extra directory contains over 100 other applications, including GUI front-ends for applications such as SoX and playmidi, as well as software not reviewed in the book.

Packages are named as presented in the book (for instance, *package-name-latest.tar.gz*) and each file is linked to the (properly named) package itself. Thus, *RTcmix-latest.tar.gz* is actually a link to *RTcmix-3.0.1.tar.gz*.

If available, binaries in RPM format have been included.

The disk is organized as follows (directory names are in parentheses):

2 Setting Up Your System (/Chapter_2)

ALSA 0.5.7

OSS/Linux drivers 2.2.x

3 Mixing, Playing, and Recording (/Chapter_3)

aumix

yarec

SoX

4 Soundfile Editors (/Chapter_4)

DAP

MiXViews

Snd

Kwave

Broadcast2000

Ceres

5 MOD Files and Linux (/Chapter_5)

SoundTracker

MikMod

Demos: Loop and State Of Mind

6 The Linux MIDI Studio (/Chapter_6)

Brahms

Jazz++

TiMidity++

11   Music Notation Programs (/Chapter_11)

Common Music Notation

Rosegarden

Mup

12   Network Audio Software (/Chapter_12)

Icecast

Speak Freely

NAS

13   Linux and the Digital DJ (/Chapter_13)

Oolaboola

terminatorX

Green Box

Freebirth

14   Linux Games (/Chapter_14)

Quake

Roll 'Em Up

Clanbomber

15   Operating System Emulators (/Chapter_15)

DOSemu

WINE

Executor

The Linux Music & Sound Applications Pages

This contains the most recent edition of my Web site, including links to more than 700 sites containing Linux audio and MIDI software, documentation, and discussion groups. Open linux_soundapps.html to view the site's main page.

Documents (/docs)

Sound HOWTO

Sound Playing HOWTO

Audio Quality HOWTO

Sound Blaster AWE HOWTO

Quake HOWTO

MP3 HOWTO

ALSA Mini-HOWTO

Extra Programs (/extra)

This directory contains all of the following:

LinuxPPC Audio Software

Lilypond Music notation typesetting from GNU

Snd Soundfile editor

Ceres3 Enhanced version of the Ceres spectral processor

CD Software

cdlabelgen Generates frontcards and traycards for CD cases

cdparanoia CD audio grabber

cdrecord CD recording software from Joerg Schilling

gcombust GUI for mkisofs and cdrecord

kover KDE utility for creating inserts for CD jewel boxes

ripperx GUI for cdparanoia

Csound Helpers

Rain Tcl/Tk script to convert GIF images to Csound score

SoundSpace Java GUI for the Csound space opcode

TkScore Graphic utility for combining soundfiles and/or Csound scores into one mega-score

Digital DJ

eMixer DJ-style mixer for two MP3 audio streams

GDAM (Geoff & Dave's Audio Mixer) A new mixer for the Linux digital DJ

Drumming

tk707 Software emulation of the Roland TR-707 drum machine

Trommler Excellent drum machine with Gtk interface

DSP Software

Aglaophone "A system of interconnectable modules for the recording, processing, and playback of real-time audio" (from the Aglaophone author's Web site)

ELE The "Excellent Low-latency Effects" processor

FFTW (Fastest Fourier Transform in the West) C subroutine library

Mammut Processes an entire soundfile as a single spectral analysis window

ObjectProDSP An X window GUI for DSP design and implementation

Sculptor A very nice suite of realtime FFT tools

TAPIIR A multi-tap delay effects processor with GUI

Ultra Power Effects Max II A realtime effects processor for full-duplex soundcards

Guitar Software

Dr. Fermi Tabulator Converts ASCII tablature to a standard MIDI file

eTktab An excellent program for writing guitar tablature in the typical ASCII tab found on the Internet

FX Processor Guitar effects processor

Gtune Guitar tuner

Ldse realtime guitar and dub effects processor, requires ALSA driver

StompBoxes Guitar fx processor with Gtk interface

MIDI Software

Brainstorm A MIDI daemon for capturing impromptu performances

Grammidity " . . . uses a kind of genetic algorithm based on user feedback to generate 'music' . . . in the form of a MIDI file" (from the
Grammidity author's Web site); requires Java JDK 1.1

Gseq A MIDI sequencer project

Melys A MIDI sequencer for ALSA

MusE A Qt 2.0–based MIDI sequencer

pmidi Another MIDI sequencer for ALSA

Softwerk A MIDI sequencer based on the design of the Doepfer analog
sequencer

Super Groove Master A unique composition program for AWE32/64,
OPL3 FM synth, or external MIDI

WaoN A WAV-to-MIDI converter

Wav2MID Another WAV-to-MIDI converter

Mixers

Smix A highly configurable mixer, uses Xforms for its GUI

XAMixer A Gtk-based mixer, requires ALSA

xmmixer Soundcard audio mixer with Motif GUI

MOD Software

Funktracker An FNK module tracker

Gmodplay Gtk MOD player

Mod4X MikMod with an XForms interface

SarahTracker A new console-mode tracker in development

Voodoo Tracker Full-featured tracker for the GNOME desktop environment

XMP The Extended Module Player

MP3 Software

Freeamp An open source MP3 player

Kblade A KDE front-end for BladeEnc

kmp3te Program for viewing and editing tags to MP3 files

Krio KDE interface for the Rio player

LAME An excellent MP3 encoder

mp3tools " . . . a set of utilities for working with MPEG audio files" (from the mp3tools README)

Tk3Play MP3 player with Tk GUI

Multitrack Recorders/Mixers

ecasound Hard-disk recording and audio processing from the Linux console or X

qrt A Qt interface for Rt

Rt A port of Paul Lansky's famous mixer

Musician's Utilities

Gtick Metronome with Gtk GUI

Solfege Ear training program with Gtk interface

Network Audio

EsounD (Enlightened Sound Daemon) Does network audio too

Notation Software

Denemo Gtk front-end for Lilypond

Lilypond Music typesetter from the GNU project; outputs TeX and MIDI

Players and Recorders

AlsaPlayer " . . . a new type of PCM player . . . heavily multi-threaded . . . tries to exercise the ALSA library and driver . . . " (from the AlsaPlayer Web site)

krecord Simple WAV recorder/player for KDE

xplay Multiformat (WAV, uncompressed AIFF, Sun AU, NeXT SND) player, requires Motif or Lesstif

Programming Tools

audio latency software Software to analyze scheduling latencies of programs running in realtime under high system loads

audiofile An implementation of the SGI libaudiofile

LADSPA Material regarding the Linux Audio Developers' Simple Plug-in Architecture

libsndfile Library for reading and writing many different soundfile formats

MIDIshare An open-source MIDI library initiative

MuCos An ambitious API for Linux audio

Open Source Audio Library C++ classes to handle audio functions

OSS Programmer's Guide Excellent resource for OSS/Linux and OSS/Free sound and MIDI device programming

SDL (Simple DirectMedia Layer) A library project especially suited for developing and porting games

SNACK A module to add sound I/O and visualization commands to Tcl/Tk

Sndlib Audio/audiofile library from the Snd soundfile editor project

Sound Programming Tutorial pages for programming OSS/Free, OSS/Linux, and ALSA

tritonus An implementation of the JavaSound API

Scopes and Visualizers

blurscope Audio visualization utility

Bomb An interactive A-life "visual-musical" instrument

Cthugha "an oscilloscope on acid . . . "

eXtace A superb scope/visualizer

oscope Digital oscilloscope for SVGA or Gtk

Synaesthesia A light show calculated from FFT and stereo positioning information

Software Synthesis

cmusic A port of the CARL computer-music software to Linux

Common LISP Music A Music-N style language from the crew at CCRMA

Common Music Extensive utility for creating scores for Csound, Cmix, Common LISP Music, and other Music-N style languages

gAlan A graphical audio language

Pd A MAX-like iconic audio/MIDI programming environment

STK (Synthesis Tool Kit) "A set of audio signal processing C++ classes and instruments" (from the STK Web site)

Tao Physical modeling synthesis language with Mesa/OpenGL GUI

Xsynth MIDI-controlled analog-style realtime synthesizer

Soundfile Editors

Electric Ears A soundfile editor project for the Gnome desktop

Smurf Editor for AWE32/64 soundfonts

Studio Excellent editor, requires Tcl/Tk

TAON Soundfile editor with Gtk GUI

WaveSurfer Tcl/Tk soundfile editor, requires the SNACK extensions

WaveTools A suite of small command-line programs for working with WAV-format soundfiles

Speech Software

Festival Speech synthesis system

MBROLA Console-mode speech synthesis project

OGI Speech Tools Toolkit for speech data manipulation, includes X interface, file conversion utilities, and LPC tools

rsynth Speech synthesizer

SFS (Speech Filing System) Excellent set of X-based and command-line tools

Transcriber "A free tool for segmenting, labeling and transcribing speech" (from the Transcriber Web site); requires the Snack package

Sound Examples

This directory contains soundfiles referenced in the book.

dp_example_01.xm

linus.aiff

linus.wav

linus8.wav

Supported Soundcards

This directory contains HTML-formatted lists of soundcards supported by 4Front (OSS/Linux), ALSA, and OSS/Free (the kernel modules).

alsa_soundcard_matrix.html

oss_free_soundcards.html

oss_linux_soundcards.html

BIBLIOGRAPHY

Print Resources

Anderton, C. *Home Recording for Musicians.* New York: Amsco, 1978.

Anderton, C. *MIDI for Musicians.* New York: Amsco, 1986.

Bateman, W. A. *Introduction to Computer Music.* New York: John Wiley, 1980.

Boulanger, R., ed. *The Csound Book.* Cambridge: MIT Press, 2000.

Chamberlin, H. *Musical Application of Microprocessors.* Indianapolis: Hayden, 1987.

Chowning, J., and Bristow, D. *FM Theory & Applications.* Tokyo: Yamaha Music Foundation, 1986.

Davis, G., and Jones, R. *Sound Reinforcement Handbook.* Hal Leonard Publishing, 1990.

De Furia, S., and Scacciaferro, J. *MIDI Programmer's Handbook.* Redwood City, CA: M&T Books, 1989.

Dodge, C., and Jerse, T. A. *Computer Music: Synthesis, Composition, and Performance.* New York: Schirmer, 1997.

Heckman, J. P. *Linux in a Nutshell.* Sebastopol, CA: O'Reilly, 1997.

Huber, D. M., and Runstein, R. E. *Modern Recording Techniques.* Carmel, CA: Sams, 1991.

Jaxitron. *Cybernetic Music.* Blue Ridge Summit, PA: TAB Books, 1985.

Lehrman, P. D., and Tully, T. *MIDI for the Professional.* New York: Amsco, 1993.

Mathews, M. V., and Pierce, J. R., eds. *Current Directions in Computer Music Research.* Cambridge, MA: MIT Press, 1989.

Moore, F. R. *Elements of Computer Music.* Englewood Cliffs, NJ: Prentice Hall, 1990.

Phillips, D. "Porting SGI Audio Applications to Linux." *The Linux Journal,* September 1998, 40–42.

Phillips, D. "Csound for Linux." *The Linux Journal,* February 1999, 38–44.

Phillips, D. "An Interview with Dev Mazumdar and Hannu Savolainen." *The Linux Journal,* July 1999, 90–93.

Pickett, R. "The Penguin's Song." *Electronic Musician,* June 1999, 106–116.

Pierce, J. R. *The Science of Musical Sound.* New York: W. H. Freeman, 1992.

Pohlmann, K. C. *Principles of Digital Audio.* Indianapolis: Howard W. Sams, 1987.

Roads, C., ed. *The Music Machine.* Cambridge: MIT Press, 1989.

Roads, C., ed. *The Computer Music Tutorial.* Cambridge: MIT Press, 1996.

Roads, C., and Strawn, J. *Foundations of Computer Music.* Cambridge: MIT Press, 1987.

Tranter, J. *Linux Multimedia Guide.* Sebastopol, CA: O'Reilly, 1996.

Welsh, M., and Kaufman, L. *Running Linux.* Sebastopol, CA: O'Reilly, 1995.

Journals

Electronic Musician	http://www.emusician.com
Keyboard	http://www.keyboardmag.com
The Linux Journal	http://www.linuxjournal.com
Linux Magazin (German language journal)	http://www.linux-magazin.de
Linux Magazine	http://www.linux-mag.com
Maximum Linux	http://www.maximumlinux.com
Mix	http://www.mixmag.com

Web Sites

DAM's MP3:
An excellent site for all things MP3. http://www.crosswinds.net/damsmp3

Freshmeat:
Daily listing of new Linux software. http://freshmeat.net

Harmony Central:
Superb resource for musicians, with especially good MIDI references. Mostly Windows/Mac oriented but includes pointers to Linux material as well. http://www.harmony-central.com

Linart:
Michael Stutz's organization for
Linux visual and audio artists.

http://dsl.org/linart

The Linux Artist:
Another fine site for Linux visual
and audio artists.

http://www.linuxartist.org

**The Linux Audio
Development Pages:**
The center for Linux audio and
MIDI software developers.

http://www.linuxdj.com/audio/lad

The Linux Gazette:
Excellent articles by and for Linux
users everywhere.

http://www.linuxgazette.com

The Linux Music Station:
Wide coverage of Linux music-makers,
includes interviews with software
developers and other Linux
audio/MIDI personalities.

http://www.crosswinds.net/~linuxmusic/

**The Linux Sound &
MIDI Applications Pages:**
An enormous list.

http://sound.condorow.net

United Trackers:
The #1 resource site for everything MOD.

http://www.united-trackers.org

Newsgroups

comp.dsp	A technical forum concerning all aspects of digital signal processing
comp.music.midi	Discussion group for MIDI matters
comp.os.linux.misc	Unmoderated discussion of any Linux-related issues
comp.os.linux.setup	Newsgroup to solve Linux installation problems
linux.dev.sound	Forum for general Linux audio issues

INDEX

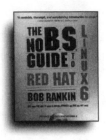

THE NO B.S. GUIDE TO
RED HAT LINUX 6.x

by BOB RANKIN

This book is a thorough yet concise guide to installing Red Hat Linux 6.*x* and exploring its capabilities. Author Bob Rankin (*The No B.S. Guide to Linux*, No Starch Press) provides easy-to-follow instructions for installing and running Red Hat 6.*x*. Through examples and helpful illustrations, the author guides readers through these topics and more:

- Installation — in ten easy steps!

- How to use and configure GNOME — the new Linux GUI

- How to write Bash or Perl scripts and use the Bash shell

- How to connect to the Internet with SLIP/PPP and how to run the Apache Web server for Linux

- How to access DOS files and run Windows programs under Linux

The CD-ROM contains Red Hat Linux 6.2 — one of the most popular Linux distributions available. It's easy to install and requires minimal configuration — you'll be up and running in a snap!

BOB RANKIN is a programmer and nationally recognized expert on the Internet. He is a columnist for *Boardwatch Magazine* and a contributor to several computer publications. His books include *Dr. Bob's Painless Guide to the Internet* (1996) and *The No B.S. Guide to Linux* (1997).

402 pp., paperback, $34.95 w/CD-ROM
ISBN 1-886411-30-1

STEAL THIS COMPUTER BOOK: WHAT THEY WON'T TELL YOU ABOUT THE INTERNET

by WALLACE WANG

"A delightfully irresponsible primer." — *Chicago Tribune*

"If this book had a soundtrack, it'd be Lou Reed's 'Walk on the Wild Side.'" — *InfoWorld*

"An unabashed look at the dark side of the Net — the stuff many other books gloss over." — *Amazon.com*

Steal This Computer Book explores the dark corners of the Internet and reveals little-known techniques that hackers use to subvert authority. Unfortunately, some of these techniques, when used by malicious hackers, can destroy data and compromise the security of corporate and government networks. To keep your computer safe from viruses, and yourself from electronic con games and security crackers, Wallace Wang explains the secrets hackers and scammers use to prey on their victims. Discover:

- How hackers write and spread computer viruses
- How criminals get free service and harass legitimate customers on online services like America Online
- How online con artists trick people out of thousands of dollars
- Where hackers find the tools to crack into computers or steal software
- How to find and use government-quality encryption to protect your data
- How hackers steal passwords from other computers

WALLACE WANG is the author of several computer books, including *Microsoft Office 97 for Windows for Dummies* and *Visual Basic for Dummies*. A regular contributor to *Boardwatch* magazine (the "Internet Underground" columnist), he's also a successful stand-up comedian. He lives in San Diego, California.

340 pp., paperback, $19.95
ISBN 1-886411-21-2

THE LINUX PROBLEM SOLVER

by BRIAN WARD

- Hands-on, practical guide solves kernel issues
- Helps solve hundreds of problems

A must-have for intermediate to advanced users who already have Linux up and running. Solves technical problems related to printing, networking, back-up, crash recovery, and compiling or upgrading a kernel. Quick and concise in approach, with over 100 problem boxes that help to solve specific problems in addition to those discussed throughout the book.

CD-ROM: Supports the book's contents with configuration files and numerous programs not included in many Linux distributions.

BRIAN WARD is a Unix systems programmer, and is the author of the "Linux Kernel HOWTO," widely circulated on the Internet. A Unix network administrator, he has worked with Linux since 1993. He is currently pursuing a Ph.D. in computer science at the University of Chicago.

350 pp. w/CD-ROM, $34.95 ($54.00CDN)
ISBN 1-886411-35-2

Phone:
1 (800) 420-7240 OR
(415) 863-9900
MONDAY THROUGH FRIDAY,
9 A.M. TO 5 P.M. (PST)

Fax:
(415) 863-9950
24 HOURS A DAY,
7 DAYS A WEEK

E-mail:
SALES@NOSTARCH.COM

Web:
HTTP://WWW.NOSTARCH.COM

Mail:
NO STARCH PRESS
555 DE HARO STREET, SUITE 250
SAN FRANCISCO, CA 94107
USA

Distributed to the book trade by Publishers Group West

Linux Journal's team of industry experts has put together a complete line of reference materials designed for Linux operating system users, programmers, and IT professionals. Visit your local bookstore or the Linux Journal Web site for other Linux Journal Press products. You may also request a free issue of the monthly magazine, Linux Journal, online at http://www.linuxjournal.com.

UPDATES

This book was carefully reviewed for technical accuracy, but it's inevitable that some things will change after the book goes to press. Visit the Web site for this book at **http://www.nostarch.com/lms_updates.htm** for updates, errata, and other information.

DESIGN SCIENCE LICENSE
FOR THIS BOOK'S CD-ROM

TERMS AND CONDITIONS FOR COPYING, DISTRIBUTION AND MODIFICATION

0. PREAMBLE.

Copyright law gives certain exclusive rights to the author of a work, including the rights to copy, modify and distribute the work (the "reproductive," "adaptative," and "distribution" rights).

The idea of "copyleft" is to willfully revoke the exclusivity of those rights under certain terms and conditions, so that anyone can copy and distribute the work or properly attributed derivative works, while all copies remain under the same terms and conditions as the original.

The intent of this license is to be a general "copyleft" that can be applied to any kind of work that has protection under copyright. This license states those certain conditions under which a work published under its terms may be copied, distributed, and modified.

Whereas "design science" is a strategy for the development of artifacts as a way to reform the environment (not people) and subsequently improve the universal standard of living, this Design Science License was written and deployed as a strategy for promoting the progress of science and art through reform of the environment.

1. DEFINITIONS.

"License" shall mean this Design Science License. The License applies to any work which contains a notice placed by the work's copyright holder stating that it is published under the terms of this Design Science License.

"Work" shall mean such an aforementioned work. The License also applies to the output of the Work, only if said output constitutes a "derivative work" of the licensed Work as defined by copyright law.

"Object Form" shall mean an executable or performable form of the Work, being an embodiment of the Work in some tangible medium.

"Source Data" shall mean the origin of the Object Form, being the entire, machine-readable, preferred form of the Work for copying and for human modification (usually the language, encoding or format in which composed or recorded by the Author); plus any accompanying files, scripts or other data necessary for installation, configuration or compilation of the Work.

(Examples of "Source Data" include, but are not limited to, the following: if the Work is an image file composed and edited in 'PNG' format, then the original PNG source file is the Source Data; if the Work is an MPEG 1.0 layer 3 digital audio recording made from a 'WAV' format audio file recording of an analog source, then the original WAV file is the Source Data; if the Work was composed as an unformatted plaintext file, then that file is the the Source Data; if the Work was composed in LaTeX, the LaTeX file(s) and any image files and/or custom macros necessary for compilation constitute the Source Data.)

"Author" shall mean the copyright holder(s) of the Work.

The individual licensees are referred to as "you."

2. RIGHTS AND COPYRIGHT.

The Work is copyright the Author. All rights to the Work are reserved by the Author, except as specifically described below. This License describes the terms and conditions under which the Author permits you to copy, distribute and modify copies of the Work.

In addition, you may refer to the Work, talk about it, and (as dictated by "fair use") quote from it, just as you would any copyrighted material under copyright law.

Your right to operate, perform, read or otherwise interpret and/or execute the Work is unrestricted; however, you do so at your own risk, because the Work comes WITHOUT ANY WARRANTY — see Section 7 ("NO WARRANTY") below.

3. COPYING AND DISTRIBUTION.

Permission is granted to distribute, publish or otherwise present verbatim copies of the entire Source Data of the Work, in any medium, provided that full copyright notice and disclaimer of warranty, where applicable, is conspicuously published on all copies, and a copy of this License is distributed along with the Work.

Permission is granted to distribute, publish or otherwise present copies of the Object Form of the Work, in any medium, under the terms for distribution of Source Data above and also provided that one of the following additional conditions are met:

(a) The Source Data is included in the same distribution, distributed under the terms of this License; or

(b) A written offer is included with the distribution, valid for at least three years or for as long as the distribution is in print (whichever is longer), with a publicly-accessible address (such as a URL on the Internet) where, for a charge not greater than transportation and media costs, anyone may receive a copy of the Source Data of the Work distributed according to the section above; or

(c) A third party's written offer for obtaining the Source Data at no cost, as described in paragraph (b) above, is included with the distribution. This option is valid only if you are a non-commercial party, and only if you received the Object Form of the Work along with such an offer.

You may copy and distribute the Work either gratis or for a fee, and if desired, you may offer warranty protection for the Work.

The aggregation of the Work with other works which are not based on the Work — such as but not limited to inclusion in a publication, broadcast, compilation, or other media — does not bring the other works in the scope of the License; nor does such aggregation void the terms of the License for the Work.

4. MODIFICATION.

Permission is granted to modify or sample from a copy of the Work, producing a derivative work, and to distribute the derivative work under the terms described in the section for distribution above, provided that the following terms are met:

(a) The new, derivative work is published under the terms of this License.

(b) The derivative work is given a new name, so that its name or title can not be confused with the Work, or with a version of the Work, in any way.

(c) Appropriate authorship credit is given: for the differences between the Work and the new derivative work, authorship is attributed to you, while the material sampled or used from the Work remains attributed to the original Author; appropriate notice must be included with the new work indicating the nature and the dates of any modifications of the Work made by you.

5. NO RESTRICTIONS.

You may not impose any further restrictions on the Work or any of its derivative works beyond those restrictions described in this License.

6. ACCEPTANCE.

Copying, distributing or modifying the Work (including but not limited to sampling from the Work in a new work) indicates acceptance of these terms. If you do not follow the terms of this License, any rights granted to you by the License are null and void. The copying, distribution or modification of the Work outside of the terms described in this License is expressly prohibited by law.

If for any reason, conditions are imposed on you that forbid you to fulfill the conditions of this License, you may not copy, distribute or modify the Work at all.

If any part of this License is found to be in conflict with the law, that part shall be interpreted in its broadest meaning consistent with the law, and no other parts of the License shall be affected.

7. NO WARRANTY.

THE WORK IS PROVIDED "AS IS," AND COMES WITH ABSOLUTELY NO WARRANTY, EXPRESS OR IMPLIED, TO THE EXTENT PERMITTED BY APPLICABLE LAW, INCLUDING BUT NOT LIMITED TO THE IMPLIED WARRANTIES OF MERCHANTABILITY OR FITNESS FOR A PARTICULAR PURPOSE.

8. DISCLAIMER OF LIABILITY.

IN NO EVENT SHALL THE AUTHOR OR CONTRIBUTORS BE LIABLE FOR ANY DIRECT, INDIRECT, INCIDENTAL, SPECIAL, EXEMPLARY, OR CONSEQUENTIAL DAMAGES (INCLUDING, BUT NOT LIMITED TO, PROCUREMENT OF SUBSTITUTE GOODS OR SERVICES; LOSS OF USE, DATA, OR PROFITS; OR BUSINESS INTERRUPTION) HOWEVER CAUSED AND ON ANY THEORY OF LIABILITY, WHETHER IN CONTRACT, STRICT LIABILITY, OR TORT (INCLUDING NEGLIGENCE OR OTHERWISE) ARISING IN ANY WAY OUT OF THE USE OF THIS WORK, EVEN IF ADVISED OF THE POSSIBILITY OF SUCH DAMAGE.

END OF TERMS AND CONDITIONS

These applications are not covered under the Design License Agreement and included courtesy of their respective authors:

Sig++ Craig Stuart Sapp
TAON the TAON development team
Roll 'Em Up The Lost Boys
RTSynth Stefan Nietschke
ARDI Executor Clifford Matthews
Cmix Paul Lansky
RTCmix Dave Topper and associates
OSS Programmers Guide 4Front Technologies
Sound Programming Tutorial Eelke Klein
Grammidity Jeffrey B. Putnam

The following HOWTOs are licensed via the Linux Documentation Project:

Sound HOWTO
Sound Playing HOWTO
Quake HOWTO
MP3 HOWTO
Sound Blaster AWE HOWTO
ALSA Mini-HOWTO

The Audio Quality HOWTO is reprinted courtesy Paul Winkler.